T4-AVA-348

SOCIETY IN ACTION

SOCIETY IN ACTION

WILLIAM F. KENKEL
University of Kentucky

ELLEN VOLAND

Canfield Press  San Francisco

A Department of Harper & Row, Publishers, Inc.
New York   Evanston   London

Library of Congress   Cataloging in Publication Data
Kenkel, William F
    Society in action.

    1. Sociology. I. Voland, Ellen, joint author.
II. Title.
HM51.K377   301   74-30314
ISBN 0-06-384487-7

SOCIETY IN ACTION
Copyright © 1975 by William Kenkel and Ellen Voland

Printed in the United States of America. All rights reserved. No part of this book may be used or reproduced in any manner whatsoever without written permission except in the case of brief quotations embodied in critical articles and reviews. For information address Harper & Row, Publishers, Inc., 10 East 53rd St., New York, N.Y. 10022.

        78   10 9 8 7 6 5 4 3

Interior design by Ann Wilkinson / Julie Kranhold
Cover by Russell Leong
Line art by Barbara Hack

Photo credits:

Chapter 1   Page x: Ansel Adams. 4: Gil Madrid, BBM. 7: Elihu Blotnick, BBM. 9: Kevin Gleason. 13: Culver Pictures. 13: Culver Pictures. 15: Culver Pictures. 15: Bettmann Archive. 17: Brown Brothers. 20: Peeter Vilms, Jeroboam. 23: David Powers, Jeroboam. 26: Jeffrey Blankfort, BBM.
Chapter 2   Page 32: Elihu Blotnick, BBM. 35: William Rosenthal. 39: Lawrence Cameron. 43: Ron Partridge, BBM. 44: Bill Owens, BBM. 48: John Pearson, BBM. 51: Lawrence Cameron. 57: William Rosenthal.
Chapter 3   Page 62: Erich Hartmann, Magnum. 66: Pana, Black Star. 69: Paul Conklin, ACTION. 71: Kevin Gleason. 73: Nacio Jan Brown, BBM. 76: Robert Kanner, BBM. 78: Kevin Gleason. 81: National Museums of Canada. 84: Steve Clevenger, BBM. 85: Elliott Erwitt, Magnum. 87: Kevin Gleason. 91: Robert Kanner, BBM. 94: Jim Harding.
Chapter 4   Page 100: Leonard Freed, Magnum. 102: Robert Kanner, BBM. 105: William Rosenthal. 107: Jeffrey Blankfort, BBM.   109: Bob Main, BBM. 111: Ron Partridge, BBM. 113: Optic Nerve, Jeroboam. 116: Gary Freedman, BBM. 120: Joanne Leonard. 122: Doug Muir, BBM.
Chapter 5   Page 126: William Ganslen. 129: Ernest Lowe, BBM. 130: Hank Kranzler. 132: Erik Weber. 135: Kevin Gleason. 137: Michael Bry. 139: Michael Bry. 141: Joanne Leonard. 145: Earl Dotter, BBM. 149: CBS TV.
Chapter 6   Page 152: Declan Haun, Black Star. 155: Susan Ylvisaker, Jeroboam. 157: Micha Bar-Am, Magnum. 161: William Rosenthal. 162: John Pearson, BBM. 164: Earl Dotter, BBM. 167: Stephen Shames, BBM. 168: Robert Kanner, BBM. 170: Earl Dotter, BBM. 173: Jeffrey Blankfort, BBM.
Chapter 7   Page 176: Candy Freeland, BBM. 180: Robert Kanner, BBM. 183: Lawrence Cameron. 188: William Rosenthal. 190: Joanne Leonard. 193: Bill Owens, BBM. 194: Bill Owens, BBM. 197: William Rosenthal. 201: Peter Goodman, BBM.
Chapter 8   Page 206: John Knaggs, BBM. 210: Marilyn Silverstone, Magnum. 212: Kevin Gleason. 214: Erik Weber. 217: Erik Weber. 219: Ilka Hartmann, Jeroboam. 220: Joanne Leonard. 223: Charles Harbutt, Magnum. 226: Thomas Hopker, Woodfin Camp. 229: John Pearson, BBM. 231: Joanne Leonard. 236: John Pearson, BBM.
Chapter 9   Page 240: Werner Bischof, Magnum. 243: Smithsonian Institution, National Anthropological Archives, Bureau of American Ethnology Collection. 246: Burk Uzzle, Magnum. 248: William Rosenthal. 251: Dave Bellak, Jeroboam. 253: H. Cartier-Bresson, Magnum. 255: Michael Bry. 257: United Nations. 260: Erik Weber. 262: Library of Congress. 265: Thomas Hopker, Woodfin Camp. 267: Nick Pavloff, Jeroboam. 272: Charles Gatewood, Magnum.
Chapter 10   Page 278: Charles Moore, Black Star. 282: William Rosenthal. 285: Michelle Vignes, BBM. 294: Roger Lubin, Jeroboam. 297: Ernest Baxter, Black Star. 302: Charles Gatewood, Magnum. 307: John Pearson, BBM. 309: Nacio Jan Brown, BBM.
Chapter 11   Page 314: Tim Eagan, Woodfin Camp. 318: Kevin Gleason. 322: Earl Dotter, BBM. 325: Elliott Erwitt, Magnum. 329: Roger Mallock, Magnum. 331: Bruce Davidson, Magnum. 334: Sepp Seitz, Magnum. 339: John Pearson, BBM. 340: Earl Dotter, BBM. 343: Earl Dotter, BBM. 346: Elliott Erwitt, Magnum.
Chapter 12   Page 350: Oscar Buitrago, Black Star. 354: Patrick Ward/Observer, Camera Press. 357: United Nations. 360: Bruce Davidson, Magnum. 362: John Nance, Magnum. 364: Burt Glinn, Magnum. 367: Ilka Hartmann, Jeroboam. 368: Doug Muir, BBM. 372: Mitchell Payne, Jeroboam. 375: Christa Armstrong, Rapho Guillumette. 376: Marc Riboud, Magnum. 378: Jeffrey Blankfort, BBM. 381: Roger Lubin, Jeroboam.
Chapter 13   Page 392: Ron Partridge, BBM. 395: Erik Weber. 397: Earl Dotter, BBM. 400: David Powers, Jeroboam. 402: Bruce Davidson, Magnum. 405: Leonard Freed, Magnum. 407: Kevin Gleason. 412: Lawrence Cameron. 414: George Rodger, Magnum. 418: Ron Partridge, BBM. 422: Pana, BBM. 425: Bob Main, BBM.
Chapter 14   Page 432: J. Eyerman, Black Star. 435: Ron Partridge, BBM. 438: Charles Harbutt, Magnum. 442: Peeter Vilms, Jeroboam. 447: Elliott Erwitt, Magnum. 449: Leonard Freed, Magnum. 452: Mitchell Payne, Jeroboam. 454: Bill Owens, BBM. 457: Kevin Gleason. 459: Dennis Brack, Black Star. 462: Ray Ellis, Rapho Guillumette.
Chapter 15   Page 466: Susan Ylvisaker, Jeroboam. 471: Fred Ward, Black Star. 475: Lawrence Cameron. 478: Leonard Freed, Magnum. 479: Hap Stewart, Jeroboam. 483: Michelle Vignes, BBM. 485: Ernest Lowe, BBM. 487: War Relocation Authority, National Archives. 489: Optic Nerve, Jeroboam.
Chapter 16   Page 494: Nacio Jan Brown, BBM. 497: William Rosenthal. 500: Roger Lubin, Jeroboam. 502: Kevin Gleason. 504: Elihu Blotnick, BBM. 510: Michael Abramson, Black Star. 516: Nacio Jan Brown, BBM. 520: Bruce Baumann, Black Star.

PREFACE

With each new sociology text that arrives to take its place among the multitudes already lining instructors' offices, many instructors must ask themselves wearily, why yet another? We believe the answers to that question are evident to most of those who ask it. Not only does the discipline of sociology itself grow and change in methods, content, and data, but each new wave of students presents its own unique problems and challenges to the instructor of sociology. We think that in its particular perspective and in its many pedagogic features this text answers the challenge posed by today's students.

In many years of teaching the sociological perspective, or what C. Wright Mills called "the sociological imagination," we have seen from experience that even well into the course students can still drift back into interpreting social behavior by "individualistic" assumptions. In this text we have tried to keep the sociological perspective in full view throughout. In addition, the project boxes, issues, and summary points and questions constantly reinforce the student's grasp of this perspective.

Since students are not likely to fully understand what sociology *is* without understanding what sociologists *do*, and why, we have tried to accomplish both descriptions in the text. And when basic concepts are presented they are vividly illustrated in ways that tie in with society as experienced by the student. The project boxes, already mentioned, are found throughout every chapter. They are exercises in sociological thinking and investigating, but framed at such a level that students can profitably handle them. While few students may be likely to complete all project boxes in one semester, even reading and discussing them in class should give everyone additional insight into the scope and methods of sociology.

The issue in each chapter is meant to stimulate the student's thinking on the subject of that chapter, and to promote active involvement in the process of defining or evaluating the data faced by the sociologist. The photographs, 170 in all, are likewise intended not only as a graphic enhancement of the text but also, by means of their captions, as an additional stimulus for the student to become involved in sociological activities. Chapter summaries also present the student with questions about each summary point.

Like the pedagogical features listed above, the arrangement of the text itself is intended to have the same illuminating effect on the student. In Part I we not only describe the sociological perspective at length but also give a brief history of the discipline and catalog the chief sociological models in current use. Our hope is to give the student an appreciation of the healthy divergencies in the field rather than to propagandize the student for a particular model. In Chapter 2 the scientific characteristics of sociology and research methodology are thoroughly described. Inclusion of case studies and participant observation methods reinforce the theme that there is no single, correct approach to sociological study.

In Part II the basic concepts for understanding social organization are treated in such a way as to clarify for students the world of their own experience. This effort to make the student's own world understandable while illuminating sociological concepts is continued through Part III, on social institutions, and through Part IV, on change and conflict in societies. At no time, however, is the sociologist's analytical concern abandoned for a "social problems" approach—even on such topics as ethnic relations, urban life, and deviancy.

Running throughout the book is the eclectic viewpoint, an effort to make the chief sociological models intelligible as scientific tools, however limited the success of each in dealing with certain topics. Repeatedly each of the chief models is tested against the sociologist's raw data to gauge its analytical effectiveness. The student is thus able to see the interplay that occurs in sociology between the things studied and the mode of study.

Any text is a collaboration of many—authors, editors, reviewers, and so on. In this particular text, Ellen Voland prepared chapters 6, 12, and 15, and William Kenkel prepared all remaining chapters except Chapter 11, which was prepared by Robert Ellis. In addition, Robert Ellis prepared the Student Guide and Instructor's Manual. We expect that users of the Student Guide will find it an aggressive supplement to the book. For each chapter of the text, the Guide presents a chapter consisting of introductory comments, an overview of the topics, treatment of key concepts, unit summaries and objectives, application exercises, a postcheck, and a popular bibliography to supplement the suggested readings in the text. The Instructor's Manual consists of two parts. Part I surveys in broad outline alternative ways of instructing students in the subject. Part II lists for each chapter specific suggestions for lecture topics, speakers, class activities, and media sources. A separate test bank is also available to the instructor.

While producing this text, we benefited immensely from the constructive criticism of many reviewers. If any one reviewer were to be singled out as having been most relied upon it would be Joan Huber, University of Illinois at Urbana–Champaign. But the text also shows the care and insights of Jane Dabaghian, American River College; Roger W. Libby, The Institute for Family Research and Education, Syracuse University; Mattye Mauldin, Angelo State University; David E. Preston, Eastfield College; and Jacqueline P. Wiseman, University of California, San Diego.

Equal gratitude is also due the many University of Kentucky faculty members who read chapters dealing with their specialties, and to Maurice Voland of North Carolina State University, who reviewed the chapters written by his wife. Two graduate students deserve recognition: Stephen Papson, who worked on the project boxes and chapter summaries, and Carolyn Sachs, who worked on the test questions. The many drafts and revisions of the manuscript were typed by Marlene Pettit, whose skill, patience, and cooperativeness can, alas, be fully appreciated only by us.

The editors at Canfield Press were a joy to work with. Sociology Editor Howard Boyer lent his rare blend of support and judicious criticism based on thorough knowledge of the manuscript. Developmental and production editor Kevin Gleason acted as a reader's advocate, so to speak, going beyond stylistic improvements to question and clarify matters of content. Photo researcher Barbara Hodder worked with Gracia Alkema to enhance the text both visually and pedagogically. And last, Gordon Light, Chris Schacker, Julie Kranhold, Molly Vaux, Nancy Stepperud, and many people at Kingsport Press worked diligently to meet a tight schedule without sacrificing the quality of the book.

CONTENTS

I

UNDERSTANDING SOCIOLOGY

If you are curious about your society (and we're supposing you are, or become so during this course), if you find just about everything around you fascinating and puzzling, familiar and at the same time mysterious—in short, if you suffer from that delightful human malady, "intellectual curiosity," a broad, constant yearning to truly understand things—how do you begin to satisfy your curiosity? The world might seem to radiate out from you in concentric circles: your family and friends, your classmates and roommates, the campus and town or city, and on and on, outward across the continent and beyond to the most distant societies.

Where do you even begin to satisfy your curiosity? How do you go about choosing the first step out of your puzzlement? Well, it's safe to say that no matter what methods you chose to use, you wouldn't be the first to use them, even if you weren't aware that you were borrowing them. Why? Because your affliction (curiosity) goes as far back into the human past as do methods of recording thoughts. And those records show remarkable variety and inventiveness in the ways of asking and answering questions about the world and the human place in it.

Oddly, many of the earliest records phrase answers rather than questions, and quite authoritative answers at that. This tendency to keep the question and thoughts about it to oneself but to make the answer public was a rather common human trait until only a few centuries ago. Nevertheless, if we go back to classical Greece, to about the fifth century B.C., we find a few people recording their questions and trying to formulate ways of measuring the reliability of their answers. That is, we find people who have become aware that appearances can be deceiving and that a method of asking and answering questions is essential for getting at the truth of whatever we're investigating. Imaginative answers, myths, and parables are no longer to be accepted at face value.

1

I

Unfortunately, despite a few glimmerings here and there (about one every five centuries that we know of), some 2000 years had to pass before, in the sixteenth century, the intuitions of the Greek philosophers began to be refined into the set of assumptions and rules that today we call the scientific method. Like our knowledge of the world, our ways of acquiring that knowledge have undergone a constant, gradual refinement. Not only did the instruments of science improve, but so did the rules that govern the scientist's ways of working and of judging the value of the results.

Success bred success, and from the seventeenth to the nineteenth century the number of scientists grew immensely, as did the scope of their investigations. More than once it was declared that science had finally solved every mystery of the physical world. Although such boasts were short-lived, they show the confidence that was placed in science and the satisfaction many felt about the work that had been done so far.

Those who had now come to be called scientists had for all previous centuries been called natural philosophers, for their methods had been much like those of other philosophers, the moral philosophers, metaphysicians, political theorists, and so on. Usually, in fact, the same people felt capable of pursuing knowledge in all of these fields of inquiry. (And the man who was known for tens of centuries simply as "the Philosopher," Aristotle, is usually also considered the father of most sciences.)

While the natural philosophers were perfecting their methods and evolving into scientists, it was rare for anyone to confuse human beings with atoms, stars, or living biological cells. The methods of studying these objects were not applied to people, and the study of societies and men and women continued to be by a mixture of logic, ethical rule-laying, and myths about our origins and nature. What is and what should be were considered inseparable. The one man who proposed to tell his prince solely about the realities of political power, Machiavelli, saw his name become synonymous with cynicism and evil.

Not until the nineteenth century did anyone seriously propose to study people and society by the same methods that had yielded so much knowledge of the physical world. Those who did were moved to do so partly by the unsettled conditions of the advanced societies of their day. For the social, economic, and political consequences of the Industrial Revolution were enormously troubling. So Auguste Comte, and soon after him a growing number of others, divorced themselves from social philosophy and pursued social science.

Each of the social sciences adapts the general methods and assumptions of science to its own field of study. The particular insight of sociologists, and the one they seek to refine and expand in detail by the use of science, is that human beings are, in the ancient phrase, social animals. That each of us is an individual is not denied by sociologists. But they are well aware that each of us is also a member of various social groupings, and that our beliefs, values, and patterns of behavior are the products of our membership in groups and our interactions with other people.

Sociologists maintain that studying the individual as an individual is like studying that person in an artificial vacuum. You may find this confusing at first, for don't you experience yourself as an individual? Aren't your joys, your fears, your frustrations your own, to be shared with others only by the effort of communication? That much is true, but it is only part of the truth. For example, suicide is surely one of the ultimate individual acts, to which a person can be driven by no less than extreme despair, unbearable physical pain, personal loneliness, or insanity. Yet the classic early sociological study, Suicide, by Emile Durkheim demonstrated that social factors play an important role in suicide rates. The kind and degree of the individual's attachment to groups could be related to the likelihood of suicide: more unmarried people than married, more Protestants than Catholics, more people in times of social confusion and unrest than in more placid times, and so on.

Since Durkheim's pioneering study, the methods of sociological research have been greatly refined and enriched. There are now a wide array of techniques, from Durkheim's own technique of statistical analysis, to interviews, questionnaires, sample surveys, and methods of direct observation.

But like any science, sociology includes a variety of other processes as well, without which data collecting by whatever methods would be useless. Without the fundamental premise that the world shows order and regularity in its workings, no science could have developed. For each science is basically a collection of interrelated methods of confirming such regularity and finding the laws by which it operates. To do this, physical and social scientists form concepts, make and confirm generalizations, and from these create theories, which in turn are the bases for hypotheses to be tested by the methods of research.

True, scientific investigation begins and ends with observation of the perceptible world, but without these mental activities there can be no true observation. Consider the myth that Isaac Newton discovered the law of gravity when a falling apple landed on his head. Now ask yourself: If Newton wasn't the first to be sitting under an apple tree when an apple fell, why was he the first to see a law of universal scope in the fall of that humble object?

So the two chapters that follow should give you the perspectives and methods you'll need as you begin to try to solve the puzzle of society. The first chapter will familiarize you with sociology, the second with the scientific method and its use by sociologists.

If each of us is unique, why is it that we are also very much alike? Sociologists trace our similarities to the group basis of human behavior, to the ways in which we interact with one another as the social animals we are. Since sociological concerns and many of its insights are as old as recorded thought, what's so special about sociology? Basically, sociology seeks to solve the ancient puzzles of human social behavior by the scientific method. In so doing, some sociologists fit society to the structural-functional model, which compares society to a living organism; others fit society to the conflict model, with conflict and change as the basic features of society; and still others take what is useful from both models but refuse to force society into the framework of either.

1

THE SOCIOLOGICAL POINT OF VIEW

> . . . the sociologist . . . is a person intensively, endlessly, shamelessly
> interested in the doings of men. His natural habitat is all the human
> gathering places of the world. . . .their institutions, their history, their
> passions. . . . And, if he is a good sociologist, he will find himself in
> all these places because his own questions have so taken possession
> of him that he has little choice but to seek for answers.
>
> Peter L. Berger

Most of us, in our humanity—or perhaps in our vanity—think first of our unique-
ness as individuals. It is only by extension that we come to recognize the unique-
ness of all people. Each person is indeed unique. Nevertheless, by focusing on
groups of people we can learn much about how individuals come to be the
way they are and why they believe and act the way they do. For example, in
your circle of friends and acquaintances there may be people who take tran-
quilizers or perhaps regularly visit a psychiatrist. If your group of friends is
statistically normal, more female friends than male friends will be doing these
things, and you may wonder why—why so many more women than men?[1] What
is wrong with these women?

The sociologist would ask a different kind of question. Instead of asking "What
is wrong with these women?" the sociologist would seek *social* explanations
for the higher rate of emotional disorders among women. The sociologist might
ask, for example, how female emotional problems might be related to a society's
expectation that women should suppress their individuality and subordinate their
interests to those of a man in their lives. Or perhaps the emotional problems
experienced by women are related to society's failure to provide women with

[1]Reliable information shows that adult women currently comprise most of the patients in community mental
health centers and in private psychotherapeutic treatment. See Phyllis Chesler, *Women and Madness* (Garden
City, N.Y.: Doubleday & Co., 1972).

meaningful roles. The sociologist may even reject the idea that just because more women than men seek psychiatric help, this means that psychiatric problems are more common among women. From the sociologist's point of view, the figures may suggest that a society can define masculinity in such a way as to make it difficult for men to admit that they need help with their emotional problems.

The sociologist would ask still more troublesome questions, such as: What really is mental illness? Is it an individual pathology, or does society's definition of proper behavior and normal thought patterns inevitably lead to the conclusion that some people's ways of coping are so unusual that they need treatment?[2] Obviously the sociologist does not have all of the answers to the problems that have plagued humanity and that continue to recur with distressing regularity. But the sociologist does have a unique way of looking at such problems. The questions asked and the answers sought are different from what one might expect on the basis of "common sense."

THE SOCIAL ANIMAL

It has been said, "Man is the only animal that blushes . . . or needs to." Perhaps so. It has also been said that humans are the only animals that drink when they are not thirsty and make love in every season. Again, perhaps so. Actually, many more important traits make humans unique and set them apart from the rest of the animal kingdom. It all depends on which slice of reality you choose, with which aspect of humanness you deal. The human's highly developed brain, upright posture, and opposable thumb clearly distinguish this animal from all others. Equally important, these physical characteristics as well as mental and emotional processes can be studied in a scientific way. And we can learn how such characteristics and processes affect overt individual behavior. For every aspect of our biological and psychological being there is a science or a discipline of study. Because the human being is also a social animal, there is a science that studies this aspect of human existence—the science of sociology.

We are social animals in many ways. To become fully human we need the nurturance of another human. Studies of children reared in isolation demonstrate that, although one can survive physically with a bare minimum of interaction, children raised away from social contact lack almost all the traits we call "human."[3] The only reason we have personalities is that we have interacted with other persons. Human beings have a deep, powerful interest in other human

[2]Thomas S. Szasz, ed., *The Manufacture of Madness* (New York: Dell Publishing Co., 1971).

[3]Kingsley Davis, "Final Note on a Case of Extreme Isolation," *American Journal of Sociology* 52 (March 1947), pp. 232–247.

Members of a community all share some basic traits, but they also reveal individual differences.

beings. We seek acceptance in ongoing human groups or establish new groupings if none exists that meets our needs. We derive satisfaction from interacting with others. We desire companionship and response from others in our groups. To be sure, we also band together to destroy people or to express our hate for them, but even here our social nature is apparent.

SOCIOLOGY AND THE INDIVIDUAL WITHIN THE INSTITUTION

To understand the behavior of individuals the sociologist looks beyond the specific behavior.[4] For example, while a couple with serious marital difficulties may view their problem as personal, it is a fact that in the United States more than one out of three marriages ends in divorce. This figure suggests that there are serious problems with the *institutions* of marriage and the family. Thus, even though a marriage counselor may be able to help a husband and wife adjust to their situation and in this sense deal with their personal problems, the sociologist would approach the issue of divorce in quite another way. From the sociologist's point of view, an important question may have to do with how the role of the woman makes her subordinate to her husband. Is the wife's inferior status

[4]For a further elaboration of this point and a good discussion of the sociological point of view generally see C. Wright Mills, *The Sociological Imagination* (New York: Oxford University Press, 1959).

Ask 20 to 50 people what they would say are the causes of divorce. How many give social explanations? How many give explanations that stress personal characteristics of individuals or habits of the couple? Instead of or in addition to divorce ask about the causes of unemployment, juvenile delinquency, or mental illness and classify the reasons as "sociological" or "individualistic."

in a marriage compatible with our expressed values of equality and democracy? Has the role she is expected to play been made obsolete by social and technological developments? In short, do society's expectations of how a wife should feel and behave make divorce almost inevitable? The sociologist would also examine how the family has declined as an educator and as a provider for the economic needs of husband, wife, and children, and how married couples are ill-prepared for marriage and burdened with glamorized, romantic myths. Thus the sociologist would state the problem and search for its explanations in the institution of marriage, not in a series of individual crises to be dealt with by the unhappy couples.

The problem of unemployment further illustrates the sociological perspective. A man or a woman who cannot find work has a personal problem, and so does his or her family. To solve this problem the job skills of the man or the woman could be matched with available employment opportunities. But when unemployment is widespread, there is no such personal solution. Recurring slumps in the economy, the automation of factories, and the changing nature of work that renders some skills and abilities obsolete are social factors in unemployment that individual ingenuity cannot change. In the same way, an individual has little power to change the system that puts down women, blacks, and other groups or that creates urban sprawl or international wars. An individual may search for ways to adjust to his or her personal situation, but the sociologist looks to broader issues and institutions in society to explain conditions.

THE STUDY OF SOCIAL CHARACTERISTICS

From what we have said it should be clear that sociology concentrates on the group basis of human behavior. Although groups obviously are made up of individuals, the fundamental unit of the sociologist's analysis is not the individual but the group. To understand human behavior the sociologist studies the family, criminal gangs, societies, religious organizations, cities, rural communities, and many other groupings large and small. In seeking to explain the behavior of

Sociologists, analyzing society by the scientific method, describe social behavior without judging it, and they don't shy away from studying certain kinds of behavior.

individuals in groups, the sociologist concentrates on the *social characteristics* shared by the individuals. It is not always easy, however, to distinguish between individual characteristics and social characteristics. For example, age is an individual trait, but society also treats age as a category and, on the basis of age, gives or withholds privileges, such as driving a car or signing a contract.

How sociologists can use social characteristics to explain human behavior is illustrated by a look at the birth rate in the United States.[5] Birth can be viewed as a biological matter, for obviously if sperm and ovum never meet there can be no conception and therefore no birth. Yet we have known for some time that education, race, and rural or urban residence are also related to the birth rate. In the United States, college-educated women have about half as many children as do women who did not go to high school—a rather striking difference. The differences in family size in a society can thus be understood by learning what social characteristics are linked with family size. Anyone seeking, therefore, to lower the birth rate of a society should try to find ways of changing the behavior, not of individuals, but of large groups of people.

[5]See Chapter 13.

Observe as inconspicuously as possible a number of men and women in a setting such as a cafeteria. Describe their gestures, facial expressions, posture at the table, touching of one another. What can you tell from their body language about how they were interacting? Do men use different gestures and expressions than women? Try this experiment before and after reading **Body Language** by Julius Fast.

SOCIOLOGY: THE STUDY OF WHAT IS

It will become clear later in this chapter and in Chapter 2 that sociology, as a social science, subscribes to the general definition of a science. And as such, sociology is a descriptive, not a normative, discipline. It is concerned with what is, not with what should be. Although sociologists study different groups' values and ideas of right and wrong, they do not, as sociologists, advocate one system of beliefs over another. Sociological knowledge can be used normatively by others, however. For instance, in the chapter on social demography we present information on our past, present, and probable future national birth rates. An organization such as Zero Population Growth (ZPG) has drawn heavily on such information to reach the normative position that our birth rate is too high and should be reduced so the total population will not continue to grow. As a citizen, a sociologist may well be in entire sympathy with the goals of ZPG, but sociologists, as sociologists, do not recommend the adoption of a particular value position. As we discuss in Chapter 2, though, not all sociologists adopt this value-free stance.[6]

A DEFINITION OF SOCIOLOGY

At this point you have some idea about how sociologists view the social world and human behavior within it. Although understanding the point of view of sociology is more important than defining the field, some definition of sociology may help you keep in mind its chief features as you study its concerns and methods throughout this book.

Sociology is the study of *interaction* among people and of the way this interaction affects human behavior. People interact whenever they respond to the actions

[6]See pp. 56–57.

of other people and whenever their actions produce responses from others. A greeting is interaction, for one person acknowledges the other person's presence, while a return greeting acknowledges the first action. A formal meeting is interaction, and so is a mugging, a casual conversation, a gesture, or a kiss. Even posture, the tightening of muscles, or other manifestations of "body language" can be interaction if these actions either respond to or affect the behavior of another.[7] The essence of interaction is that the spoken words, the gestures, the writings, or other acts of one person in some way influence another person.

The study of human interaction and how it has affected human groups and societies has fascinated scholars and scientists for a long time. To give you some sense of the origins and development of this interest, let us turn to a brief account of the history of sociology.

THE ORIGINS OF SOCIOLOGY

Sociology is as old as the efforts of humans to understand themselves and society. In ancient times many rulers and thinkers observed human behavior and speculated about its effects on society. Often they drew up codes of laws to be followed by all for the good of society. The commandments of Moses are an example of such laws, as is the code of Hammurabi, written over 4,000 years ago. Its 282 laws dealt with the treatment of children, property rights, husband–wife relations, and other matters affecting the welfare of society. In *The Republic*, written in the fourth century B.C., Plato planned an ideal society, describing in great detail his ideas about the proper organization of the government, the economy, education, and the family. Many philosophers, religious leaders, and kings have spoken, often brilliantly, on the human condition, the ills of society, and how harmonious social relations could be promoted. All who have tried to understand the behavior of their fellow humans can be thought of as forerunners of sociology. Their speculations, however, were a far cry from the daring idea that came into prominent use in the nineteenth century—the idea that society could be studied by the scientific method.[8] This was the true beginning of sociology. The man who put forth the idea of a science of society was Auguste Comte.

[7]Julius Fast, *Body Language* (New York: Simon & Schuster, 1971), pp. 9–16.

[8]For a concise history of sociology see Roscoe C. Hinkle, Jr., and Gisela J. Hinkle, *The Development of Modern Sociology* (New York: Random House, 1954). See also Floyd N. House, *The Development of Sociology* (Westport, Conn.: Greenwood Press, 1936); and Nicholas S. Timasheff, *Sociological Theory* (Garden City, N.Y.: Doubleday & Co., 1955).

AUGUSTE COMTE

The Frenchman Auguste Comte (1798–1857) is often called the father of sociology, for he developed an elaborate system for the scientific study of society. He called this discipline *sociology*. His writings, which appeared between the years 1830 and 1854, in many important ways were the foundation of the discipline. Comte divided all of human history into three great stages: the theological, the metaphysical, and the positive. During the first epoch, Comte maintained, people gave theological explanations for everything and believed that all phenomena were "produced by the immediate action of supernatural beings."[9] In the second or metaphysical stage, abstract principles of man's own creation, such as the idea of "goodness," were thought of as ultimate causes. During the final, positive stage "the mind has given over the vain search after Absolute notions, the origin and destination of the universe, the causes of phenomena, and applies itself to the study of their laws."[10] *Positivism*, Comte's system of thinking, stresses invariable laws and the need for observation, experimentation, and comparison to discover and interpret the causes of events.

Thus, the idea that society should be studied scientifically was expressed well over a hundred years ago. Comte was mainly concerned with social order, or "social statics" as he called it, which he saw as the forces that held the parts of society together and governed the relationships of one part to the other. But he also sought laws of "social dynamics" or social change, thinking these laws would explain the progression of society to an ideal state.

Comte's dual interest in social order and social change is still the core of modern sociology. Sociology deals with social order by describing the regularity in social interaction that tends to keep human groups together. Unlike Comte, however, modern sociologists view change and conflict as normal processes of ongoing groups rather than as necessary steps in social progress toward an unchanging utopia.

HERBERT SPENCER

Herbert Spencer (1820–1903) was a wealthy, straitlaced English gentleman. He employed numerous secretaries to collect facts on human behavior from all over the world while he was content to remain in his library and write an elaborate theory of society. But Spencer, like Comte, was a positivist and, again like Comte,

[9]Auguste Comte, *The Positive Philosophy, Vol. I* (New York: D. Appleton, 1853), p. 2.

[10]Comte, p. 2.

August Comte (1798–1857)   **Herbert Spencer (1820–1903)**

believed that the scientific study of society would solve man's social problems and maladjustments.

Spencer held that sociology is "the study of evolution in its most complex form."[11] He believed in the existence of a "natural law" (a law operating unyieldingly through the processes of nature) that would guide societies through progressively higher stages and lead eventually to "the survival of the fittest," a phrase later borrowed by Darwin. In keeping with his ideas on social evolution, Spencer opposed aiding the poor and the dependent, for to do so would interfere with natural selection. And he was against free education, holding that those who truly wanted to learn would find a way to do so.

Modern sociologists no longer propose elaborate schematic explanations for the progress of all societies. Spencer's evolutionary model of social development has been abandoned, for a mass of evidence has shown that societies do not pass through a fixed and definite number of stages. Spencer's individualistic ideas on the survival of the fittest were adopted by a few early American sociologists but were generally not well accepted. Yet his strong conviction that the scientific method could be applied with great benefit to the study of society was readily accepted by many early sociologists.

[11]Herbert Spencer, *The Study of Sociology* (New York: D. Appleton, 1873), p. 350. See also Herbert Spencer, *The Principles of Sociology*, 3rd ed. (New York: D. Appleton, 1910).

KARL MARX

While Spencer used an evolutionary model of social development to support conservative, laissez-faire political arguments, Karl Marx (1818–1883) used a similar model to buttress political theories of the extreme left.[12] According to Marx's evolutionary model, each stage of civilization contained within itself "the seeds of its own destruction." Each must inevitably be followed by the next, higher stage. But because each stage resisted the coming of the new, revolution was necessary to achieve the next step in the evolutionary process.

Marx was an "economic determinist." He explained history, society, and social change by the economic relationships between people and between groups. Marx defined groups basically by their economic characteristics—that is, according to whether they owned "the means of production" (factories, machines, investment capital). He saw the capitalist system as plagued with injustices and "internal contradictions," and felt that a struggle between the workers and the capitalists—that is, between those who did not own the means of production and those who did—was inevitable. Because the system resisted change, Marx believed that only a major revolution could achieve a classless society.

Modern sociologists are indebted to Marx for his focus on conflict within society. Although Marx's ideas on resistance to social change are generally considered extreme and seem to be discredited by history, they are nevertheless a useful reminder that change is not always orderly and that people and groups often find it difficult to accept and adjust to social change.

EMILE DURKHEIM

Another early social theorist, the Frenchman Emile Durkheim (1858–1917), also developed an evolutionary model of society.[13] Durkheim focused on the division of labor, the degree of specialization within society. According to Durkheim, societies could be arranged on a scale from those with little specialization to those with much specialization. In smaller communities with little division of labor, people are held together by the strong bonds of their personal, intimate groups such as the family and the village church. Durkheim called this type of social cohesion "mechanical solidarity." In larger societies with greater division of labor, social cohesion rests on the formal contracts and common interests that bind persons to one another. Durkheim called this form of social cohesion "organic solidarity."

[12]Karl Marx and Friedrich Engels, The Communist Manifesto, ed. Samuel H. Beer (New York: Appleton-Century-Crofts, 1955); and Karl Marx, Capital, ed. Friedrich Engels (New York: International Publishers, 1967).

[13]Emile Durkheim, The Division of Labor in Society, trans. George Simpson (New York: The Free Press, 1949).

Karl Marx (1818–1883)   **Emile Durkheim (1858–1917)**

Other sociologists have typed human societies in ways similar to Durkheim's, suggesting that by describing the different kinds of bonds between people Durkheim was getting at a basic feature of human groups. You will note the similarity, too, between Durkheim's notion and the concept of *primary group* discussed in Chapter 6. Primary groups are characterized by intimate, personal, and usually face–to–face relations among members, whereas secondary groups are bound by more formal ties. Although contemporary sociologists do not accept Durkheim's notion of evolution as a fixed, unchangeable course of movement from one type of society to another, they do accept as fundamental the change in societies from primary, personal relations to impersonal, secondary ones.[14]

Durkheim's study of suicide, published in 1897, can be considered the first scientific study in sociology.[15] In this work Durkheim sought to discover whether the degree to which people were integrated into cohesive groups was related to suicide rates. According to his theory, people who have strong emotional ties to an enduring group, such as the family or the church, should, as a *category*, have a lower suicide rate than those without such ties. Durkheim collected

[14]Sacred versus secular and folk versus urban have been developed by Becker and Redfield, respectively. See Howard Becker, *Through Values to Social Interpretation* (Durham, N.C.: Duke University Press, 1950); and Robert Redfield, *The Folk Culture of Yucatan* (Chicago: University of Chicago Press, 1941). See also Tonnies' distinction between *Gemeinschaft* (community type of society) and *Gesellschaft* (urban type of society) in Ferdinand Tonnies, *Fundamental Concepts of Sociology*, trans. Charles P. Loomis (New York: American Book Co., 1940).

[15]Emile Durkheim, *Suicide: A Study in Sociology*, ed. George Simpson (New York: The Free Press, 1951).

statistics on suicide for many years and from many European countries. The results of his study showed that single people did indeed have a higher rate of suicide than the married.

Earlier we discussed how sociologists use social characteristics to explain human behavior. You can see how in his study of suicide Durkheim was the first to set forth this idea and also the first to demonstrate the validity of the sociological approach. He did not try to explain individual acts of suicide by the person's mental illness or emotional stress or imbalance; rather, he studied how the *rate* of suicide varied among different *categories* of people. This method of study is an excellent example of the sociological perspective.

MAX WEBER

The German sociologist Max Weber (1864–1920) received his academic training in economics and law. He taught at the University of Heidelberg, but because of a severe breakdown in his health dropped out of academic work for eighteen years. Because he was independently wealthy, Weber used this time for travel and scholarly research.

Weber's contributions to sociology were enormous.[16] Many of his important ideas on the nature of sociology are contained in writings that deal with concrete problems. He had no grand scheme of society like Comte's, Spencer's, or Marx's but instead wrote widely on such social topics as religion, economics, bureaucracy, the city, and social history. (In Chapter 7 we deal with Weber's ideas on power and social class.)

One of Weber's most important studies is *The Protestant Ethic and the Spirit of Capitalism*.[17] His methods and logic are as fascinating as the findings. The data that he collected, indicating that the Protestant areas of Germany were wealthier than the Catholic sections, suggested to Weber that a relationship existed between the economic and religious systems of society. Capitalism, as Weber saw it, is a system of profit–making enterprises that are bound together. Mature capitalism, the rise of which he sought to explain, is more than just profit–making; it is a rational activity that stresses order and discipline. Success in profit–making is seen as an indication that the organization is functioning smoothly and efficiently.

[16]*From Max Weber: Essays in Sociology*, trans. and ed. H. H. Gerth and C. Wright Mills (New York: Oxford University Press, 1946); and Max Weber, *The Theory of Social and Economic Organization*, trans. A. M. Henderson and Talcott Parsons (New York: Oxford University Press, 1947).

[17]Max Weber, *The Protestant Ethic and the Spirit of Capitalism*, trans. Talcott Parsons (New York: Charles Scribner and Sons, 1958).

Max Weber (1864–1920)

In the Calvinist form of Protestantism, salvation was thought to be predetermined; that is, a person was born already saved by God or damned to an eternity in Hell. But Calvinists also believed that one's worldly success was a sign that one was chosen. Calvinism stressed that people should work hard at their worldly callings and should practice self–discipline. To work hard and to achieve worldly success were thus important elements in Calvinist doctrine.

Weber noted that the kind of behavior promoted by the religious doctrines of Calvinism closely fitted the behavior needed for the success of mature capitalism. As he saw it, if general economic conditions are ripe for the development of mature capitalism, the Protestant ethic will stimulate its emergence. Not content to rest his case with Western societies, Weber studied the economic systems and religions of India and China. These studies led him to conclude that economic conditions cannot in themselves guarantee the development of capitalism; another ingredient is necessary—an ethical or moral system that promotes behavior conducive to capitalistic success. Weber's study is not merely of historical interest. A recent research article compared the occupational histories of 161 fathers and sons and found that Protestant men tend toward greater occupational and educational achievement than do Catholic men.[18]

[18]James W. Crowley and John A. Ballweg, "Religious Preference and Worldly Success: An Empirical Test in a Midwestern City," *Sociological Analysis* 32 (Summer 1971), pp. 71–80.

Max Weber's definition of sociology as "a science which attempts the interpretive understanding of social action in order thereby to arrive at a causal explanation of its course and effects"[19] is close to our definition of sociology as the study of social interaction. Note, too, that Weber held sociology to be a science and that he saw sociology's mission as the explanation, not merely the description, of human behavior. Many modern sociologists share these ideas.

MODELS IN CONTEMPORARY SOCIOLOGY

Sociology is a young science. As the field developed, the ideas and theories of the early founders were not always useful for explaining the conditions and problems of human society that later sociologists saw around them. For example, the evolutionary model, with its assumptions that all societies progress through immutable stages of growth toward some kind of utopia, does not square with the known facts. Ancient China, once more advanced than many other cultures, later slowed down in its development and was surpassed by European civilizations. The many primitive tribes studied by anthropologists show a variety of change patterns proving that they grow in different ways and at different rates. Thus, the early assumptions about rules of social progress were abandoned and new ways of studying the social world were developed. Even today different models of society guide research and determine what aspects of social reality the researcher will study.[20]

A model is a set of integrated assumptions about some system we wish to understand. A model can be in one's mind, as with the farmer who relates his assumptions about market conditions, grain prices, and his financial resources to the decision of whether to increase his livestock holdings. Physicists use a written model with mathematical symbols to express the relationship between factors that affect a problem at hand. Sociological models are most frequently expressed in words that explain the ordered set of assumptions the researcher uses to understand human interaction and its results. The two most common sociological models are the structural–functional model and the conflict model.

[19]Weber, *The Theory of Social and Economic Organization*, p. 88.

[20]For a concise treatment of different models used in sociology see Alex Inkeles, *What Is Sociology?* (Englewood Cliffs, N.J.: Prentice-Hall, 1964), ch. 3.

THE STRUCTURAL-FUNCTIONAL MODEL: HOW SOCIETY HOLDS TOGETHER

The *structural-functional* model implicitly compares society to a living organism.[21] Just as your body has its digestive, circulatory, and reproductive systems, a society has interacting systems, called *structures*. The family system, the religious system, the educational system, and the political system are the major structures of society.

How a structure contributes to the survival and well-being of the total society is its *function*. Structural-functional analysts thus examine the total society in order to determine how the structures that make up the whole affect that society. In Chapter 8, for example, we analyze the functions of the family; we look at the consequences that different aspects of this institution have for the survival of the society and the solution of social problems. An obvious function of the family is to care for dependent infants and to train and educate them so that they will be acceptable adults. If any society is to endure, this function must be performed in one way or another. Here again the sociologist's point of view is clear. Although a man or a woman may like to rear children and may get married to make this possible, the sociologist is less concerned with personal satisfactions and motivations than with the social functions served by child-rearing.

Structural-functional analysis yields insights into the workings of human society in many ways. It can reveal how the various structures work together to keep the society in operation, for example, how the family and the school share the task of childrearing. Structural-functional analysis also shows that social customs are more than merely interesting practices with no relation to the whole of society. For example, although the custom we call dating may be something that people do because it is fun, it also has a functional importance within the larger institutions of marriage and family. In our society we expect that a husband and a wife will like each other and get along well together. Dating serves this expectation by allowing a man and a woman to test their

[21]For major works on functionalism see Talcott Parsons, *The Structure of Social Action* (New York: The Free Press, 1949); Talcott Parsons, *The Social System* (New York: The Free Press, 1941); and Robert K. Merton, *Social Theory and Social Structure* (New York: The Free Press, 1957). Among the many other works dealing with the topic are: Bernard Barber, "Structural-Functional Analysis: Some Problems and Misunderstandings," *American Sociological Review* 21 (April 1956), pp. 129-135; Harry C. Bredemeier, "The Methodology of Functionalism," *American Sociological Review* 20 (April 1955), pp. 173-180; Francesca Cancian, "Functional Analysis of Change," *American Sociological Review* 24 (December 1960), pp. 818-827; Kingsley Davis, "The Myth of Functional Analysis as a Special Method in Sociology and Anthropology," *American Sociological Review* 24 (December 1959), pp. 757-772; Harold Faulding, "Functional Analysis in Sociology," *American Sociological Review* 28 (February 1963), pp. 5-13; and Carl G. Hempel, "The Logic of Functional Analysis," in Llewellyn Gross, ed., *Symposium on Sociological Theory* (Evanston, Ill.: Row-Peterson, 1959), pp. 271-307.

In the structural-functional model, society works because certain functions are performed by specific structures. What example(s) of this model can you observe here?

compatibility before committing themselves to marriage. Dating, therefore, is not an isolated social custom but is a functional part of the mate–selection process. In former years in India, for instance, marriages were arranged by parents with the expectation that love and personal attraction would come after the union. There was no need for a couple to test their compatibility before marriage, and the custom of dating did not exist.

The structural–functional model also allows us to compare different societies as well as different stages of the same society. These points are related. In studies of other societies structural–functionalists may discover various structures for performing the same social functions. They may find that in another society children are reared by more specialized persons than their parents—in day–care centers, for example. They would then explore how performing the function in this way fits in with other group values, such as a greater stress on communal values. They could also compare how at different points in the history of a given society the same structure performed different functions. For example, the family structure at one time might have performed the function of caring for the elderly as well as for the young, whereas now it cares only for the young.

THE MODEL AND ITS CRITICS

The structural–functional model is not without its critics.[22] One criticism is that the model is an oversimplified view of social reality. Something may be called functional simply because it seems to work. For example, the pre–Civil War institution of slavery could be labeled either functional or highly *dysfunctional.* As a means of producing goods slavery was "functional." But can any system that virtually tore the country apart and degraded human beings be called functional? The system was actually harmful to the Southern economy in that cheap labor retarded the development of better agricultural practices and non-agricultural pursuits. And, of course, the social problems left in its wake have been with us for more than a century.

Another criticism of structural–functionalism is that it has a conservative bias. By focusing on how certain practices help keep society running, it is an easy step to conclude, critics say, that such practices are therefore good. Slavery could illustrate this point, but so can the current economic system. Concentrating on how the economy works to produce and distribute goods can ignore unemployment, poverty, and great differences in income, all of which are also part of the system. Because structural–functionalism stops the motions of society at a given time and examines how various structures contribute to the society at that time, the model tends to emphasize stability rather than change, even though it does not assume that society is unchanging.

The severest criticism of structural–functionalism is that it does not give a true picture of social reality. Proponents of the *conflict model* claim that it is a serious misconception to view society as being in a state of equilibrium with all of its parts contributing to the harmonious balance of the whole. While this notion overstates the functionalist position, the idea that conflict, and not order, is the dominant social condition is worth considering.

THE CONFLICT MODEL: SOCIETY IN STRIFE

When a conflict theorist looks at society, he sees group struggling against group and clashes of interest everywhere. Karl Marx, as we have seen, was an early conflict theorist. His theory of the inevitable struggle between workers and those who own the means of production, the capitalists, is an early example of the conflict model of social interaction.

No single capitalist today owns a modern factory system. Nevertheless one group, the board of directors, manages the system, while another group works

---

[22]The major criticisms have been by those who developed or hold to the opposing conflict model. See the references cited under that topic.

Write a short essay on the university as it would be described by a structural–functionalist sociologist. Then do the same from the conflict theorist point of view. Which essay was easier to write? Which represents your real opinion? A debate in class could substitute for the essays.

---

for a wage. At times there are strikes, and between times there is much negotiating involving bargaining between workers and managers, threats of strikes, and the establishment of numerous rules and regulations specifying the rights and obligations of each party. These expressions of disagreement are important to the conflict theorist. Yet because the system is in operation most of the time, it is reasonable to ask what holds it all together. The conflict theorist sees the order that exists as the result of one group's ability to control the other.[23]

Clash of interests and the *unequal distribution of power* are thus two main concepts for the conflict theorist. Labor unions, associations of manufacturers, lobbies, and pressure groups are vivid proof of differences of interests within society, but many less organized groups differ with one another over who should get what share of goods and social privileges. Clearly power, that is, the ability of persons or groups to get their own way even when opposed, is unequally distributed in society; some have more "clout" than others. Thus, society can be divided into those who have power and those who do not, with the "haves" seeking to retain power and the "have nots" seeking to get it.

Conflict and power struggles are easy to find in modern American society. Riots in cities and prisons are frequently coupled with demands by the dissenters, a clear indication that one group wants more control over its life and living conditions. Consumer groups are formed to secure truth in advertising and to obtain redress from shoddy manufacturing. Environmentalists clash with energy interests over such matters as the Alaska pipeline. Anti–abortionists vie with those who favor legal abortion on demand. School boards clash with parents over what should be taught and who should decide the issues. The list could be continued. In every nook and cranny of society we find group pitted against group in an unending struggle to determine which shall have the power to achieve its goals at some other group's expense. Although not always violent or noisy, conflict must be considered a part of social reality.

[23]Important works in conflict theory are many, including: Lewis Coser, *The Functions of Social Conflict* (New York: The Free Press, 1956); Ralf Dahrendorf, *Class and Class Conflict in Industrial Society* (Stanford, Calif.: Stanford University Press, 1959); Alvin W. Gouldner, *The Coming Crisis of Western Sociology* (New York: Basic Books, 1970); Irving L. Horowitz, ed., *The New Sociology* (New York: Oxford University Press, 1964); Peter Weingart, "Beyond Parsons: A Critique of Ralf Dahrendorf's Conflict Theory," *Social Forces* 48 (December 1969), pp. 151–165.

When a conflict theorist looks at society, he sees group struggling against group and clashes of interest everywhere.

THE NEED FOR DIFFERENT MODELS

Modern sociologists are not disturbed by the different models employed in the study of social interaction. The discipline is not at the stage where a single, all-encompassing model can guide sociologists in each of their studies. As we build toward such a stage, each existing model can act as a corrective or cleansing mechanism for others. Overemphasis on what holds society together and what promotes stability is corrected by focus on conflict and change. Overemphasis on the structure of groups, which in a sense ignores the individual, is balanced by the *humanistic* and the *symbolic interaction* models.[24]

[24]Alfred McClung Lee, *Toward Humanistic Sociology* (Englewood Cliffs, N.J.: Prentice-Hall, 1973); and Herbert Blumer, *Symbolic Interactionism: Perspective and Method* (Englewood Cliffs, N.J.: Prentice-Hall, 1969).

If sociologists differ among themselves about which model yields the most valid knowledge of social interaction, it is both understandable and desirable that such differences exist in a young discipline. As the sociologist Morris Cohen puts it, "Science means the rigorous weighing of all evidence, including a full consideration of all possible theories."[25]

THE ECLECTIC VIEWPOINT

Eclecticism is the selection of elements from various models rather than strict adherence to a single model. It has an obvious advantage in a field that studies broad, complex phenomena but that has not yet developed stable, incontestably proven theories. Different sociologists can approach their studies from different viewpoints, thus adding various dimensions to our knowledge of human interaction. A single model is neat and precise, but if certain kinds of studies cannot be performed because they do not fit that model, valuable knowledge can be lost. Eclectism can be confusing if one is prematurely concerned with what is the best model, but not if one views it as a necessary stage in the development of a comprehensive theory.

The approach followed in this book is eclectic, but with a heavier reliance on structural–functionalism than on other models. However, some issues are better handled by other models. In Chapter 10, for example, we start off with a structural–functional analysis of the educational institution, analyzing how this institution fits in with the rest of the social order. But to deal with such issues as who should control the schools, the conflict model is more appropriate. The modern American city could scarcely be handled without reference to conflict, nor could minority group relations. Throughout this book the various models will not be labeled when they are used. Elements of each are simply applied to each issue, concept, or topic being discussed.

WHY STUDY SOCIOLOGY?

Anyone who has felt intellectual curiosity about the world can understand the sociologist's motivation. For sociologists are simply men and women who are curious about how people interact with one another and form themselves into enduring groups and societies. They are interested in people and have decided to study them in a scientific way.

[25]Morris Cohen, *Reason and Nature: An Essay on the Meaning of Scientific Method* (New York: Harcourt, Brace and World, 1931), p. 347.

With the help of your instructor, or as a class project, develop a definition of sociology that you will consider correct. Interview 20 people, 10 college students and 10 people who are not connected with a college, and ask them what the word sociology means to them. Record their answers as carefully as possible. (Have a small group of students in the class analyze and score the answers.) In a table show how many had correct definitions.

The sociologist's laboratory is wherever people are gathered. The sociologist is not really concerned with who these people are or why they are gathered together, but only with how they interact with one another. Every kind of human interaction among every kind of human being is interesting to sociologists because they have questions about human behavior that press for answers. Sociologists seek to learn as much as they can about human interaction and to impart this knowledge to others because they feel this is the most relevant way they can spend their lives.

As a student, what will you get from the study of sociology? Will you learn anything that will be useful to you? We could dodge the question by saying that it all depends on how much you put into your studies. But how much you put into studying sociology depends in part on what you think you will get out of it. Chiefly what you should get out of an exploration of sociology is an understanding of the sociological point of view—that sometimes frustrating but always exciting way in which sociologists view reality. The study of sociology should develop your ability to examine human behavior objectively and to appreciate the need to get information that is as complete as possible. The sociologist seeks, as the courtroom oath puts it, the truth, the whole truth, and nothing but the truth.

Surely all reasonable people believe that it is good to see things without bias or prejudice. Or do they? At times sociology is unpopular precisely because its findings conflict with what people would like to believe. Sociologists are not really cantankerous people with a sadistic streak, but they seek the truth, and the truth can be quite disturbing.

Sociological studies have shown, for example, that on college campuses it is quite common for unmarried couples to live together. Many middle-aged and older people find this practice to be a disturbing and serious threat to their cherished values. Even more threatening is the sociologist's discovery that couples living together are happy and that they find in their relationship trust, com-

The sociologist's laboratory is wherever people are gathered. What questions might a sociologist ask about these men gathered in the streets of Rome?

panionship, and involvement with another person, and not just a simple opportunity for sexual satisfaction.[26] It would be more comforting to believe that such couples are a handful of sexually depraved neurotics who soon recognize the error of their ways, come to their senses, and opt for conventional marriage. It may be more comforting, but to the best of our knowledge it is not true.

We should not conclude from this example that sociologists study only controversial behaviors and interactions. As we have shown, sociologists study all human group behavior. And what sociologists have discovered about human interaction and human societies will be found throughout this book. We will consider information dealing with such matters as births, income, education, crime, and church attendance. But one course in sociology cannot provide you with all the findings of sociological research. Your introductory study of sociology should direct you to the sources of reasonably accurate information on human

[26]Judith L. Lyness, Milton E. Lipetz, and Keith Davis, "Living Together: An Alternative to Marriage," *Journal of Marriage and the Family* 34 (May 1972), pp. 305–311; and George Thorman, "Cohabitation: A Report on Couples Living Together," *The Futurist* 7 (December 1973), pp. 250–254.

SHOULD ANY SOCIAL ISSUES BE OFF-LIMITS
TO THE SOCIOLOGIST?

Whole societies or particular groups have held certain beliefs as virtually sacred, and scientists have often disagreed with these beliefs only at their peril. Centuries ago, the Ptolemaic theory of the universe fitted with the teachings of the Catholic Church, and the Church was not interested in any changes. But in 1632 Galileo Galilei published research support for the upstart Copernican theory. The Inquisition promptly invited Galileo to denounce his own findings. He pondered his alternatives (which included a very good chance of burning at the stake) and accepted the invitation.

Many sociologists have come up against a modern-day version of Galileo's choice. They have noted broadening political interference in their research and in the treatment of their reports. Many universities have set up review panels to limit the boundaries of research. And the United States Department of Health, Education, and Welfare issued in 1973 a lengthy report on a broad system of control that now applies to all federally funded research.

The area of research where sociologists feel most threatened is race relations. Apparently a combination of factors is at work. Minority problems and proposed solutions have, of course, long been sources of controversy. Minorities have developed their own identities and have sought to reestablish their own cultures. But they have also become conscious of themselves as victimized groups. In effect they have become politically significant.

In the politically charged atmosphere of recent years, violent controversies have been triggered by certain sociological reports. To name only a few, the Moynihan report of 1965 concluded that a major black problem was the matriarchal family inherited from the slave past; in 1966 James Coleman reported on the inequality of achievement between black and white school children; and, perhaps most notorious, the so-called Jensen report (see the issue in Chapter 15) of 1969 concluded that blacks seemed innately inferior to whites in intelligence.

Many sociologists have been condemned not only for their conclusions but even for having conducted and published their studies. They have gotten the message that "the scientist represents a threat to politically motivated interpreters of reality, and certain things are best left unsaid." The goals of sociologists and politicians appear to be in conflict, and in 1972 sociologist Wilson Record reported that most sociologists who had been specializing in race relations no longer were. Is this a gain for social harmony or a loss for social knowledge? And can you really have the first without the second?

interaction. Maybe you will want to seek out such information, and in doing so you will better equip yourself to understand your society and do your part in solving its problems.

From this brief history of sociology we can see that man has been investigating and speculating on society for centuries but that sociology itself is only about a century old. What creates this sharp distinction between social speculation and evaluation, on the one hand, and sociology on the other is the use of the scientific method in analyzing society. The scientific outlook and its method of research are the fundamental traits of any social science, and the sociologist employs these traits to study human interaction and groups. How this is done is the topic of the next chapter.

SUMMARY POINTS AND QUESTIONS

1. The sociologist searches for social explanations for human behavior and concentrates on social characteristics shared by individuals.

> *Explain the difference between a social and an individualistic interpretation of human behavior.*

> *What social characteristics might a sociologist investigate to explain why some people go to college and others do not?*

2. Sociology approaches its subject matter from a scientific position rather than from a normative position. Sociology does not make value judgments.

> *What is a value judgment?*

> *Why can't values be substantiated by science?*

3. Sociology studies social action—that is, people communicating, responding, and interacting with other people—and the social institutions that emerge from this interaction.

When is an action social action?

What are some types of action that are not social?

4. Sociology traces its roots back to Auguste Comte, who coined the word *sociology.* Comte divided human history into three stages, the theological, the metaphysical, and the positive, and called for the scientific study of society.

How would a positivistic explanation of social conditions differ from a theological and metaphysical one?

How does the view of the modern sociologist differ from that of Comte on the issues of change and conflict?

5. Three classical sociologists were Herbert Spencer who viewed evolution as the survival of the fittest, Karl Marx who believed that change is the result of conflicting classes, and Emile Durkheim who saw society becoming increasingly specialized. All of these writers were interested in social change.

Which of these social theories do you think best accounts for social change?

What evidence is there to support or reject each of these theories?

6. One of Max Weber's important studies is *The Protestant Ethic and the Spirit of Capitalism.*

What similarity did Weber note in the kind of behavior stemming from capitalism and Calvinism?

How does Weber's study fit the proposition that sociologists use social characteristics to explain human behavior?

7. One model of social reality used by sociologists is the structural–functional model. It conceptualizes society as a living organism having various structures that perform functions necessary for the survival of that organism.

What are some functions that must be performed if a society is to survive?

Does every structure have a function?

8. Another model is the conflict model. This model views society as a composite of groups with different interests that come into conflict with each other.

What are some of the opposing groups in our society?

In what ways and over what interests do these groups come into conflict?

9. One might also study social reality by selecting elements from various models. This is called eclecticism.

> *If you were an eclectic and were attempting to construct a model of society, what elements would you select from the structural-functional model? From the conflict model?*
>
> *Do you think it is better to use a single model or to draw on several to explain social reality? Why?*

10. Sociology is useful in that it offers a scientific perspective for the study of human behavior and by so doing makes us aware of the effect of groups, institutions, and society on our behavior and on the behavior of others.

> *Why did you choose to study sociology?*
>
> *What do you personally expect to get out of a sociology course?*

SUGGESTED READINGS

Aron, Raymond. *Main Currents in Sociological Thought,* vols. I and II. New York: Doubleday & Co., 1970. An excellent secondary source on the major classical theorists.

Berger, Peter L. *Invitation To Sociology: A Humanistic Perspective.* New York: Doubleday & Co., 1963. Constructs a humanistic sociological perspective to understand the relationship of man to social institutions and to society in general.

Bottomore, T. B. *Sociology: A Guide to Problems and Literature.* New York: Random House, 1972. Begins by defining the scope of sociology, then integrates major theoretical perspectives, and finally shows how these perspectives can be used to understand social problems.

Faris, Robert E., ed. *Handbook of Modern Sociology.* Chicago: Rand McNally, 1964. Provides a wide range of essays covering the various theoretical positions of the main schools of sociological thought.

Gouldner, Alvin W. *The Coming Crisis of Western Sociology.* New York: Basic Books, 1970. Essentially a critical review of the development and present stance of modern sociology. It concludes by calling for a reflexive sociology.

Hinkle, Roscoe C. and Gisela Hinkle. *The Development of Modern Sociology.* New York: Random House, 1954. Traces the development of American sociology from 1905 to 1954, specifically taking into account the influence of classical European sociology on American sociology.

Mills, C. Wright. *The Sociological Imagination*. New York: Oxford University Press, 1959. Criticizes bureaucratic or establishment sociology by calling for a sociology that takes into account the effects of both history and social institutions on man.

Nisbet, Robert. *The Sociological Tradition*. New York: Basic Books, 1967. Integrates the classical social theorists around five conceptual areas: community, authority, status, the sacred, and alienation.

Stein, Maurice and Arthur Vidich, eds. *Sociology on Trial*. Englewood Cliffs, N.J.: Prentice-Hall, 1963. A collection of essays dealing with problems that have plagued the discipline of sociology. Deals with such problem areas as value neutrality, bureaucratic sociology, and historical sociology.

Wallace, Walter L., ed. *Sociological Theory: An Introduction*. Chicago: Aldine, 1969. A collection of articles dealing with the major conceptual approaches of sociology. There are several especially good articles comparing the structural-functional model to the conflict model.

How can anyone pretend to learn anything scientific about unpredictable human beings? Well, sociologists have learned much about us by using the scientific method. Sociology (like any other science) begins and ends with observations of the real world, by sample surveys, by participant and nonparticipant observations, and by interviews, questionnaires, and census reports. But sociologists engage in a complex sequence of other steps as well. Conceptualization, generalization, theorizing, and the formulation of hypotheses are all based on the firm assumption that the social—as well as the natural—world shows order and predictability.

2

SOCIOLOGY AS A SCIENCE: GOALS AND METHODS

When we run over libraries . . . what havoc must we make? If we take in our hand any volume—of divinity or school metaphysics, for instance—let us ask, "Does it contain any abstract reasoning concerning quantity or number?" No. "Does it contain any experimental reasoning concerning matter of fact or existence?" No. Commit it then to the flames, for it can contain nothing but sophistry and illusion.

David Hume

I often say that when you can measure what you are speaking about and express it in numbers, you know something about it; but when you cannot express it in numbers, your knowledge is of a meagre and unsatisfactory kind; it may be the beginning of knowledge, but you have scarcely, in your thoughts, advanced to the state of science whatever the matter may be.

Lord Kelvin

We noted in the first chapter that sociology, as distinct from social speculation, involves the application of scientific principles and methods to the study of human behavior in groups. The ultrascientific views expressed in these quotations may imply that sociology has a cold and unfeeling approach to human interaction. Yet humans live in and are part of a world that can be explained by scientific principles. It is difficult to imagine living in an unpredictable world, in which all features and events in the environment, and human behavior as well, occur haphazardly. Fortunately we can predict that night will give way to day, that the oceans will keep their water, and that our clocks will continue to run forward.

PREDICTION AND ORDER IN SCIENCE

We do not know with absolute certainty that any of these things will happen, but our knowledge allows us to predict that they will probably do so. This predictability is inseparable from the notion of regularity or order in the universe. The fundamental assumption of science is that there is such order in the universe. All scientists believe that no event occurs by chance and that no elements of the universe are arranged haphazardly. Only if there is order in the universe can the scientific goals of understanding and predicting phenomena be achieved.

We do not know when, in the dim past, man first began to sense order in his surroundings. No doubt man was early aware of the regularity of periods of dark and light, of the inflexible sequence of seasons, and of the growth cycle of his own and other species. But we will never know which food gatherer, faintly sensing a regularity in nature, first mentally classified fruits as edible and inedible, or which ancient shepherd pondering the night skies first speculated that system and harmony were up there.

Almost everyone knows enough about human behavior to predict many sorts of social interaction. No one knows with certainty what will be the interaction pattern tomorrow between student and teacher, clerk and shopper, or doctor and patient, but we can predict with good accuracy these and other patterns.

Prediction is both an application of knowledge and a test of our knowledge or understanding. That is, if an event is correctly predicted before it happens, the principle that yielded the prediction is confirmed. If the event does not occur as predicted, then for some reason the general principle does not apply to the specific event.

SCIENTIFIC UNDERSTANDING: BUILDING GENERALIZATIONS

The scientific meaning of *understanding* is a more rigorous application of what the word usually means in the everyday world. If we understand the behavior of a close friend in a particular situation, we've applied our knowledge, our past familiarity with his or her personality and temperament, to the particular facts: We can say why our friend behaved as he or she did. From general knowledge about our friend—for our notion of his or her personality is a generalization built from our own observations and/or reports from other friends—we can explain the particular facts.

Sociologists try to discover the principles by which all human interaction can be described and how these principles interrelate.

The scientific meaning of understanding is not fundamentally different. From careful observation of particulars the scientist builds generalizations that both explain later particular happenings and are tested by those happenings. Each generalization is tested by how well it fits the particulars and how accurately it predicts each occurrence. The sociologist believes that human interaction and the formation and maintenance of groups are governed by *principles*, by descriptive generalizations. The scientific task of the sociologist is to discover these principles and explain how they work and how they relate to one another. All of the many principles in sociology are tentative: New knowledge could cause them to be qualified or even discarded.

ELEMENTS OF SCIENTIFIC RESEARCH

To understand a phenomenon we must gather and assemble much information about it; that is, we must do research. The basic elements of research are the same for all sciences, whether the exact, the natural, or the social.[1] The simplified scheme in Figure 2-1 shows the flow from one element of the scientific method to another.[2] Let us take a quick overview of the scheme and later we will elaborate on its parts.

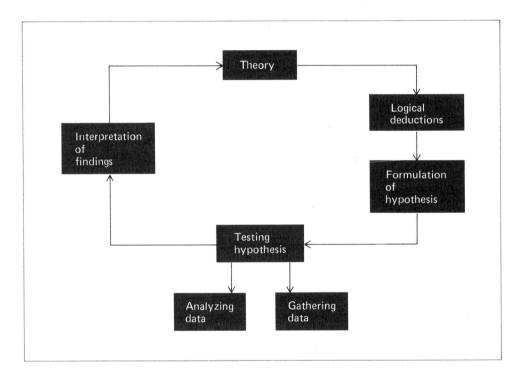

Figure 2–1.   This diagram shows the flow of elements in the research process. Sociologists do research by applying an already established theory to a specific problem. Following this procedure of deduction, hypothesis formulation, and hypothesis testing, they arrive at a result that either confirms the original theory or suggests ways in which the theory should be modified.

[1]For a good overview of the basic research steps see Delbert C. Miller, *Handbook of Research Design and Social Measurement* (New York: David McKay, 1970); and Walter L. Wallace, *The Logic of Science in Sociology* (Chicago: Aldine, 1971).

[2]Adapted and modified from Wallace, p. 18.

Good research begins and ends with *theory,* at the top of the figure. Every science has sets of systematically related propositions. These propositions are the theories of the science. A simple illustration of propositions can be taken from family sociology: "The greater the conflict between parents, the greater the inconsistency in the parents' treatment of a child; the greater the inconsistency in childrearing, the poorer will be the personal development of the child." Knowing these propositions, a researcher may want to test whether marital conflict is related to juvenile delinquency. It would appear from the theory that such conflict should affect children's behavior, for it is related to poor childrearing and poor personal development of the child. Thus, after choosing a research problem, researchers review the theories in the field, choose one of them, and, to put it simply, go through the process of *deduction.* That is, reasoning from the general theory, they state a relationship they expect to find in a particular situation (in other words, they predict). This predicted relationship is the *hypothesis.*

Next the hypothesis must be tested to see whether it is true. Hypotheses are tested by *observation,* which may consist of watching, counting, weighing, asking questions, and so on, depending on what is being observed. (Often various instruments may be used for better and more precise observations.) Researchers must first be satisfied that they have adequately observed the phenomenon. Then if what they observed squares with what they expected to find, they accept the hypothesis; if it does not, they reject the hypothesis.

In either case it is important that researchers relate their conclusions back to the theory. If the results of a particular hypothesis test support the general theory, then there is added evidence that the theory is true. If the results don't support the theory, this too provides valuable information. It indicates that the theory must be modified or replaced by another theory that can account for the facts. Beginning with a fuller explanation of theory, let us take a closer look at the various elements in the research process.

THEORY: THE GENERALIZING TOOL

In popular speech the word *theory* is often used to mean simply speculation or conjecture—for example: "My theory is that he must have been stoned when he had the accident." The scientist does not use theory in this sense. A scientific theory is a systematic statement of propositions or ideas that are logically related and give general descriptions of phenomena and relations among phenomena. A theory enables us to understand, explain, and predict situations or events that are more specific than the relationships contained in the theory. It also provides us with an order into which we can fit observations or newly discovered facts.

Charles Darwin's theory of evolution, despite its weaknesses, illustrates how a theory can be used. From Darwin's general theory of evolution by random mutation and natural selection it would follow that, among fish that migrated from open waters to cave waters, those fish having mutations most compatible with life in a cave would survive and reproduce their kind. Small eyes are less likely to be injured than large ones, so eventually fish with no eyes should evolve in the cave species. This is exactly what is found in Mammoth Cave and similar places.[3] When tied to a theory, the cave fish's blindness takes on greater meaning and is not just a random bit of information.

When the principles of gravitational theory were applied to the orbits of the known planets, the astronomer Percival Lowell concluded that there was a planet in our solar system that had not yet been discovered. Unless the theory was wrong, something out there was exerting the pull that gave Uranus its irregular movement. Using theory, Lowell mathematically proved in 1905 that another planet existed, and he even fixed the planet's approximate location; it was not until 1930 that Pluto was first sighted. Thus gravitational theory provided both an explanation for the behavior of planets and the correct prediction of a new phenomenon. Moreover, Lowell's predictions, based on theory, alerted other astronomers to look for a planet in an area they had previously presumed empty.

A theory that does not explain the known facts is replaced by one that does. In the 1800s physicists sought to explain how light waves travel. The knowledge of the time led them to believe that light needs a medium or substance in which to travel. Physicists developed the theory that an invisible substance called ether fills all space and provides the medium through which light travels. An experiment designed to measure the relative motion of the earth and ether was conducted by the physicists Albert Michelson and Edward Morley in 1887. Michelson and Morley found no support for the ether theory. Later the theories developed by Albert Einstein provided an explanation for the movement of light. Thus the ether theory could not explain the events it was supposed to, while the new theory could.

SOCIOLOGICAL THEORIES—PREDICTION AND LIMITATIONS

As a young science, sociology hasn't yet developed theories like those of Lowell, Darwin, or Einstein. Nonetheless, sociological theories work in basically the same way. For example, in 1945 the sociologists Kingsley Davis and Wilbert Moore

[3]Thomas C. Barr, Jr., "Cave Ecology and the Evolution of Troglodytes,"in Theodosius Dobzhansky, M. K. Hecht, and William C. Steere, *Evolutionary Biology*, vol. 2 (New York: Appleton–Century–Crofts, 1968), pp. 35–102.

From what he knows about stratification and social order, what survival chances would the sociologist predict for this group's alternate life style?

presented a theory to explain how stratification or class systems relate to the rest of the social order.[4] Beginning with the need to fill different positions in a society and the unequal distribution of talent in any society, the theory proposed that a system attaching more rewards to some positions than to others is universally necessary. Although this theory requires some modification, we can deduce from it that in a utopian community established on the principle of uniform rewards it would be difficult to get people to accept jobs that were more demanding or that required considerable training. As a result, with its important jobs unfilled, the community would fail to survive. Now, what if we find a society with uniform rewards that manages to get its positions filled and is surviving? Because such a finding would be contrary to what our theory predicts, we would examine the society closely to understand how it operates. Perhaps the society is a religious group, and one of their religious beliefs is that some people will work harder than others or will have to undergo long years of training for a position while others will not, but all will get the same rewards. The original

[4]Kingsley Davis and Wilbert E. Moore, "Some Principles of Stratification," *American Sociological Review,* **10** (April 1945), pp. 242–249.

theory would have to be modified to exclude this presumably unique case. But the theory would still be presumed generally to hold.

Perhaps in another society, such as in the Israeli communal societies called *kibbutzim,* we might discover that the society operating without a system of differential rewards was not a complete society but depended on other groups for medical services and technical improvements of various sorts.[5] These social tasks, according to the original theory, would be difficult to accomplish without a system of unequal rewards. Although the results of observing this community basically support the theory, it would be necessary to refine the theory still further to apply only to completely self-sufficient societies.

Any science needs the generalizing activity we call theorizing in order to make sense out of accumulated facts and predict new events. For example, if a sociologist were asked to consult with a group that had fairly complete plans for a unique classless society, he could say, in effect, that although there has never been a society exactly like the one proposed, his theory predicts that the group will have some problems to overcome if it is to survive.

We should bear in mind that the theories of sociology are neither as well developed nor as well tested as those of the older sciences. Sometimes sociologists have no good theoretical base for predicting a certain kind of human behavior. Or they predict behavior incorrectly because existing theory is not an adequate guide for prediction. According to *exchange theory,* for example, persons who interact are guided by the principle of seeking the most favorable cost–benefit ratio; that is, we would expect a person who is given a choice between two relationships to choose the one that promised to yield greater rewards or satisfaction than the other. As the family sociologist and theorist William Goode has suggested, exchange theory can be used to predict whether women with one child will remarry sooner after divorce than will those with several children.[6] From exchange theory we would probably predict that women with several children would be less of a bargain in the marriage market and thus would take longer to remarry than would women with only one child. The data suggest exactly the opposite, however. Probably women with several children, who are in more need of financial help from a male and more desirous of a father figure in the home, work harder at finding a new husband than do women with only one child. The liability of having several children is thus offset by their mate-seeking efforts.

[5]Melford E. Spiro, *Kibbutz: Venture in Utopia* (Cambridge, Mass.: Harvard University Press, 1956).

[6]William J. Goode, Elizabeth Hopkins, and Helen M. McClure, *Social Systems and Family Patterns* (New York: The Bobbs-Merrill Company, 1971), p. x.

CONCEPTS: THE BUILDING BLOCKS OF HYPOTHESES

From our observations of, say, many tables each of us has built an idea of "table." This idea includes only what is common to all tables, not all the many variations among tables. We then can communicate about the concept "table" knowing that it does not refer to any specific item in its class, that is, any particular table. A concept is thus a way of summarizing a large number of experiences we have had with an object or idea about which we are developing a concept. Every science has developed concepts—for example, in physics the concepts of mass, volume, velocity, and so on; in zoology the concepts of organism, of living and nonliving, and the like.

A sociological concept is a generalized idea about human interactions, a shorthand method of summarizing observations by a label or name. The labels applied to sociological concepts are frequently everyday words, such as *role, group, family, class, culture,* and *deviant.* But just as *work* has a technical meaning to the physicist, *demand* a technical meaning to the economist, and *reaction* a technical meaning to the chemist, so the definitions of sociological concepts are technical and frequently differ considerably from the same term as it is used in everyday life. The development and use of proper sociological concepts is important for research, for we must be as precise as possible about what we are attempting to measure or observe.

HYPOTHESES: KNITTING THEORIES TO FACTS

A hypothesis states a relationship that one expects to find between facts. A hypothesis is more than a guess or a hunch, for it is derived from theory, or at least is based on previously observed phenomena or previously discovered generalizations.

Researchers typically will first use general concepts to phrase a hypothesis. For example, they might state as a hypothesis, "The higher the social class, the better will be the quality of marriages." This hypothesis, you will notice, predicts a certain relationship between two concepts: social class and quality of marriage. This prediction is possible because we know some things about marriage and because we know some things about the behavior of people in a particular social class. For instance, it is known that upper-class people tend to marry at a later age than middle-class or working-class people. And we know too that people who marry later in life are less likely to get divorced than are those who marry young. These two facts alone might lead us to expect that there will be fewer divorces among the upper class. But we also have some other facts about upper-class people, and these increase the likelihood that our hypothesis will be correct. We know, for instance, that upper-class people tend to stress kinship ties and to be more concerned than other classes with the larger family group of which the married couple is a part. Upper-class people, by definition, have money, and so financial problems are unlikely to interfere with their marriage. Therefore, later marriages, concern with the extended family, and financial security are all characteristics of upper-class people. Knowing these characteristics allows us to predict that there will be fewer divorces among the upper class than among other classes of people.

REFINING CONCEPTS AND HYPOTHESES

So that the hypothesis can be tested, the next research step is to specify what is meant by the two basic variables in our hypothesis: *social class* and *quality of marriage*. Let us just consider one of the concepts, the quality of marriages. To measure this concept one might be tempted to use official divorce statistics. However, the divorce rate would not include couples who have informally separated, who for their own reasons are putting up with a tension-filled marriage, or who, as the common expression has it, are married in name only. If we are actually interested in discovering whether the quality of the marriage relationship varies with social class, then divorce statistics would tell only part of the story. Although there are sound data to support the hypothesis that the divorce rate does decrease as social class increases, sociologists are not certain that the quality of upper-class marriages is actually better than that of middle- or working-class marriages.[7]

Furthermore, the hypothesis should specify the group or society in which a relationship is predicted to exist. Otherwise, unless this information is clear from the context of the study, it would be assumed that the hypothesis had general application. Continuing with our example, we note that some societies do not even allow divorce, so obviously the hypothesis does not apply to such groups. In other societies divorce is expensive and hard to obtain. There is good reason to believe, based on previous research, that in such places divorce and social class are not inversely related. As a matter of fact, in such societies wealthier people are more likely to divorce than poorer ones.

Thus, if our hypothesis did not specify the society or kind of society to which it applied, the test of it would show that it is supported in some societies, not

[7]William F. Kenkel, *The Family in Perspective*, 3rd ed. (New York: Appleton-Century-Crofts, 1973), pp. 314–316; and U.S. Bureau of Census, *Current Population Reports*, series P-20, "Marriage, Divorce and Remarriage by Year of Birth: June, 1971" (Washington, D.C., U.S. Government Printing Office, 1972), p. 4

If this couple's social class were known, what could a sociologist say about the quality of their marriage?

supported in others, and in still others could not even be tested. It is difficult to handle findings such as these. What is required, then, is a hypothesis that clearly states what is meant by "quality of marriage" and one that specifies the society and the time period during which the hypothesized relationship is expected to exist.

COLLECTING DATA

To test a hypothesis facts are needed. The hypothesis to be tested will determine what facts or data are appropriate and also how this information will be collected. A researcher may use the *survey research* method, mailing questionnaires or asking questions in personal interviews. For some studies it might be better to use an *observation method*.

In large–scale survey research, no matter what groups are being studied, it is usually neither feasible nor necessary to gather data from the entire group, so the technique of sampling becomes essential.

To obtain a good example of homes in this suburb, each house
should be as likely to be selected as every other house.

SAMPLING: SOME REPRESENT ALL

If you wanted to discover how many marbles of each color were in a large
barrel filled with marbles of several different colors, you could of course dump
the barrel and painstakingly sort and count the marbles of each color. But often
such precision is not necessary, and a properly drawn sample would give approximately the same results as would a total count.[8] Obviously it is easier, quicker,
and less costly to use a sample than to do a complete count.

Before drawing a sample the researcher must define the group about which
he wishes to generalize. This group is called the *universe* or *population*—for
example, people over sixty-five years of age who live in Austin, Texas; all college

[8]For a discussion on sample size needed see Julian L. Simon, *Basic Research Methods in Social Science* (New
York: Random House, 1969), pp. 421–423.

TABLE 2–1. Comparison of a Probability Sample and
Actual Population of the United States[a]

| Region | Percentage Distribution | |
	Actual Adult Population	Completed Interviews in Sample
East	27.6%	25.6%
Midwest	29.9	29.8
South	28.9	31.3
West	13.6	13.3
	100.0%	100.0%

[a]Sample size, 4,933. From Samuel A. Stouffer, *Communism, Conformity, and Civil Liberties* (New York: John Wiley & Sons, 1955), p. 237.

students in the United States; the patients in City Hospital. To be good, a sample must give an unbiased picture of the total universe under study. One method of obtaining a good sample is *random sampling*. Every unit in the universe is given the same chance to be selected as every other unit.

The major advantage of·random sampling is that a simple statistical formula indicates what size the sample should be to give confidence that, within a given margin of error, it resembles the universe. Suppose that we wanted to know whether the adults of the United States favor the legalization of marijuana. A properly drawn random sample of 2,500 people would be enough to give us an answer accurate to within 5 percent. That is, if it was found that 60 percent of the sample was in favor of legalizing marijuana we could be confident that the true percentage for the nation ranges from 55 to 65 percent.

The data in Table 2–1 are taken from an actual study. They compare the proportion of interviews completed in different sections of the country with the proportion of the population determined by Census to be living in those sections. The biggest difference is that 2.4 percent more people from the South were interviewed than the proportion of people living in that area would indicate. All in all, the sample in the national study resembled the regional distribution of the people of the United States to a remarkable degree.

RESEARCH BY OBSERVATION

The survey research method, however, is not the only way in which sociologists study human interaction. Another basic method is *observation*. In *nonparticipant* observation one carefully witnesses interaction from outside the group. In *participant* observation, one is or becomes a member of the group and takes part in the interaction to be observed. Nonparticipant and participant observation

Select a random sample of a group such as the students in your class. Get some information from them such as religious preference or whether they were born in the state they are now living in. Next, get the same information from the rest of class. Compare the findings from the total group and the sample. Are the differences between the sample and the total group acceptable?

are not clear–cut categories. As a sociologist you might approach a commune, for example, and explain that you would like to live with the group and conduct a sociological study of it. If you are housed with the group, eat your meals with them, and accept work assignments as others do, you are obviously not observing the group from the outside. Still you are not a full member of the group, but rather a sort of sociologist in residence. As a true participant observer you would actually be a member of the group you are studying. You would join a dance band, as did one sociologist, move into a community and join groups as do other newcomers, or take a job in a factory as a normal employee and not as a sociologist conducting a study.[9] The basic techniques are similar, however, for both nonparticipant and participant observation.

SOCIOLOGICAL OBSERVATION: FOR A PURPOSE

Anyone can observe a group in action and give some kind of report of what was observed. The differences between an average person's observations and those of a trained sociologist lie in three areas: why the observation is made, how the observation is conducted, and what is done with the findings.

Sociologists observe for a purpose: They would like more knowledge about some aspect of social interaction. In designing a given study sociologists specify what they want to observe, and often they write out in advance what they expect to find. For example, sociologists living in or joining a commune may want to learn whether the phenomenon of territoriality exists and, if so, how it is handled. Territoriality is the tendency of individuals and cliques to stake off physical space that becomes in a sense their own. A corner of the cafeteria may be the meeting place of a certain group of students, a woman may have her favorite chair in the living room for reading her paper, a given park bench may be informally reserved for the daily use of several older men, or designated city blocks may be the turf of a boys' gang that will be vigorously defended

[9]For a good discussion of observational techniques see Jacqueline P. Wiseman and Marcia S. Aron, *Field Projects for Sociology Students* (Cambridge, Mass.: Schenkman Publishing Co., 1970), chs. 1 and 4.

from invasion by rival gangs. Such possessive attitudes toward space would seem to conflict with the idea of communal living, but since territoriality is a basic trait of human groups and is found among many animal species as well, sociologists are intrigued by the question, How does the commune deal with it?

We should not assume that the participant observers restrict themselves to only one research problem at a time. Sociologists studying communes, for example, may also want to investigate how the group gets the necessary work done without passing out rewards, whether problems of personal jealousies arise, or whether leaders tend to emerge. All of these problems are sociologically important and the results of the observations would thus contribute to sociological knowledge.

SOCIOLOGICAL OBSERVATION: SYSTEMATIC

Just as participant and nonparticipant observers are systematic in their statement of a research problem, they are also systematic in their observations. While they do not know what they will find, they know what kinds of interaction they are interested in, and so they focus their attention on the people and the situations that will provide them with relevant information. They must be alert to subtleties of interaction as well as to the more obvious spoken word and physical action. Some years ago, for example, one of the authors conducted an observational study on family decision-making.[10] In their own home couples discussed how to spend a hypothetical gift of money. To make it easier for them to allocate the money to different purchases, they were given 300 dollars in stage money. The money was given to the couple and physically placed between the husband and wife. The focus of the study was on whether the husband or wife would have more influence on the use of the gift. Careful records were made of how much each partner talked and how frequently each submitted ideas. It was of more than passing interest that in all cases the man took physical charge of the stage money, counted it, and sorted it into piles. This occurrence illustrated and helped to explain the man's influence in decision-making. It would be interesting to repeat this study and see whether male dominance prevails among young couples today.

Participant observers are not usually able to take notes while observing. As soon as possible, however, a written record must be made of the sociologically relevant facts observed. It is desirable to go over these from time to time while in the group being observed, to be sure one is getting the kind of information needed or to detect an area where more observation is needed to verify an earlier one.

---

[10]William F. Kenkel, "Influence Differentiation in Family Decision Making," *Sociology and Social Research* 42 (September–October 1957), pp. 18–25.

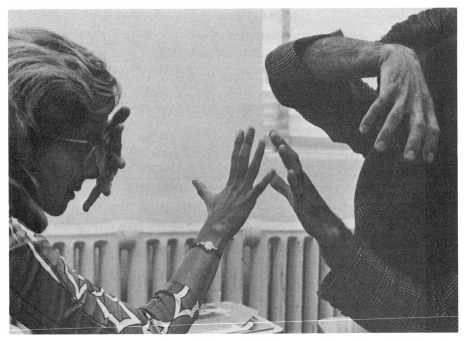

Subtleties of interaction might tell the sociologist more about the subjects under study than their conversations or physical acts.

Participant and nonparticipant observation are particularly fruitful methods to use in research areas that have not been well explored and to get a thorough description of the interaction patterns of a group. The sociologist Jacqueline Wiseman, for example, composed a description of the typical day spent by men on Skid Row by repeatedly and thoroughly observing their activities.[11] Sometimes observational and other research methods are combined. Another sociologist, Lloyd Birch, had an organist in a funeral home record specific points in ministers' sermons, such as whether they mentioned the deceased by name.[12] A few months later Birch interviewed the ministers witnessed and asked what they *would do* at hypothetical funerals closely resembling ones they had actually conducted. The earlier observed behavior of ministers differed from their reports of how they said they would conduct a funeral.

The raw findings of observational research usually consist of copious written notes. These findings need to be analyzed. What this analysis often amounts to is a systematic presentation of the findings as answers to the questions that guided the research.

[11]Jacqueline P. Wiseman, *Stations of the Lost* (Englewood Cliffs, N.J.: Prentice-Hall, 1970).

[12]Lloyd Birch, "A Comparison of Observational Data and Interview Data: A Validity Study," Unpublished Ph.D. dissertation. Lexington, Kentucky, University of Kentucky Graduate School, 1971.

Try the participant observation method in a situation in which you are a part, such as the floor of your dorm or the crowd at a sports event. Write down everything that happens. Try to develop some generalizations concerning how people characteristically behave.

ANALYZING DATA: FINDING THE MEANING IN FACTS

Facts do not speak for themselves. Modern research techniques typically give numerical codes to the answers to many different questions answered by each respondent. These numbers can be put onto punch cards or tape, and the computer can be programmed to furnish a printout. If we stopped at this stage, we would have a meaningless array of numbers. What we must do is to use these numbers to test our hypotheses.

Suppose that a sociologist wished to discover whether more women than men favored the Equal Rights Amendment. A sample is drawn of 500 men and 500 women to whom a questionnaire is given. On this questionnaire are items asking the respondents' age and sex, and also a five–point scale, ranging from "strongly approve" to "strongly disapprove," on which the respondent can indicate his or her position on the Equal Rights Amendment. All these responses can be converted to numbers and fed into a computer.

What then? Let us assume we have access to a computer, which can give us a frequency count by sex. We would then know how many men and how many women gave each response on the attitude scale. In the imaginary distribution presented in Table 2–2, more women than men gave favorable responses. But everyone knows that if a coin is tossed 100 times, by chance alone it will turn up heads more than fifty times in some trials and less than 50 times in others. So is there a real sex difference in attitude to the Equal Rights Amendment or could the difference be due to chance? Fortunately a statistical test answers this question.[13] When we use this test, it turns out that the sex difference discovered would occur by chance fewer than once in a hundred times. We can safely conclude, then, that chance alone does not explain the difference we discovered.

[13]We are referring to a test called Chi Square. This and other tests and their usage can be found in Hubert M. Blalock, Jr., *Social Statistics* (New York: McGraw–Hill, 1960).

TABLE 2–2. Attitudes of 500 Men and 500 Women Toward Equal Rights Amendment[a]

	Strongly Approve	Approve	Neutral	Disapprove	Strongly Disapprove
Women	225	90	75	60	50
Men	150	80	60	110	100

[a]Data are simulated.

In the same hypothetical study another researcher might reason that older people would resist change more than would younger ones. The researcher might then hypothesize that the older one is the less likely he or she is to favor the Equal Rights Amendment. This hypothesis could be tested by the data, but numerical values would need to be assigned to the responses. For example, a value of "5" could be assigned to the "strongly approve" response, "4" to the "approve" response, down to "1" for the "strongly disapprove" answer. Assuming that age is found to be related to support of the amendment, still another test could be applied to determine which factor, age or sex, is more strongly related.

INTERPRETING FINDINGS: FITTING NEW WITH OLD

Once data have been analyzed, either statistically or otherwise, there exists a collection of facts. On the basis of the study a certain relationship, given the facts, can be said to exist or not to exist. But a science does not develop by a mere accumulation of facts. The ultimate goal of any science is the discovery of principles or rules that explain certain *classes of facts* rather than isolated facts or relationships. Not every research finding will yield a general law or principle. What we call interpretation of the findings should at the very least include an effort to relate the findings to previous research. Do the new findings support the old? If not, is it because the present study was made at a time so far removed from earlier studies that circumstances have significantly changed, or because the study used different methods, or perhaps because a different kind of sample was studied? Whatever the explanation, the finding must be fitted into the existing body of knowledge. Only in this way will laws be formulated that specify the conditions under which certain categories of relationships will prevail.

PITFALLS IN ANALYZING AND INTERPRETING

Our description of the scientific method used by the sociologist may seem deceptively simple because it has been outlined in steps labeled with one word: First you pick a *theory;* then form a *hypothesis,* choosing from your array of *concepts;* then collect *data;* then *interpret* the data. But as in any science, each of these steps is complex and can involve many steps and many choices. For the subject of the sociologist's research, human interaction, is itself extremely complex. The intellectual process of interpreting and analyzing data, like all the steps that go before it in research, poses for the sociologist many hazards of error. For example, in our everyday life we commonly talk of *causes:* "Why did you do that?" "What caused the energy crisis?" and so on. But in sociology it is not common practice to speak of the *cause* of human behavior, partly because the concept of causality is loaded with philosophical complexities and ambiguities.

Is this woman bored or alienated or lost in her own thoughts or listening to the music? Can you be sure without further observation?

For example, a newspaper account of a fire says that the fire was caused by a person smoking in bed. Perhaps if the man had not been drinking, he would not have fallen asleep with a lit cigarette; and if his boss had not been unusually rough on him, he would not have gotten drunk. If the mattress had not been made of flammable material, it could not have caught fire, and of course if our atmosphere did not contain so much oxygen, neither the cigarette nor the mattress could have burned. What, then, was the cause of the fire?

Why worry about it? Often it is sufficient to talk about an *association;* that is, our knowing that a certain relationship exists allows us to predict human interaction and, if it is so desired, to control it. Let us say we know, for example, that people of different social classes live in different parts of a city and that the lower the social class the more children are in a family. Then we can predict in which section of the city schools will be needed even if we do not believe that having a low income is what makes a woman pregnant. If a study discovers that minority-group children learn more in racially integrated schools than in segregated ones, we could control the outcome of the educational process by integrating the schools even without knowing the whys and wherefores of the relationship. If we know that the younger a couple is when they marry the more likely they are to divorce, we could reduce the divorce rate by discouraging marriage at a young age. Of course, the better we understand why a relationship exists, the sounder will be our basis for predicting or controlling the behavior in question.

SPURIOUS RELATIONSHIPS: SEEMING CAUSES AND LOST CAUSES

There is always the possibility that two factors may be statistically associated but that the relationship is *spurious*—that is, false or accidental. A may appear to be related to B when actually it is not; it may be that C is linked to both of the others. Let us suppose a study found a relationship between the sale of Bibles and the sale of alcoholic beverages. As Bible sales increase so does the sale of alcohol, and as less of one is sold so is less of the other. Does reading the Bible turn one to drink, or does drinking turn one in remorse to the Bible? Neither. The sale of many goods is related to economic conditions; the more money people have the more they spend on lots of things, including Bibles and booze.

Studies have found a positive relationship between college grades and smoking pot; the average grades of marijuana users are higher than those of nonusers.[14]

[14]Mary K. Gergen, Kenneth Gergen, and Stanley J. Morse, "Correlates of Marijuana Use Among College Students," *Journal of Applied Social Psychology,* Vol. 2 (January–March 1972), pp. 7–8.

Which causes which, and why? Does smoking pot expand the mind or otherwise make it easier to learn, or does studying hard for high grades lead one to seek relaxation and tension-release in smoking grass? Perhaps neither of these is true. It may be that pot-smoking and high scholastic achievement are two causally unrelated results of growing up in a modern suburban family marked by permissive childrearing. In such an environment we may expect a tolerance for smoking pot as well as good elementary and high schools that provide sound preparation for college. Or perhaps the academically more successful students have more self-confidence and are thus less inclined to follow social rules without first testing alternatives for themselves.

To date we do not understand how marijuana use and college grades are related. We suspect that the explanation is complex and that the association does not indicate a simple causal relationship.

DANGEROUS EXTRAPOLATIONS

It should be obvious that we cannot take a trend and mathematically extend it indefinitely. That the birth rate is going down in the United States does not mean that in the foreseeable future no one will be having babies. That the divorce rate is going up does not mean that everyone getting married will someday divorce. Anyone with elementary skills in arithmetic could take current trends on birth or divorce, extrapolate them, and reach startling but farfetched conclusions. Mark Twain gave all the warning necessary to avoid this misuse of data:

> There is something fascinating about science . . . the wholesale returns of conjecture out of such a trifling investment of fact. . . . In the space of one hundred and seventy-six years the lower Mississippi has shortened itself two hundred and forty-two miles. That is an average of a trifle over one mile and a third per year. Therefore, any calm person, who is not blind or idiotic, can see that in the old Oolithic Silurian period, just a million years ago next November, the Lower Mississippi was upwards of one million three hundred thousand miles long, and stuck out over the Gulf of Mexico like a fishing rod. And by the same token any person can see that seven hundred and forty-two years from now the Lower Mississippi will be only a mile and three quarters long, and Cairo and New Orleans will have joined their streets together.[15]

[15]Mark Twain, *Life on the Mississippi* (Boston: J. R. Osgood, 1883), p. 129.

Find a research report in a sociology journal. Assume that you want to repeat the study in order to verify the findings. Does the article provide you with the information you need? Can you design a study of your own based on·the information contained in the research report? If not, what is missing that you would need?

REPORT OF THE RESEARCH

The final step in the scientific method is to make a written record and report of the research. The results of sociological research may be reported in a paper read at the meetings of the American Sociological Association. They may appear as an article in the *American Sociological Review* or in one of the more specialized journals such as the *Journal of Marriage and the Family* or *Social Problems*. For many reasons it is important to report research findings. A science grows by the steady accumulation of knowledge. Once in a while, to be sure, a major discovery or breakthrough is destined to have a major impact on the discipline. Not too often, however, does an Archimedes of sociology run naked down the street yelling "Eureka" upon gaining some sudden insight into the workings of reality. Generalizations and laws usually grow gradually as the findings of one research effort add to the existing body of knowledge, or as an existing generalization is modified by more recent research. If research findings are to contribute to the general body of knowledge they must, therefore, be carefully and fully reported. Not only must findings be reported but the methods of research and the interpretation must be described. Only then can others conduct similar studies to verify the findings or to discover whether a relationship found to exist in one group can be generalized to other groups.

Many research findings in sociology ultimately have implications for the lives of people. This is another reason why such findings need to be reported. Research results with such immediate implications reach the public in various ways. Formal courses in sociology, such as *Juvenile Delinquency, The Family,* or *Race Relations,* are continually updated to take into account the most recent findings and generalizations. The results of some studies reach still wider audiences through newspapers and magazines. That youthful age at marriage is associated with divorce has received fairly good coverage in the popular press. So also has the finding that the greater the density of a housing unit the smaller the space with which people identify and the greater the crime rate. This particular finding has been vulgarized as "the taller the building the higher the crime rate," but at least it is out in the open where citizens and city officials can, if they wish, take it into account when planning multiple-family housing units.

Thus the research process that begins with the formulation of a problem ends with the report of the findings. It is exciting and intellectually stimulating, even though it involves much tedious work. There are frustrations, such as when it is not feasible to get the sample size one would like or when there is not enough money to use the computer. The many instances when the judgment of the researcher comes into play can be a source of worry to him or her. Did the researcher phrase the questions so that people understood what he or she meant? What should be done about the fact that 5 percent of the sample failed to respond to a question? All these questions, and more, are counterbalanced by the realization that one is making a contribution to the field and adding to the ever-expanding store of knowledge.

PREDICTION AND CONTROL: LIVELY CONTROVERSIES

Despite the sociologist's use of scientific principles, some people question the scientific nature of the discipline, particularly its ability to predict human behavior. Others, including professional sociologists, argue over what should be done with research findings. These points are related, for if accurate prediction is not possible, it would be foolish—even dangerous—to use the findings of sociological research in an attempt to control future events.

Some people claim that patterns of human interaction and behavior in groups are too elusive and complex ever to be predicted and that the scientific nature of sociology is questionable. Yet sociologists can and do predict the rates of birth, marriage, divorce, death, and other social phenomena. Although lacking precision, a method to predict the success or failure of marriages has been worked out and tested.[16] We can predict where in a city the number of arrests for juvenile offenses will be the highest. In these and many more instances we can state what will probably occur because we think we understand the phenomenon or have a grasp—sometimes admittedly slight—of an underlying principle.

[16]For a discussion of the research on predicting marital success see Charles E. Bowerman, "Prediction Studies," in Harold Christensen, ed., *Handbook of Marriage and the Family* (Chicago: Rand McNally, 1964), ch. 6.

PROPHECIES: SELF–FULFILLING AND SELF–DEFEATING

It is true that sometimes predictions about human behavior can affect the outcome and lead us to conclude that a false prediction was correct or that a true one was wrong. The sociologist Robert Merton adapted to sociology the concept of the "self–fulfilling prophecy," meaning that an originally false prediction can come true simply because it was made.[17] For example, a teacher might wrongly predict that a certain group of boys are predelinquents and then act as if they were by watching their behavior carefully, cracking down on their infringements of minor rules and perhaps segregating them from the "good boys." If the teacher's activity were sufficiently intense, the close scrutiny could impair the boys' self–images or provoke their hostilities toward a suspicious authority figure, sparking the boys to rebellious activities. Thus the boys would have become delinquents simply because the teacher had predicted it. In addition to the obvious harm to the boys the false prediction come true could confuse our understanding of the roots of delinquency.

There seems also to be a similar concept of the "self–defeating prophecy"—that is, forecasts that may not come true precisely because they are made.[18] For example, if it is predicted that the spring rains will bring flooding in the suburbs, the citizens can construct better storm sewers. Therefore, the prediction, because it was made, will not come true. Although the self–defeating prophecy may pose a methodological difficulty for the sociologist, it can also be used strategically by those wishing to bring about social change. For example, Zero Population Growth has actively publicized predictions of a future world plagued with over–population, massive famine, and shortages of materials and energy. It may be that as people become aware of the dangers of unrestrained population growth, they will decide to limit the number of children they have. Thus the prediction becomes self–defeating, and the goal of ZPG—the reduction of population growth—is achieved.

CONTROL: SCIENTIFIC NEUTRALITY VERSUS SOCIAL RESPONSIBILITY

We have seen that the goals of every science are understanding and prediction. Along with prediction comes the possibility of control. The practitioners of pure science exclude control from their activities and concerns. But the fact cannot be ignored: The better our knowledge and ability to predict, the better able

[17]Robert K. Merton, *Social Theory and Social Structure* (New York: The Free Press, 1949), p. 121.

[18]Merton discusses the self–defeating prophecy as in the case where overconfidence in winning a game produces a loss. This is different from our use, here and elsewhere, of self–defeating prophecy. See Merton, *Social Theory and Social Structure*; and William F. Kenkel, "Marriage and the Family in Modern Science Fiction," *Journal of Marriage and the Family* 31 (February 1969), pp. 6–14.

Prediction allows control. Could computer technology joined with sociology someday be used for social manipulation?

we are to control matters. If we know when a swollen river will crest, we can build dikes or at least evacuate the area. The better we understand the causes of a disease, the more likely we are to be able to cure or prevent it.

But we do not have to use the knowledge. Or do we? This is one of the controversies in sociology today, and it has been with us for some time. What responsibility, if any, do we sociologists have to study issues related to the welfare of society or to see that the findings of our studies are applied to the improvement of social ills?

One position is that sociologists should take a neutral stance. We may want to investigate, for example, the factors associated with divorce. But we should not judge the morality of divorce, nor should we feel compelled to see that our findings benefited couples with marital difficulties.

Physicists, chemists, astronomers, and other scientists pursue knowledge in their fields without applying it or being concerned—at least in principle—with its application. Sociologists, it is held, are scientists, even if their field is society and their theories are not as rigorous as those in other sciences. As scientists they should report what is; it is not their concern to say what should be or to show how their findings can be used to change conditions in society. They do not work for "the establishment" or against it; science is their only master. This value-free position was well expressed in 1947 by the sociologist George

---

Survey your classmates to determine their opinions on value-neutrality and social responsibility. Then divide the class into two teams and debate the issue. After the debate, survey the class again. Did the debate make any difference in people's opinions?

Lundberg in his book *Can Science Save Us?*[19] It is probably the dominant position of sociologists in the United States today.

Others claim that sociologists have a moral responsibility to choose research problems that have a bearing on the welfare of society and to see that the findings of their research are applied to the common good. The sociologist should take a stand for or against such social phenomena as a high birth rate, a low infant mortality rate, or increase in the rate of extramarital sexual relations, and so on. The sociologist should be involved in changing society, not just in studying it. In 1939 the sociologist Robert S. Lynd argued, in his book *Knowledge for What?*, for the position that sociologists should apply their knowledge to the solution of human ills.[20] More recently other sociologists have supported this position.[21]

The controversy between adherents of value-neutrality and social responsibility is not the sort that will be easily resolved. The main thing is to recognize that the controversy exists. Both types of sociologists continue to "do their thing"—and actually do much of it in the same way. They differ in the stance they take toward the responsibility of the sociologist for determining how sociological knowledge is used.

In the following chapters we will not be referring to the controversy over the uses of the studies that will be mentioned, nor will we discuss in any detail the methodologies of such studies. We should recognize, however, that these studies followed in a general way the procedures set forth in this chapter. You should by now be getting a feel for what sociology is and how sociologists go about their work. In the chapters of Part 2, we come to grips with the basic sociological concepts of human interaction and the effects of the process on human groups and societies.

[19]George A. Lundberg, *Can Science Save Us?* (New York: Longmans Green, 1947).

[20]Robert S. Lynd, *Knowledge For What?* (Princeton, N.J.: Princeton University Press, 1939).

[21]Howard S. Becker, "Whose Side Are We On?," *Social Problems* 14 (Winter 1967), pp. 239–247; Robert W. Friedrichs, "Choice and Commitment in Social Research," *American Sociologist* 3 (February 1968), pp. 3–7; Alvin W. Gouldner, "Anti-Minotaur: The Myth of Value-Free Sociology," *Social Problems* 9 (Winter 1962), pp. 199–213; C. Wright Mills, *The Power Elite* (New York: Oxford University Press, 1956).

SOCIOLOGICAL RESEARCH:
SOMETIMES A FORM OF DEVIANT BEHAVIOR?

Presumably every science has limits to its permissible areas of investigation and methods of research. What are the limits sociologists must respect? Their scope of study is all social behavior, and different kinds of studies respond to some methods of research and resist others. Can a sociologist choose a research topic that interests him or her and then adapt any method of investigation to suit the topic, with the only limitation being perhaps that no outright physical or social harm come to the human subjects of the research?

The sociologist Laud Humphreys, in the late 1960s, undertook to study "impersonal sex in public places," homosexual activities in "tearooms" (homosexual slang for public restrooms used for homosexual encounters). To conduct his study, Humphreys used a modification of the participant observer method. Concealing the fact that he was a sociologist, he allowed himself to be used as a "watchqueen," a third person who acts as a lookout during homosexual encounters to protect the participants from discovery by the police or a nonparticipant.

By recording license numbers of cars, he was able to get the identities of many participants (these identities Humphreys scrupulously kept concealed). He "took notes on their homes and neighborhoods and acquired data on them from the city and county directories." A year later, his appearance deliberately changed, he interviewed many of those participants ("often in the presence of their wives") on subjects unrelated to their homosexual activities.

Using these methods, Humphreys drew up a sociological profile of people otherwise mysterious to society, people whose activities, motives, and characteristics had so far been described only by the police.

Despite Humphreys' care that his subjects' identities would never become known, and despite the possible social value of his study as a guide for future public policy, Humphreys has created some controversy, chiefly for his method of research.

Should sociologists allow themselves to invade the individual's privacy without his or her knowledge? Many nonsociologists say no. Humphreys himself says, "You do walk a . . . tightrope in regard to ethical matters in studies like this, but unless someone will walk it, the only source of information will be the police department, and that is dangerous for a society."

SUMMARY POINTS AND QUESTIONS

1. As a scientific enterprise, sociology accepts the assumption of science that the universe is orderly.

> *Would science be possible if you did not make this assumption?*
>
> *Can you think of a subject matter that is not orderly and to which science cannot be applied?*

2. Because we assume there is order to social behavior, we can *understand* the principles that govern this order, we can test our understanding by making *predictions,* and if our predictions hold we have the potential to *control* this behavior.

> *Can you think of any principles that apply to social behavior?*
>
> *How have or could these principles be used to control social behavior?*

3. Understanding evolves in the process of constructing, testing, and if necessary modifying social theory.

> *Can you give an example of a social theory that has been tested and modified?*
>
> *What is the relationship between a hypothesis and a theory?*

4. In order to test a theory, it is necessary to collect data. Sampling is a convenient method of collecting data because it allows us to gather data about part of a group in which we are interested, and then allows us to generalize our findings to the entire group with a known degree of confidence.

> *What is a biased sample?*
>
> *What are some ways that bias enters into a sample?*

5. Sociologists generally avoid the concept of causation and talk about the association between facts, rates, and so on.

> *What is the difference between causation and association?*
>
> *Can we ever be certain that one event causes another?*

6. A spurious relationship exists when one variable appears to be related to another variable but the relationship is actually the result of a third variable.

> *Give an example of a spurious relationship.*
>
> *How can we be certain that two variables are actually related, and that the relationship is not spurious?*

7. One method of research is participant observation. Here, the sociologist actually becomes involved in an ongoing situation in order to understand what is happening.

> *What are the advantages and disadvantages of participant observation compared to survey research?*
>
> *What are some of the problems a sociologist might face by becoming too involved?*

8. The final steps of sociological research are the interpretation of findings and the reporting of these findings.

If certain findings appear to be detrimental to the people you studied, would you report them? Why or why not?

Give a hypothetical example of research findings that would be harmful to a minority or oppressed group in society.

SUGGESTED READINGS

Braybrooke, David, ed. *Philosophical Problems of the Social Sciences.* New York: Macmillan, 1965. A collection of essays dealing with the meaning of social reality and the extent to which the social scientist might intrude into that reality.

Forcese, Dennis and Stephen Richer, eds. *Stages of Social Research: Contemporary Perspectives.* Englewood Cliffs, N.J.: Prentice-Hall, 1970. A collection of essays on the basic issues in the area of methodology. The issues include the scientific approach, conceptualization of research problems, measurement, research strategy, sampling, data collection, analysis, and interpretation.

Matson, Floyd W. *The Broken Image.* New York: Doubleday & Co., 1966. A critique of the relationship of the scientific enterprise to man and society. The thesis that science has reduced and destroyed the image of man is forcefully presented.

McCall, George J. and J. L. Simmons, eds. *Issues in Participant Observation.* Reading, Mass.: Addison-Wesley, 1969. Essays dealing with the methodological issues specifically related to qualitative research. These issues include the relationship of field workers to their subjects, the quality of the data, and the difficulties of generating and evaluating hypotheses.

Philips, Bernard S. *Social Research: Strategy and Tactics.* New York: Macmillan, 1971. A comprehensive work on the research process, data collection, and the analysis of data. Contains an especially good section on measurement and scaling.

Rosenberg, Morris. *The Logic of Survey Analysis.* New York: Basic Books, 1968. Aims at constructing a logical method for the interpretation of survey research data. Especially helpful to those interested in learning how to analyze statistical tables.

Schoeck, Helmut and James Wiggins, eds. *Scientism and Values.* Princeton, N.J.: D. Van Nostrand, 1960. These essays question whether a science of man is possible.

Simon, Julian L. *Basic Research Methods in Social Science: The Art of Empirical Investigation.* New York: Random House, 1969. One of the better works on sociological research. The author views social research in terms of the problems and obstacles that particular approaches have to overcome.

Zetterburg, Hans. *On Theory and Verification in Sociology.* Totowa, N.J.: Bedminster Press, 1965. Develops a scheme for the conceptualization of theory and for the deduction of working hypotheses from theory. A good source on what is known as axiomatic theory.

II

UNDERSTANDING
SOCIAL ORGANIZATION

We've already seen that sociologists conceptualize as part of their research method. But rarely, if ever, do sociologists conceptualize about anything so simple as the table we used as an example in our discussion of concepts. Their subjects are infinitely more ambitious and difficult, for they have to set society and everything that is part of society into a single conceptual framework. That framework, in turn, must give rise to descriptions and explanations that sociologists can test for accuracy and completeness.

The conceptualizing done by sociologists often begins with commonsense ideas, and these ideas are designated by such familiar words as culture, society, role, and institution. But the very familiarity of these words may lead to misunderstanding. For, as sociologists have developed their concerns and a descriptive vocabulary with which to discuss these concerns, familiar words have taken on specialized meanings. For example, when you hear the word culture you probably think of the arts: music, literature, and painting. The word may suggest boredom and pretension or excitement and discovery. But does it suggest your ten-speed bike, or your car, or the hot plate in your room, or the belief that men and women should marry before having sexual relations? Do you think of your individual rights and freedoms, your love of fried chicken and loathing of grasshoppers as food?

Probably the word culture suggests none of these things to you, but sociologists include all of these objects, ideas, beliefs, and preferences in their concept of culture. Just about everything you believe, every idea you cherish, every object you own or would like to own is part of your culture, for the sociologist defines culture very broadly as ". . . a historically derived system of explicit and implicit designs for living, which tend to be shared by all or designated members of a group." As little as this definition may convey to you right now, you should still be able to see that culture pervades our society.

You will soon see also that your "humanity" is a product of your culture. We think of ourselves as human beings. However, if by some process of abstraction we were able to remove from ourselves the beliefs, ideas, values, and feelings *that we derive from our culture, the only human characteristics remaining to us would be our bodies and our basic physical and psychological needs.*

How did we come to be so dependent upon culture that it determines who we are and whether or not we survive? Sociologists would reply that we have reached this point through socialization, the complex process of bringing us from the helpless condition of the newborn to the state of being full-fledged functioning members of our society. As you can see, the process begins at birth. Childrearing in any society is both the collection of techniques for ensuring the infant's survival and the process of teaching the child the first rudiments of social behavior. During childhood we learn to feed ourselves, to control our bowels and bladders, and to dress ourselves.

Even in early childhood, however, we are not learning only techniques for self-sufficiency. We are also learning attitudes, beliefs, values, rules, and all of the elements that make up a personality. Some of these are taught us deliberately; others we learn through no one's apparent effort. By observing those around us, particularly our families, we pick up ways of behaving; attitudes towards others; and values about life, society, property, and work. We augment our observations by imitating others as well.

Despite the immense human capacity for learning, we would not become true members of a human society were it not for one other crucial element in the human makeup, the capacity to develop a self. Without this capacity societies probably couldn't survive. Individuals could then simply play at being responsible, functioning members whenever it suited their purposes, and they could violate the needs of others whenever to do so was more profitable. True, almost every society has a certain portion of members who do disregard the people around them, and the rest of us are not always angels and good little scouts. But enough of us are dependable enough of the time so that we do not jeopardize society.

What is this crucial self? It is simply the product of our internalization of our culture's basic values. Early in this century, the sociologist Charles Horton Cooley developed the notion of "the looking-glass self." This concept stresses how much social interaction enters into even the privacy of our own personalities to make us what we are, or what we think we are. The process of forming the looking-glass self can be artificially divided into three steps: (1) I imagine what you see when you look at me; (2) I then imagine how you judge what you see; (3) I then have feelings about myself according to how I imagine you judged me.

Thus, socialization has not only given us ideas, values, and norms. It has so formed us that we are committed to the things it has given us, and we identify with them. But to say that we are now members of a society tells us as little as to say that we are human beings. You're a young man or woman, a son or daughter to parents, brother or sister, college student, a friend to many. Perhaps you're already a parent yourself, or have been in the armed forces as a soldier, sailor, or pilot. The sociologist calls all of these capacities social positions. You are no doubt aware that as a son or daughter, college student, soldier, or even friend, you are expected to act in certain ways and not in others. You are expected to be obedient and respectful to your parents, to give them affection (and you expect to receive it in return), to be studious at college, and to make an earnest effort. The behavior demanded of you in any of your positions is what the sociologist calls your role.

Just as you're born into one or more positions and begin early to learn roles, you're born into what sociologists call a group. Groups have three basic traits. They allow physical and symbolic interaction, or communication, among members, who are aware of one another. They are made up of people who think of themselves, and are thought of, as members. Their members accept roles and obligations as well as privileges and rewards. Your family clearly fits this definition. Sociologists consider societies to be held together by groups and by institutions (your family is also an institution), which are defined as sets of interwoven folkways, mores, and laws built around one or more functions. Part III of this book is devoted entirely to a study of the five basic institutions of society.

Nearly all societies are divided not only into different groups and institutions, with their positions and roles, but also into classes that vary according to the social rewards their members receive. These rewards can take the form of wealth, prestige, power, or all or any combination of these. Although most societies need most of the positions and roles they encompass, they seem to consider some worthy of more rewards than others, as you can easily observe in our own society. Doctors, lawyers, and other professionals are handsomely rewarded in money and prestige.

Our social class affects more about us than simply how much money we make or how much social prestige and political power we have. Class plays a crucial role in our lives, for it affects our life chances, for example, the likelihood that we will marry early or late, will get divorced or not, will continue long in school or not, or will have larger or smaller families. We are therefore more fortunate than members of many other societies in that our society allows a relative degree of vertical social mobility—the possibility of moving up (as well as down) the strata of social classes—and thus the possibility of improving our own or our children's life chances.

Why call culture the human invention? Because only humans have developed tools, beliefs, and values to help ensure survival. Like many inventions, culture can call necessity its mother, for our lack of instincts to guide our behavior is counterbalanced by our great capacity to learn and communicate. Since we rarely survive outside of groups, cultures include ways of living harmoniously together and meeting our psychological needs. Because cultures are the inventions of many minds, they vary from one to another, and each one is constantly changing. Cultures change in response to environmental changes and through transmission from one generation to the next. Such change, however, is not always smooth, for often we change our tools and methods more readily than we change our ideas and values.

3

CULTURE: THE HUMAN INVENTION

It is important to realize that man is an animal, but it is even more important to realize that the essence of his unique nature lies precisely in those characteristics that are not shared with any other animal. His place in nature and its supreme significance to man are not defined by his animality but by his humanity.[1]

George Gaylord Simpson

Humans share their ability to create, use, and transmit culture with no other animal. Culture gives humans their unique place in nature, and indeed their humanity. So profoundly does culture influence the lives of humankind that it is almost impossible to imagine man or woman as we know them without culture. Perhaps if we stretch our imaginations we can envision humans without culture. Then we can begin to see why culture is a basic concept used to explain the forms and results of human interaction.

A WORLD WITHOUT CULTURE: NOT HUMAN

Imagine that in probing into space, we happened to anger aliens living on a distant planet. Imagine that these aliens returned the visit and sprayed the entire earth with a substance that erased all human memory of everything that had been learned from previous generations. Men and women would remain intelligent and in other ways human, but they would have no memories of the customs, habits, or abilities passed on by their predecessors.

Within a month most people in our cities would be dead, and the remaining few would probably last less than a single year. Shortly after the attack, hunger and thirst would abound, but not one person would be able to communicate

[1]George Gaylord Simpson, *The Meaning of Evolution* (New Haven: Yale University Press, 1952), p. 284.

his needs to his fellows, or tell others about chance findings of food or water. Grunting, upright apes would wander aimlessly in search of food. The stronger would snatch from the weaker what little was found in a desperate effort to survive. Perhaps after many had already died some would explore the supermarkets that smelled of rotting meat and vegetables, but they would have no way of knowing that the many boxes and cans contained food.

Sanitation would be a gigantic problem because it would never occur to anyone to bury the rapidly increasing dead. Disease would be rampant. A broken arm would lead inevitably to death. On the farms, people would probably be afraid of the larger animals. But they would survive for a time by eating all the smaller ones and any foodstuffs that were stored up or ready to harvest. In the northern and temperate zones, the few people who survived for six months or so would perish during the winter. Perhaps some primitive groups in the tropics, where there are fewer threats to physical survival, could stay alive long enough to develop some simple way of life. These primitive people might be all that would stand between the human race and utter extinction.

CULTURES: STOREHOUSES OF LEARNED BEHAVIOR

Life without culture is not pleasant to think about, for without culture we would not be human. We desperately need the culture we have created. Only by responding in one of two ways can any living thing survive in its environment: by *instinct* or by *learned behavior*. Among the lower animals instincts are supreme. Although animals do learn, by trial and error and sometimes by imitation, they are governed mainly by instinct. Learned responses have a tremendous advantage over instincts, for what has been learned can be either modified or replaced by a new and better response. Particularly if the learning capacity is high, as in humans, reliance on learned responses provides a truly remarkable advantage in the struggle for survival.

Our tremendous capacity to learn sets us apart from every other animal. Our learning ability is so much greater than that of any other species that this difference between humans and other animals becomes not merely one of degree but one of kind. Equally important in setting humans apart from other animals is our ability to use language. One person's ideas can be shared with others, and all of the ideas that a group creates and collects can be passed on from generation to generation. In the dim past, for example, one person's chance discovery of how to make fire could be quickly shared with others and eventually taught to the children, who in turn could teach it to their children.

The ability to communicate by language, to share ideas and learned behaviors, is what sets man apart from all other species.

This ability of human beings to store and pass on what has been learned allows each generation to take advantage of the experiences of previous generations. Without this ability to learn and to communicate what we have learned, each new generation would have to start from scratch. The capacity to make and use fire, to distinguish edible foods from poisons, and all other learned skills required for survival would have to be rediscovered by each new generation.

CULTURE AND THE FOCUS OF SOCIOLOGY

Humans, therefore, have a remarkable ability to discover, to invent, and to improvise. With language we can transmit all that we have learned to the next generation. These two characteristics, intelligence and language, give us the ability to create, use, and transmit culture.

Sociologists start from the human ability to create culture, and they pursue answers to three broad questions:

Why do humans create culture? – *to solve problems*
How do humans create culture? – *by environment & studying cultural change*
How does culture affect human interaction?

Our chapter-opening fantasy about humans without culture provides a clue to the answer to the first question. Stated simply, humans need culture to solve their problems. In a later section we classify these problems and indicate what sociologists have discovered regarding human attempts to deal with them.

How humans create culture has been studied by sociologists. This question can be approached in two ways. One is by studying the forces, such as geographic environment, that affect the building of culture. The other is by studying cultural change. Because no human group lacks culture, we cannot observe how one would start from scratch and develop its culture. We can, however, study how a group changes the behavior and ideas that form its culture.

Answers to the third question, about how culture affects human interaction, appear throughout this chapter and throughout the entire book. In this chapter, how culture affects interaction can be seen with particular clarity in the sections on cultural variability. Culture's effect on interaction can also be seen in the discussion of human ingenuity in devising ways to meet group needs. Later chapters that deal with the family, religion, and the class system, for example, indicate how profoundly culture affects our lives.

Culture is created by humans as they interact with one another, and in turn human interaction is strongly conditioned by culture. Thus, it is clear that culture is a basic sociological concept. Before going more fully into why and how culture is created, we must provide a somewhat fuller treatment of what this important concept means to the sociologist.

THE MEANING OF CULTURE

Culture was defined by anthropologist Clyde Kluckhohn as "a historically derived system of explicit and implicit designs for living, which tend to be shared by all or specifically designated members of a group."[2] Kluckhohn's phrase "historically derived" means that at any given time a society's designs for living have come down to the group from earlier generations. In other words, culture is

[2]Clyde Kluckhohn, *Mirror of Man* (New York: Fawcett Books, 1957), p. 23. More than 160 definitions of *culture* have been found in use by sociologists and anthropologists. See A. L. Kroeber and Clyde Kluckhohn, "Culture: A Critical Review of Concepts and Definitions," *Papers of the Peabody Museum of American Archaeology and Ethnology* (Cambridge, Mass.: Harvard University Press, 1952).

This random group in a New York park intermixes racial and ethnic backgrounds, languages, and social classes. Could these people share a common culture?

learned. It is transmitted from generation to generation by the process of *socialization* (a concept treated more fully in the next chapter).

In any culture the designs for living are so extensive that most of the behavior and characteristics we consider human come from culture rather than from our biological makeup. Thus, much of what we consider normal or natural is not really so in any ultimate sense. For example, while Americans think it natural to be competitive in economic affairs, we are competitive only because we have learned to be. It is no more natural for a person to be economically competitive than it is for him to be cooperative. From our culture we can learn to worship many gods or only one, or to love several wives or only one, and so on.

In Kluckhohn's definition, culture is "shared by all or specifically designated members of a group." The idea that culture is shared is very complex, fraught with semantic and other difficulties. How many people must hold a belief or follow a practice before that belief or practice can be considered a shared cultural element of the group? For example, Americans supposedly share a common language. But do we? A narcotics agent would show little interest in a middle-aged person's remark that he intended to cut the grass. The same statement overheard coming from a college student would elicit quite a different reaction from the same agent. Furthermore, there are regional differences in pronunciation and vocabulary within the United States, and some ethnic minorities use the English language very little. Nevertheless, if we think of the similarities rather than the differences, it is apparent that a common core to our language permits adequate communication. It is therefore appropriate to say that Americans really do share a language. In a similar way other cultural elements can be considered shared if they provide a dominant thread in the goals and destinies of a group, even if not all members of the group make equal use of them.

Although some aspects of a culture are fully shared by only "specifically designated" members of a society, the elements nevertheless belong to that culture. For example, although attitudes and behavior are now changing, much of the behavior of women around the home and in connection with childrearing is still not shared by men. A society's religious leaders have specific knowledge, beliefs, and practices that are unique to them and are not shared by society as a whole. Political leaders, steam fitters, farmers, and many others share knowledge and behavior among themselves but not with the entire society.

All or most members of society frequently have a general knowledge of the culture shared by a category; therefore, all in a way share those aspects of culture. Many Americans of both sexes, for example, have a general idea of what is involved in replacing the pistons in an automobile engine even if most men and women do not share with mechanics the knowledge and skill required to perform the job. City people have a general knowledge of what is involved in farming even though they probably do not know enough to be very good at it.

SHARING CULTURAL ALTERNATIVES

A society that shares a common culture also shares alternatives. In other words, a given culture may provide more than one belief or practice for use in a given situation or to achieve a certain end. These beliefs and practices can be used by almost any member of the society. As an example, the culture of the United States contains a wide range of religions, with no cultural requirement to select a certain one. Likewise, the culture provides a range of alternative techniques of childrearing from which parents are free to choose.

Yet even the widest range of alternatives excludes some of all the possible choices. Thus, our variety of religious beliefs and practices does not include human sacrifice to the gods or polygynous marriage, the marriage of one man to two or more women at the same time. We can choose to travel by airplane, train, or automobile, but our culture does not offer us the choice of ox cart or camel. The examples should make clear that some things are prohibited in a culture—human sacrifice, for example—while others are absent through neglect. An ox cart or camel are of no real use in our culture, but they are not prohibited.

In what ways could you say that street artists share elements of this society's common material and nonmaterial culture as well as its alternatives?

The cultures of most large, industrialized societies provide more alternatives for the solution of life's problems than do small, nonliterate groups. In addition, because large societies usually have a more intricate division of labor, it is more common that some aspects of the culture are shared fully only by certain groups of people, not by everyone. For example, the *Dictionary of Occupations* lists tens of thousands of jobs practiced in the United States; obviously we cannot all share the skills and attitudes that go along with all these jobs. This multitude of both specialties and alternatives makes it difficult to describe accurately and thoroughly the entire culture of a large, industrialized society.

CULTURE: MATERIAL AND NONMATERIAL

The designs for living shared by a society can be either tangible or intangible. Most of our examples have so far been of intangibles, such as language, culturally prescribed roles, and religious beliefs. These and other intangible products of the human mind are nonmaterial aspects of culture. Material aspects of culture are artifacts, the things that humans have produced. Material and nonmaterial culture are closely related. The automobile, for instance, is the result of ideas, even though it is itself quite tangible. The automobile would be useless without systems of learning how to drive and repair it, ideas on traffic control, and

> **Each family can be said to have its own culture. Write an essay on the culture of your family emphasizing how your family's way of life is different, in some degree, from that of other families. Use illustrations of expressions that have meaning only to family members, unique rituals or customs, punishments and rewards, food habits, attitudes toward beauty, cleanliness or work, and anything else that will show your family's distinct way of life.**

so on. Only if both the material and the nonmaterial aspects of the automobile are taken into account can we understand how this part of our culture fits into the total way of life of American society.

CAUTION: CULTURE IS AN ABSTRACTION

Before we study culture further, an important distinction must be made. Culture is an abstraction: an idea, not a thing. We form an abstraction by the same mental process that we use to form concepts. We form an idea about the properties or qualities of an object, or about the relationships between objects, and then we mentally separate this idea about the objects from the objects themselves, much as we did earlier with the concept of table in Chapter 2.

The important step in forming an abstraction, whether the abstraction represents things or people, is that we mentally separate the idea from the actual things or people. The abstraction can be thought or spoken about without reference to particular people or objects. We can think of tallness without having a person, a building, or a tree in mind. Likewise, honesty is an abstraction. We can observe honest behavior, but we cannot observe honesty. Yet we can talk about honesty, and we believe we know what we mean when we do so.

The abstraction *culture* was invented by early sociologists and anthropologists to stand for the system of shared beliefs and practices of an enduring group and for the material objects that are the products of group behavior or are in some way related to it. As an abstraction, culture is not the behavior or the objects. It is an idea about them. The idea of culture was derived from observing behavior and objects and thinking about what was observed. In this sense, the idea of culture is much like that of honesty, blueness, or tallness.

Although everyone knows the differences between an idea and a material object, we sometimes tend to think of the ideas that we create as real objects. This tendency is called *reification*. When we reify an abstraction we treat the idea as if it had material substance. Reification may be convenient, but the danger is that we may not always be fully aware of what we have done. For example, we talk of a changing culture. Yet since culture is an abstraction it cannot change, for an idea has no ability of its own to change. Again, no culture can compel people to act in any manner. And yet we talk of behavior that is prescribed or dictated by culture. We say, for example, that the practice of female infanticide is prescribed by the culture of some nonliterate group. However, the culture does not drown the babies; some person does, probably the baby's own parent. The various expressions that tend to ascribe life or substance to culture are figurative statements: They are not to be taken literally.

Although the people of a society behave in ways that implement their culture, and although people transmit their culture from one generation to the next, culture can be studied without reference to specific people. Culture tends to persist over long periods of time, while individuals do not. Not everyone in a society behaves in a way that implements all aspects of the culture. We therefore can study culture in the abstract, charting the changes of a given culture, comparing the culture of one group to that of another. At a more general level, we can determine the functions of all cultures, as we will now do.

THE UNIVERSALS OF CULTURE

We humans are idea-making animals. We think up ideas on how to wrest a living from our environment, how to regulate our lives in society, how to amuse ourselves, and how to explain the order of things in nature. Often these ideas produce material objects. For example, early humans not only invented the idea that it would be good to build fire, they also invented the fire saw and fire drill to produce fire. We "modern" humans not only have elaborate systems of ideas that we refer to collectively as our religions, but we have also produced temples, priestly vestments, and sacred objects.

Material objects are inventions, but so are the ideas behind these objects. It would seem logical, therefore, to suppose that no two groups would develop exactly the same culture, either material or nonmaterial. Such is indeed the case. Because culture has come from human minds, with countless people helping to shape and modify it, it is unimaginable that even two young cultures could be alike in every detail.

On the other hand, although no two cultures could be exactly alike, all cultures should have some features in common. Cultures are invented by men and women, and as biological creatures all men and women have common needs. We may expect, then, that everywhere basically similar ways will be invented to meet basically similar needs.

The needs of all men and women are for survival and the well-being of society, but each culture has its own ways for how people meet those needs.

The function of any culture is to assure the survival and well–being of the society. All societies face basic problems that interfere with the groups' survival and well–being if they are not solved by the culture. The common problems of people in society everywhere are how to ensure physical survival, how to maintain orderly and satisfactory group living, and how to provide for the psychological needs of the society's members. The results of efforts to solve these problems constitute the three *universal functions of culture.*[3]

IDEAS FOR PHYSICAL SURVIVAL

Every culture contains ideas about securing food, providing shelter from the elements, and assuring protection from enemies. The culture directs how people should behave in order to achieve these fundamental goals. Culture further dictates what objects people should make for physical survival and how these

[3]Anthropologists and sociologists have developed different ways of classifying social needs and consequently have different conceptions of the universal functions of culture. Our classification parallels but is not as extensive as Linton's. See Ralph Linton, *The Tree of Culture* (New York: Alfred A. Knopf, 1955), pp. 34–37.

objects should be made. The primitive digging stick and the combine of modern wheat farmers are both material culture objects developed to assist people to secure food. In a similar sense, the knowledge of how to construct a thatched-roof hut or a split-level suburban home, or techniques of weapons making are expressions of the function of culture to help people survive.

A society could not long survive unless it replaced members who got old and died. People are easily taught how to make babies. But they also must be taught how to take care of these babies so at least some of the offspring will live to adulthood. Thus, in every culture there are ideas about who should assist the mother during a birth and how the newborn should be treated. The culture also specifies who will provide food and other necessities for the mother, what and how often the young child should eat, and so forth.

Furthermore, these new members of society must be trained or socialized so that they will know how to function in their society. Not only what a child learns, but also how it learns, is determined by culture. For example, if a child is to survive, it must receive nourishment. But what to eat, when to eat, and how to eat—whether with chopsticks, fingers, or knives and forks—are all culturally determined. How this learning takes place is also a matter of cultural determination. In some societies, parents reward their children for culturally approved behavior. In other societies, children are punished for behaving in inappropriate ways. Many societies, including our own, use both reward and punishment. Still other societies depend mainly on imitation: The child learns by watching the behavior of adults and older children.

IDEAS FOR LIVING TOGETHER

If a group merely worked out ways to secure its food and shelter and still allowed extreme friction, rivalries, fighting, and killing among its members, the society would be doomed to extinction. Every culture must contain ideas that allow the people of a society to live together without undue friction. Ways of behaving must be established that result in orderly relations between individuals, between groups within a society, and often between one society and others.

One of the cultural techniques invented to promote harmonious relations among people is position. Fireman, doctor, medicine man, husband, daughter—all of these are positions. With each position comes a role, a kind of behavior that is expected or demanded of the person in that position. (The concepts position and role are explained more fully in Chapter 5.) If all members of society learn their roles and how these roles relate to other roles, each person's behavior will contribute to the needs of the group. Each person's conduct will mesh—and not conflict—with the behavior of others. Of course, such a state of affairs is hypothetical and idealistic. For not even the smallest society has been able to

For survival of the group, ideally all social positions and roles mesh; each person thus contributes to the functioning of society.

develop a network of positions and to define roles in such a way that there are no areas of ambiguity or conflict. Also, no society has been able to get everyone to accept all positions as they are defined or to learn all of the behavior expected of them.

Positions and roles are not by themselves enough to ensure orderly behavior within the group. We have referred already to the need for socialization to teach behavior and attitudes appropriate to various roles. Every society must impose a system of morality, rules of right and wrong, and a system of reward and punishment designed to enforce good behavior. Rules of conduct, like positions and roles, share something important with fire-making tools, thatched-roof huts, and animal-skin clothing. All are human inventions produced to meet human needs, and all of them have developed and changed over time. But not one of them was developed as a conscious donation to culture, by a cultural committee as it were. In other words, we should remember that culture is an abstraction invented by social scientists. It is not a thing that people consciously serve, contribute to, or organize.

Construct a questionnaire directed toward finding out what
Americans value most in life and whether or not Americans orient
their behavior toward these values. Administer this questionnaire to
two age groups, those under 25 and those over 25, in order to see if
cultural values are changing.

IDEAS TO MEET THE PSYCHOLOGICAL
NEEDS OF INDIVIDUALS

Every social science provides strong evidence that all human beings have basic
psychological needs. A society that fails to meet deep-seated human needs will
produce discontent among its members and will endanger its own survival. The
sociologist William I. Thomas has developed one system for classifying human
needs.[4] In Thomas's view, the needs of humankind produce four basic wishes.
These are the desire for new experience, for security, for response from other
individuals, and for recognition. A culture thus contains diversions, play, creative
activities, and other ways for the members of a society to escape boredom and
find new experiences. Various aesthetic activities—painting, dancing, writing
—provide new experience and an opportunity to gain recognition and response
from other members of the group. Security of a long-term sort is provided by
the culturally prescribed behavior, beliefs, and rituals that deal with unknown
forces and the meaning of life. We derive (sometimes) a sense of security, too,
from our government and economic systems, which provide a regularity to life,
physical protection, and a means of satisfying our many wants and needs.

We need look no further than our own society to see the discontent that
can arise if human needs are not adequately met. Some of the complaints of
women, as articulated by those in the women's liberation movement, are that
women have been systematically deprived of equal opportunities for new experience, for response from individuals other than their children, and for recognition
in occupations and professions.[5]

The three functions of providing for physical survival, orderly group living,
and fulfillment of individual needs are performed by the total culture, not just
a single element. In addition, a given element, whether a material object like

[4]William I. Thomas and Florian Znaniecki, *The Polish Peasant in Europe and America*, Vol. II (New York: Alfred
A. Knopf, 1927), p. 1859.

[5]Robin Morgan, ed., *Sisterhood is Powerful* (New York: Vintage, 1970).

a sports car or a complex institution like marriage, may have a variety of functions. A sports car may serve as a student's mode of transportation, but it also may be a source of recognition among his or her peers if it is one of the latest models. Its owner may very likely find it a thing of beauty, and keeping it clean and in good condition may help to satisfy his or her aesthetic urges.

To take another example, the cultural rules and practices of marriage and the family serve many functions. By living together in a small, intimate group, individuals can meet their needs for response and recognition from other people. Permitting or encouraging sexual intercourse between marriage partners not only meets the needs of husband and wife, it also provides the society with new members. The family provides a sense of security, particularly for the young but also for adult members. Regardless of which specific tasks are considered the man's work, which the woman's, and which are shared, the culture of a group contains some ideas on the division of labor within a family and these ideas, in turn, help to assure that society's members meet their needs for physical survival.

It is also true that the same general function, such as physical survival, is usually served by more than one aspect of culture. The cultivation of food, the construction of dwellings, and the manufacture of clothing are different aspects of culture. But each of these activities contributes to the function of assuring physical survival.

WHY A SPECTRUM OF CULTURES?

Even though all cultures serve the same three functions for society, their methods vary considerably. Digging sticks and tractors are two very different tools with the same function: to help people secure food. Earlier, we suggested one explanation for cultural diversity. Since every culture and element within it is an invention of human minds in response to basic needs, it is unfathomable to suppose that the collective ideas of any two groups will be exactly alike. Other influences account for cultural diversity, however. Among these are geographic environment and race. We now look at these two explanations and later return to a further consideration of human versatility.

GEOGRAPHIC ENVIRONMENT

Most geography school books show Eskimos living in igloos and South Pacific islanders in their thatched-roof huts. They present pictures of Chinese junks on the Yangtze River; scantily clad, spear-throwing bushmen on the African

The Eskimos' methods of hunting, living, and traveling respond to their environment.
So why can't we say that determined their culture?

plains; and the great cities of Western civilization. The notion of cultural variability, that humans secure their food and protect themselves from the elements in many different ways, is learned early. But this textbook presentation can lead to a false conclusion. Having learned that geographic environments vary considerably and that cultures also vary considerably, you might conclude that geography somehow produces the cultural variability. Such a conclusion is wrong or at best a gross exaggeration.

Geographic environment imposes some limits on culture. A particular environment poses certain problems and usually limits the variety of possible solutions. To survive, people must somehow reckon with the temperature, terrain, animal and plant life, and other features of their environment. Eskimos could not have invented bamboo dwellings because bamboo is not available to them. And bamboo would not provide an effective arctic shelter even if it could be obtained. Tribes deep in the interior of Africa, no matter how hungry they become, could not develop new and better ways of harpooning whales. The presence of wild fruit–bearing trees might well have tempted people to taste the fruit and much later perhaps to cultivate them. Fur–clad animals in the environment may have given our shivering ancestors the idea of slaying the animal and wrapping the fur about themselves.

Even for early humans, the mere presence of certain resources in the environment by no means guaranteed that these resources would be used at all, let alone used in a certain way. The American Indians did not see in the Great Lakes the possibility of a great inland water route, nor did they feel obliged to improve on nature by digging the Erie Canal. The forests of our continent did not suggest to them a lumber industry or the processing of wood pulp for newspapers. They never used the coal that lay beneath their campgrounds to warm a dwelling or cook a meal. Groups in the Siberian Arctic, such as the Chukchi and Yukaghir, live in an environment quite similar to that of the Eskimo, yet they have never built an igloo. Instead of using the snow around them, they make shelters of skin attached to a framework of wood. And they do this even though wood is scarce around the Arctic Circle.[6]

Even when geographic features suggest certain functions, the environment does not tell people how to carry out these functions. River and lake dwellers may eventually try water transportation, but rivers and lakes do not tell them what kind of boat to build or how to build it. Different groups along the same river can and do develop different types of boats. Only the available animals can be hunted, but they can be killed in many different ways. Only the available fruits and vegetables can be eaten, but they can be carried home in a basket, wrapped in an animal skin, or eaten on the spot. The environment of early humans, therefore, placed some limits on early culture and suggested some strategies for survival, but it did not determine cultural development for these people.

The nonmaterial aspects of culture seem even less traceable to geographic environment than do the material ones. It is indeed farfetched to think of the presence of mountains or rivers as accounting for man's religions, even though both have been personified and worshipped. Neither trees nor rainfall nor temperature can explain the variability of marriage systems throughout the world. Only in a loose sense can the physical environment affect human artistic endeavors or play activities. There is, then, only a very limited connection between the physical environment and the strategies developed by different cultures for assuring their survival.

RACE AND CULTURE

By the same reasoning that derives cultural variety from geographic variety, we can observe that there are different physical types, or *races*, of humans and that humans have different cultures. You will recall from Chapter 2 that to propose a relationship between two observations is to state a hypothesis. In this case, we observe that people differ in their physical make-up and that cultures differ from one another. When it is maintained that the physical differences cause the cultural differences, we have a hypothesis. A hypothesis is

[6]Melville J. Herskovits, *Cultural Anthropology* (New York: Alfred A. Knopf, 1955), p. 98.

not a fact, but it can be tested. That is, we can gather evidence and discover whether the hypothesis is true or false. As for the hypothesized relationship between race and culture, the evidence strongly suggests that differences in race do not cause differences in culture.

By *race*, we mean major groupings of people who share inherited physical characteristics. The peoples of the world are often classified into three major races: Mongoloid, Negroid, and Caucasoid. Chinese, Japanese, Koreans, Okinawans, and many smaller groups make up the Mongoloid race. From this short list alone it is immediately obvious that different cultures have been developed by people of the same race. The corollary to this is also true: Different races can both participate in and help develop the same culture. We need look no further than our own society for evidence of this. Caucasians, Negroes, and Mongolians share a common culture. Could this be possible if a given race customarily produced a single type of culture?

The hypothesis that race determines culture could be true only if one of two conditions prevailed. Because culture exists to satisfy human needs, either the different races have different physical, psychological, or social needs, or the different races have different abilities to satisfy their needs. Long ago social scientists proved both assumptions false.[7] It is no accident, therefore, that the same race can produce different cultures or that different races can contribute to and participate in the same culture. Most differences among races are superficial ones and are not of the sort that would lead to the development of different cultures.

HUMAN INVENTIVENESS IN MEETING NEEDS

Remember that culture is invented, maintained, and transmitted by human behavior. So to explain the variability of culture, perhaps we should first look at the human species. Two of its characteristics make it highly unlikely that any two groups would develop precisely the same way of life: its intelligence and its physiological flexibility. First, human intelligence allows the invention of more than one solution to almost any problem. Second, human physiological characteristics are such that many different solutions to a given problem will all work.

Food: A Biological Need and a Cultural Artifact Like the lower animals, humans need food to survive. But unlike lower animals, humans have surrounded their

---

[7]Juan Comas, "Racial Myths," *The Race Question in Modern Science* (New York: William Morrow and Co., 1956); and Ashley Montagu, *Race, Science and Humanity* (Princeton, N.J.: D. Van Nostrand Co., 1963).

All people share the need for food, but what they eat and how they prepare and serve it varies greatly from culture to culture.

procuring, processing, and consuming of food with a variety of meanings. No dog or chimpanzee seems to have developed the idea that it is wrong to eat certain foods. Yet in modern as well as primitive societies food taboos abound. Jews eat no pork, Hindus eat no beef, until recently American Catholics ate no meat on Fridays, and many sects and individuals eat no meat at all.

Not only what people may eat, but even what is considered to be food, varies from culture to culture. We may not choose to eat, say, chicken, beef, or pork. Whatever our taste, though, we recognize these items as food. But what about snakes, eels, grasshoppers, and rats? Many Americans would maintain that these are not food. Yet for other people—and even for some Americans—these foods are rare delicacies.

Just as humans have come up with different meanings for the food sources they see around them, so have they invented a host of ways to process their food. They fry their fish, smoke it over a fire, or eat it uncooked—with chopsticks, with a knife and fork, or with their hands. They have regular meals, two or three a day, or eat whenever hungry. They may designate that only certain foods are appropriate for feasts or parties. These values, attitudes, meanings, and emotions associated with food and the eating of it are the inventions of humans.

Comparing the two photos on these pages, which one would you select as a better example of food as "cultural artifact"? Why?

Once acquired and shared by a group, these meanings tend to be transmitted to later generations so that great cultural variability develops with respect to food.

Sexual Variability No known society is completely indifferent to the sexual behavior of its members. All cultures contain values, regulations, and emotions concerning sexual behavior. And again, from culture to culture great variety is found in how this behavior is handled.

Societies must both permit sexual behavior and limit it. Without sexual reproduction the society would die out from lack of replacements. In addition, total prohibition of expression of the adult sexual drive would provoke serious discontent and thus jeopardize the society. But at the same time, a society completely indifferent to its members' sexual behavior would be in jeopardy. (As we said, no such group is known. This is probably because the human sexual drive and its expression have the potential for so much conflict, jealousy, and guilt that without regulations the harmony of group life would be seriously threatened.)

All societies, therefore, must reckon with the identical biological facts of human sexuality. True to form, humankind has been extremely ingenious in the variety of ways it has invented to cope with the dual social needs for permission and prohibition of sexual expression. To be sure, as a legitimate relationship for sexual expression, marriage has been a universal invention. But the forms this invention has taken are various.

Marriage takes a greater variety of forms than can be listed here, but some of its major variants include the following: monogamy, one man married to one woman, a common but not universal form; polygyny, one man married to more than one wife at a time, common in the *Old Testament* and often found today, particularly in nonliterate societies; polyandry, one woman with more than one husband at a time, found less frequently than polygyny; and there are possibly a few instances of true group marriage—that is, several men and several women living together as a family group.

Marriage is only one way that societies have invented to deal with human sexuality.[8] Other customs and regulations show the same variety as marriage. For example, every culture prohibits sexual intercourse with close relatives, but the definition of *close relative* differs widely. First cousins may be either tabooed as marriage partners or considered the best possible mates. Premarital sex relations may be tolerated under some circumstances, always severely punished, or even expected. Adultery may be either mildly criticized or punished by death. Prostitution may be part of religious rites, may be condoned or defended, may be considered a great social ill, or may be completely unknown. Human ingenuity has resulted in a wide range of sexual practices, customs, and values.

The diversity that societies show in food practices and control of the sexual drive extends into every area of social life—political systems, economic systems, and so on. Our ability to invent various ways to satisfy our needs explains most of the differences between cultures. But only principles of *cultural change* can supply a satisfactory explanation for the variety of cultures in the world today. For even if two or more cultures happened to be similar at the time of their origins, the principles of cultural change assure that they would not be similar today.

ALL CULTURES CHANGE

By its very nature culture must change. Since culture is a human invention, there is no reason to assume that the development of a certain culture will end inventiveness. On the contrary, it is much more reasonable to assume that the same general processes of invention that formed the culture will continue to change the culture. Second, culture is transmitted from one generation to the

[8]For a discussion of the variety of regulations of sexual behavior based on a survey of 250 societies, see George P. Murdock, *Social Structure* (New York: The Macmillan Co., 1949), Chapters 8 and 9.

**Only a few years ago most American girls desired
such a slip; today it is an exotic curiosity.
Has our nonmaterial culture changed as fast?**

next. But culture does not transmit itself; people transmit it. Furthermore, each person has his or her own interpretation of what is to be transmitted. So even if faithful transmission were attempted, changes would be introduced. Finally, culture is developed to satisfy human needs. But needs change. As people learn more about their environment, they come to have different expectations. Contact with new groups may introduce new needs into a society. To provide for these new needs and expectations, a culture must be able to change.

You will recall that late nineteenth-century social theorists—Comte, Spencer, Marx—developed theories on how societies progressed from one stage to another. At about this same time there were other attempts to establish theories of cultural evolution comparable to Darwin's theory of biological evolution. These early theorists were correct in noting the changing nature of culture. But they were incorrect in their assumption that natural law dictated that all societies have passed or would pass through a fixed number of stages. While sociologists and anthropologists have largely abandoned the search for fixed, universal stages of cultural evolution, much has been learned about cultural change.

Different cultures change at different rates. Since World War II, for example, the culture of Japan has changed much more rapidly than that of Spain. Moreover, the same culture will change more rapidly at some times in its history than at others. We can see this by looking at how the rate of change during the hundred years before the Industrial Revolution in the United States or England contrasts with the rate of change in the hundred years following industrialization.

Also, not all parts of the same culture change at the same rate. The sociologist William Ogburn introduced the theory of *culture lag* to explain how imbalance may result when one part of a culture fails to keep pace with another part.[9] In general, according to Ogburn, our ideas and ways of thinking tend to lag behind technological aspects of culture. For example, a study in New Mexico found that the introduction of high–yielding, good–grade hybrid corn was not successful because the people did not like the color and texture of the corn dough used to make tortillas.[10] This group's aesthetic ideas on what was good corn lagged behind what was good from the agricultural and nutritional points of view. As another example, a case could certainly be made that our ideas on how to use the automobile safely and conveniently have lagged behind our ability to mass produce it and to improve it technically. To understand culture lag and other aspects of cultural change, we must understand the processes of cultural change.

PROCESS OF CULTURAL CHANGE

There are only three essential ways in which a culture can change. New elements can be added; elements can be dropped; or elements can be redefined or reinterpreted so they have a new meaning to the group. At times the three methods are intertwined, but it is well to look at them separately.

Adding a Cultural Element Whether it is a complex, intangible pattern like Christianity or a simple cultural object like the longbow or the airplane, any new item is added to a culture by the same three-step process:

1. The society learns of a potential addition to its culture.
2. The element is accepted by the group.
3. The new element is integrated into the existing culture.

[9]William F. Ogburn, *Social Change* (New York: B. W. Huebsch, 1923).

[10]Anacleto Apodaca, "Corn and Custom: The Introduction of Hybrid Corn to Spanish American Farmers in New Mexico," in E. H. Spicer, ed., *Human Problems in Technological Change* (New York: Russell Sage Foundation, 1952), pp. 35–39.

A society can learn about a potential addition to its culture in several different ways. The new item can be discovered, invented, or borrowed from another group. The result of each process is similar. Some new idea or artifact has been presented to a society for inspection by its members.

Invention and Discovery "Necessity is the mother of invention." If there is a problem, human ingenuity will be turned to solving it. History gives us many examples of this sequence. Machines are developed to release people from toil, medicines or surgical techniques are sought to fight disease and restore health, and systems of traffic control are invented to ease movement in a large city.

It makes equal sense, however, to reverse the proposition and claim that "invention is the mother of necessity." In other words, the invention may create the need. Television provides an excellent example. Before its invention there was no need for it. Today millions are highly dependent on it and find it difficult to imagine life without television. The giant field of advertising, of course, rests on the assumption that once something has been invented, people can be convinced that they need it.

Discovery is often like invention. The New World, for example, was discovered because a shorter trade route was being sought to the Indies. But consider that in fact Columbus rediscovered a continent that the Scandinavians had discovered centuries earlier. (Obviously, the Native Americans had discovered the continent earlier still.) Apparently the Scandinavians had little need to incorporate their discovery into their culture. But the fifteenth and sixteenth century Spanish, Portuguese, French, and English were at a stage of economic and social development that made Columbus's discovery immensely useful to them.

Not all inventions and discoveries are made to fill needs, or even to create needs. The private notebooks of Leonardo da Vinci, who died in 1519, are filled with detailed scale drawings of such military things as the machine gun, the helicopter, and the tank. Apparently da Vinci invented these ideas for his own entertainment, and they were not even made public within his lifetime. In our own society, many longstanding needs remain unfilled. Despite immense efforts, we still do not have a cure for cancer. Nor have we managed to alleviate poverty and great economic inequality.

Cultural Diffusion: Borrowing Among Cultures New cultural elements can be introduced into a society when ideas or practices spread from one society to another. This process, which is the borrowing of cultural traits, is called *cultural diffusion.* Probably every society that has come into contact with another one has borrowed cultural traits. If this is true, almost all human societies owe parts of their culture to other groups.

Contemporary industrialized societies that have been in contact with many other groups sometimes seem to have a hodgepodge of cultural traits liberally borrowed from a host of groups over many years. For example, the dominant religion in Western Europe and the United States came from the Middle East, our alphabet from the Phoenicians, the dishes we eat on from China, and so on. It is important to remember, however, that every cultural trait that is diffused was invented by someone, somewhere.

Particularly when we deal with complex ideas, it can be difficult to trace the diffusion of cultural elements. For example, the concept of democracy shows its roots in the Athenian Constitution of 508 B.C., while the Magna Carta of A.D. 1215 guaranteed specified rights and liberties to the English people. Many more specific democratic experiences or notions could be found that in one way or another have influenced democracy in the United States. Then, of course, many of our own people have added to and modified the principles of democracy. By now it is almost impossible to say how much of the current American meaning of democracy was borrowed and how much was invented. So it is with other ideas and practices. Many are widely dispersed throughout the world.

The process of cultural diffusion is essentially the same whether the new ideas are actively sought by a society or are brought into it by an outside group. Thus, almost a thousand years after Christianity had spread throughout Europe it was still practically unknown in Russia. Prince Vladimir sent emissaries to both Rome and Constantinople to learn more about this unknown religion. Following the emissaries' glowing reports, he embraced the Greek Orthodox religion and persuaded other princes to join him. They, in turn, brought their subjects into the church. A new culture pattern, one that was destined to have a profound effect on the lives of the masses, was thus deliberately sought out and brought into the culture from another society.

At other times, the initiative for cultural diffusion rests with a group that attempts peacefully or otherwise to teach its way of life to other peoples. A little more than a hundred years ago Commodore Perry sailed into Yokohama Bay and opened the ports of Japan to world trade. A nation that had long shut itself off from the rest of the world became a world power in about fifty years. Today most Americans are acquainted with the various kinds of economic, technological, and agricultural assistance that their country is providing to the developing nations. On a smaller scale, our own and other countries have for years been sending religious missionaries, doctors, and teachers to less developed nations for the purpose of teaching them aspects of our way of life.

At times, a conquering group will attempt to eradicate parts of the culture of a defeated group and teach the people a new way of life. During the Japanese occupation of Korea, for example, the Koreans were forced to change many aspects of their life, including even the long braided hair styles of the men.

A vivid instance of borrowing among cultures. The culture of the Japanese is such that they readily embrace many foreign cultural elements.

Many decades earlier, it seemed that the manifest policy of the European American was to force the Native American Indians to change their way of life to conform with that of the invaders. Diffusion, therefore, is not always a slow and peaceful process but can occur relatively quickly and by force.

Acceptance of a Cultural Element Whether a society learns of a cultural trait by invention or diffusion, that trait must be accepted by the group before it becomes part of the culture. It is sometimes difficult to explain why a group will accept some new traits but not others. Late in the eighteenth century a commission of French scientists developed a new system of weights and measures, called the metric system. This system seems objectively superior to the English system of inches and feet and is now used in most industrialized countries. Certainly the idea of the metric system was diffused to the United States a long time ago, but it has not yet been accepted as a part of our general culture. Very likely we will adopt the metric system, and possibly soon, but we have not yet done so.

The source of a new idea can sometimes influence whether a trait will be accepted or rejected. This may explain our prolonged resistance to the metric system. For countries under English control or influence were not prone to accept foreign ideas, particularly from a political enemy like eighteenth-century France. As another example, imagine the fate of a congressional bill to broaden our social security program if its backers were to say that they got the idea from the Russians. Japan's reputation before World War II as an exporter of cheap, inferior merchandise accounts for resistance in recent years to its acceptance as a producer of high-quality optical and electronic goods.

Little is known about why some cultural elements are accepted and others are rejected. As we saw with the metric system, the sheer utility of an element does not guarantee its acceptance, for the element must be seen as useful by the potentially borrowing·group. Also, new elements that seem to fit in with the existing culture, that are not contrary to the group's values, are more likely to be accepted than are other types. The Eskimo is not likely to borrow the bikini bathing suit, nor the Hindu to borrow some new technique for preparing beef. Yet much is unknown. Just a few decades ago it would have seemed ludicrous to predict that Japan would adopt democracy so quickly and with so much enthusiasm. The introduction of Christianity in some primitive societies has also met with outstanding success despite its apparent contradiction with existing religious beliefs.

Integration of the New Element The third step in the addition of a cultural element is the integration of the new element into the existing culture. If a new element comes by borrowing, new meanings often are assigned to merge it with the existing culture. Thus, in some areas where Catholicism has been introduced and accepted, the gods and spirits of the native religion have become fused with the saints of the Catholic church. In Haiti, converts to Catholicism merged the personalities of the Dahomean rainbow serpent with Saint Patrick, who is often portrayed amidst snakes. The Haitian god Lagba, who dressed in rags, was fused with Saint Anthony, the patron of the poor.

Invented cultural elements also must be integrated into the culture. The element must be assigned meanings and its relationship with existing elements must be defined. Consider the invention of television. As TV became integrated into our culture, radio and its functions and meanings had to be redefined. Daytime soap operas and evening drama and variety shows shifted to the new medium, leaving radio with music, news, and call-in shows. In addition, new rules of etiquette for visiting patterns have been developed. For many the meaning of family mealtime has been altered by the fact that some meals are taken in front of the television set. Schools, churches, airlines, and bars all have developed

> **Ask a person who was living in a family as a young or middle-aged adult when television was introduced (late 1940s) to describe how this invention affected family life. Ask lots of questions; follow up leads from answers; listen carefully and record as much as you can. Be particularly concerned with testing Ogburn's cultural lag theory. Was there strain in developing habits and rules for watching or selecting programs? How did these people work TV into their daily life?**

ways to integrate this invention into their particular segment of the culture. Many more aspects of our culture have been changed as we have worked television into our total way of life.

Loss of Cultural Element For some reason, how and why cultural elements are lost have been studied less than how these elements are acquired. Perhaps a trait is dropped by a culture because a new one is introduced that performs a similar function better or more efficiently. But not all elements are dropped when a new and better one is introduced, and some traits are lost without being replaced by an invented or borrowed one.

When a society learns of a new and better idea or thing, it may reluctantly drop the older element or refuse to give the older element up altogether. The old order Amish are the only group in the United States today who use the horse and buggy as their exclusive form of transportation. For everyone else the horse and buggy has for all practical purposes been dropped from the culture. Newer methods of transportation have supplanted it, so that all that remains is its history. But this does not necessarily always happen.

The fireplace is still a very real part of our society's culture. It is found in inns and public buildings, lodges, camps, offices, and most of all in quite a number of American homes. When more effective ways of heating homes were developed the fireplace was not dropped. The existing cultural element was reintegrated into the culture when new ones were developed. New meanings have been assigned to the fireplace, and new functions have been developed for it. Today, the fireplace is used because it is considered attractive, because it serves as a focus of interest in room decoration, or perhaps because its fire symbolizes psychological warmth and comfort.

Someday, unless the energy crisis becomes more severe or is taken more seriously, the electric table fan will be widely replaced by air conditioning. But the fan is not likely to be kept for some aesthetic reason or otherwise reintegrated

Just as cultural values can predispose some groups to rapid cultural change, they can cause others, like the Amish, to reject many changes.

into the culture. What is the difference between the table fan and the fireplace? Quite possibly the fireplace had other meanings even when it was valued chiefly for its utilitarian functions. The aesthetic and other meanings came to be emphasized as the utilitarian meanings decreased. The more numerous the different functions a given culture trait serves, the more likely the trait is to be retained when one of its functions is replaced by a newer trait.

Although our examples have focused on simple material culture traits, it can be seen that it is difficult to establish basic principles that explain the loss of cultural traits. With more complex matters—and particularly in the area of ideas —the task of explaining cultural losses is more difficult still.

DIRECTION OF CULTURAL CHANGE

Because any culture is a pattern of traits, it follows that elements are not added or dropped at random. There always is a certain regularity in the direction in which a culture changes. Having first taken care of the basic necessities of life, cultures seem to go off in different directions. They specialize, as it were, in certain kinds of endeavors. Once having developed certain emphases, the changes in the culture will tend to be consistent with the culture's specializations. Thus, generations ago the Indians of the Southwest had a culture marked by rituals and ceremonies. The culture continued to develop to the point where most of the time and resources of the people not needed for basic survival were spent

THE TASADAY: THE STONE AGE AS
THE GARDEN OF EDEN

Any scientific statement, whether it is theory, hypothesis, or prediction, can be described roughly as a statement that can be disproven, disproven rather than proven because the history of science is one of refinement by correction. But theories and concepts that describe and explain our complex world rarely yield to a single stroke of the axe. We don't often discard an idea because of only one instance of disproof. Just as scientists do not adopt theories too hastily, they don't abandon them unless the evidence is conclusive.

Since the vague beginnings of the social sciences, workers in the field have gathered from around the world evidence that all societies and cultures share certain fundamental traits. It had long been thought by anthropologists and other social scientists that primitive peoples who subsisted by food gathering, and therefore spent all their time scrounging for the bare essentials, would not be settled enough to invent a technology.

But in 1971, in the dense mountain jungle of the Mindanao rain forest on one of the Philippine Islands, anthropologists made contact with the Tasaday, a tiny, peaceable tribe of twenty-four persons who did no hunting or farming, and who knew neither war nor hatred. Their food could be gathered in a few hours each day, and the rest of their time was leisure. Yet they had not developed a technology beyond the classic Stone Age tools of the stone axe for opening roots and sharpening bamboo tools, and a fire-making tool.

Except for a bamboo version of the jew's harp for music, they exhibited no arts, living in natural, unadorned caves. They had some fears and taboos, such as fear of thunder and a taboo against venturing far from their caves at night, but they had no articulated religious beliefs or myths to explain to themselves where they came from and why they were here. Asked if they had souls, their young spokesman said, "We don't know."

When a hunter and trapper of a neighboring tribe had accidentally come upon some Tasaday in 1966, he gave them various hunting tools and weapons and taught them how to trap. But they remained nonhunters and became only casual trappers, using their new steel blade knives in their old food-gathering pursuits, adding only two edible plants to their diet. About animal flesh they said, "We found that their meat is good, but we do not need it."

Although this newly discovered tribe has been little studied, we can tentatively state that, while extreme adversity retards technological development, the absence of adversity makes such development unnecessary. And this rule might also apply to the nonmaterial elements of culture such as religious beliefs and creation myths.

Take a 2 to 3 hour segment of TV time (such as morning game shows, daytime soap operas, or nighttime variety shows) and analyze the segment in terms of the following questions: What are the themes of the shows? What cultural values underlie these themes? What kinds of stereotypes are created by these shows?

---

in ceremonial observances. In the Pacific Northwest some Indian cultures emphasized the importance of wealth. The host of a lavish ceremonial feast, called a *potlatch,* would give large amounts of property to his guests, obliging them to stage a bigger and better *potlatch* at some later date. Conspicuous waste and the ostentatious display of wealth were the specialty of these societies.

The culture of the United States has a specialty that helps to determine its continued direction. We emphasize the production of material objects and collectively spend a great deal of time and effort in making buildings, automobiles, and a host of other things. In keeping with this cultural emphasis, we reward those who make material inventions or improvements or otherwise aid our specialty. New ideas in other areas are, of course, produced, accepted, and rewarded, but not to the same degree as are ideas in the mainstream of our cultural emphasis.

In nature there have been examples of specialized developments that had unfortunate results for the survival of the species.[11] The Irish elk, a majestic animal now extinct, is an example of evolution that was carried too far. Gradually, over generations, the antlers of the Irish elk became bigger and bigger. Ultimately they became a heavy, massive structure measuring over eleven feet across. They were too big and heavy for the elk's own good. Metaphorically speaking, the Irish elk chose to specialize in antler development, and its overspecialization proved to be *dysfunctional,* that is, harmful to its needs.

Although the tendency for cultures to specialize does not always lead to the fate of the Irish elk, overspecialization may make it difficult for a society to cope with its own persistent problems. Solutions outside the cultural emphasis are more slowly invented or accepted. In the United States today, for example, attempts to solve the problems of the urban slum often seem to revolve around tearing down old buildings and erecting new ones. Seldom do we hear new ideas for redistributing our national wealth so nobody needs to live in slums in the first place. Large government subsidies—or gifts, if one prefers—to any family not able to afford decent housing might be an effective means of ensuring

[11]Linton, *op. cit.,* pp. 50–51.

rapid vacancy of the urban slums. We cannot be sure that such an approach would work better than bulldozing and rebuilding. But the point is that our present cultural emphasis produces more technological solutions than social, political, and economic ones. For coping with our environment, our specialization in some areas has manifest disadvantages.

We have seen in some detail how culture is a group enterprise. Knowledge and practices are shared with others and passed on to succeeding generations. What culture is and how it operates illustrate the primary themes of sociology—human interaction and behavior of men and women in groups. Only by social interaction is culture developed, only by interacting with others can we learn our culture, and only by interacting within groups is culture passed on. We are members of a group that shares a culture. But at birth we are simply individuals who have been *born* to members of a group. How we ourselves become members, the process of *socialization,* is the subject of Chapter 4.

SUMMARY POINTS AND QUESTIONS

1. The ability of humans to create, use, and transmit culture is what makes the human unique among animals. This fact leads to the sociological questions:

> *Why do humans create culture?*
>
> *How do humans create culture?*
>
> *How does culture affect human interaction?*

2. Culture is an historically derived system of designs for living. It is learned and transmitted from generation to generation through the process of socialization. And it is shared by the members of a society or group.

> *What is meant by* historically derived?
>
> *Explain how culture can be shared while not all members of a society use all of the available cultural elements.*

3. Culture consists of material aspects such as artifacts and objects. It also consists of nonmaterial aspects such as ideas, norms, and language.

> *How are ideas and artifacts interrelated?*
>
> *How are they necessary for each other?*

4. Culture is an abstraction. It is not behavior or objects but ideas about behavior and objects.

> *What is meant by* reification?
>
> *How is culture often reified?*

5. There are three universal functions of culture. Culture supplies the ideas necessary for physical survival, for living together, and for meeting psychological needs.

What is meant by universal functions?

In what ways does American culture fulfill each of these functions?

6. The diversity of culture is illustrated by different practices for attaining food and by different sexual norms found among societies. Cultural diversity might be explained by geographic environment, race, or man's inventiveness.

Which of these factors do not explain cultural diversity? Why not?

Which factor is the most important? Why?

7. One way in which a culture changes is through the addition of a new element. The addition of a new element follows a three–step process: the group becomes aware of the new element, it accepts it, and it integrates the new element into the culture.

In what ways are new elements introduced into a culture?

Why may a new element not be accepted?

How does a new element become integrated?

8. Two other ways by which a culture changes are the dropping or loss of an element and the redefinition or reinterpretation of the meaning of an element.

Why are some elements dropped from a culture? Give some examples.

Give an example of the meaning of a cultural element being redefined.

9. The direction which cultural change takes is not random. Once a culture develops a certain emphasis or theme, change usually follows that theme.

What are the major themes in American culture?

How do these themes direct cultural change by eliminating certain alternatives?

SUGGESTED READINGS

Barnett, H. G. *Innovation: The Basis of Cultural Change.* New York: McGraw–Hill, 1953. An analysis of the conditions that allow new additions to culture.

Barnouw, Victor. *Culture and Personality.* Homewood, Ill.: Dorsey, 1973. A complete text on culture. It defines culture and its basic concepts, surveys the various classic studies on culture, and also includes a section on methodological approaches to culture and personality research.

Duncan, Otis Dudley, ed. *William Ogburn on Culture and Social Change.* Chicago: University of Chicago Press, 1964. A collection of essays by William Ogburn, which deal with various forms of sociocultural change and explanations for change, such as the cultural lag theory.

Edgerton, Robert B. *The Individual in Cultural Adaptation.* Berkeley, Calif.: University of California Press, 1971. A comparative study of the people in four tribes in East Africa. A good treatment of the emergence of similar and unique cultural patterns in a common physical environment.

Linton, Ralph. *The Study of Man.* New York: Appleton-Century-Crofts, 1936. Drawing from a wide variety of cross-cultural materials and examples, the author deals with the functions, components, and universals of culture. A basic anthropological treatment of culture.

Marcuse, Herbert. *One Dimensional Man.* Boston: Beacon Press, 1964. A critical approach to the organization of thought and ideology in modern America. Argues that mass-produced culture has restricted the alternatives necessary for desirable qualitative changes in modern society.

Miner, Horace. "Body Ritual Among the Nacirema." *American Anthropologist* 58 (June 1956): 503–507. A satirical essay on American culture and behavior. It pokes fun at many of our customs and practices.

Roszak, Theodore. *The Making of a Counter Culture.* Garden City, N.Y.: Doubleday, 1969. An historical reconstruction of the counterculture in the 1950s and the 1960s. Shows along what issues and to what extent the youth culture conflicted with the dominant culture.

Slater, Philip. *The Pursuit of Loneliness.* Boston: Beacon Press, 1970. A critique of the emphasis placed on individualism in American culture. Argues that while Americans seek community involvement and dependence, these needs are frustrated by American values and norms.

At birth we know nothing and have everything to learn. Who sets about the awesome task of teaching us? Our parents do. They're better teachers than they know, for we learn from them more than they imagine. In fact, we learn a great deal from many people during childhood. We learn ways of doing things, beliefs, values, norms, prejudices. We learn not only by instruction from others but also by observing and imitating. Rewards and punishments help us want to learn what others think we should know. Meanwhile, we're developing a self, which is a social creation that we derive from others with the help of our imaginations. Socialization and development of the self are most intense in our preadult years, but neither of these processes ends when we reach adulthood. Most of us are constantly assuming new roles or changing old ones, and we remain subject to rewards and punishment, promotion or dismissal, happy homelife or divorce.

4

SOCIALIZATION: THE SCHOOL WITHOUT WALLS

Most of the mental traits we think of as constituting the human mind are not present unless put there by communicative contact with others.

Kingsley Davis*

A long look inside a beehive will teach us a few things about the individual development and social organization of bees. First, the infant bee, newcomer to the complex society of the hive, will mature to adult size and assume a distinct adult role. Moreover, it will do this without ever having been taught how to behave as a bee. It does not need to learn how to fly, to seek and carry back food, to signal its findings to other bees, or to do a certain kind of work in the hive. These skills are gained by every bee without any transmission of knowledge from an adult bee to a young, maturing bee. No learning takes place. Biology is all.

Built into every bee is the genetic program for its general behavior as a bee and for its special role in the society. Furthermore, if we observed the hive for a long time, we would notice that the social organization of the hive remains unchanged. Because individual behavior is so rigidly determined by biology, innovations or inventions of new ways of doing things are impossible. Generation upon generation of bees will be born, mature to adult roles, and later die. But the number of social positions and roles and the kind of behavior required in each generation will remain the same.

If bees were to study humans, how different would be the conclusions. They would note that biology alone cannot account for adult human behavior; rather, it has something to do with how the mature members interact with and teach

*Kingsley Davis, *Human Society*. New York: Macmillan, 1949.

In Japan, as everywhere, many hands aid in socializing children to the values and traditions of society.

the immature. They would further note that knowing the genus and species of the animals they were observing would not allow them to predict their intricate patterns for social living. But yet human infants do become functioning adults; and their cultures, while ever changing, do tend to endure. If biology cannot account for these phenomena, what can? The concept *socialization* can explain both the development of the individual and the perpetuation of society.

SOCIALIZATION: THE HUMAN ALCHEMY

This year in the United States alone three million babies will be born. Think for a minute—three million creatures who are human only biologically but are otherwise like little animals: They are all born naked but unashamed; they are born male or female but ignorant of the difference or of its profound effect on their lives; they are born black or white or brown or yellow, but neither care nor judge; they are soon hungry but are totally unable to get food or prepare it or even to get it into their mouths; they have no status aspirations, no religious faith, and no political convictions. They are not really very human. Most of all, they are utterly helpless. (Alas, only their lungs and bladders seem to work persistently and well.) They would survive only a few days, or perhaps hours without the care of other people.

Most of these little animals will someday be human adults. They will be able to feel shame, pride, guilt, love, anxiety, hate, and ecstasy. They will have a great many mental and physical skills, attitudes and values, beliefs and judgments. Each will be different, but each will share with all the others a remarkable number of traits and characteristics.

The helpless infant undergoes the fantastic metamorphosis into the human adult through *socialization,* the learning process that prepares a person to take his or her place in a group.[1] Socialization is a lifelong process of learning that does not end with infancy or childhood. But the child learns a great deal and undergoes dramatic changes from a barely human, helpless animal to a fully participating member of a human society. Socializing the infant so he or she will be an acceptable member of adult society is a vital task that no group can ignore. Childrearing practices are everywhere the first element in the complex, ongoing process of socialization.

CHILDREARING: THE FIRST STEP INTO SOCIETY

No society leaves to chance or to the whims of parents how children are to be raised.[2] All people seem to understand, no matter how vaguely, that childrearing practices shape the personality of the future adult. As the saying goes, "As the twig is bent, so the tree inclines." Every culture approves only certain kinds of behavior, attitudes, and specific childrearing techniques for the parents or guardians of the newborn child.

A catalog of all the many different childrearing practices throughout the world would be nearly endless. In fact, the rules for child care begin even before birth. In our society a woman is expected to begin regular visits to an obstetrician as soon as her pregnancy is certain. And she is to follow the doctor's instructions faithfully in matters of diet, rest, physical exertion, and so on. If she neglects to visit a doctor or ignores the doctor's instructions, many will consider her irresponsible. If she is too poor to see a doctor regularly, she and the baby

[1]A tremendous amount of research has been conducted on socialization. See Edward Z. Dager, "Socialization and Personality Development in the Child" in Harold T. Christensen, ed., *Handbook of Marriage and the Family* (Chicago: Rand McNally & Co., 1964), pp. 740–781.

[2]See Beatrice B. Whiting, ed., *Six Cultures: Studies in Childrearing* (New York: John Wiley & Sons, 1963) and Urie Bronfenbrenner, *Two Worlds of Childhood: U.S. and U.S.S.R.* (New York: Russell Sage Foundation, 1970).

are likely to be considered victims of social inequality. But in many industrial societies, and indeed in parts of the United States, a doctor is rarely or never seen. Instead, a midwife may be visited occasionally and may actually deliver the baby. In some societies a woman may deliver her baby alone. In others she may be helped by female relatives. In still others she may have the aid of shamans (magic–using priests) and their rituals.

Culture begins to influence the infant at birth. In one society babies are tightly swaddled, while in another they can kick freely. In our own society newborn babies usually are taken from their mothers and placed in cribs in the hospital nursery. In other societies the infant spends most of the first days in its mother's arms, the two warm bodies in intimate contact.

FEEDING AND TOILET TRAINING: THEIR VARIOUS WAYS

The infant's need for food is universal. But it is culture that dictates infant–feeding behavior and attitudes. Feeding practices have been extensively studied by social scientists. These practices are of particular interest because they are the infant's first introduction to how other people respond to its strong, urgent needs. In many societies an infant will be breast–fed for a year or more, while in our society few mothers breast-feed their children at all, and those who do usually continue it for only a month or two.[3] With bottle feeding, an object is interposed in the mother-child relationship, the first of many objects that will come between individuals and their relations with others.[4] Infants born into one society will be nursed whenever they show hunger, while infants in another society will be nursed only on a schedule. Culture also determines at what age a child should be weaned and whether weaning should be swift or gradual, harsh or gentle.

Birds do not foul their nests, nor do wolves foul their dens. Likewise, all human societies believe that the living quarters should be kept free from excrement, and no society seems to believe that this can be accomplished by instinct. No infant, therefore, escapes entirely what in our society we call toilet training. Societies vary greatly, however, on when to start training the child and on what training methods should be used.

In some societies children must begin to learn bowel control before they are a year old. Elsewhere they will be two years old or more before they begin. In some societies severe punishment is part of the training, while in others training is gentle. In still other societies shame and ridicule are used.

[3]Robert R. Sears, Eleanor E. Maccoby, and Harry Levin, *Patterns of Child Rearing* (White Plains, N.Y.: Harper & Row, 1957), p. 71.

[4]See the cross–cultural studies of infant feeding in John J. Honigmann, *Personality in Culture* (New York: Harper & Row, 1967).

Direct instruction is an important way of learning, not only in school but at home and everywhere else.

LEARNING IN CHILDHOOD SOCIALIZATION

As a child, you were not just taught how to control your bowels and how to feed and dress yourself. Nor were you left to pick up values, beliefs, and rules of behavior by sitting and watching your elders. (Recall how many times you heard, "Do as I say, not as I do.")

Teaching by Instruction   Many skills, attitudes, and kinds of behavior were taught to you by *direct instruction*. For example, when you first started school at five or six years of age, your parents probably told you that you must be attentive and obedient to the teacher and nice to the other children. In preparation for his role as a hunter, an Indian boy is shown how to estimate the freshness of a moose track by inspecting the torn soil.

As a child you were taught many kinds of behavior. You had to learn the behavior appropriate to particular roles, such as how to behave as a student, a son, a sister, or a friend. And you had to learn more specific kinds of behavior as well—how to hold a fork, how to dress yourself, and how to speak your language. You were also taught many facts and beliefs about the world, such as "berries like these are poisonous," "the snake is to be feared," or "the stove is hot."

Rewards and Punishments To be instructed is not necessarily to learn. Sometimes you must be instructed over and over again before you learn a skill or piece of knowledge. Rewards or punishments or both can encourage learning. Rewards and punishments may be large or small, tangible or intangible. Your mother's smile or approving nod may have been reward enough for you to repeat a desired response. Her frown may have stopped you from behaving in a disapproved manner. To be effective, rewards or punishments need not be immediate, especially with an older child. An American teenage boy may wash the car in the morning to win approval from his father in the evening or to increase his chances of using the car next weekend.

Learning by Imitation Not every detail in socialization is taught or learned by direct instruction. Parents and other adults can unwittingly teach the child important lessons about himself or herself, about the parents, or about the society. The child seems to absorb meanings from the observed behavior patterns of others. By acting out their roles, by expressing their attitudes and beliefs to one another, the adults of a society unwittingly and inevitably influence their children's behavior.

Such unconscious teaching and learning partly explains the transmission of attitudes and values from one generation to the next. For instance, the child in Alor observes how careful his parents are not to waste food. The child hears them talking to one another about recurrent food shortages in the past. Before anyone deliberately teaches this child the proper attitude toward food, the child has learned that food is something precious and scarce. Food is not to be taken for granted. In the child's mind a sense of uncertainty will be associated with the idea of food.

Some American parents, to take another example, appear mystified when their children display racial prejudice, and they stoutly deny that such beliefs were taught in the home. What the parents mean is that they never sat their children down and told them that blacks are untrustworthy, inferior, or whatever. Such direct instruction is not necessary, though. The child may have observed that blacks were never guests in the home. Perhaps the only blacks seen around

Adults, often unknowingly, provide the models for children's behavior; finger-shaking is something this boy has learned by watching others.

the house were those employed by the parents to do menial and undesirable work. And the child may have noticed how the parents talked about and interacted with blacks. In these ways—and without any direct instruction—a child may quite easily absorb the attitudes and prejudices of the parents.

Children are influenced not only by what their parents say and do. They also learn values and attitudes from their parents' gestures, tone of voice, and emotional reactions. A child is quick to learn when its mother is angry. By the emotions the mother shows as she describes how the supermarket clerk almost cheated her out of fifty-nine cents, the mother teaches her child much about the meaning of money and financial injustices. Adult reactions to a child handling a snake or worm are picked up by children even if the adults try to conceal their true feelings. The parents' amused reaction to a little boy's announcement that he would like to be a garbage man when he grows up may teach him that this is a goal that they—and therefore he—should not take seriously.

Interview a number of students in order to find out the range of specific childrearing practices used by these students' parents. See if the different ways that persons were reared vary systematically, for example, by family income, sex of the child, or birth order of the child.

THE CHILD: A PERSONALITY IN THE MAKING

A worldwide survey of societies would produce a full spectrum of emotional attitudes held by parents for their children. In some societies children are merely accepted as necessary burdens and receive little affection from their parents or from anyone else. Among the Alorese, for example, children are commonly frightened, teased, and ridiculed by adults. In other societies children receive abundant love from all around them. In still others, especially advanced, industrial societies, a complex and often contradictory pattern can be found. In our society, over the decades since World War II, children (particularly adolescents) have gained enough freedom and financial support from their parents to evolve what has been called a youth culture. At the same time, movies and TV have dramatized the social problems of the young. Crime, drug abuse, unwanted pregnancy, and other problems of the young have often been blamed on the parents. Parents have also been blamed for giving their children material goods and freedom instead of the love and guidance the young wanted. Receiving love has a great effect on the later ability to give love. Early in life, therefore, culture begins to influence personality through the lessons the child learns on the importance or unimportance of love and how it is to be expressed. (The child's ability to love is affected more or less unwittingly, and not because the people who have developed the childrearing system know that it will be affected.)

Despite the individual differences among parents in a given society, the prescribed childrearing practices and attitudes of the culture will generally prevail. Social scientists are not yet able to say what effects different childrearing methods and attitudes have on personality development.[5] Nevertheless, because children in any one society will have similar experiences with training and with parental and adult attitudes, they will come to have elements of personality in common.

Before we provide more evidence on the cultural influences on personality, it is necessary to look into a problem that arose early in the history of sociology.

[5]Dager refers to over 150 studies in his summary article. These are but a fraction of those that have been conducted. See Dager, *op. cit.*, and David A. Goslin, ed., *Handbook of Socialization Theory and Research* (Chicago: Rand McNally & Co., 1969).

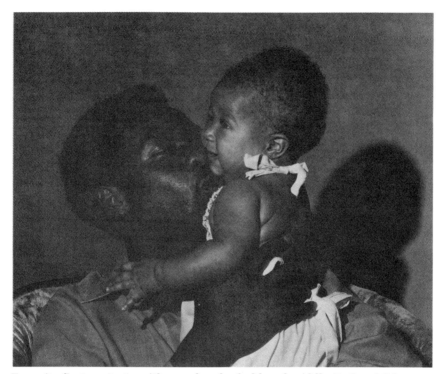

From its first contacts with people who hold and cuddle it, the child learns whether love is important in its culture, and how to show it.

It concerns the essential duality of human nature, the fact that humans are both biological and social creatures. The problem can be stated in many different ways: nature versus nurture, heredity versus environment, biology versus culture, and so on. What are we born with and what do we learn?

THE PERSONALITY: HOW MUCH IS BIOLOGICAL?

It is not as easy as it might at first seem to determine once and for all which individual personality traits are inherited and which are learned, or to discover how biological inheritance and learning interplay.[*] For instance, much of what is commonly called musical ability clearly is learned. But is any of it due to inherited biological characteristics? Perhaps some features of the hearing apparatus make it much easier for some people than for others to discriminate and repeat musical tones.

[*]John Watson, *The Ways of Behaviorism* (New York: Harper & Row, 1928), p. 35.

The old "heredity versus environment" debate is still very much with us, and social scientists remain undecided about the importance of each as factors in personality development. In the later nineteenth century, for example, the importance of heredity in personality development was greatly stressed. "Blood will tell" was a popular phrase. Gradually, however, evidence began to accumulate to suggest that different life experiences affect personality development. By the 1920s emphasis on the importance of environmental factors had become so extreme that the psychologist John B. Watson could say: "Give me a dozen healthy infants, and my own world to bring them up in, and I'll guarantee to train any one of them to become any kind of specialist I might select—doctor, lawyer, artist, merchant, chief, and even beggar man or thief."[7]

Neither Watson nor anyone else carried out such an experiment, and social scientists no longer believe that Watson's guarantee could have held. Although much is still unknown, social scientists today are trying to achieve in their theories and research some kind of balance between inheritance and environment as factors in human behavior.

FITTING THE MOLD AND BREAKING IT

Each person is human in his or her own unique way. This means two things, one of which is often missed. If we are each human, then we all share many traits and characteristics with humans everywhere. If each of us is human in our unique way, then each of us is in some way different from everyone else. How much of the sameness, and how much of the difference, is a result of our inherited characteristics?

Each normal human has basically the same body—the same number of organs located in the same places in the body and performing identical functions. We share the same basic reflex actions, such as the eye-blink or the knee-jerk. And we all have the same basic needs for sleep, food, and sexual satisfaction.

Our essential sameness is, of course, why we can be called human. But we each inherit a physical appearance that is a unique combination of such physical traits as body size, hair type, and eye color. Even the capacity to learn is an inherited characteristic, so that one person will learn more easily than will another person. It also seems, although with less certainty, that traits of temperament such as excitability or lethargy (quickness or slowness to react) are inherited.

[7]Witness the reopening of the issue of the role of heredity in the alleged racial differences in intelligence. See Arthur R. Jensen, "How Much Can We boost I.Q. and Scholastic Achievement?," *Harvard Educational Review* 39 (Winter-Summer, 1969), 1–123.

Our sameness is why we are all called humans. How much of this sameness, and how much of our difference, is inherited?

BIOLOGY PROPOSES; CULTURE DISPOSES

Your inherited characteristics do not determine what you will become, but they do determine what you can (or cannot) become. Most of us have the inherited capacity to fill many roles and perform many tasks in our society. To give a few simple exceptions, though, a mentally slow person cannot become a notable scientist; a very short man cannot become a basketball player; a tone-deaf person cannot become a professional musician.

Tone-deafness and short stature are certainly not barriers to many other roles in society. But certain inherited characteristics will be selected for attention by a given culture. For instance, an extremely tall French or German boy may not receive any special attention, except perhaps teasing. But an extremely tall American boy, if he is physically adept, will be encouraged by his high school physical education teacher to play on the basketball team. If he is good, he will probably be offered one or more college athletic scholarships. If he excels at college basketball, he may be offered a place on a professional team at a very tempting sum of money.

In college, this young man may have developed a passionate interest in medicine, law, agronomy, or any of a number of fields. In our society he will be faced at college graduation with choosing between the immediate prestige and money rewards of the professional athlete and the rigorous study and riskiness of building a career based on his other interests. The choice is his to make, but the culture of his society has presented the choice to him.

Just as a culture can favor certain inherited characteristics, it can disfavor others, not necessarily because, like tone-deafness in a musician, these characteristics are inherent disabilities. Only in the recent past, and only after much personal and social struggle that is still going on, have women begun to enter the professions in any number. Their numbers are growing, but women lawyers, doctors, architects, and stockbrokers are still a small percentage in their respective professions. The same is true of blacks, chicanos, American Indians, and the other minorities.

This interplay of social roles and cultural values with individual traits makes it extremely difficult for the social scientist to isolate what is biologically inherited from what is culturally learned. Say, for example, the social scientist wanted to discover how much given levels of intelligence are inherited. The scientist would choose young subjects, test their intelligence, and then would have to test the intelligence of the parents. For thoroughness, grandparents and others in the family should be tested.

How does one construct tests that are proven to isolate some concept like intelligence from differences in age, education, motivation, attitudes toward tests and toward social scientists, and so on? Clearly the scientist's material is riddled with ambiguity—that is, with findings that can be equally well interpreted in two or more ways, often diametrically opposite ways.

Lively controversies are raging today both in the popular media and in the social sciences about such questions as inherent differences of blacks (of both sexes) and women (of all races) from their racial and sexual opposites. Some say that blacks as a group are inherently less intelligent than whites, and even that their way of thinking differs from that of whites. Others say this is nonsense, that the data are being naively and wrongly interpreted. They argue that such basic factors as poor diet, cultural disadvantages, apathy and low self-esteem adversely affect the performance of test subjects.

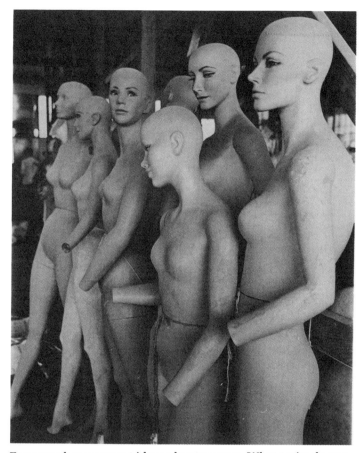

Everyone has some set ideas about women. What traits do you ascribe to females? Are they based on culture or biology?

Many claim that basic biological traits make women inherently different from men in their personality traits. Women are said to be more emotional than men and less able to reason and to guide their behavior by reason. They are considered vain and flighty and largely helpless without men, and so on. Others say that this is nonsense, that women who fit the stereotype have simply learned how to act in accordance with cultural expectations. A woman's culture, not her biology, has taught her to act in these ways and to think of herself as having these traits.

The fact that the contributions of heredity and environment are so far impossible to isolate does not make the problem any the less a lively issue for the scientist and layman alike. Debates over the claim that one sex is inferior to the other or that one race is inherently less intelligent than another are not trivial academic exercises. For the outcome of such debates cannot help but have a profound effect on a society like ours, which is based on the presumed equality of all people.

THE INFLUENCE OF CULTURE ON PERSONALITY

In Chapter 3 we noted that culture is the "way of life" of a society. We found also that there is an extreme variability among the cultures of the world. Herein lies the clue to the influence of culture on personality. Everywhere a child is born into some ongoing society with its established way of life, but each society has its unique culture that it presents, as it were, to the newborn.

The culture of any society contains the definitions and descriptions of the many roles and positions in the society. Culture contains the beliefs of the people concerning the world about them. Culture contains their values, their definitions of the natural and the supernatural, and the norms that govern their behavior. These and other aspects of culture are shared by the members of a society. The shared patterns constitute at the same time a fund of common experience for the infants and children of the society.

As the adults enact their roles of parents or providers, as they express their beliefs through their magical or religious practices, as they conduct their court-ships and engage in play, and as in many other ways their behavior expresses or reflects their culture, they are in a sense acting out their culture for the newcomer. They are providing him with what is his first and may be his only experience with a society in action. As the culturally prescribed behavior is repeated over and over again, the developing child gradually comes to accept the fact that what he sees around him is the way of all life, or at least the way life should be led.

Since no two cultures are precisely the same, nowhere is the fund of experience to which a given newborn will be exposed exactly the same as it is in his society. Each child, usually, sees but one drama of life acted out before him, the one of his society. Merely by being born in Samoa, for example, the total experiences of a child will in some measure be different than the total experiences of all of the children in the world who were not born in Samoa. As he witnesses, and later participates in, the Samoan culture in action he gradually learns to talk, to think, and to act like a Samoan. His personality, which at one time had the potential for being like the personalities found in any society, will become instead like the personalities found in Samoa.

Even though culture exerts a strong influence on personality development, the members of a society are not identical. They nevertheless do have certain basic traits in common and exhibit a general personality pattern more frequently than do the members of another society. Thus, if we say that the Arapesh are cooperative, it does not mean that an uncooperative Arapesh cannot be found. It does mean that life in the Arapesh society calls for considerable cooperation. Consequently, cooperation is so stressed in socialization practices that it becomes incorporated in the personalities of most members of the society. It has proved difficult for sociologists and other behavior scientists to conduct research to discover the commonalties of personality traits within a society, but some efforts have been made. We often hear, for instance, that Americans are materialistic and competitive. Imagine what a gigantic research effort would be needed to demonstrate, or refute, the fact that these two personality traits are indeed commonly found among our people, let alone to determine whether Americans are more materialistic and competitive than people in other societies.

THE SELF: A SOCIAL CREATION

While you are learning the elements of your culture and how to fit into society, at the same time that you are developing a personality you are acquiring a *self*. Odd as it may seem at first, no one is born with a self. The self is developed only through social interaction during which you are gradually forming attitudes and beliefs about yourself—for example, that you are smart or not so smart, good-looking or plain, bold or shy, and so on. These beliefs and attitudes develop as you compare yourself with others and become aware of how others see you.

Your self is you as you perceive yourself. When you consider your self, you are both subject and object. It is as if you stand back and view yourself as an object. That is, you attempt to look at yourself from the standpoint of another person. For instance, if you are ashamed of yourself, you have mentally gone outside yourself and are looking at your behavior as others might view it; and you feel a sense of shame before these mental others. When you talk to yourself, you are both speaker and listener, taking the roles of yourself and another.

THE LOOKING-GLASS SELF

The self we each develop is an inevitable product of socialization. It follows from the human trait of not merely learning values, beliefs, and rules but also of *internalizing* them. That is, we come to describe and judge ourselves by how well we meet these cultural standards of belief and behavior. Thus, our development of a self is inseparable from our experience of socialization and from our interaction with others.

Our image of ourselves determines much of how we act around other people—and, in turn, their reaction reinforces the self-image.

Soon after the turn of the century Charles Horton Cooley developed the theory of what he called the *reflected* or *looking-glass self* to describe the feelings about ourselves that result from our imagining how others view us or our behavior.[8] Cooley thought that the looking-glass self has three parts: (1) What *I think you see* when you observe me. As if in a mirror, we see ourselves in the mind of another. (2) What *I think you think* upon observing me. We imagine not only what another sees when looking at us, but also how the other judges us. (3) How *I feel about myself* because of how I think you see me and judge me. Having imagined how I am seen by another and how I am judged, I feel pride, joy, shame, or some other emotion. Self feelings results not from how we appear or behave but from how we think another judges our appearance or behavior.

We begin to develop a looking-glass self when we are two or three years old. From then on, throughout our lives, we gradually build up, reinforce, or modify

[8]Charles Horton Cooley, *Human Nature and the Social Order* (New York: Charles Scribner's Sons, 1902).

For a simple test of Cooley's theory of looking-glass, select two people: one who knows you very well, and one who knows you only slightly. Ask both of these people the following questions:

1. How do you see me?
2. How do you think I see you?

Now ask yourself the following questions about the two people you have selected:

3. How do I think he or she sees me?
4. How do I think he or she sees me seeing him or her?

Compare the answers to (1) and (3), and (2) and (4).

a great many attitudes about our self. Through repeated perceptions of how we are judged by others, we conclude that we are good-looking or plain, smart or dull, good or bad, short or tall, poised or clumsy, well versed or ill informed, emotional or stable. Whether these perceptions are completely right or partially or totally wrong, they will influence our self appraisal. Thus, someone who has an "inferiority complex" is actually judged more highly by others than by himself or herself.

Our attitudes and beliefs about ourselves influence how we act. If I feel that I'm not terribly smart or informed I may not add my opinions to a discussion. A man who thinks that women find him unattractive does not ask them for dates. Often we may act in ways that conceal how we really feel about ourselves. For example, you may feel insecure enough to refrain from expressing your opinions, but the expression on your face may suggest knowledgeable agreement with a particular person, or perhaps superiority and boredom at the silliness of it all. Or an insecure person who is uneasy at a party may be too talkative and perhaps too loud. We may not know what the person's true self-feelings are, but we can see that they are influencing his or her behavior.

THE SOCIAL STEPS TO THE SELF

Two decades after Charles Horton Cooley had contributed his looking-glass theory to sociological thought, the great sociologist George Herbert Mead made important theoretical contributions to the *stages of development* through which the individual goes on the way to the self.[9] Cooley showed that the self is a social creation in that the looking glass reflects our own imaginings about how

[9]George Herbert Mead, *Mind, Self, and Society* (Chicago: University of Chicago Press, 1967).

Many groups have ritualized practices for socializing new members into the group. Analyze the practices of some group such as a fraternity, sorority, armed services, church, etc. that you have joined. If a number of students can do this, find out if there are common, intended purposes for the rituals. Are there other purposes?

---

others see and judge us. Mead theorized about how various stages of social interaction contribute to the development of the self. Mead stressed language, play, and games as essential to this development.

Language and Ideas All animals interact and communicate with one another, but only humankind has a true language.[10] A bee that returns to the hive and dances to communicate to other bees the direction and distance of food is guided by a built-in, instinctive *code* of movements. The code is fixed, and it can communicate only the kind of information that other bees by instinct are able to receive.[11] But the human mind and its product, language, are capable of creating and communicating *ideas*.

These abilities to create and communicate ideas are essential to the development of the self. For example, as children we learned the meaning of the word *happy*. Once we had the idea of happy, we could apply that word (idea) to our own experience of the feeling it describes or stands for. When we saw the outward signs of happiness in another person we could apply the word to them. We could now think about our own happiness or that of another person. Although as children we at first had only simple understandings of simple ideas, we had acquired a basis for developing the self. We were now able to go outside ourselves to see how our behavior would appear to someone else.

Play: Being Others Once we can imagine how others react to our behavior, we can behave in ways that elicit the reaction we want. We are beginning the actual development of a self. In Mead's description, we pass into a *play* stage, in which we act out specific roles that we have observed. More or less indiscriminately we will act out the role of mother, father, cowboy, or even cat or dog. We pretend to be these people or animals. We behave as though we were in their positions. We have imagined what is expected of someone who occupies a certain position and we have acted out the role as we interpret it.

[10]An interesting discussion of how language affects our thinking process can be found in Ralph Ross, *Symbols and Civilization* (New York: Harcourt, Brace, Jovanovitch, 1957), pp. 11–26.

[11]Karl von Frisch, "Dialectics in the Language of Bees," *Scientific American* 207 (August, 1962), pp. 78–87.

RIDING INTO THE SUNSET—AND A DIVORCE BEYOND?

"Big boys don't cry" is a piece of advice many little boys have been given when they're crying. A great many big boys also refrain from expressing several other emotions besides the unhappiness, fear, grief, or whatever it is that crying might express. In our society few boys are allowed to express what have long been treated as feminine emotions, fear, tenderness, sadness. "To be a man" means to be tough, aggressive, brave, and competitive. To be a woman is to be weak, dependent, and "emotional."

By the process of socialization, we begin at infancy to become boys and girls and later men and women. We are taught, that is, how to act, and what we may and may not admit to feeling. Remember, just about every human trait you might consider biologically based is in fact culturally based. This has been proven time and again. For example, Margaret Mead applied our sex role stereotypes to several primitive societies in New Guinea 30 years ago. She found that Arapesh women and men were "feminine"; that Mundugumor men and women were "masculine"; and that Tchambuli women were "masculine" and Tchambuli men were "feminine."

Sociologists cannot say in any absolute sense that our sex role stereotypes are "right" or "wrong." But they have gathered evidence that our divorce rate (one out of every three marriages) is at least partly due to the inexpressiveness of males. The male sex role, say sociologists Jack Balswick and Charles Peek, is proving increasingly dysfunctional for contemporary marriages.

As you will see in later chapters, the social function of the family has gradually been reduced in our society. Its chief function has come to be affectional. Other social functions that once gave families their purpose are no longer there to give the family stability. At the same time, for various reasons, women have come to expect more expression of affection from their husbands. Many men learn to break with their socialization and are able to be emotionally expressive with their wives. But many other men are unable to make the change. Is this because they have been so well socialized that they simply fail to experience the emotions their wives feel? Or can some feel emotions but not express them? Whatever the reason, the inability now often leads to the divorce court.

Games and the Generalized Other At the play stage we became able to take the roles of others—but only one role at a time. According to Mead, we next pass into the *game* stage. To take part in even a simple organized game like hide-and-seek, we must learn to imagine the roles of several people simultaneously. We must imagine where each of the other children will hide, where the child who is "it" is likely to look, and we must take all these facts into account when choosing our own hiding place.

We have thus begun to view our behavior as we imagine it is viewed by the group, and we begin to regulate it accordingly. In responding to a group instead of to an individual, we are responding to what Mead calls the *generalized other*. While at the *play* stage we chose our behavior to fit how we imagined

Playing is an important aspect of socialization as we learn to assume different roles and imagine how others would act in similar situations.

Watch Saturday morning children's programs. See what values are presented to children and to what extent commercials are oriented toward children. Try to assess the effects of TV on what children know and believe.

---

it would appear to a single other person, at the *game* stage we behave according to how we think it will appear to a collective or generalized other, such as our play group. As we mature, we gradually expand the idea of the generalized other until it includes the society. In this way, society has entered each of us and has become part of our self.

SOCIALIZATION IN ADULT LIFE

If our socialization has been reasonably complete and successful, we will have the requisite skills, abilities, and feelings to take on adult roles when we reach adult age. We become members of new groups and will probably continue to join new groups throughout much of our lives, for example, by moving to a new community, taking a new job, or attending a new school. To be successful members of these new groups we must continue to learn new skills and acquire new attitudes.[12]

Adult socialization is not much different from that of childhood.[13] Those who are doing the socializing—the members of the ongoing group that we join—are both instructors and models for our imitation. As newcomers, we listen to instructions, observe what is going on around us, and adjust our behavior and attitudes in accordance with our imagined reactions of the generalized other.

When we enter college we must be socialized. As freshmen we learn to adjust our actions and feelings to the expectations of the group. Perhaps not until we go home for the holidays will we notice the changes we have undergone. We think of ourselves as college students, and consciously or unconsciously we have discarded attitudes and modified values that we feel are inappropriate to the new role. Soon we will be no longer obvious newcomers and can ourselves serve as models for the next group of freshmen.

[12]Adult socialization in learning how to use marijuana and becoming a patient in a mental hospital can be found in Howard S. Becker, "Becoming a Marijuana User," *American Journal of Sociology* 59 (1953), pp. 235–242 and Erving Goffman, "The Moral Career of the Mental Patient," *Psychiatry,* 22 (1959), pp. 123–142. See also a novelist's powerful description of learning the role of a patient in a mental hospital in Ken Kesey, *One Flew over the Cuckoo's Nest* (New York: The Viking Press, 1962).

[13]A good account of adult socialization can be found in Orville G. Brim, Jr., "Socialization Through the Life Cycle," in Orville G. Brim, Jr. and Stanton Wheeler, *Socialization After Childhood: Two Essays* (New York: John Wiley & Sons, 1966).

**Would you say these two patrolmen are susceptible to attitude
change, or instead that adults in general have inflexible self-images?**

The Self in Adult Life Although adult socialization produces fewer and less
drastic personality changes than occur in childhood socialization, the adult
personality does not escape some change. But the self is not a sort of chameleon,
assuming new colorations with each new interaction with another. Once
self-feelings have been built up gradually during childhood, they become relatively fixed. In later life, reactions to the generalized other strike against already
established solid self-images.

If as children we were consistently accepted and liked for what we were,
we probably developed a basic self-respect that will not be altered by an occasional contrary looking-glass encounter later in life. Also, as we get older,
we generally become more selective in receiving looking-glass reflections. For
one thing, our personal associations are likely to be with those who think and
feel more or less as we do. Such people are unlikely to give us reflections seriously
at odds with our prior self-conceptions. Few business executives comfortably
frequent truckers' bars, and few truck drivers will feel comfortable in an extremely elegant and snobbish restaurant. A timid left-wing intellectual is not
likely to seek out the company of right-leaning, aggressive construction workers.

As children we discriminate little among the array of looking–glass reflections we perceive, except to give most weight to those from our parents and teachers. As we mature, though, we pay more attention to some and less to others. Adults can become quite effective at screening out reflections of themselves that are incongruous with previously established self-feelings. For example, even though a doctor may know that a few people in his community think that medicine is a fraud and that doctors are unscrupulous charlatans, he does not alter his image of himself as a member of an important profession. Most parents firmly maintain their beliefs, values, and self-image despite conflict or criticism from their teenage children. Thus, the looking–glass process operates differently with adults, whose personalities are relatively fixed, than it does with children in the formative years of personality development.

During the process of socialization, we learn much of what makes up our culture—our beliefs, values, and rules of behavior. We develop a personality, and we acquire a sense of self. Just as *socialization* is a single term covering this series of interrelated changes in us from squalling infants to adult members of a society, the word *society* itself covers a complex whole made up of inter-related parts. Even before we are aware of the fact, we have assumed certain roles or positions in society; we are sons or daughters, brothers or sisters, students, and so on. In Chapter 5 we examine closely the network of roles and positions that make up any society.

SUMMARY POINTS AND QUESTIONS

1. *Socialization* is used in two senses. It refers both to the process by which the individual learns the way of life of the society into which he is born, and also to the process of becoming human.

> *How are these two aspects of socialization interrelated?*
>
> *What role does social interaction play in these two processes?*

2. The personality of the individual is shaped both by heredity and by culture. The individual inherits not only physical traits but also, to a certain extent, psychological traits.

> *What specific psychological traits do you think are inherited?*
>
> *How do culture and heredity interact in forming an individual's personality?*

3. Although certain traits might be inherited, the importance of these traits is culturally determined. Culture contains the definitions and descriptions of many roles and positions, and emphasizes certain personality traits over others.

> *What personality traits does the American culture emphasize?*
>
> *What are some societies that emphasize completely different traits?*

4. Socialization is a continuing process. Socialization during infancy and early childhood, however, appears to be most important, as evidenced by the interest shown in childrearing practices in all societies.

> *What general categories of childrearing practices do sociologists study?*
>
> *What difference do these practices make to the personality of the individual?*

5. Language is necessary for socialization. Language permits the formation and communication of *ideas*.

> *If we did not have language, how could socialization take place?*
>
> *If we did not have language, would we be different from other animals?*

6. Socialization takes place both through direct instruction and through unconscious learning.

> *What are some examples of each?*
>
> *Can you think of a situation in which these two aspects of learning could present contradictory instructions?*

7. One's sense of self is developed through social interaction as one learns to stand back and view himself or herself as an object.

> *At what age do individuals begin to develop a sense of self?*
>
> *Do some persons develop a truer conception of themselves than others?*

8. Charles Horton Cooley developed the concept of the looking-glass self to describe the self-feeling that results from one's imaginations of how others view oneself or one's behavior.

> *What are the three principal stages in the formation of the looking-glass self?*
>
> *Why do individuals sometimes form the wrong conception of themselves?*

9. George Herbert Mead pointed out the importance of the *play* stage in which the child acts out roles, and the *game* stage in which the child views his behavior from the standpoint of the group or the generalized other.

> *How does the play stage prepare one for the game stage?*
>
> *How are each of these stages important to the development of self?*

10. As individuals join new groups they must learn new roles and new expectations of behavior; the process of socialization thus continues through adulthood.

> *Can you give some illustrations of adult socialization?*
>
> *How does adult socialization differ from that of childhood? What particular problems may this cause?*

SUGGESTED READINGS

Cooley, Charles H. *Human Nature and the Social Order.* New York: Schocken, 1964. Originally published in 1902. In this classic work Cooley develops his concept of looking-glass self. There are also some interesting chapters on the social aspects of conscience, emulation, personal ascendancy, and personal degeneracy.

Danziger, K., ed. *Readings in Child Socialization.* New York: Pergamon Press, 1970. A collection of essays on the process of socialization during early childhood. Deals with the role of the family, and shows how different value orientations become a part of the child.

Devos, George. *Socialization for Achievement.* Berkeley, Calif.: University of California Press, 1973. Essays on the cultural psychology, basic value orientations, and achievement motivation of the Japanese. An excellent cross-cultural study on socialization.

Goslin, David A., ed. *Handbook of Socialization Theory and Research.* Chicago: Rand McNally, 1969. A comprehensive volume of essays on socialization. It is divided into four sections: theoretical approaches, content of socialization, stages of socialization, and special contexts such as the socialization of the mentally retarded.

Hoppe, Ronald A., G. Alexander Milton, and Edward C. Simmel, eds. *Early Experiences and the Processes of Socialization.* New York: The Academic Press, 1970. A collection of readings dealing with genetic, psychological, and sociological factors that affect personality development.

Langton, Kenneth P. *Political Socialization.* New York: Oxford University Press, 1969. Focuses on the agencies in the political socialization process, specifically the family, the school, and the peer group.

McNeil, Elton B. *Human Socialization.* Belmont, Calif.: Brooks/Cole, 1969. An excellent treatment of socialization. It provides a wide view of concepts, factors, agents, and consequences that are necessary to understand socialization.

Mead, George Herbert. *Mind, Self, and Society.* Chicago: University of Chicago Press, 1934. A collection of lectures and essays on social psychology, the development of self, and the interaction that forms the basis of human society.

Skinner, B. F. *Beyond Freedom and Dignity.* New York: Random House, 1972. Presents an extreme behaviorist position on socialization. Many consider it an assault against freedom and human dignity. Thought-provoking.

Wrong, Dennis H. "The Oversocialized Conception of Man in Modern Sociology." *American Sociological Review,* 26 (April 1961): 183–193. A critique of modern sociology's over-emphasis on environmental factors as explanations for personality. Points out the need to be aware of biological and instinctual factors as well.

After a childhood of socialization, we're members of society, right? Yes, but that only begins to tell the story, because ever since birth we've been playing parts in a complicated system. We've been sons or daughters, brothers or sisters, friends, students, and so on. Sociologists call these parts positions, and each position includes a role, or the kind of behavior expected of us. In addition, as we carry out these roles, we must act according to our culture's values by following society's norms or rules of behavior, both society's mores and folkways, that is, both its important and trivial rules of behavior. How well does this social subdividing work? Usually, pretty well, but not always. Roles can fail, either as discrepancies or conflicts. They fail chiefly because someone was inadequately prepared for a role or was unable to overcome discontinuity in socialization, which is the need to unlearn one role before learning another.

5

POSITIONS AND ROLES IN SOCIETY

A woman on her way to her daughter's wedding, to be held in a beautiful spruce grove in the Colorado mountains, couldn't help asking herself a number of questions: "Will the minister *really* change the vows to read that they will remain together 'for as long as there is love'?" "What am I supposed to do at this wedding, anyway, since there will be no receiving line to stand in and no reception to supervise?" And even the silly question (she thought), "What will I do when they offer me the honey-in-the comb, rose-petal soup, and all those natural foods I don't like?"

Jane and Jim are a modern young couple, but at the moment do not seem to be getting along any better than some of their elders. He says that he is not trying to put her down but since she is better at cooking she ought to do more of it than he does. She says that he will never be better at cooking unless he gets more practice. He says that she needs more practice working on the car and can start with the brakes that need relining. She says that he . . .

Now Joe wished that he had not volunteered for the job. When he agreed to act as chairman of the picnic committee, all he was told was that he should choose a committee and plan a picnic for the club. He wasn't even sure how many people he needed, nor what he should ask them to do. "Let's see," he mused, "I'll need someone in charge of games, someone to pick up the keg, and maybe someone in charge of transportation. What things should I do myself, and what things should I ask someone else to do?"

Although these three cases may at first glance seem to have little in common, all are concerned with the actual or anticipated behavior of individuals in groups. More than this, each problem is about the part the individual is expected to play in a certain position in a specific group. The mother of the bride is unsure of how to act in an unfamiliar but emotionally important situation. The young married couple is having trouble agreeing on the parts that each spouse should play. The picnic committee chairman must decide what positions to set up in the new group and what duties and responsibilities to assign to each position.

THE SOCIAL SYSTEM AND ITS PARTS

Three basic sociological concepts—*social system, position,* and *role*—must be understood before the behavior of people in groups can be analyzed.[1] In this chapter we define and explore these and related concepts. We show how these concepts relate to one another and how sociologists use them to analyze human interaction. These sociological concepts can be used to study large and small groups and to analyze the problems individuals face as they attempt to act out their parts as members of a group. Even though we will concentrate mainly on understanding the concepts, we will obtain some idea of their significance for interpreting, or even changing, behavior in the real world.

SOCIAL SYSTEMS: PATTERNS OF HUMAN INTERACTION

A *system* is some unity or whole made up of interdependent parts.[2] Thus, we can speak of the solar system, or a supply system, or the digestive system of the human body. What these systems have in common is that each is made up of a number of parts, and that these parts interact with one another in a patterned and predictable way. But a system, we must remember, is an abstraction. What we actually observe are the component parts and their effects on one another. From these observations, however, we can establish the system's rules of interaction. Once we know these rules, we can predict behavior that never may have actually been observed. For example, we know that the planetary orbits are maintained by a balance between gravity and centrifugal force. An orbit, therefore, results from a certain relationship between a planet and the sun. If either the sun or the planet changes, the orbit will change. If the change is great enough, the planet will either crash into the sun or fly off into outer space. We can say this with some certainty even though we have never seen it happen. But we know that under certain circumstances it will happen because we know about the solar system's rules of interaction.

[1] Our presentation of these concepts follows that of Gross and his associates. See Neal Gross, Ward S. Mason, and Alexander W. McEachern, *Explorations in Role Analysis* (New York: John Wiley & Sons, 1958).

[2] James G. Miller, "Living Systems: Basic Concepts," *Behavioral Science* 10 (July 1965), 193–237; and Talcott Parsons, *The Social System* (New York: The Free Press, 1951).

A game of touch football symbolizes the pattern of interaction: Parts connect to one another in special relationships.

Sociologists use the concept *social system* to describe the pattern that exists or could exist whenever two or more people interact. The elements or parts of a social system are not the particular people but rather the *positions* they fill in the system. Of course, real people fill the positions and act out their parts with other people who are filling different positions. But the social system itself, the abstraction, is simply the network of interrelated positions. (Some sociologists use the term *status* for what we will call position.[3] Because many people find it difficult to separate status from the idea of a high or low ranking, though, position seems the less confusing term.)

POSITIONS AND THE NETWORK OF RELATIONSHIPS

A position, therefore, can be described and studied without studying the individuals or their particular behavior, just as the positions on a basketball team—guard, forward, and center—and the relationships among them can be described without

[3]Frederick Bates, "Position, Role, and Status: A Reformulation of Concepts," *Social Forces* 34 (May 1956), 313–321.

Positions in the real world are not as formalized as those in Caesar and Cleopatra, but they create the network of relationships in culture.

ever referring to the particular players. Although a position exists apart from the person who fills it, a position cannot exist without at least one other position. For positions are part of a system and a system is a collection of relationships. You cannot occupy the position of son or daughter unless someone else occupies the position of father or mother. You cannot be an employer unless there are employees. And teachers would not exist were it not for students. (Even a hermit occupies a social position, for the word comes from the Greek for *lonely;* the hermit has adopted the social position of avoiding all other social positions.)

The network of positions in a social system can be simple or complex: from two campers in the wilderness to a giant industrial bureaucracy with its many different positions. In such a complex system as the latter, not only are there many different kinds of positions, but also many people who simultaneously fill, or could fill, a single position. There may be twenty men filling the position of foreman, but we can think of this system as having a single position called foreman rather than twenty. This is possible because all persons in the position of foreman stand in the same relationship to persons in the position of plant

---

Obtain permission to observe several small groups in action, or eavesdrop on several groups, such as the people at the next table in a cafeteria. Considering each sentence spoken an action, make a record of who talks the most, and who, regardless of how much talking, did the most to keep the group functioning smoothly. Did one person dominate in the sense of suggesting ideas or bringing up new topics of conversation? Two people should observe the same group to check results.

---

manager, inspector, or assembly-line worker. Many other social systems also have more than one person in a single position. In a college class there are usually only two positions, instructor and student. Although usually only one person occupies the position of instructor, the position of student can have anywhere from four or five in a small seminar, to hundreds in a large lecture.

ROLES: SETS OF EXPECTED BEHAVIOR

Just as positions can be studied apart from the people who fill them, the *behavior* expected of people who fill the positions can be separated for analysis from the positions themselves and from the particular people who fill them. Some positions have titles that describe what a person filling them would be expected to do: drill instructor, shop manager, street cleaner, housekeeper. But whether the title is descriptive or not, each position in any social system carries with it a set of expectations. The *incumbent,* the person who is filling the position, is expected to do certain things. We expect, for example, that a person who fills the position of drill instructor will in fact teach his troops close-order drill. We expect that the housekeeper will keep house and that the street sweeper will sweep streets. We also have expectations about what the incumbent will be like, apart from what he or she will do. In our society a mother is expected to feel love and affection for her child and concern for the child's well-being, health, and safety. And she is expected to know pretty well how to act on these concerns. In addition, the incumbent of any position will have expectations about how other people in other positions will behave toward that incumbent—what they will do to or for him or her. To be effective, the mother must expect obedience and cooperation from her child, as well as love and respect. The holder of any position thus has rights and privileges as well as duties and obligations. Others expect certain things of the incumbent, and he or she in turn has legitimate expectations of them.

**For the smooth functioning of the society, each position incorporates a role—
a set of expected behaviors.**

The sum of what we expect from someone who occupies a position, and what he or she can expect of others, is called a *role* (or sometimes a *social role*). A *role* can be defined as the sum of culturally prescribed duties, characteristics, and rights expected of and granted to the incumbent of a particular position.[4] For every position there is a role, and for every role a position. Although role and position can be studied separately, in real life the two concepts are inseparable.

ROLES: ENACTMENTS OF A SOCIETY'S CULTURE

To thoroughly understand the functions of roles in society we must again separate for sociological analysis what are inseparable in real life. We enact roles in *society,* but we draw much of what goes into every role from our *culture,* through *socialization.* Our behavior in just about every accepted role in our society is guided by certain of the nonmaterial elements of our culture (elements that every culture has): *values* and *norms.*

[4]Bruce J. Biddle and Edwin J. Thomas, eds., *Role Theory: Concepts and Research* (New York: John Wiley, 1966).

Construct an organizational chart for some formal group, organization, or institution. In this chart show the various positions, the expectations associated with these positions, and the flow of orders, directions, and communication between positions.

VALUES: THE ABSTRACT BASES OF NORMS

Our cultural ideas about what is right and wrong, our concepts of the desirable that guide our behavior, are known as *values*. Values are the most abstract ideas we have. In fact, we often have trouble expressing or describing them. Yet through our socialization we have learned these values. Once learned, these values guide us in deciding what is important and unimportant or what is right and wrong. As well as guiding how we function, values set limits within which we function. They help us to choose between alternatives.

As children we begin developing values and attitudes about these values. During our most impressionable years they become deeply ingrained in us. Even though we can modify them somewhat, these basic values stay with us throughout life.

Values permeate all aspects of social life as well as the individual's life. To the extent that they are shared by members of a society, they provide a certain common sense of purpose among those members. In a capitalistic society, for instance, children learn to compete for grades in the classroom and for a trophy on the ball field, while their parents compete in the economic arena for prestige and material success. Thus, competition is a prevailing value in such a society. We also find in our society fewer girls than boys playing with trucks and dreaming of being engineers. Fewer boys than girls play with dolls and dream of becoming kindergarten teachers. And few American women really feel guiltless about leaving the dishes for their husbands, even if they both work. Each of these observations suggests that the value of sexual equality is not yet fully held by many in our society. We still hold the traditional image of masculinity and femininity. Until this image changes, our *social norms* will continue to confine males and females to playing roles based on increasingly outmoded concepts of masculinity and femininity.

NORMS: ACTING ACCORDING TO VALUES

Norms are the rules, formal and informal, that regulate our behavior. Somewhat less abstract than values, norms are our means of putting abstract social values into action. That is, norms consist of our ideas about how we should behave in our society.

Mores and Folkways Sociologists differentiate between two kinds of norms: *mores* and *folkways*. *Mores* are deeply internalized, expected ways of behavior that are severely punished if violated. *Folkways* are the more customary social behavior patterns that are unpunished or only mildly punished if violated.

Our society stresses mores such as monogamy rather than polygamy, honesty rather than theft and cheating, and so forth. To us, monogamy seems as right as polygamy does to a sultan with a harem of wives. Our mores are more basic and deeply ingrained than our folkways, and they are less apt to change as radically as our folkways. Folkways do change, and as they do the corresponding mores and values from which they stem are sometimes modified, though usually only slightly. Folkways lend diversity to our society. As an example, young people are now trying variations on the folkways of social relations between males and females, but changes are occurring slowly if at all. In recent years female college sociology students have tried experiments in which they played the aggressive, more traditionally masculine role of arranging a date with a man. The woman would pick him up at his apartment, help him on with his coat, light his cigarette, and perform all the other customs or folkways that women are perfectly capable of doing, but which traditionally have been reserved for the male. The results of these experiments have consistently been that the men have felt threatened and have cut off their relationships with these female students. (In fairness it should be noted that these dating experiments were based on the traditional prearranged dating customs. Many current dating patterns are more casual and spontaneous and might naturally evolve into essentially more egalitarian relationships.)

VALUES AND NORMS: THE CEMENT OF SOCIAL INTERACTION

We can see that norms play a strategic role in integrating a society. They put into practice the values that are at the very core of social interaction. Norms give meaning to life in society since they evolve directly from social values and goals. Our own society tolerates considerable diversity. For instance, an overall social goal could be to instill within each person a feeling of worth as an individual, a feeling that he or she belongs to the society and is needed by it, a feeling that he or she can and should participate in it according to its prescribed norms.

If we are socialized to play the traditional male and female roles, we will feel most comfortable doing this and will see ourselves as contributing members of society. On the other hand, if we are socialized to see sexual differentiation of roles as unimportant or as wrong, we will probably act accordingly and modify

In every one of our roles, no matter how casual or insignificant, we enact the cultural values and norms.

some of our society's mores. The growing practice of couples living together without marrying exemplifies just such a change of mores in one segment of society. Whereas many people object to such arrangements as a violation of our mores against premarital sexual relations, those who favor the practice maintain that such a prohibition is artificial or hypocritical. They say that it singles sex out from all of the other ways in which people achieve relationships of intimacy and mutual respect.

CHARACTERISTICS AND SOCIAL USES OF RULES

The values and norms of a society generally permeate every position and role in that society. If a society values human life and the right of a person to an expression of individuality, then norms dictating behavior that safeguards those values will apply to most roles in the society. Yet it will be clear by now that all positions and roles, while having these basic norms in common, also have basic elements that distinguish them from others. The role of a shop foreman is readily distinguishable from that of a nurse or a guitarist in a rock band. Just as norms assure stability of the society, roles assure stability of the group.

List five different roles that you have played (for example, son, sister, student, friend, and so on). For each role, list the norms, values, and expected behavior that go with it.

ROLES AND GROUP STABILITY

Almost anyone can think of a group that has had to replace a member. Perhaps it was a small rock group that had to find a new guitarist. After the position was refilled, the group continued to function more or less as it had previously because the role in the group remained the same even though a new person had to be found to enact it. Roles not only give a certain stability to human groups, they render human behavior fairly predictable. The new guitarist can be expected to behave in predictable ways and to have certain skills, attitudes, and values. It can be expected that the new guitarist will come to practice, read music, follow directions, and play the guitar. Such expectations and others will influence how the old members of the band interact with the new one. They will know what to do and what to say to him or her because they know what behavior is associated with the role of guitarist. Because of the relative stability of the roles in the group, the band will continue to perform its functions in more or less the same way as before.

A single role can be played by different people. In our history almost forty different men have acted the role of President of the United States. The role of junior partner in a business firm may be enacted first by one person, then by someone else. Almost everyone has positions in many different social systems and thus enacts that many different roles. Even a preschool child plays several different parts. Certain characteristics and behavior are expected of a little girl or boy as a child of parents, as a little sister or brother of an older child, as a playmate among neighborhood children, and so on. Children learn that when a grandfather comes for a visit they have a position in still another social system, for interaction with a grandfather is somehow different from interaction with a father.

ROLE CHANGES

Throughout our lives in society the roles we play can change in four different ways: (1) New roles can be added to the cluster of roles; (2) roles can be given up, willingly or otherwise; (3) one role can be substituted for another; (4) the nature or content of one or more roles can change over time.

A dancer waiting in the wings will not much change the dance. So it is with roles: Each has set boundaries.

As children grow older they enact more and more roles: student, church group member, club member. In adulthood they continue to acquire roles—positions of employment, husband or wife, member of a professional society. Any person can add new roles to existing ones or substitute one role for another—by changing jobs, by divorcing, and in many other ways. One can lose roles, as a person does who retires and gives up not only a job but also union and other job-related memberships.[5]

Not only does a person's number of roles change, but the content and nature of each role can change over time. What is expected or demanded of a three-year-old son or daughter is not what is expected of a teen-age or adult

---

[5]Being *required* to give up a role can be quite distressing. Goffman refers to it as a person losing one of his social lives. See Erving Goffman, "On Cooling the Mark Out," *Psychiatry* 15 (November 1952), 462–463.

Watch at least five different types of TV programs and concentrate on how one particular role is played (child, parent, husband, wife, female worker, teenager, etc.). In a report, discuss whether or not it is possible to generalize about the kinds of behavior associated with a given role.

---

son or daughter. The roles of newlyweds differ so clearly from those of spouses who have been married for a while that even a casual observer can usually distinguish among the two groups, even if all the couples are about the same age. Thus, roles change even while a person is enacting them.

Changes in roles over time in the same society can be studied. And a role in one social system can be compared with a similar role in another system. For instance, changes in the role of women in the United States over the last one hundred years could be studied. Such a study would note that in the earlier period women were expected to possess certain domestic skills, to observe the strictest decorum in speech and dress, and to be subordinate to men. The study would note that over time these expectations were modified, and new abilities and attributes came to be expected of women.

Such a study of the changes in the role of women could have important practical implications. It might explain why two generations of women, even a mother and her daughter, frequently have a difficult time understanding one another. In times when roles are changing rapidly, a woman who attempts to teach her daughter the role she learned in her youth is indeed "old-fashioned."

No less valuable than a historical study of roles would be one that compared roles in different societies. As an example, the role of the adult male in the United States requires that men not cry when sad, that they not hug male friends in greeting, and the like. In other societies, such as in France, males are freer to express their emotions and their feelings of friendship. By such a comparison we learn that different cultures have different role expectations for the same position.

ROLE LEARNING

In Chapter 4 we found that roles are learned as part of the socialization process. Since so much of a child's life consists of learning, it is usually impossible to separate the various learning processes. But because many problems in role performance can be traced to improper or incomplete role preparation, a closer look at the mechanisms of role learning will help us to understand and deal with the various role problems to which we later turn.

Playing with dolls and instruction from older women are the primary ways a little girl is taught about the role of mother.

INSTRUCTION AND OBSERVATION

Remember from Chapter 4 that some aspects of roles are learned by direct instruction. A little girl will be taught part of the traditional role of wife and mother by instruction from her own mother and probably also from high school courses such as home economics. She will be taught by her mother how to make beds, how to cook, and how to clean house. She will be *taught* how to act out certain portions of a role.[6] She will be learning at one and the same time certain skills and certain expectations that others will have of her if she assumes the position of housewife.

Instruction is required for many roles throughout life: members of the armed forces, clergymen, office workers, and so on. Even prostitutes, as a study by

[6]Formal instruction has been used to induce people to play acceptable social roles. See Martin R. Haskell and H. Ashley Weeks, "Role Playing as Preparation for Release from a Correctional Institution" in Donald M. Valdes and Dwight G. Dean, eds., *Sociology in Use* (New York: The Macmillan Company, 1965), pp. 110–120.

James Bryan has shown, must be instructed in the many elements of their roles. The novice call girl is taught by an established prostitute or pimp. She must learn how to solicit potential customers, how to converse with them, and how to collect the fee. She must also learn what not to do: as one woman put it, "Don't take so much time, the idea is to get rid of them as quickly as possible."[7] Bryan concludes that what makes the prostitute's training period necessary is not the level of the skills that are required, but rather the secrecy of the occupation.

We learn also by observing people who are playing certain roles. Those who may one day play a certain role usually have early opportunities for observing how others play that role. By continued observation over the years of her childhood, a girl will enlarge her knowledge of the traditional role of wife and mother. Through observing her father's reaction to the way in which his wife plays her role, the daughter may modify her ideas on how the role of wife should be played. She will also learn by observing how other women interact with their husbands, either in real life, as at a friend's house, or in novels or television programs. All of these observations over the course of many years will influence how she later acts out this role, if she chooses the position of wife and mother.

PLAYING A RECIPROCAL ROLE

Some roles can be partly learned by playing the *reciprocal* or *counter role* in a specific social system. Even though it may sound odd at first, a boy learns to play the role of father partly by playing the role of son. Playing a reciprocal role differs from observation in that the boy is not merely watching someone act out the role of father; rather, he is interacting with the person in the other role. He learns not only what a father does in interacting with his son but also how he, the son, reacts to what the father does or says. In other words, he evaluates the role performance of his father in terms of his own reaction to that performance. The boy will remember both how the role of father was played and how well he thought it was played.

If when the boy becomes an adult he chooses the position of father, his own performance of the role will depend partly on how he evaluates his father's role performance and partly on what he has learned elsewhere about the role of father. Even when a man is determined to act as much unlike his father as possible, he nevertheless has learned the role of father partly by playing the reciprocal role of son. He may, therefore, choose elements of his role performance because they are unlike his father's.

[7]James H. Bryan, "Apprenticeships in Prostitution," *Social Problems*, 12 (Winter 1965), 287–296.

The world of a child's imagination is peopled by many performers, and play-acting is a major way of learning roles.

A person learns roles by playing counter or reciprocal roles in many areas of life. As people act out their roles as members of a church congregation they are learning about the role of minister. The role of teacher is learned partly by being a student. The role of boss is learned by being bossed.

GENERALIZING AND IMAGINING ROLES

Sometimes we learn how to play a role largely from having had experience in similar roles. Often we can recognize tasks and functions common to different groups and then apply what was learned in an earlier group experience to a later one. As an example, at a children's summer camp one evening just before dark, a child is discovered to be lost. A search party is formed at once but the camp director is unavailable. The immediate task is to organize a search party in a way that best ensures finding the child. It is quite possible, though, that no one at the camp has ever had experience in doing such organizing. Quite likely, however, one or more of the counselors have had experience organizing or administering other groups. Without necessarily realizing that he was doing so, such a person could draw on his previous experience. He could select the members of the search party, instruct them in what had to be done, assure that there was adequate communication within the group, solicit the reactions and advice of group members, and so forth.

We can partly learn to enact roles by using our imagination and mentally trying out one role or another. A person may plan out in imagination what to do when he or she arrives home an hour and a half later than expected. The person will probably also imagine the role of the other person in the interaction and may mentally develop his or her own response to the other person's behavior—"Then he'll say . . ., then I'll say. . . ." People can mentally rehearse various kinds of roles they anticipate enacting. Although some experience, observation, or instruction may be furnishing the materials used in the imaginative role playing, part of the learning process will consist of mentally trying out the role, rejecting some ideas on how it should be played and keeping others.

Although we learn in these various ways the behavior, attitudes, and knowledge expected of a person who enacts a certain role, what we actually do in a particular role is not necessarily the same as what is expected. Such differences between expectation and performance lead to the distinction between *role* and *role behavior*. When a person's actual behavior in a role deviates sharply from the expected behavior for that role, then a *role failure* is said to have occurred.

ROLE FAILURES: KINDS AND CAUSES

In any type or size of social system things sometimes go wrong. In the family, the husband and wife or a parent and child may be having difficulties. Every day people are dismissed from jobs in the factory or office for their failure to perform adequately their roles. Even though the individual is surely affected in such situations, the sociologist may understand the problem by considering it a social rather than a personal problem. The sociologist, that is, looks not at the individual but at the role. Sociologists commonly distinguish the main types of role failure as *role discrepancy* and *role conflict*. They see the main causes of role failure as inadequate role preparation and discontinuity in socialization. We look at each of these in turn.

Find three people to represent three different roles (for example, a student, a foreman, a teacher, etc.). Ask these people how they learned the role they are now playing. Note especially if they mention each of the five methods of role-learning mentioned in this chapter. Ask them about any of the methods which they may have failed to mention—for example, "Did you ever imagine yourself playing this role?"

ROLE DISCREPANCIES

As we have discovered, the simplest social system consists of two positions that in some way relate to one another. Each of the two people filling the positions attempts to enact the proper role with only partial success. Sometimes the difficulty is a *role discrepancy*, the failure of one role enactment to correspond with what is expected by the actor in the reciprocal position. For example, if a college couple marry or live together, what the woman does will not necessarily conform to what the man expects her to do, or vice versa. She may want to have friends over to study with her, but the man may consider this an infringement on his need for a quiet place to study.

Often there is not much point in trying to discover who is right and who is wrong. Each time that a person attempts to act out a role, his or her behavior may be inconsistent with what the person in the counterposition expects. Because roles are learned, there is no guarantee that two people who one day enter reciprocal roles will have learned them in exactly corresponding ways. Even if a man and woman had similar experiences as students, had talked with other college couples, and had known each other for some time before marrying or deciding to share an apartment, they could still enter the arrangement with different conceptions of the proper roles of man and woman. Each would bring his or her unique expectations of how the roles should be played. These expectations would serve as a guide to the person's own behavior and as a standard for evaluating the other person's behavior.

Resolving Role Discrepancies The first step in resolving role discrepancies is to accurately appraise them. Which of the three possible ways of resolving discrepancies should be used depends on the nature of the role discrepancy.

the specific social system in which it occurs, and the willingness and ability of the role incumbents to modify their behavior or expectations. The role behavior of a given actor can change; the expectations of the person in the counter position can change; or both behavior and expectations can be modified until they are compatible with one another. For instance, the woman could change her behavior by not having friends over to study with her; the man could accept her point of view and go to the library to study. Or perhaps role behavior and role expectations could be modified by an agreement that except on weekends neither will have friends in unless it will not inconvenience the other.

ROLE CONFLICTS

Although a role discrepancy results from an incompatibility of role expectations between two or more persons, sometimes the incompatibility occurs within a single person.[8] A *role conflict* occurs when one role of a person conflicts with one or more other roles the person plays at the same time. Since each person plays many roles, it is understandable that now and then serious role conflicts will arise. The conflict is internal and personal, for it is the individual who must act out the parts or refrain from doing so. But the conflict is also social because the conflicting demands come from a social system or systems in which the person has positions. For instance, several years ago cadets at the Air Force Academy discovered that some of their friends had been cheating on examinations. In the role of students under their honor system, the cadets were required to inform their superiors of the cheating. As members of friendship groups, however, the cadets also had to play the role of friend and remain silent. The roles were clearly in conflict; one could not successfully play both roles.

Most of us have experienced role conflict at some time or another. Often teen-agers cannot simultaneously be both the child their parents expect them to be and the group member their friends expect. The demands of the role of wife may conflict with those of mother, and both may conflict with the demands of a woman's job. As a worker she is expected to be efficient and productive. As a mother, she is expected to give her child the time, attention, and guidance required for proper childrearing. Her husband may expect her to cook and look after the house. It is the rare woman who can fill all these roles without experiencing at least some conflict.

Resolving Role Conflicts Role conflicts are seldom easy to resolve. One method is to *avoid* or give up one of the conflicting roles. Another is to *compromise* between the two roles to minimize conflict. A third method is to *rationalize*

---

[8]See, for example, Ernest Q. Campbell and Thomas F. Pettigrew, "Racial and Moral Crisis: The Role of Little Rock Ministers," *American Journal of Sociology* 64 (March 1959), 509–516; and Jack J. Preiss and Howard J. Ehrlich, *An Examination of Role Theory: The Case of the State Police* (Lincoln, Neb.: University of Nebraska Press, 1966).

Would you expect these black policemen to have role conflicts? If so, how would you think they resolve them?

the conflict and reduce its importance in one's own perceptions. Or one can try to live with both conflicting roles, pursuing at proper times each role as if the other were nonexistent. The choice of method will depend on the circumstances. A man whose religion requires pacifism can avoid the role of combat soldier by not enlisting in the military. But even while the draft was still in effect, he could apply for conscientious objector status. And if all else failed and he firmly wished to avoid a combat role, he could elect prison or self-imposed exile as a preferable alternative.

Another man may have a conflict between the role of father and that of provider. The more time and energy he spends on the job, the less he has for his children, and vice versa. Compromise is one of the commonest resolutions of such a conflict. But compromise may be unsatisfactory if it leads to the feeling that both of the conflicting roles are being neglected.

Rationalization is another common resolution of role conflict. To rationalize is to think the problem away, to rearrange one's ideas so the conflict appears either unreal or unimportant.[9] A person concerned about pollution of the envi-

[9]Wispé's study of the role of insurance salesman found that traits necessary for success in that role conflicted with traits related to being accepted as a friend but that the salesman interviewed were apparently not aware of the conflict. Lauren G. Wispé, "A Sociometric Analysis of Conflicting Role-Expectations," *American Journal of Sociology* 61 (September 1955), 134–137.

Conduct a study in role conflict. Ask a number of persons, "What do you think makes for a good worker and family provider?" and "What do you think makes for a good husband (or wife)?" Do the roles conflict? How many persons recognized the conflict as they described the second role?

---

ronment may work for a company that is a source of pollution. Such a person may think up all sorts of reasons why "for now" pollution is inevitable. That person may also come to feel that it would be futile to express any objections, since it would not change the situation and might result in the loss of the job.

Let's return now to the woman who is at once an office worker, a mother, and a wife. Her office job may demand as much time, attention, and energy of her as her husband's job demands of him. The demands of her job and her husband's expectations of her role in the home may be in conflict.

Suppose that avoiding either role is impossible (the second income is essential to the family, and divorce is unthinkable). Compromise has failed, for her husband is thoroughly socialized into the traditional male–female distinction. Rationalization is impossible because there is nothing for it to work on. She will not give up either role, and the conflict is produced outside of her, by her husband's refusal or inability to change his expectations of her role. Her only choice, then, is to live as best she can for as long as she must—or for as long as she *can*—with both conflicting roles. She must try in effect to handle each role as if the other were nonexistent or not conflicting. This is the fourth way of handling conflict, and one that is probably quite widespread in our society.

INADEQUATE ROLE PREPARATION

A common cause of the role failures we've studied is that the incumbent was not prepared to fill the new position and its role. If the behavior and attitudes of the new role can be learned quickly, there will be temporary and probably only mild role strain. But sometimes so much preparation is required for a role that learning to enact it before failure occurs is extremely difficult or impossible.

All around us we see examples of role failures caused by inadequate preparation. At many colleges and universities every fall a small but predictable number of freshmen drop out of school after only a week or two of their first semester. Many students who leave so soon are not yet able to direct their own lives. They miss classes and appointments, fail to complete their assignments, and in various other ways prove unable to take care of themselves without supervision and direction. Others have never left home emotionally. Still others have never learned how to get along in small groups of their peers. Many young couples marry with as little preparation for marriage as such students have had for college.

146

POWER CORRUPTS?
OR ONLY IF YOU'VE BEEN TOLD IT DOES?

Whether or not we think the prison system is in need of reform, we should all be familiar with certain criticisms frequently leveled against the prisons: They punish rather than rehabilitate; many guards are insensitive at best, brutal and sadistic at worst; the prisoners are dehumanized by life behind the walls, treated like animals and only made less fit to reenter society.

Many proposals have been made to improve the system, from locking up only those convicted of violent crimes, to giving applicants for guard positions psychological tests. But a possible kink in the entire notion of prison reform comes out of an experiment conducted by Professor Philip Zimbardo of Stanford University.

Zimbardo and his colleagues set up an experiment to study deviant behavior. They built a mock prison in a laboratory basement. They selected twenty-two young volunteers from those who answered an ad offering fifteen dollars a day for participating in a prison experiment. They administered personality tests to be sure all twenty-two were emotionally stable. By random selection, eleven volunteers became prisoners and eleven became guards. The guards were instructed only to maintain order.

The experiment was to last fourteen days. It lasted six. Prisoners and guards quickly began to show the behavior attributed to their counterparts in actual prisons. Prisoners became passive and anxiety-ridden; guards became abusive and cruel. Several prisoners had to be released after only a few days. Almost all the remaining prisoners were desperate enough for release that they were willing to sign away the right to the money they had earned so far. The guards, on the other hand, were eager to continue the experiment. Several guards worked for longer than their regular shifts without extra pay. As one guard later said, "Power can be a great pleasure."

Why did middle-class college students so quickly and thoroughly fall into roles that were alien to their experience? A psychologist might answer that most personalities respond in similar ways to certain conditions of experience, for example, having power over others or completely lacking power. But the sociologist would say that, through our socialization, we carry around in our heads many roles beside those we've already enacted. Could it be that these students knew of no other way to act as guards and prisoners than to follow popular stereotypes?

Inadequate role preparation frequently appears to be the fault of the ill-prepared individual. Some individuals do fail to perceive what is required of them or are otherwise unable or unwilling to prepare for a new role. But often poor role preparation can be traced to the specific social system in which the person is supposed to take a new role, or to the social system that should have prepared the person for that role. Perhaps the college was forbidding to certain students in its size and its apparent demands or in its seeming impersonality. Or perhaps the person's family or high school counselor urged the person on to college without taking seriously his or her expressions of doubt or lack of self-confidence, or without making clear the immense difference between high school and college.

DISCONTINUITY IN SOCIALIZATION

Ideally, our preparation for life's sequence of roles will have a certain continuity. The characteristics we acquire while enacting a given role can be carried over into our next role, allowing us to go from one to the next with little strain. At times, though, there are *discontinuities* in the sequence of roles we play. That is, before we can enact a new role we may have to unlearn earlier appropriate behavior or attitudes. When the tendency toward discontinuity is society-wide, it is a *discontinuity in socialization,* or a discontinuity in cultural conditioning.[10]

In the United States we find discontinuity in socialization in the many contrasts between the role of the child and that of the adult. Most children today are not supposed to be responsible for their own maintenance and welfare; almost always someone will take care of them. Children are not expected or allowed to be truly independent, make their own decisions, and direct their own lives. Yet as adults they are supposed to be responsible for their own welfare and usually for that of others. They are expected to be autonomous, free agents capable of directing their own adult lives.

All adults were once children, and everywhere children become adults. The transition from one role to another can be smooth or harsh, and the time for role change can be clearly marked or left ambiguous. In our society discontinuity in socialization prevails because the contrast in successive roles is great. There is much unlearning involved before the adult role can be fully assumed, and often enough there is no clear-cut signal to the incumbent that the time has come to change roles.

Only a few decades ago many more children than now were introduced to the adult world in early or middle adolescence, when they got their first real jobs. They entered a transitional stage in which they had to please employers, hold down a job, bring home wages, and yet they still kept for a while some of the benefits (and liabilities) of being dependent offspring. In fact, it was once

---

[10]The anthropologist Ruth Benedict pointed out a number of discontinuities in role preparation in American society. See Ruth Benedict, "Continuities and Discontinuities in Cultural Conditioning," *Psychiatry* 1 (May 1939), 161–167.

In **Death of a Salesman,** Willy Loman personifies the concept of role failure—he has failed as provider, husband, and father.

fairly common for offspring to live at home until they married, no matter what their age. But since World War II our higher standard of living has freed many teenagers from the need to work. Our insistence on a college education for so many jobs and careers has prolonged the dependency of adolescence. (This account is not intended to suggest that child labor laws be repealed, that the standard of living be lowered, or that you quit college. The point is that in our society there is no smooth transition from childhood to adulthood.)

In this chapter, we have seen how, through socialization, our behavior is shaped to fit the roles, norms, and values of our society. First as children, then as adult participants in such institutions as school, church, family, and community, we hold the attitudes and behave in the ways expected of us by others. But we are part of larger groupings as well. These larger units of social organization are our subject in the next chapter.

SUMMARY POINTS AND QUESTIONS

1. To analyze human behavior in groups, it is necessary to understand three basic concepts; social system, position, and role. *Social system* refers to the patterns of behavior that exist, or could exist, whenever two or more persons interact.

>*What are some ways that the concept of system has been used in science?*
>
>*What is meant by the statement that the term system is an abstraction?*

2. Social systems are composed of positions. *Position* refers to a location in a network of social relationships that can be occupied by a person or by a class of persons.

>*What is an example of a position?*
>
>*Show how it is related to one or more positions in a social system.*

3. For every position there is a role. A *role* is defined as the totality of culturally prescribed duties, attributes, and rights expected or demanded of the incumbent of a particular position.

>*Write out a partial description of a specific role.*
>
>*Describe how you would go about comparing a role in one group or society with a similar role in a different social system.*

4. Norms include mores and folkways. They are the rules that regulate an individual's behavior and are based upon the underlying values of society.

>*List a few important, current American norms.*
>
>*Compare and contrast these norms with ones governing the same type of behavior when your parents were your age.*

5. The roles a person enacts can change by adding a new role, by giving up a role, by substituting one role for another, and by the nature of a role itself changing.

>*Give an example of each of the processes by which the roles a person plays can change.*
>
>*Discuss the proposition that in our society too little attention is given to helping people learn how to give up roles.*

6. It is possible to distinguish between *role* and *role behavior*. While the former refers to what is expected of a person occupying a position, the latter refers to what the person actually does as he attempts to act out these expectations.

>*Do some persons play roles better than others?*
>
>*Can you think of a situation in which a person did not play his role very well? What happened?*

7. Roles permit the members of a group to come and go while allowing the group to remain stable.

>*How does this process work?*
>
>*What occurs when a new member enters a group but does not play the role he was expected to play?*

8. Because roles impose common expectations on those who perform them, they tend to standardize behavior.

   Because of these common expectations, do roles inhibit individuality?

9. Roles are learned by formal or informal instruction, by observation, by playing a reciprocal role, by generalizing from similar roles, by imaginative role playing, and by combinations of the above.

   How does each of these processes operate to facilitate role learning?

10. Two types of role failure are *role discrepancy*, which exists when the role behavior of an actor in a social system does not correspond to what is expected by the actor in the reciprocal role; and *role conflict*, which exists when there is inconsistency between two or more roles an individual is expected to play.

   What is an example of each of these types of role failure?

   How are these role failures resolved?

SUGGESTED READINGS

Dobriner, William M. *Social Structures and Systems.* Pacific Palisades, Calif.: Goodyear, 1969. Emphasizes the concepts of social systems and community, and their components from a functional perspective.

Glaser, Barney G. and Anselm L. Strauss. *Status Passage.* Chicago: Aldine, 1971. A discussion of the movement of persons from one status position to another and the institutional mechanisms that facilitate or inhibit such passages.

Goffman, Erving. *The Presentation of Self in Everyday Life.* Garden City, N.Y.: Doubleday, 1959. Using the theatrical performance as a model to study social behavior, Goffman provides an insightful view of man the actor performing for various social audiences.

Lopata, Helena Znaniecki. *Occupation: Housewife.* New York: Oxford University Press, 1971. A study of the many roles played by the housewife, socialization into these roles, and the areas in which role conflict occurs.

Merton, Robert K. *Social Theory and Social Structure.* New York: Free Press, 1968. A thorough discussion of role conflict and the mechanisms that operate to reduce various types of conflict.

Simmel, Georg. *The Sociology of Georg Simmel.* ed. by Kurt Wolff. New York: Free Press, 1964. A collection of Simmel's most important essays. It includes his essays on the dyad, triad, collective behavior, rituals, the secret society, the stranger, and the city. One of the most insightful works in classical sociology.

Smelser, Neil J. and William T. Smelser, eds. *Personality and Social Systems.* New York: John Wiley & Sons, 1970. Readings on the relationship of social systems to individuals. They deal with both macroscopic systems, such as society, and microscopic systems, such as small groups.

Whyte, William Foote. *Street Corner Society.* Chicago: University of Chicago Press, 1955. A classical participant observation study of a neighborhood group of young men. It focuses on the way in which group membership affects the individual's behavior.

At your age you've directly experienced most of what we've already discussed. But culture, socialization, and values and norms do not by themselves define and hold together a large, complex society. For such purposes, according to sociologists, we belong to groups of several kinds, and to institutions. To sociologists, groups are enduring modes of human interaction, ranging from the intimate and emotionally rewarding, like the family, to the formalized and impersonal, like the voluntary association or the bureaucracy. Whatever the group, roles are integrated to ensure that all functions are performed. And just as most of us have extragroup linkages by being members of more than one group at a time, so communities are linked to one another by commerce, government jurisdictions, and the news and cultural media.

6

SOCIAL INTEGRATION AND ORGANIZATION

What would life be like in a society in which there were no sex-role differentiation and the equality of the sexes was a fact? One must start with the assumption that the family system would be retained, that sexual behavior would continue to be basically heterosexual, and that monogamous marriage would still prevail. As often as not, however, one would expect to find husbands tending children and doing housework while wives worked at careers. One would find entrance into occupations in which both sexes are equally capable to be irrespective of sex. Women locomotive engineers and male kindergarten teachers would be as common as their sex counterparts. Divorce would never provide for the support of the wife. When married, couples would take the wife's name as often as the husband's, move for the convenience of her education or her job as often as for his. While middle-class women now consider it part of their role as wives to contribute to the husband's career development, one might expect husbands to be equally concerned with the development of their wives' full potential. Today it rarely occurs to a man that he has any such responsibility.

In the last decade, sociologist J. Richard Udry created this model of a hypothetical society embodying the value of sexual equality.[1] His model exhibits many features of the sociological method. First, it is a *model*—an intellectual creation that reduces a complex system to its essential features. Although it is a model, it strongly resembles a technique used by sociologists on real world phenomena; by describing a hypothetical society it implicitly makes, or invites us to make, comparisons between our society and another. A model thus resembles a *comparative study,* a common sociological method. Udry points out the similarities between the hypothetical society and ours (monogamy, prevalence of heterosexuality, the family) as well as the differences between the two.

[1] J. Richard Udry, *The Social Context of Marriage* (Philadelphia: J. B. Lippincott Co., 1966), p. 55.

Conduct a descriptive survey (like a Gallup Poll) to determine differences, if any, in career aspirations of boys and girls at various age levels (ages 4, 8, and 10). Try to select an equal number of boys and girls at each age level. Ask each person what he or she wants to be when he or she grows up. Present your findings in a table. Analyze your results. Are any jobs chosen exclusively by one sex? Which careers are selected by both sexes? Are there noticeable differences by age levels? If you combine your findings with those of your classmates, your samples may be large enough to make generalizations such as, "Career aspirations tend to become less traditionally sex-role oriented as age increases."

Udry applied his imagination to our society and to the question of sex roles to create his hypothetical society. Perhaps we can do the same and imagine that his creation is an actual society somewhere on our planet. How, we might wonder, could he have gathered the information about sex roles? Because he has generalized from voluminous data, we can assume that he used quite an array of methods. Probably not every one of these methods was intended to gather unique information. Some were probably used to test other sources of data or other conclusions or hypotheses. Because roles are not separable from norms and values in the real world, we assume that he would be studying all three as a way of cross-checking his findings about any one. After all, a society like his very possibly has had at least one woman president. For if there is no discrimination of roles by sex, values based on belief in the biological inferiority of women's minds or emotional capacities are not likely to be prevalent.

Let us look briefly at a few of the methods Udry might have used to study sex roles throughout his society. He might, for example, have studied government census figures to ascertain the composition of occupational positions by sex. By properly interpreting the statistics he could discover why people moved from one area to another—to pursue a job for the husband or one for the wife. He could also tell how many husbands were helping their wives through school and vice versa. By proper sampling techniques he could choose people with whom to conduct structured interviews about their attitudes, values, and beliefs; or he could use questionnaires for the same purpose. He could use participant observation in many ways. He could live with a family in order to gather data on sexual equality in the husband and wife roles. He could find out how the children are socialized (what values and norms they are consciously and unconsciously taught), how smoothly monogamous relationships operate with sexual equality of roles, and many other facts useful in a comparative study with our own society.

All the methods mentioned above, and others as well, could have been used by Udry in his investigation of sex roles. These very methods—and others—have in fact been used to study sex roles in our own society. As a result of these studies, we know that we are pretty far from having a strongly held, universal value of sexual equality. For the norms that apply to almost every role in our social institutions are based on the belief that women are inferior to men. To see how well you have been socialized into what is called the "sexist" mentality, consider honestly your reactions to Udry's hypothetical description. Whether you're male or female, even if you weren't shocked or scandalized, you still probably felt uncomfortable with this or that detail ("Equal pay for equal work, sure—but men playing the housewife?").

Yet we say briefly in the last chapter that our folkways are changing in many ways that affect relations between the sexes. For example, many women now feel free to initiate a relationship with a man. Also, the women's liberation movement, no longer considered a joke by many, is growing stronger. The Equal Rights Amendment seems to be gathering the state ratifications necessary to eventually make it a part of the Constitution. The combined effect of all these changes is to make many more women aware of their feelings about their roles in society, roles they had once taken for granted as regrettable necessities. As

We are not yet a sexually egalitarian society, though we are making progress. Test yourself: What's your reaction to this young woman's doing physical labor?

Conduct a survey among students on campus to determine differences, if any, in students' attitudes toward true sexual equality. The more data you collect on each student—age, sex, rural or urban background, marital status of parents, size of family, income, occupation of parents—the more inferences you can draw from your data (assuming your sample is large enough). You could ask questions such as "Assuming both husband and wife work full-time, should they both share equally in the household tasks?" "If a husband earns enough to amply provide for his wife and children, should he agree to his wife's working too, if this is what she wants to do for her own self-fulfillment?" "If the wife has a good job, should the husband stay home to care for the house and children?" Combine your data with those of others in your class into a table. See how many generalizations you can make—for example, "Students from rural backgrounds are more (or less) liberal in their views toward sexual equality."

the folkways continue to change on an ever-broadening front, our mores on sexual roles cannot remain unaffected. (Recall that only a few years ago most abortions were illegal throughout this country, and that pressure generated and built mainly by *women* produced this change in our mores and our attitudes.)

Only the future will reveal whether our society will evolve into the twin of Udry's model. Meanwhile, we can wonder whether such forces for change in our values, norms, and institutions can succeed without provoking major disturbances in our society. In its history, our society has gone through many profound and sweeping changes. Probably even our founding fathers, many of whom were men of foresight, would find our society today far stranger than Udry's model might seem to you. Change will be studied thoroughly in Chapter 12, but we can ask here, How do societies *survive* change and remain intact? What holds them together? Are roles, norms, and values enough by themselves to hold together a large, complex society?

SOCIAL INSTITUTIONS AND GROUPS

Just as we saw in the first chapter that the sociologist's concerns are as old as history and recorded thought, so are the basic insights about the functioning of societies. Thousands of years before the beginnings of sociology, philosophers and social theorists were aware that any society was more than a mere collection of people located in a defined area, who somehow managed to stay together.

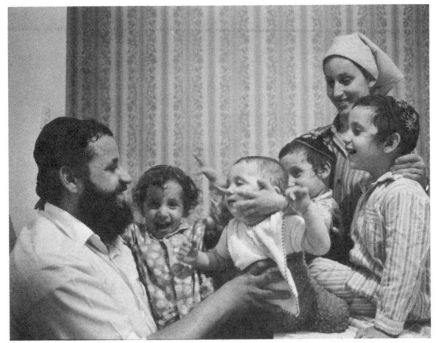

What are the criteria for categorizing a family as a group, and which of those criteria are visible in this photograph?

They knew that societies were integrated, that they possessed organization and sources and modes of unity. It remained for sociologists to conceptualize these modes of integration and organization so they could be studied scientifically.

Sociologists conceptualize two larger units of social interaction than we have so far studied. The family, which played an important role in our treatment of socialization, is an example of both of the larger units: It is an *institution and it is a group*. In your mind your family is a concrete collection of specific people, but to the sociologist it is also the representative of these two social units. Your family is a *group* not because it is a collection of people in the same place at the same time, but because it satisfies the three criteria sociologists have set up for their special definition of a group: It allows physical and symbolic interaction (communication by words, gestures, etc.) among mutually aware members; it is made up of people who think of themselves as members and who are thought of by the others as members; its members accept roles, privileges, and obligations within the group.

The family also fits the sociological concept of an *institution*, which is, in Kingsley Davis's definition, "a set of interwoven folkways, mores, and laws built

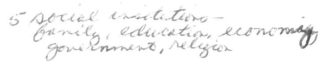

around one or more functions."[2] Sociologists commonly number the basic social institutions at five, corresponding to the five broad areas of human needs that are considered universal. Each institution has the social function of fulfilling those needs. For example, the family fills the infant's needs for rearing by providing food, shelter, protection, and emotional interaction. And it fills society's need to control sexual behavior, to assure constant replenishment of its membership, and to acquire fully socialized members.

The other four social institutions are education, which also functions as a socializing agent; the economy, which fills our material needs for goods and services; government, which meets society's need for constant forms of social control; and religion, which fulfills our need for a sense of meaning in life. Sociologists have ample evidence that every human society has some version of these five basic social functions and their attendant cluster of cultural elements. This is true even though the corresponding institutions of two different societies may not appear similar in their collections of norms and folkways. For example, our economic institution is dominated by gigantic corporations and conglomerates, and by advertising agencies that persuade us to participate heavily in the economy as consumers. There is not much likeness here to the economy of the African bush people, which consists of hunting by the men and searching for edible roots by the women. These are deliberately extreme examples to show you that wholly dissimilar activities in very different societies can be related to each other through the sociological concept of the institution.

THE GREAT MESHING:
INDIVIDUALS, GROUPS, AND SOCIETY

During socialization we learn one of our most basic skills: to develop and maintain social relationships with other human beings. We learn to trust others, to communicate with them, to want to be like them in many ways, and to get along with them. We usually want to be part of the social interaction we see going on around us. Because we must interact with others in order to learn about ourselves and our society, establishing and cultivating social relationships is a survival skill that we learn early and maintain throughout life. Sociologists differentiate between two general kinds of social relationships: primary and secondary group relationships.

[2]Kingsley Davis, *Human Society* (New York: Macmillan, 1949), p. 71.

PRIMARY GROUP RELATIONSHIPS

Early in the history of American sociology, Charles Horton Cooley developed the concept of the *primary group*.[3] A primary group offers its members intimate, face-to-face relationships and open and meaningful communication. Members of a primary group value each other as whole persons. The resulting personal satisfactions lead the members to identify with the group and to feel a sense of belonging. Primary group interaction is generally spontaneous, yet continues regularly over a long period of time, so its impact is deep and long-lasting. Our first experience of a primary group is of course the family. Later, our childhood play groups and our school friendship groups and cliques become primary groups too.

Primary groups, then, play a major part in the formation of our individual self-concepts and our character development. Thus, the people in our primary groups, whether consciously or unconsciously, significantly affect our total personality development. The emotional bonds in primary groups are a key element in our socialization because the values and norms we are taught are not merely abstract social rules. We seek to do what we are told is good and right in order to gain approval and sustained emotional support.

Because of this importance of primary groups to socialization, sociologists have been concerned in recent years to note that the primary group relationships in our society have been weakening. With increased urbanization, our relationships have become more impersonal. At one time, whole communities, neighborhoods, and extended families (families including grandparents and often aunts and uncles in the same or a nearby home) served as primary groups in the socialization of young people. Most mothers in a neighborhood once felt it was their responsibility to deal with any child caught deviating from community norms. Today, however, we rarely become involved in raising anyone's children but our own. Many social scientists, Urie Bronfenbrenner among them, believe that today's children are socialized more by their peers and by television than by their parents.[4] Whether or not this is true, the shift from the extended to the nuclear family structure has meant that our children have fewer primary group members with whom they can identify and from whom they can learn. Consequently, they also have fewer sources of motivation and social control. In short, our society as a whole appears to be moving closer to the end of the scale where secondary, rather than primary, group relationships are predominant.

[3]C. H. Cooley, *Social Organization* (Glencoe, Ill.: Free Press, 1956), pp. 23–29.

[4]Urie Bronfenbrenner, "Split-Level American Family," *Saturday Review*, October 7, 1967; pp. 60–66.

SECONDARY GROUP RELATIONSHIPS

Sociologists following Cooley perceived a set of traits basic to groups other than the primary, and classified them as *secondary groups. Secondary group* relationships are impersonal rather than intimate, superficial and businesslike rather than deep, meaningful, and spontaneous. Unlike primary relationships, they affect only one aspect of an individual rather than his total personality; interaction takes place between roles rather than between persons. For example, a taxi driver acts out a role and takes you to your desired destination; you in turn perform your role by paying for the driver's services.

A society like ours must have positions such as taxi driver and passenger, store clerk and customer, business executive and client in order to function smoothly. Because we cannot possibly know everyone with whom we come in contact, as we might in a small group, we must rely on expected role behavior when dealing with others in a more impersonal secondary group situation. But secondary groups are inferior to primary groups as socializing agents, for they lack the emotional bonds and the influence on our self-concepts that lend so much force to the socializing role of primary groups. Social roles and positions tend to bind our secondary groups together, while face-to-face relationships in primary groups give more personal meaning and direction to the lives of individuals.

SOCIAL PROPERTIES OF GROUPS

We have already gained some idea of the social properties of groups. The basic property of groups is interaction among their members. In some groups this interaction is quite spontaneous and informal. In others it is based on roles and on the way that the roles of each person are integrated with those of others. Sometimes this interaction is carried beyond the group and forms extragroup linkages. These are the three social properties of groups that we now discuss more fully: interaction, role integration, and extragroup linkage.

SOCIAL INTERACTION

During interaction each participant acts upon and somehow affects the behavior of another participant. But sociologists who try to observe this process in a large group find many complicating and competing factors that obscure what actually is going on. So instead of trying to study interaction in a large group, sociologists often study the *dyad,* two persons interacting with each other. There is a special closeness and openness between two persons that is not so readily attainable

Select one primary group to which you already belong and play the role of a participant observer. You would need to continue your normal behavior in this group while at the same time, without the knowledge of the others in your primary group, you would observe objectively what is going on. You would need to determine ahead of time the kind(s) of things you intend to observe and record them later on in privacy. You might want to keep track of the number and kinds of interaction that occur. Are there seeking/giving assistance patterns, leadership patterns, and so on between certain members? Do these patterns shift? How does the group cope with problem situations and/or problem members? Whatever you decide to investigate, do so objectively, recording your observations as soon as you can after each time you meet with the group. You may add your own background interpretations, but keep them separate from your objective observations.

Secondary group relationships are impersonal rather than intimate, and superficial and businesslike rather than deep, meaningful, and spontaneous.

The dyad, two people interacting with each other, allows for a special closeness hard to achieve in larger groups.

in larger groups, primarily because interactions between more than two individuals are more complex. When a dyad is increased by the addition of one more person, creating a *triad,* the number of relationships jumps from one to three. A dyad, for example, of a wife and husband is one set of relationships. But add a child and there are three sets of relationships: (1) mother and father, (2) mother and child, (3) father and child. If two children were added to the original dyad there would be *four* persons but *six* sets of relationships: (1) mother and father, (2) mother and child A, (3) mother and child B, (4) father and child A, (5) father and child B, and (6) child A and child B. And if we extrapolate to a group of twenty members, often the sociologist's upper limit for small groups, we find *190* relationships![5]

ROLE INTEGRATION

The second social property of groups is *role integration.* How roles become integrated through interaction is again more apparent in the dyad. The husband and wife usually play separate and distinct roles, yet through the give and take

[5]James H. S. Bossard and Eleanor Stoker Boll, *The Sociology of Child Development* (New York: Harper & Row, 1966), p. 69.

> **Choose a number of famous people, such as Gloria Steinem, Richard Nixon, Elvis Presley, and so on. Using the members of your class and their connections with people in other groups, see if you can form a chain of extragroup linkages between yourself and some famous person. For example, one of your classmates might belong to the Young Republicans. The head of his group might know someone in Washington. And that person in Washington might know someone who knows John Dean. And John Dean, of course, knows Richard Nixon. See how many groups you have to go through in order to reach the person whom you've selected.**

of their interactions their roles mesh together. In a traditional arrangement the husband will work to earn the couple's income and the wife will remain at home and keep house; or both spouses will work to earn income and will share household chores between them. Of course a couple may enter a marriage relationship with discrepant role expectations for each other, which could lead to role conflict rather than role integration. If their interaction is open and their communication honest, however, the differences in role expectations frequently can be reconciled and integration of roles achieved.

In larger groups, differences in role expectations could likewise be reconciled through free and open communication, but too often such honesty, concern, and intimacy is lacking in large secondary groups. This lack of intimacy, coupled with the enormous potential number of interrelationships, quite often calls for more formal means—rules and regulations, outside mediators, or other procedures—for reconciling roles or managing conflicts. Later in this chapter we see how role integration is handled in highly structured organizations, such as bureaucracies with their flow charts and chains of command. But for now it should be clear that within any group, roles must be integrated if interaction is to solidify a group and help it move toward its goals.

EXTRAGROUP LINKAGE

A third property of most social groups is *extragroup linkage*. Each member of a group establishes relationships with other individuals and other groups, thus forming an intricate network of relationships contributing to the integration of our society. Let us begin with the simple dyad and assume that a teacher and student have established a dyadic relationship during the semester. Most likely each has other dyadic relationships, such as with good friends, members

The complex network of interrelationships that society is based on starts with the friendships of individuals.

of their families, and other significant persons in their lives. In addition to these one–to–one relationships, each would have established relationships in larger groups at school, work, and in the community. Some of these extragroup linkages would be primary while others would be secondary.

Individuals in these other groups would have their own constellations of dyadic and extragroup linkages. Individuals participate in their society through this interlocking system of groups. Therefore, when we look at our whole society, it becomes apparent how intricately this complex network of interrelationships is established among individuals, between individuals and groups, and among groups.

THE STRUCTURE OF GROUPS

Groups differ widely in how loosely or tightly organized they are. Bureaucracies such as General Motors or the Army characteristically have written job descriptions and a certain status of authority and prestige for each position. There is a definite hierarchy of jobs, which leaves no doubt as to who has direct authority over whom. Bureaucracies, the most highly structured of secondary groups, predominate in our society. Most corporations, government agencies on all levels, most religious groups, and almost all schools and school systems are bureaucracies. But other significant types of secondary groups are more loosely structured. Of the two others besides bureaucracies that we will study—social movements and voluntary associations—social movements are the more loosely organized.

SOCIAL MOVEMENTS

Inequalities have existed for hundreds of years in our and other societies. Throughout history organized efforts to cope with perceived injustices have been triggered by certain events or circumstances. Social movements often barely fit the definition of groups. They are frequently so loosely structured, especially in their beginnings, that they closely resemble a mob or a spontaneous gathering. To be considered a social movement, however, a group must be longer–lived than a mob. Indeed, the beginnings of an active social movement sometimes can be traced to something as specific as a riot or mob action (although this can be a dangerous oversimplification if the collective desires for social change that predated such a riot are not kept in mind). For example, it has been argued that the gay liberation movement of homosexuals took shape in one week in the fall of 1968 in and around a gay bar in Greenwich Village. It began when homosexuals started to forcibly resist what they considered to be arbitrary police harassment of homosexual frequenters of the bar. On successive nights in one week, they staged confrontations with the police that brought many homosexuals together and suggested to them the possibilities of solidarity and organization.

The civil rights movement that began in the early 1960s is the classic example of a contemporary social movement. It started with a few small organizations and many highly dedicated, active people. Its aims were both broad and specific, including integration of public facilities, exercise of the right to vote, reform of the political and economic structure, and radical improvement of the self–image of blacks.

The women's liberation movement can be seen as a revival of the nineteenth–century woman's suffrage movement. But it encompasses a much greater sweep of social issues related to sexism, including sexual prejudice and discrimination in all of society's institutions. Although women are a numerical majority in our society they have the economic, political, and social status of a minority.[6]

VOLUNTARY ASSOCIATIONS

Many years ago Margaret Sanger was fighting to convince society that there was a dire need to limit family size, to recognize the morality of birth control, and to legalize it. She and her followers constituted a social movement. Once their goals were accepted by a major segment of our society, however, Planned

[6]Helen Mayer Hacker, "Women as a Minority Group," *Social Forces* 30 (October 1951), pp. 60-69.

Parenthood became a more established and formally organized association, which carried on and extended the work of Margaret Sanger.

The trade union movement illustrates a similar sequence. It began as a broadly based, loosely organized movement. It is now a collection of voluntary associations of workers. Union leadership is now represented and consulted in the highest quarters of government.

Political parties go so far back in our history and for so long have been integral with our political institutions that their classification as voluntary associations may at first be surprising. Nevertheless, in their origins as social movements and in their current state as bureaucracies, the major parties fit the category.

Sociologists have traced the evolution of social movements into associations with economic and social bases. During this evolution several things generally happen within the group. The original charismatic leadership is replaced by a bureaucratic structure, and original goals yield to more moderate goals that fit those of the greater society.[7] Professionals are hired either to replace the volunteers or to help them keep the organization functioning. Voluntary associations often have a national or international membership and branch councils that maintain uniformity in all sectors. Thus, a leader or consultant trained in one geographic area could easily perform the same role in another area without having to start anew with basic training courses. This uniformity allows progression and continuity for both the individual and the organization. However, this very same uniformity may make the bureaucracy insensitive to local conditions and unable to cope with unusual situations. How this bureaucratic structure works is discussed more fully in the next section.

DUAL SOCIAL FUNCTIONS OF GROUPS

Although the extent of involvement in voluntary associations varies from culture to culture, most sociologists agree that voluntary associations play an important role in the socialization of individuals in our own rapidly changing society. Arthur M. Schlesinger, Sr., believes that "voluntary organizations function to train individuals in democratic self-government, to help integrate the nation, to provide a safety valve for tensions and ambitions generated by modern life, to educate the public, and to promote social reform."[8]

Many persons who join groups either would not admit to the functions outlined by Schlesinger, or would be unaware of them. If asked why they joined a group, they would more than likely quote as their reasons the group's formalized objec-

[7]F. Stuart Chapin and John Tsouderos, "The Formalization Process in Voluntary Organizations," *Social Forces* 34 (May 1956), 342–344.

[8]Arthur M. Schlesinger, Sr., as paraphrased in *Voluntary Associations: Perspectives on the Literature,* ed. Constance Smith and Anne Freedman (Cambridge, Mass.: Harvard University Press, 1972), p. 22.

**In what ways did the Vietnam war protest fulfill the
functions of voluntary organizations outlined by Schlesinger?**

tives. Nevertheless, the sociologist Robert Merton first distinguished between
two distinct functions of a group: *manifest* functions and *latent* functions. Functions whose consequences are "intended and recognized by participants in the
system" (that is, the group's objectives) are *manifest*. Those functions "which
are neither intended nor recognized" are *latent*.[9] For example, our social institution of education has the manifest functions of transmitting knowledge, providing
equality of opportunity, and creating new knowledge through scholarship and
research. Its latent functions include keeping children out of the home for nine
months of the year and out of the full-time labor force for eighteen or more
years. These two functions were not originally intended for education, but they
are latently functional for both the family and economic institutions.

[9]Robert K. Merton, *Social Theory and Social Structure* (Glencoe, Ill.: Free Press, 1957), p. 51.

A hard fact, perhaps, but in any bureaucracy or large organization, the position, not the individual filling it, is indispensable.

BUREAUCRACIES

As we have seen, the people in a society usually organize themselves into various kinds of associations or groups, many with goals that carry out specific aspects of a society's norms. Each of these associations is further structured into roles and positions, which determine how the members will behave. These positions and roles are relatively permanent, changing slowly as social change occurs in society.

Formal Structure Every characteristic bureaucracy has a division of labor, chain of command, and coordination. The division of labor, essential to proper functioning, corresponds to the integration of roles mentioned earlier. All of the tasks essential to achieving the organization's goals and to sustaining the organization must be described and allocated to minimize waste of time, effort, and money, and to maximize the efficiency of their use. Each position within the structure must have a job title. And each corresponding role must have a detailed job

> **Select a bureaucratic organization with which you are familiar or to which you have access. This organization can be a bureaucracy with economic goals or one with social goals, such as clubs, Red Cross, and the like. Determine the major division of labor in your bureaucracy, its line of command and methods of coordination. If possible, differentiate between its formal and informal structure. If you are unable to use the participant observer method of research, then you could use the interview method. Be sure you have thought carefully about what you want to find out. Write down the questions you want to ask so you can elicit the information you need efficiently and effectively.**

description that clearly outlines duties, responsibilities, and privileges, as well as the qualifications required for the job. For the proper functioning of the bureaucracy, it is the position, not the individual filling it, that is important. The individual is dispensable and can be replaced by another individual with the same training and expertise. But the position or job is indispensable to the functioning of the organization, and its accompanying role must be fulfilled. Interaction occurs between positions rather than between persons. For instance, in the United States Army bureaucracy, a soldier salutes the rank, not the person. In a corporation, the vice president in charge of purchasing issues instructions that are followed, not because of his or her personal reputation as a decision maker, but because of the specific authority that accompanies the position.

The clear-cut *chain of command* eliminates questions as to which position has authority over another. Most bureaucracies have "red tape regulations" to control the flow of communication. For example, if an official wants to communicate with another official two or more levels above him in the bureaucratic hierarchy, he cannot do so directly. Rather, he must go through his immediate supervisor, the person directly above him in the chain of command. This control of communication helps to assure that the incumbent of every position is aware of everything that goes on within his or her jurisdiction.

Because each bureaucracy or large-scale organization has specific goals toward which the combined roles of all employees must be directed as efficiently as possible, there is an overall plan of action. As a result of the strict and narrow specialization of each job, though, the individual employee may not be aware of the company's goals or of how his or her own job fits into the plan of action. Thus, some person or persons must coordinate each separate position and its role so it contributes to the overall plan of action.

In any bureaucracy or large organization, bosses are needed to coordinate the activities of the workers to meet the company's goals.

Informal Structure Several years ago, partly at the request of big businesses to discover ways of improving productivity, sociologists began applying their methods of study to large bureaucracies. Using such techniques as participant observation, checking office records for levels of productivity, and questionnaires and interviews, sociologists gathered intimate data about the actual day-to-day operation of a bureaucracy. Some of these studies produced *sociograms*—maps of how members of a department, or of several coordinated departments, actually interacted according to personal preferences.

The results of these many studies conducted over the past decades have revealed that inside the highly formal, secondary structure of the organization there exist informal primary groups and relations. Informal regulation of production levels was a common discovery. That is, it was found that employees frequently worked out maximum and minimum quotas of production and applied sanctions (punishments) to those who worked outside the quotas. Because the impersonal goals of the formal structure provided no fulfillment of personal needs, the workers found satisfaction among themselves, providing each other with acceptance, recognition, and so on.

Many large corporations have responded to such discoveries in recent years by incorporating into the formal structure elements that encourage productive primary interactions at all levels. Executives have been urged to join sensitivity training groups. Tennis courts and golf courses have been made available by

ARE COMMUNES AN ANSWER TO BUREAUCRACIES?

Since the 1850s the commune had been neglected as an unworkable idea. Then, in the late 1960s, the idea was given a revival. But the latest communes have goals somewhat different from the goals of the earlier ones. The preindustrial world had never been a paradise for most people, but the Industrial Revolution introduced multitudes to new depths of economic exploitation and suffering. The new urban populations lacked even their former pittance of land from which to wrest a meager existence.

The first communes were born out of religious or moral outrage. Their founders believed that the world did not have to be as it was. Despite the variety of their designs, these communes shared the intent to put into practice various Utopian visions. Most of these "new societies" died fairly quick deaths. The rest died very quick deaths. (For a robust exception see the issue in Chapter 13.) Their members usually fell short of the idealistic expectations of the founders. Some communities even rejected machinery as being the root of social evil. They harked back to some imagined preindustrial agrarian ideal, which they never found.

Today's communes spring from a variety of different sources. True, there is still economic poverty and social injustice, but today's communes are only partly an effort at socio-economic equality. Many of the new communes seek to radically overturn the immense depersonalization in our society. From childhood on, secondary groups and relationships dominate our lives. And most of us feel alienated from society to one degree or another. So some people seek to prove, once again, that our society does not have to be depersonalizing.

Some communes are designed to fulfill religious values, or to revive Utopian efforts of over a century ago. But a few communes are experimental in a different sense; they are based on scientific theory. For example, the Twin Oaks community, outside Richmond, Virginia, is an attempt to put into practice the theories and purposes of the behavioral psychologist B. F. Skinner. The rules by which "interpersonal relations" are conducted are based on what some behaviorists call "behavioral engineering." Is it possible that sociology could likewise yield theories and hypotheses for use in extended experiments in alternative forms of social integration? Could something called "group engineering" produce a less stressful society and richer lives for everyone? Can science lead us to Utopia?

the corporations to all their employees. And the coordination of positions within departments has been made more flexible to accommodate, and benefit from, the primary relations that arise.

COMMUNITIES AND SOCIAL INTEGRATION

To most of us the word *community* suggests a town or a village—something concrete and self-contained, a more or less self-sufficient collection of people. Indeed, communities are small societies within the larger society, but societies that are less abstract than the immense complex of the larger society. So if we understand how communities work, we should have a better understanding of societies.

All communities include homes, churches, schools, court houses or municipal buildings, hospitals, and a variety of businesses, banks, and office buildings. All of these components are performing in their locality one or more of the major social functions we discussed earlier. In any true community all of the groups and institutions discussed in this chapter are integrated. The larger cities, of course, contain more of these interacting social units and, owing to sheer numbers of people and groups, their integration is more complex.

Social integration in the small town is often much like that of primary groups. People share many secondary relations, but the small scale of a town or village both enables and requires its people to constantly interact either directly or through intergroup linkages. (Our symbols of such a community are the cracker barrel or the pot-bellied stove of the old country store, where everyone gathers to swap yarns and gossip.)

Cities, on the other hand, are much more dominated by secondary groups and impersonal relations. (Consider, for example, that in many cities a single school will have far more children in it than live in an entire small town.) This predominance of secondary relations in cities is not merely the result of their size, however. It is part of their history. Cities, we must remember, began as commercial centers, places of trade and industry. Secondary relations, therefore, are the city's reason for being.

Secondary relations are chiefly what tie communities, large and small, together into the larger network of a society. We are not bound merely by values, norms, and so on. We are bound by the actual day-to-day roles that the physical representatives of our institutions play in our lives. The railroad passes through the town (or the city) with goods and people; we get foodstuffs from farms and ranches further out in the country or in a different geographic region; our ministers, rabbis, and priests are assigned by distant synods or bishops; our local government is part of the county, state, and federal governments; and our schools may be part of a larger system.

Big cities are communities, but within the larger community exist many smaller ones, such as San Francisco's Chinatown.

So you can see that we are not integrated as a society merely by the abstractions we've studied. Those abstractions are the sociologist's attempt to isolate for study the behavior of real people in observable situations. Societies are generally too large to be seen as a whole, but they are composed of unabstract people and groups engaged in much unabstract interaction. In the next chapter, we will study one further category used by sociologists in their attempt to understand human interaction: the social class.

SUMMARY POINTS AND QUESTIONS

1. Two major functions of groups are to be (1) the vehicle through which the individual can cope with society and (2) the mechanism for carrying out the values, goals, and norms of the greater society.

Into which function(s) would your college class fit? Explain.

What group(s) do you belong to that helps you participate more in society?

2. Social relationships are of two main kinds, the primary group relationship that involves the individual's total personality, and the secondary group relationship that pertains more to a certain aspect of an individual's personality, such as a role he or she is playing.

> *What primary groups had a significant impact on your life?*
> *Do you believe there is a trend toward using more primary group*
> *relationships in otherwise secondary group situations? Cite examples.*

3. The social properties of groups include interaction between members, an integration of their roles, and a carry-over of relationships to other groups by individual members.

> *Apply these properties to your college class. What are the linkages*
> *between your class and other groups?*

4. Groups tend to vary according to their degree of structural organization with collective behavior at one end of this continuum and bureaucracies at the other. In between lie social movements and voluntary associations.

> *What social movements are active on or near your campus?*

> *Which ones, if any, are becoming organized to the extent that they*
> *might remain functional and eventually evolve into voluntary*
> *associations?*

5. The manifest functions of a group refer to goals and objectives that are intended and recognized by a group; latent functions are those that are unintended, may be byproducts of interaction, and are not considered the reasons or purposes for the group's existence.

> *What are some of the manifest functions of your college? Your class?*
> *Your dorm?*

> *For each of these groups, list several latent functions they seem to be*
> *performing.*

6. Bureaucracies are associations designed to carry out specific tasks. They have a formal structure that is characterized by a division of labor, chain of command, and coordination.

> *Using a specific bureaucratic organization as an example, show how*
> *these different aspects of the formal structure are realized.*

> *Bureaucracies are often criticized as being impersonal and*
> *inefficient. Why is this so?*

7. Bureaucracies also have an informal structure in which members form attachments to other members. Often the roles that members play and the amount of work that they do are governed by this informal structure rather than the formal structure.

> *How might the informal structure inhibit the attainment of goals of*
> *a bureaucracy? How might it help goal attainment?*

> *Give an example of an informal structure in a bureaucracy in which*
> *you have participated.*

8. Communities are another form of social organization. Often the type of social integration within a community is determined by the size of that community. Small towns are seen to be characterized by primary relations, while cities are seen to be characterized by secondary relations.

> *What are the differences between living in a small town and a city?*
>
> *What are the advantages and disadvantages of each?*
>
> *How might living in a suburb be characterized compared to living in a small town? In a city?*

SUGGESTED READINGS

Blau, Peter and Marshall W. Meyer. *Bureaucracy in Modern Society.* New York: Random House, 1971. A study of the meaning of bureaucracy, the organization of bureaucratic authority, and the operation of particular bureaucracies.

Cartwright, Dorwin and Alvin Zander, eds. *Group Dynamics.* New York: Harper and Row, 1968. A reader on small group research. It covers leadership, power, structural properties of groups, pressures to conformity, and group membership.

Cooley, Charles Horton. *Social Organization.* New York: Scribner, 1909. A classical treatment of social organization both on the macroscopic level and the microscopic level. Especially important is the chapter on primary groups.

Hinton, Bernard L., ed. *Groups and Organizations.* Belmont, Calif.: Wadsworth, 1971. A collection of articles on small group formation and processes. This reader is especially oriented to understanding small groups that exist in the context of formal organizations.

Liebow, Elliot. *Tally's Corner.* Boston: Little, Brown, 1967. A participant observation study of black street corner men, their relationships to their wives and children and to each other, and the effects of their economic situation in their lives.

Report of the National Advisory Commission on Civil Disorders. New York: Bantam Books, 1968. A comprehensive source on the 1967 urban riots. The study centers on three questions: "What happened?," "Why did it happen?," and "What should be done?"

Stein, Maurice. *The Eclipse of Community.* Princeton, N.J.: Princeton University Press, 1960. Synthesizes the findings of a number of community sociologists into a macroscopic view of American society. Theorizes that the processes of urbanization, industrialization, and bureaucratization have resulted in the breakdown of communities and the rise of mass society.

Warren, Roland. *The Community in America,* 2nd Ed. Chicago: Rand McNally, 1972. Presents the various perspectives for studying community and then deals with sociological processes that are now affecting American communities.

We've seen that roles are designed to complement each other, like pieces in a jigsaw puzzle, so every needed task is performed. All tasks may be necessary, but not all tasks are considered equally important. Whether a chief of a primitive tribe, a priest of ancient Babylonia, or a physician or advertising executive today, some people receive greater rewards in wealth, prestige, power, or some combination of these than others do. Using these rewards as measures, we find that even our supposedly egalitarian society has social classes. Your class determines more than your income and prestige; it sets your chances for a long life, adequate education, mental health, marital stability, and many other things.

7

SOCIAL STRATIFICATION AND MOBILITY

> Throughout recorded time, and probably since the end of the
> Neolithic Age, there have been three kinds of people in the world,
> the High, the Middle, and the Low.
>
> The aims of these groups are entirely irreconcilable. The aim of the
> High is to remain where they are. The aim of the Middle is to change
> places with the High. The aim of the Low, when they have an
> aim—for it is an abiding characteristic of the Low that they are too
> much crushed with drudgery to be more than intermittently
> conscious of anything outside their daily lives—is to abolish all
> distinctions and create a society in which all men shall be equal.[1]
>
> George Orwell

High, Middle, Low; Upper Class, Middle Class, Working Class; the "haves" and the "have nots"—all of these expressions describe inequalities in human societies, and *inequality* is what social stratification is based upon. The dream of living in a classless society is ancient and persistent, but the real world in which people live is marked by inequalities in rewards, privileges, prestige, and power.

In the quotation above, George Orwell states not only that social stratification is found in all human societies, but that people are concerned with what sociologists call *social mobility,* movement up or down the social status ladder. Those at the top, Orwell claims, want to prevent their own downward mobility; others want to achieve upward mobility. Orwell describes those at the bottom as being "crushed with drudgery," an accurate description of the lives of people who are, as we put it in the United States, "below the poverty level."

[1] George Orwell, *1984* (New York: New American Library, 1949), p. 166.

177

There are many questions about social stratification with which sociologists have dealt, among them:

1. What kinds of inequality exist in the United States? How much inequality is there? What difference does it make?
2. Why does stratification exist? What theories can explain it?
3. To what extent are places in strata inherited? What is known about the process and extent of social mobility?

Many sociology departments devote entire courses to the study of social stratification. In this chapter we cannot possibly deal comprehensively with the extensive research and theory on the subject, but we can look into the three sets of questions above. And we can look into the basic concepts sociologists use in their studies of social stratification.

CLASS, STRATUM, AND RANK

Early sociologists borrowed the term *strata* from geologists, who use it to describe *layers* of rock. A vertical cut into a mountainside reveals these layers, each one more or less distinct and laid atop one another. The early sociologists saw the term as descriptive of societies in which people could be placed in different categories, and the categories themselves could be ranked one above the other. The criterion that separated each layer, or *class*, from the others was its level of social rewards—wealth, power, prestige, and other related social traits.

The analogy is more descriptive of some societies than of others. Under feudalism, for example, there were noblemen, freemen, and serfs. Although some differences in privileges and rewards could be found within each group, nevertheless feudal society clearly had three distinct classes of people. Everyone knew to which class he or she belonged, and all agreed on which class was highest and which was lowest.

All complex societies distribute privileges, rewards, power, and prestige to their members in different amounts. The society's members can be *ranked* from highest to lowest according to the amount of society's rewards and privileges they receive. This ranking system is commonly called *social stratification*.

A large, complex society does not exactly fit the analogy to geologic strata. In a society like ours, the vertical hierarchy of social rank does not seem to break into a given number of distinct categories or strata, as it did in feudal times. In the United States, differences in prestige, wealth, and other variables seem more to shade into one another as we go up or down the status hierarchy.[2]

---

[2]The smooth gradations in the status hierarchy are technically referred to as the continuum theory of social stratification. For one of the earlier discussions of the continuum theory see John F. Cuber and William F. Kenkel, *Social Stratification in the United States* (New York: Appleton-Century-Crofts, 1954), pp. 132–155 and 303–314.

Compare the ways that different classes of persons are treated by different community institutions. For example, visit a state or city mental hospital and a private mental hospital, and make an assessment of the type of hospital care provided.

Without distinct, separable strata, it is not literally correct to talk of social classes in the United States, but the concept of social class is still useful for our society. We can talk of the upper, middle, and lower class in much the same way that we speak of old age, middle age, and youth. That is, fine lines may not be possible between such categories, but broad differences are discernible. For some purposes, finer gradations, such as upper–upper or lower–lower class, may be desirable. So long as some approximate portion of the status hierarchy is being distinguished from other segments, there should be no confusion in calling these portions social classes.

Although we have talked about social stratification as if it were a single system, the sociologist Max Weber distinguished among stratification systems in society: (1) the economic order, (2) the honorific or prestige order, and (3) the power structure.[3] According to Weber, each of us has not one rank in society but *three,* and our three ranks do not necessarily match one another. The same person could rank very high in the power hierarchy, not quite so high in prestige or esteem, and lower still in economic position. Our behavior would be affected by each of our three positions. To understand the totality of our behavior, the sociologist would have to determine all three of our ranks.

Much of the stratification research in the United States today concentrates on two of the dimensions discussed by Weber, the economic and the prestige dimensions. Further, there has been considerable research into *status consistency*—that is, into how similarly a person ranks on different dimensions of social class.[4] It has been proposed, for example, that people whose incomes place them lower in the status hierarchy than does their education would probably feel a certain dissatisfaction. This dissatisfaction, in turn, would affect their ideas and their behavior, such as how they vote or the likelihood of their joining a protest movement.

[3]See Hans H. Gerth and C. Wright Mills, *From Max Weber: Essays in Sociology* (New York: Oxford University Press, 1946), pp. 180–195; and A. M. Henderson and Talcott Parsons, *Max Weber: The Theory of Social and Economic Organization* (New York: Oxford University Press, 1947), pp. 424–429.

[4]See, for example, K. Dennis Kelly and William J. Chambliss, "Status Consistency and Political Attitudes," *American Sociological Review* 31 (June 1966), 375–382; Andrzej Malewski, "The Degree of Status Incongruence and its Effects," in *Class Status, and Power,* 2nd ed., ed. Reinhard Bendix and Seymour Martin Lipset (New York: Free Press. 1966), pp. 303–308.

All societies show some kind of stratification. Some societies, like India's, have rigid caste systems.

SOCIAL MOBILITY VERSUS SOCIAL RIGIDITY

As we see in some detail later in the chapter, ours is a society that offers *social mobility*, the possibility of moving up (as well as down) in the ranks of privilege, prestige, and power. But some societies today, like many societies in past history, have rigid systems. A society with a rigid stratification system—marked by classes clearly set apart from one another and with practically no movement among them—is said to have a *caste system*. A person born into a certain caste is restricted to its life style, its privileges (if any), and its occupation or range of occupations. A person's friends and possible marriage partners come from the same caste, and one's children will be born, grow old, and die in that same caste.

For most of the Middle Ages, the feudal system was close to being a pure caste system. The caste system of India, which was ended by law only a little over a decade ago, was one of the oldest in the world.[5] There were originally four castes in India. From highest to lowest, these were the priestly, warrior, merchant, and worker castes. Over time, thousands of castes developed, each based primarily on a particular occupation. An intricate system of approach and avoidance governed social interaction between members of different castes. For example, if a lower caste person were to come closer than a certain distance to a higher caste person, the higher caste person would be polluted. A high caste person would also be polluted if the shadow of a low caste person fell on him, and he would have to be ritually purified.

In the ideal *open class system,* although differences in prestige and privilege would exist, the higher ranks could be readily attained by anyone with the ambition and abilities. The occupation of physician, for instance, might carry high prestige and financial rewards. But if one could get into medical school, then one's ability to learn and to perform would be the only requirements for becoming a doctor. In such a system we would expect to find many people moving up and down the status hierarchy from the classes into which they were born, for there would be no arbitrary or artificial barriers to such movement.

There is no known society with such an ideal open class system. Some industrialized societies are certainly far closer to the open class than to the caste system. And it is possible to designate where in the range from caste to open class any given society falls. Later in this chapter, we deal with mobility and the barriers to it in the United States.

DIFFERENTIAL REWARDS IN THE UNITED STATES

In any stratified society, the people at different ranks receive different rewards, that is, different amounts of something. Almost anything that is valued by a group, is scarce, and is distributed unequally can be considered a reward.

COMMON SOCIAL REWARDS

In industrialized societies, the three common rewards are money, prestige, and power. Money enables a person to compete in the acquisition of scarce, valuable goods, and to obtain privileges, such as hiring someone to perform undesirable tasks. *Prestige* is the quality attributed to a person by others because he or she does something, has something, or is something that is valued by the group. An individual receives prestige, admiration, or esteem by occupying a position

[5]There have been many studies of the caste system in India. For succinct accounts see Noel P. Gist, "Caste Differentials in South India," *American Sociological Review* 19 (April 1954), 126–137; and John H. Hutton, *Caste In India: Its Nature, Function and Origins* (Cambridge, Mass.: The University Press, 1946).

Using census data, indicate the average income of census tracts in your city. If you cannot find census data, ask a knowledgeable person to mark off upper, middle, and lower class areas. Visit the different areas and report on the physical environment (streets, crowdedness, trees, etc.), the class of people living in the area, and other features or observations that could be used to rank the prestige of the areas.

---

or having possessions that are valued. *Power,* the ability of a person to control the behavior of other persons, even over their opposition, is also distributed unequally in society. The sociologist Gerhard Lenski sees power as the basic element in a stratification system, for with power one can acquire privileges and be granted prestige.[6] Lenski sees prestige as a function of both power and privilege; the more power and privilege people have, the more esteem they have.

The relationships among the basic inequalities—wealth, prestige, and power—are quite complex. Money, for example, can be translated into power. A wealthy person may win election to a political office because of a well-financed campaign. The power that comes with the office can, in turn, be used to increase that person's wealth. Furthermore, someone with high prestige will have an easier time getting a loan than someone with low prestige. The loan can be used to finance a business enterprise, which will increase the person's wealth. Or it can be used to finance a political campaign which, if successful, will increase the person's power. It is relationships like these among prestige, wealth, and power that give credence to the saying, "The rich get richer while the poor get poorer."

INCOME INEQUALITIES

Income inequalities are a fact of American society. Adding some of the percentages in Table 7-1 shows that almost a third of white families have an income of $15,000 or more, while almost 20 percent have less than $6000 (about $115 per week). Ten percent of the white families are very poor, making less than $4000 a year; 8 percent of the white families are quite well off, with $25,000 or more in annual income.

The table also shows that race is part of our stratification system. About 45 percent of black families, as compared with less than 20 percent of white families,

---

[6] Gerhard Lenski, *Power and Privilege* (New York: McGraw-Hill, 1966), p. 46.

Money, power, and prestige—for these social rewards, members of most societies compete. These three kinds of rewards usually go together.

have an income of $6000 per year or less. A much higher percent of blacks than whites fall below $4000 annual income. At the other extreme, less than half as many black families as white families have a yearly income of $15,000 or more.

Table 7-2 presents the median annual income of workers. (In a ranking from highest to lowest, *median* is the midpoint. Half earn more and half earn less than the median.) The data show that not only race but also sex is part of our stratification system. Although those with little education would not be expected to earn as much as those with much education, the data in this table indicate otherwise. With the same education, women, whether black or white, earn less than men.

In part this inequality results because women often drop out of the labor force to bear and rear children, and upon their reentry into the job market find that the value of their work skills has diminished. This inequality, however, is also built into the stratification system. In general, it is the skills of women, and not those of men, that lose value. Moreover, women are more likely than men to be underemployed—that is, working at less than their full capacity, as

TABLE 7-1. Income Distribution in the United States, 1972

Total Annual Income	Percent of White Families	Percent of Black Families
Under $1000	1.1	2.8
$1000–$1999	1.7	6.7
$2000–$2999	3.1	9.3
$3000–$3999	4.1	9.4
$4000–$4999	4.5	8.7
$5000–$5999	4.7	7.6
$6000–$6999	5.0	6.5
$7000–$7999	5.4	7.0
$8000–$8999	5.5	4.7
$9000–$9999	5.8	5.7
$10,000–$11,999	11.8	8.3
$12,000–$14,999	15.2	9.2
$15,000–$24,999	24.2	12.2
$25,000–$49,999	7.1	1.9
$50,000 and over	0.9	0.2

Source: U.S. Bureau of the Census, *Current Population Reports*, Series P-60, No. 85, pp. 48–49.

is the case with the female college graduate employed as a typist. The under-employment of women is also a part of our stratification system.

The truth of the claim made by some that income inequalities in the United States are narrowing can be tested by comparing the shares of total national income received by various income groups at different times. We can discover, for example, whether the 20 percent of the families with the lowest incomes now receive a larger or smaller share of the total national income than they did 10, 20, or 60 years ago.

TABLE 7-2. Median Annual Income of Persons 25 Years Old and Over by Race, Sex, and Years of Schooling, 1972

Years School Completed	Median Annual Income			
	White		Black	
	Male	Female	Male	Female
Elementary				
0–7 years	$4491	$1705	$3119	$1498
8	5844	2014	5322	1975
High School				
1–3	8297	2668	6037	2758
4	10,182	3745	7316	3827
College				
1–3	11,228	4039	7817	4796
4 or more	14,385	6632	10,654	7978

Source: U.S. Bureau of Census, *Current Population Reports*, series P-60, No. 90, p. 124.

TABLE 7-3. How the Total Income is Distributed: Percentage Share Received by Each Fifth of Families, 1910-1972

	Lowest Fifth	2nd Fifth	3rd Fifth	4th Fifth	Highest Fifth
1972	5.4	11.9	17.5	23.9	41.4
1970	5.4	12.2	17.6	23.8	40.9
1960	4.8	12.2	17.8	24.0	41.3
1950	4.5	11.9	17.4	23.6	42.7
1910	8.3	11.5	15.0	20.0	46.2

Note: While generally the distribution has remained about the same, the lowest 20 percent of all families now receive a smaller share of the national income than they did in 1910.

Sources: Data for 1910 from Gabriel Kolko, *Wealth and Power in America* (New York: Frederick A. Praeger, 1962), p. 14. Other data from U.S. Bureau of the Census, *Current Population Reports,* Series P-60, No. 90, p. 45.

For all of the years shown in Table 7-3, it is apparent that the top 20 percent of income recipients receive a larger share of the national income than does the bottom 60 percent. What is more, the lowest 20 percent has experienced a definite loss in its share of the income as compared with 1910, even though it has regained a little of it in the last decade. In general, for the last 60 years the extent of inequalities in income has remained about the same.

PRESTIGE INEQUALITIES OF OCCUPATION

Many sociologists who study the effects of the stratification system on social interaction and human behavior use *occupational prestige* as an indicator of a person's rank in the system. The scales measuring occupational prestige were developed by determining through questionnaires how samples of Americans rate selected occupations.

The prestige scores of occupations in the United States, as displayed in Table 7-4, have changed very little between 1947 and 1963, including up to the present. The prestige of the policeman and the nuclear physicist have increased a little, while the radio announcer's prestige has dropped some, but basically the prestige system has been remarkably stable. As a matter of fact, the sociologists who conducted the 1963 study report that the prestige of occupations in the United States has not changed very much since 1925.[7]

Cross-cultural studies suggest that an occupation carries essentially the same prestige in different societies. Alex Inkeles and Peter Rossi studied the prestige of occupations in six industrialized societies (the United States, Great Britain,

[7]Robert W. Hodge, Paul M. Siegel, and Peter H. Rossi, "Occupational Prestige in the United States: 1925-1963," *American Journal of Sociology* 70 (November 1964), 286-302.

TABLE 7-4.   Occupational Prestige Ratings, 1963 and 1947

Occupation	1963 Score	1947 Score
U.S. Supreme Court Justice	94	96
Physician	93	93
Nuclear physicist	92	86
Scientist	92	89
Government scientist	91	88
State governor	91	93
Cabinet member in the Federal Gov't.	90	92
College professor	90	89
U.S. Representative in Congress	90	89
Chemist	89	86
Lawyer	89	86
Diplomat in U.S. Foreign Service	89	92
Dentist	88	86
Architect	88	86
County judge	88	87
Psychologist	87	85
Minister	87	87
Member of the board of directors of a large corporation	87	86
Mayor of a large city	87	90
Priest	86	86
Head of a dept. in state government	86	87
Civil engineer	86	84
Airline pilot	86	83
Banker	85	88
Biologist	85	81
Sociologist	83	82
Instructor in public schools	82	79
Captain in the regular army	82	80
Accountant for a large business	81	81
Public school teacher	81	78
Owner of a factory that employs about 100 people	80	82
Building contractor	80	79
Artist who paints pictures that are exhibited in galleries	78	83
Musician in a symphony orchestra	78	81
Author of novels	78	80
Economist	78	79
Official of an international labor union	77	75
Railroad engineer	76	76
Electrician	76	73
County agricultural agent	76	77
Owner-operator of a printing shop	75	74
Trained machinist	75	73
Farm owner and operator	74	76
Undertaker	74	72
Welfare worker for a city government	74	73

Source: Robert W. Hodge, Paul M. Siegel, and Peter H. Rossi, "Occupational Prestige in the United States: 1925-1963," *American Journal of Sociology*, 70 (November 1964), 286-302.

TABLE 7–4 (continued)

Occupation	1963 Score	1947 Score
Newspaper columnist	73	74
Policeman	72	67
Reporter on a daily newspaper	71	71
Radio announcer	70	75
Bookkeeper	70	68
Tenant farmer—one who owns livestock and machinery and manages the farm	69	68
Insurance agent	69	68
Carpenter	68	65
Manager of a small store in a city	67	69
A local official of a labor union	67	62
Mail carrier	66	66
Railroad conductor	66	67
Traveling salesman for a wholesale concern	66	68
Plumber	65	63
Automobile repairman	64	63
Playground director	63	67
Barber	63	59
Machine operator in a factory	63	60
Owner-operator of a lunch stand	63	62
Corporal in the regular army	62	60
Garage mechanic	62	62
Truck driver	59	54
Fisherman who owns his own boat	58	58
Clerk in a store	56	58
Milk route man	56	54
Streetcar motorman	56	58
Lumberjack	55	53
Restaurant cook	55	54
Singer in a nightclub	54	52
Filling station attendant	51	52
Dockworker	50	47
Railroad section hand	50	48
Night watchman	50	47
Coal miner	50	49
Restaurant waiter	49	48
Taxi driver	49	49
Farm hand	48	50
Janitor	48	44
Bartender	48	44
Clothes presser in a laundry	45	46
Soda fountain clerk	44	45
Share-cropper—one who owns no livestock or equipment and does not manage farm	42	40
Garbage collector	39	35
Street sweeper	36	34
Shoe shiner	34	33
Average	71	70

The garbageman's income is usually higher—sometimes much higher—than his occupational prestige.

the Soviet Union, Japan, New Zealand, and Germany).[8] Robert Hodge and others at the National Opinion Research Center compared occupational prestige in the United States and twenty-three other countries, both industrialized and developing ones.[9] All of them found a striking similarity in the prestige of occupations from country to country. (Hodge and his associates caution, however, that only occupations found in all of the societies studied can be used in comparative analyses.)

[8]Alex Inkeles and Peter H. Rossi, "National Comparisons of Occupational Prestige," *American Journal of Sociology* 61 (January 1965), 329–339.

[9]Robert W. Hodge, Donald J. Treiman, and Peter H. Rossi, "A Comparative Study of Occupational Prestige" in Bendix and Lipset, p. 311.

Hodge's study concludes with the intriguing hypothesis that rather than being a *consequence* of economic development, the similarities in the prestige of occupations may actually *enhance* development: "Development hinges in part upon the recruitment and training of persons for the skilled, clerical, managerial, and professional positions necessary to support an industrial economy. Thus, acquisition of a 'modern' system of occupational evaluation would seem to be a necessary precondition to rapid industrialization. . . ."[10] A further implication of the study is that it may be *functionally necessary* to have a system of unequal prestige to assure that the important positions in society are filled.

THE IMPORTANCE OF SOCIAL CLASS

The study of social stratification is one of the most significant areas of sociological research. This is so partly because knowledge of a person's social status is extremely crucial in understanding and predicting his or her other behavior. From birth to death, in almost countless ways, our social status affects what will happen to us, what we will do, and even how we will think and believe. Because social traits are generally so closely linked to social class, it was once commonly believed that the linkage was biological, that social traits were genetically determined. Ample sociological evidence proves otherwise. And we now know that a person's social traits will tend to change if that person moves from one social class to another. Nevertheless, the social class into which we are born affects both our *life chances* and our *life styles*.

SOCIAL CLASS AND LIFE CHANCES

When we say that *life chances* vary by social status we mean that the odds of receiving an advantage or suffering a disadvantage in some important aspect of our social lives are dependent on our social status. For example, we know that juvenile delinquency occurs less frequently in the upper class than it does in the lower class. We know too that more lower than upper class people will be hospitalized as schizophrenics.[11] (This does not mean, however, that schizophrenia and juvenile delinquency occur *only* in the lower class. It is a matter of probability. Schizophrenia and juvenile delinquency are not evenly distributed in our society. Although both occur in all classes, it is also true that both occur more frequently in the lower class.) Many other disadvantages and advantages vary with social class. Sociologists generally restrict the concept life chances

[10]See Hodge, Treiman, and Rossi, p. 320.

[11]August B. Hollingshead and Frederick C. Redlich, *Social Class and Mental Illness* (New York: John Wiley & Sons, 1958).

Being black and female will have a significant effect on this girl's life chances. Can you explain why?

to important events and to characteristics that have fairly high social approval or disapproval, even if all of these terms must be rather loosely defined.

It may be inhumane to inform a group of new mothers that the probability that their child will survive its first year depends on their social class, but it is statistically true. For a long time the infant mortality rate has varied inversely with social class.

For over the last 100 years in the United States, family size has varied by social class; the higher the social class, the fewer the children in the family, although the size of this difference is now narrowing.[12] A child's life chances are affected by this inverse relationship because the scarce financial resources of the lower class family have to be spread over many people, while the greater resources of the middle and upper class families are distributed among fewer people.

[12]There has been considerable research on social class and childbearing. For a review of the findings and sources of the subject see William F. Kenkel, *The Family in Perspective,* 3rd ed. (New York: Appleton–Century–Crofts, 1973), pp. 198–206.

Using about twenty different occupations, construct an occupational prestige scale. To do this, write down each occupational title on a card and give the set of cards to a number of persons, asking them to rank the prestige of each occupation high, medium, or low. Score all "high" responses 5 points, all medium ones 3, and all low ratings 1. Total the ratings for each occupation, arrange the occupations from highest total score to lowest score. How does your scale compare to the one presented in this chapter?

Throughout our lives our destinies are affected by social status. Lower class children are less likely than upper or middle class children to do well in school. From their parents they have probably already picked up the notion that school is dull and that education is not really important. From parents, too, children learn how to speak and dress and relate to adults. Lower class children often do not speak correct (that is, educated) English. Nor are they as clean and well dressed as their middle class teachers think they should be.

Thus, while middle class children meet with a certain consistency in their lives—for parents and teachers reinforce one another and seem to agree on what is important in life and what is necessary to get ahead in the world—lower class children meet instead with contradictions. Their teachers are not like the other adults they know. The teachers speak differently, dress differently, and most of all, expect different behavior of children. It is not surprising, then, that lower class children do not like school and are more likely than middle or upper class children to decide that school is not for them.[13] The school dropout rate has a strong inverse relationship with social class.

The lower the social class, the younger the age at which people will marry, the more children they will have, the greater the chance that they will divorce, and the younger they will be when they die. (For despite the presumed tensions, businessmen and professionals live longer on the average than unskilled and semiskilled workers.) As we look over the cycle from birth to death, it is quite apparent that the lower classes receive more of the disadvantages of life and fewer of the privileges than the higher classes. We must remember, though, that the relationship between social class and life chance is a matter of probability, and therefore that it may not hold true for any particular individual. Nonetheless, we may whimsically conclude that the best advice to give a child is "Choose your parents carefully."

[13]Interestingly, sociologists noted the class bias in the school system over 30 years ago. See W. Lloyd Warner, Robert J. Havighurst, and Martin B. Loeb, *Who Shall Be Educated?* (New York: Harper & Row, 1944). See also August B. Hollingshead, *Elmtown's Youth* (New York: John Wiley & Sons, 1949).

SOCIAL CLASS AND LIFE STYLE

Although there are many differences in the life styles of people at different status levels, it must be remembered that not all lower class people think or act one way, all of the middle class people another way, and all of the upper class people still a third way. Rather, there is a gradual shading in life styles as we ascend or descend the status ladder, and at every status level there are exceptional individuals.

Nevertheless, knowing a person's social status allows us to predict many aspects of his or her style of life. In various significant ways, people of different social statuses think and feel differently, behave differently, and have a different way of life.

Material Possessions One of the more obvious differences among people of different classes is in their possessions, the things that money can buy. Homes, automobiles, and clothing are among the more conspicuous possessions that differentiate the social classes. These and many other goods are not distributed uniformly either in amounts or in quality. Some goods become *status symbols*, outward signs that the possessor has attained a certain economic or social rank. Those who are moving up usually are quick to acquire the symbols of their new rank. They buy a bigger home in a more prestigious area, trade their modest car for a larger one, and perhaps purchase fur coats for the women of the family.

The effects that material possessions have on a person's way of life also constitute major differences among the classes. Living in an overcrowded tenement is different from living in a modest ranch house or a spacious mansion. One may have no fine clothes, only one set of Sunday clothes, or many fine clothes. The poor person may have to buy a worn-out used car, while the wealthy person can buy a new Lincoln or Cadillac and trade it in regularly. Such differences in material possessions affect how we feel about ourselves, how others see us, and how we behave.

Political-Economic Attitudes Questionnaires, opinion polls, area analyses of voting patterns all yield ample sociological evidence that people of different social classes think differently about political and economic issues; they perceive the world and its problems in different ways.[14] The lower the social class, the more likely one is to favor labor unions. Working class people view various government regulations of business and industry as desirable, while the upper

---

[14]Many stratification theorists have stressed the different political and economic attitudes expressed by people of diverse ranks; this phenomenon has been called the interest group theory of social classes. For an early study in this area see Richard Centers, *The Psychology of Social Classes* (Princeton, N.J.: Princeton University Press, 1949).

Some goods become status symbols, outward signs of a certain economic or social rank. People moving up are quick to acquire such goods.

classes regard them as unnecessary interference. On the other hand, political scientists and sociologists have discovered that the exercise of constitutionally guaranteed civil liberties is positively related to social status. One study found that about two-thirds of professional and semiprofessional men had tolerant attitudes toward civil liberties, while about half of the clerical and sales workers and only 30 percent of the manual workers expressed tolerant attitudes.[15] Another study revealed that 66 percent of college graduates said that they voted in the last presidential election. Yet only 58 percent of the high school graduates and 43 percent of those who did not go beyond grade school voted in that election.[16] What is more, there is a strong tendency for working class people to vote Democratic, and for upper class people to vote Republican.

The list of specific differences in political and economic attitudes among the social classes could be extended considerably. Actually, it is not hard to under-

---

[15]Seymour M. Lipset, "Democracy and the Working Class Authoritarianism," *American Sociological Review* 24 (August 1959), 486.

[16]For persons reporting that they voted in 1968 and 1970 by income level, education, age, race, and sex see U.S. Bureau of the Census, *Statistical Abstract of The United States, 1972* (Washington, D.C.: 1972), p. 374.

Could the social class of these people have something to do with their parading on the 4th of July?

stand why the "haves" and the "have nots" perceive society and its problems differently, and why they hold different beliefs concerning how to correct the economic and political ills they perceive.

Social Participation In many ways our relations with others are affected by social class. The higher our social status, the more likely we are to belong to and participate in formal organizations, and to hold leadership roles in them. Yet lower class people do not seem to compensate for their low participation in formal groups through informal contacts with close friends. One study found that while 30 percent of unskilled workers reported that they had no close friends,

---

Have your class construct a questionnaire designed to probe the social, political, and economic attitudes of people. Give this questionnaire to people in different social classes—manual laborers, white-collar workers, professionals, and so on. See if the results show any consistent similarities within a class or any consistent differences between classes.

---

only 13 percent of the skilled workers and 10 percent of the professional and business men reported the same.[17]

The range of social contacts also varies by social class. Typically, upper class people travel extensively, in this country and abroad; their social sphere is often international. They may maintain several homes in different parts of the United States. Upper-middle class people may once in their lives have vacationed in Europe, but their sphere of activities is usually within their own section of the country. Many lower class people live out their lives in one geographically restricted area.

In part, the patterns of social participation differ among the classes according to the differing availability of money for traveling, joining formal groups, and giving and attending parties. Also, the knowledge and skill required to seek out compatible groups in one's own town or city are not distributed evenly by social class. And the social activities of the classes differ according to the values placed on belonging to groups and on interacting with others.

SOCIAL MOBILITY

Social mobility refers to the movement of a person from one position to another—*horizontal* when the change in position does not change prestige, *vertical* when movement is up or down the status hierarchy. By *social mobility* sociologists usually mean *vertical* mobility. Most Americans believe that there is, or should be, a great deal of social mobility in the United States. "There is room at the top." "Any boy can grow up to be President." Although probably few believe the second claim anymore, if indeed they ever did, many people seem to believe that most people can improve their lot in life and rise above their parents' social position. Before turning to the social mobility pattern in the United States, we must look first at some basic concepts, and at how social mobility is measured.

[17]Joseph A. Kahl, *The American Class Structure* (New York: Holt, Rinehart and Winston, 1957), pp. 137–138.

MEASUREMENT OF SOCIAL MOBILITY

Vertical social mobility can be either of two kinds of vertical movement. First, and most commonly, we can move above or below the social status of our parents; this is called *intergenerational* mobility. One way that our status could be compared with our parents' is by means of an occupational prestige scale, like that in Table 7–4. It could be seen whether our occupational status is higher or lower than that of our parents, and if so, by how much. Although occupation is only one of many status characteristics, it can be used to determine how many mobile people there are. Further, if the data were available, we could compare the rates of vertical mobility in different societies or in one society at different periods of time.

Intragenerational mobility refers to movement upward or downward within a person's own working lifetime. We are compared with ourselves at different periods of our work lives to see whether in the course of our careers our status rose or fell. Not all career lines provide the same opportunities for advancement or promotion, so a rise in income or prestige that is normal in one type of job may be unusual upward mobility in another type. For this reason, intragenerational studies of upward mobility do not tell as much about the open or closed nature of the stratification system as do intergenerational studies.

Measurement of social mobility is more difficult than it might seem, particularly in specific cases. As an example, the son of an uneducated, unskilled worker graduated from high school and operated a small business for a time. When the business eventually failed, the son accepted unskilled employment much like his father's. The son was upwardly mobile, then downwardly mobile, while the net lifetime result was no mobility at all. Studies of the same person at different times would reach quite different conclusions. Or what about the rise or fall of an entire occupation in the prestige hierarchy? We saw in Table 7–4 that the prestige of policemen rose and that of radio announcers declined from 1947 to 1963. Should a person who remains in either profession during that period of rise or decline be considered vertically mobile? These and other measurement difficulties make our conclusions about social mobility less precise than we would like them to be.

TECHNOLOGICAL CHANGE AND VERTICAL MOBILITY

When a society becomes industrialized the expanded need for workers is usually filled by taking people away from the farms. Industrialization, then, is bound to change the occupational structure of a society by creating new kinds of jobs. As it continues, industrialization moves people about in the stratification system.

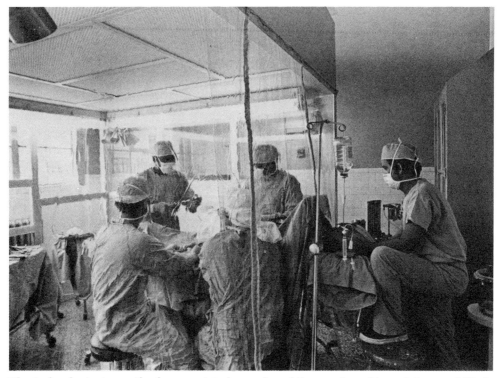

The technological growth of our society has reduced the number of low status, unskilled jobs and enlarged the proportion of skilled workers.

At the present stage of industrialization in the United States, more top level, high prestige positions are being created, and low status, unskilled jobs are becoming increasingly scarce. People to fill the new top level executive positions can come only from some place lower in the status hierarchy. The growing complexity of our industrialized society demands more skilled workers and foremen, who come chiefly from the ranks of the unskilled. Thus, technological changes in the United States today have assured social mobility, much of it upward.

FERTILITY DIFFERENTIALS AND VERTICAL MOBILITY

Traditionally, social status has been inversely related to family size. At times, the higher economic, educational, and occupational classes were not even replacing their numbers, and for a long time they have not contributed their proportional share to the total population growth. This circumstance alone has made some room at the top. For example, assume that a society needs a certain proportion of professional workers in the general population. As the population grows, more professional workers are needed to fill that need. Even if the children of every professional worker became professionals themselves, if there were not enough children, there would be unfilled professional positions. These positions could be filled only from below, thus assuring some upward mobility. In recent years, the differences in family size by social class have narrowed, but they have not disappeared. Class differences in reproduction thus still help assure that there will be some mobility in the United States, although these differences are not as strong a factor as they once were.

EXTENT OF OCCUPATIONAL MOBILITY

Entrance of blacks and women into many areas of the labor market is so recent and is still on so minor a scale (although it is growing) that the best evidence on social mobility is about *men*. The best estimate is that one-half to three-fourths of those in professional, business, clerical, and skilled labor positions have a higher position in the occupational prestige hierarchy than did their fathers. Collectively, this includes a high proportion of the male workers in the United States. Half or more of the men at any one of these levels see around them men like themselves, men who have been upwardly mobile from the status of their fathers. It is no wonder that the stratification system appears to be open and fluid.

At the higher levels both the total number of workers and their percentage of the total work force are relatively small. Even recruitment of half the professional workers from below produces upward mobility for only about three percent of the male labor force. It is true, too, that the sons of upper level fathers tend to stay at that level. Their chances of remaining at the top are from five to eight times greater than for those who fill top positions from below. Thus, technological change, and not the downward mobility of the sons of high status fathers, has produced upward mobility.

Between any two generations, advances in the status hierarchy are more likely to be short moves rather than dramatic "rags to riches" changes. This fact results in more mobile people. For when one new top level position is created, the odds are that it will be filled by someone from the middle ranks, thus creating a new vacancy in the middle. Perhaps three or four sons can be mobile because of one new top level position. If the new high level position were filled by someone from the very bottom, as occasionally happens, only one son would be mobile. Although such major intergenerational changes do sometimes occur,

MUST SOME ALWAYS BE MORE EQUAL THAN OTHERS?

Social stratification appears in some form in all societies. The social rewards may vary among societies, but differences in the distribution of these rewards are found everywhere. Even in the People's Republic of China, where the differences in financial rewards are kept to a minimum, it is clear that prestige is differentially bestowed. All students and professionals are required, at least at some point in their lives, to join the peasants in the fields during planting and harvests.

Even physicians, who are among the best-rewarded noncorporate entrepreneurs in our society, have strictly limited incomes in China. But their prestige is clearly more than that of, say, a coolie. And of course the leaders and bureaucrats high up in the state apparatus have far more power and prestige, and presumably more wealth, than anyone else in China. If even such a rigidly egalitarian society as China's is not without differentials in reward, can any society expect to be?

Clearly, a socialist society is not likely to be egalitarian. A government that represents the people, that holds almost all property in the name of the people, cannot function without immense authority and power. And it is almost impossible to imagine power and authority without prestige. Apparently only an anarchist society could ever achieve complete equality of all social rewards. On the face of it, however, an anarchist society is the Utopian vision least likely to succeed.

Perhaps the question is better rephrased: Can societies operate efficiently and beneficially with only a minimum of differences among social rewards of wealth, power, and prestige? To this question there seems to be an affirmative answer. Sociologists are beginning to find some agreement on points that relate to this question.

For one thing, immense differentials in wealth are not functional. A corporate executive who annually earns $100,000 or more, or even far less than that, is receiving at least a partially symbolic reward. Is the executive motivated to perform by the spending power of his or her earnings? Or is he or she motivated by the prestige built into such a salary? It would seem that the salary, or much of it, symbolizes the executive's worth more than it represents that person's physical needs.

There is evidence from many societies, besides the government-imposed egalitarianism of China, that people can be socialized to perform necessary and valuable social functions without the promise of immense financial and symbolic rewards. Would our society benefit from efforts to socialize its members in such a direction?

Do an intergenerational study on social mobility. Select 25 people and compare the occupations of the person's grandparents and parents to that of the person. How often was there upward social mobility? Downward mobility? How often was it impossible to determine whether there was mobility caused by the changing nature of occupations?

---

the more modest rises of the masses are what produce our relatively high rate of vertical mobility.

Although international comparisons are difficult, the rate of social mobility, as determined by occupational changes, appears to be only slightly greater in the United States than in most European countries. This suggests that wherever massive technological change is found, it results in a certain amount of social fluidity.

The surest pathway to upward social mobility is through education—at least for white males. Even though education has not yet worked so well for blacks and females, the data presented in Table 7–2 indicate that even in these categories the better educated earn more than the less educated. It is true that education alone will not allow a person, even a white male, to reach the very top, for it is almost impossible to enter the upper class except by birth. For the masses, however, the more education one has, the better are one's chances of moving upward and of competing successfully for the economic rewards of society. Current programs like Headstart and massive efforts to reduce the school dropout rate should make the educational avenue of mobility available to more people. To the extent that such programs work, in the future there should be more competition for middle and high level positions.

IS SOCIAL STRATIFICATION NECESSARY?

Are the differential rewards and the impact of the stratification system on the lives of people necessary? Must group living inevitably bring about a system of unequal distribution of rewards and privileges? The functional theory of stratification holds that no society could exist or survive without a system of differential rewards and privileges; for every society has division of labor, and

The reality for an overwhelming majority of adults is that they must work to earn a living, often at jobs they dislike. Can you think of any alternative to this reality?

people do not fill identical positions or perform identical jobs.[18] Some jobs are more pleasant than others, some are more difficult than others, and some are more necessary than others. Because in all societies talent and intelligence are distributed unevenly, every society must have some system of differential rewards to motivate the most talented people to prepare themselves to fill the most important positions. Lesser rewards are attached to less important positions, and the fewest rewards are attached to those positions requiring the least talent or training. Although this reasoning may seem persuasive, there is no guarantee

[18]Kingsley Davis and Wilbert E. Moore, "Some Principles of Stratification," *The American Sociological Review* 10 (April 1945), 242–249.

that a system of differential rewards and privileges is the only way to motivate talented people to undergo the training and to accept the important jobs.

The kibbutzim, communal settlements in Israel, hold that all necessary work is good and that everyone should work for the good of the group, without regard for personal gains.[19] Each does what he or she is able to do in accordance with the needs of the group, and all are rewarded equally. These small communal societies have been able to avoid a stratification system up to a point. Thus, it seems that differential rewards are not the only way to fill the various positions in a society. But the Israeli kibbutz is not a complete, self–sufficient industrialized society, for its members depend on the larger society for some key services, such as those of physicians and dentists.

CRITICS AND VARIABLES

The functional theory of stratification has been sharply debated by some sociologists. Melvin Tumin, for example, has dealt in detail with the dysfunctions of a stratification system.[20] Such a system, Tumin maintains, limits the discovery and use of talent because the talented among the poor are unlikely to develop or to be found. Thus, the productivity of society is impaired. In addition, according to Tumin, social inequalities encourage hostility, suspicion, and distrust among the social classes. These criticisms of stratification, however, have not persuaded functionalists that systems of differential rewards are not necessary or inevitable, and the debate continues.[21]

Even if stratification is considered a necessity, the necessity alone does not dictate the *kind* of stratification system. Honorific rewards can be stressed instead of tangible rewards such as income. Nor must there be great differences in the rewards, whatever they are. The system can be relatively open, allowing people to readily move up or down, or it can restrict movement. In any or all of these respects the stratification system of a society can change over time.

In the last several chapters, we have studied how societies are organized and held together. We have looked at the process of socialization and at the ways

[19]Melford Spiro, *Kibbutz; Venture in Utopia* (Cambridge, Mass.: Harvard University Press, 1956), pp. 19–31.

[20]Melvin Tumin, "Some Principles of Stratification: A Critical Analysis," *The American Sociological Review* 18 (August 1953), 387–393.

[21]Kingsley Davis, "Reply to Tumin," *American Sociological Review* 18 (August 1953), 394.

in which we become contributing members of our society. We have looked, too, at the positions we fill and the roles we play in groups, institutions, and social classes. It is now time to study in more detail the five major institutions whose function it is to meet our enduring physical and social needs. The next part of this book, Part III, takes up each institution in turn, beginning, in the next chapter, with the institution of the family.

SUMMARY POINTS AND QUESTIONS

1. *Social stratification* refers to a social and economic ranking system in which a society's members are arranged from highest to lowest according to the rewards and privileges they receive.

> *What is the difference between rank and a class?*
>
> *What are some of the possible dimensions on which a person may be ranked?*
>
> *What is meant by status consistency?*

2. A rigid stratification system in which there is little or no movement from level to level is referred to as a *caste system*.

> *How does the open class stratification system differ from a caste system?*
>
> *Give an example of each.*

3. In a stratified society, members receive differential rewards. In most industrial societies, these rewards tend to be money, prestige, and power.

> *What is meant by prestige?*
>
> *How can power be considered a reward?*

4. In the United States, there is a wide range of income and prestige inequalities. Some are along racial and sexual lines.

> *On what is occupational prestige based?*
>
> *Do the same jobs always carry the same prestige? If not, why not?*

5. Social class affects one's life chances. This is exemplified by differential rates of mental illness, infant mortality, the number of children per family, educational success, and the age of marriage.

> *What other indicators of life chances also differ by class?*

6. Social class also affects life style variables such as the material possessions one owns, the political–economic attitudes one holds, social participation, and socialization practices.

> How do each of these variables differ from class to class?

7. *Functional theory* holds that stratification is necessary to assure that the most important positions are filled by persons willing and capable of performing the duties of the positions.

> How does this process work?

> How might stratification be dysfunctional to a society?

8. *Social mobility* refers to movement from one position on the social ladder to another. It might be measured in terms of *intergenerational mobility* or *intragenerational mobility*.

> How do these differ?

> Which do you think is the better measure of mobility?

9. *Verticle mobility* is possible when there is an inverse relationship between class and family size, and when technological change results in the creation of new high status occupations.

> What are examples of technological changes which have resulted in
> a high incidence of upward mobility?

> Has technological change ever resulted in downward mobility? Give
> an example.

SUGGESTED READINGS

Bendix, Reinhard and Seymour Lipset, eds. *Class, Status and Power.* 2nd ed. New York: Free Press, 1966. A collection of essays on theoretical approaches to class, differential class behavior, social mobility, and stratification issues in post–industrial society.

Bottomore, T. B. *Classes in Modern Society.* New York: Pantheon Books, 1966. Offers an interesting discussion of the basis of class, the effects of class on technology, and the development of modern class ideologies.

Davis, Kingsley and Wilbert E. Moore. "Some Principles of Stratification." *American Sociological Review* 10 (April 1945): 242–249. An article that summarizes the functional approach to stratification.

Dollard, John. *Caste and Class in a Southern Town.* Garden City, N.Y.: Doubleday, 1957. A study of a southern town highlighting the aspect of stratification along racial lines. It points out the gains of whites from segregation.

Domhoff, G. William. *Who Rules America?* Englewood Cliffs, N.J.: Prentice-Hall, 1967. A study aimed at discovering whether or not the upper class is also a governing class. Shows the extent to which the upper class controls the corporate structure, the political institutions, and institutions that affect public opinion in the United States.

Heller, Celia S., ed. *Structured Social Inequality*. New York: Macmillan, 1969. A reader in comparative social stratification. It presents a wide variety of essays on the theories, types, dimensions, and consequences of stratification.

Lopreato, Joseph and Lawrence Hazelrigg. *Class, Conflict, and Mobility*. San Francisco: Chandler, 1972. A comprehensive volume on stratification. Begins with the theories of Marx, Pareto, Dahrendorf, and Weber and shows how these theories have been applied to social phenomena.

Lundberg, Ferdinand. *The Rich and the Superrich*. New York: Grosset and Dunlap, 1968. A brilliant analysis of the upper class in American society. It focuses on how the rich got their wealth and the institutions in American society that allow the rich to keep control of their wealth.

Veblen, Thorstein. *The Theory of the Leisure Class*. New York: Random House, 1934. Originally published in 1899, this classical work in American sociology critiques the upper class for their failure to perform any meaningful function for society.

Warner, William Lloyd. *Yankee City*. New Haven: Yale University Press, 1959. A classical community study. It focuses on the stratification system of Newburyport, Massachusetts and the effect of bureaucratization on that system. It is an excellent source on the methodology used to analyze stratification.

III

UNDERSTANDING SOCIAL INSTITUTIONS

Since all the social elements are indispensable to society, none can be said to be more important than the others. But one set of social elements—social institutions—perform such a variety of complex and interlocking functions that as a group they demand lengthy study on their own. Once again, sociologists adopt a familiar word to stand for, perhaps, an unfamiliar concept. Whatever their importance to sociologists, institutions usually assume humble enough disguises in the real world. The cathedrals, magnificent university campuses, gigantic industrial plants, the White House, and Capitol Hill are not common to the everyday experiences of most of us. We are far more familiar with supermarkets and hardware stores, neighborhood churches, banks, schools, and our families' homes or apartments.

Yet each of these is part of an institution, for sociologists define institutions as those enduring social groupings and their interwoven folkways, mores, and laws built around one or more functions. The functions of institutions are as old as human life, for they correspond to permanent human needs. And once again, although we can use the sociological method to isolate the social institutions, in the real world these institutions are interdependent, interlocking, and interacting. Several will combine to perform one function, and any one institution will perform, in whole or in part, more than one function.

What are the basic functions that institutions combine to fulfill? There are three functions, and we've seen them before in this book. The first function is to ensure physical survival; the second, to maintain order and harmony within the group; and the third, to provide for the individual's psychological well-being.

Sociologists find the same five institutions in every society, although in many societies two or more institutions may overlap in the same group of people. For example, in many primitive tribal societies that subsist by hunting game and gathering roots, the institution of the family and the economic institution may be the same group. This group might also be the educational institution.

In our own society large bureaucracies, division of labor, and specialization make the five social institutions visible as distinct, separate entities. The family, education, religion, government, and the economy, while interwoven in a complex network, are each nevertheless separately recognizable. However, over the last couple of centuries, and especially in the past several decades of our century, each institution has changed markedly.

The family, for example, although still the major socializing agent, has given up much of that role to education. It has even given up part of the socializing role to television, thus accelerating the entrance of secondary groups into our lives. Marriage was once the unchallenged regulator of sexual conduct. Premarital and extramarital sex go back at least as far as Biblical times, but they were considered immoral, and in most societies were illegal. In our society notions of acceptable sexual conduct are changing; more and more people think sex outside of marriage is not wrong.

The immense changes in our economic institutions over many generations gradually made the education institution stronger as a socializing force in our lives. To be productive members in society, we have to know much more than our ancestors had to know. At the same time these economic changes have gradually shrunk the economic importance of the family. The family has been transformed from a productive unit to a consumer unit. And although the extended family was common in our agrarian past, it is virtually nonexistent in our present urban, industrial society.

The increased importance of education and its growth into a major bureaucratic institution have made the schools an arena of perpetual controversy. Traditionalists maintain that schools are meant only to impart information and train the young in mental skills essential to the economically productive good citizen. Progressives maintain that the schools must live up to their recently acquired duties as socializing agents. They must deal not only with minds but with the whole person. Still others attack the schools for failure to provide equality of opportunity. Blacks, most minorities, and the poor of all races get less from our schools than does the white middle class.

As you can conclude from the chapter on stratification, education is not the only institution that is doing a less than perfect job in fulfilling its basic social functions. As we have grown from our agrarian roots into an advanced industrial society, we have also become a mass society. More and more, gigantic industrial, business, and government bureaucracies have come to dominate our lives and determine our fates. As our industrialized economy spawned immense trusts and monopolies, government necessarily began to grow in order to control them.

Government itself reached its bureaucratic maturity in the Great Depression of the 1930s, when the economy broke down and left millions in utter poverty and misery. The government took upon itself the task of running the economy, and to this day it still tries to manage the economy. Once government stepped into the economy, not only did it never step entirely back out, it began to assume other social responsibilities as well. A survey of current government regulatory and social agencies would be staggering, especially if compared with a survey of 1930, or even of 1950.

Much of what happens in society, from the economic, political, and social welfare of minorities to the relations between consumer and producer, is no longer left to the conscience of the individual or the group. Government has assumed a significant role as the conscience of society. Whether this is good or bad is not for sociologists to say. But they can ask, among other questions, where this puts the institution of religion in relation to the social functions that institutions are supposed to perform.

In the past several centuries religion has undergone constant changes in its social power and importance. In the early Middle Ages in Europe, religion was society. In those disjointed times after the fall of the Roman Empire, the Church was the only institution with unquestioned power and authority. The Church possessed the word of truth, and it was the earthly representative of God.

The situation of religion in our own society is clearly quite different. Our constitutional separation of church and state protects each religion or sect from the others. But it also limits the social power of religion itself. Over the centuries, religion has surrendered one area after another of secular authority. Few in Western societies take the Biblical account of creation literally. The Church once burned at the stake people who claimed that the earth is round or that the sun, not the earth, is the center of the solar system. Today a scientist can say that many planets in the universe are likely to have intelligent life, and not a murmur of objection is heard from churchmen.

What, then, is the social function of religion in our present-day society? Religion offers to its believers the solace of ultimate answers to the questions that we bewildered humans have always raised. Its beliefs and rituals, its sacred objects and prayers enable believers to face life and its tragedies as something other than meaningless and cruel. But can't religion, by its claims to supernatural sources of truth, create problems if society is changing against the wishes of a powerful religious body? It can and it has, as you will see. But religions have also been the sources of social change, often when society has not been living up to its professed cultural values. Ministers, priests, and nuns were in the forefront of civil rights activities in the 1960s and the antiwar movement of the late '60s and early '70s. But whether religion, or any other institution, group, or person, resists or promotes change, it is not for sociologists to say that the change is desirable or undesirable.

Remember how, as a child, you learned from your family to be increasingly self-reliant and to live harmoniously with others? And how you also received and returned love and emotional support? In every society families have such functions, and they serve other purposes as well. Marriage and the family regulate the sexual impulses of a society's members and assure the physical survival of the young. Beyond these common functions, families can differ greatly among societies. All societies have nuclear families (parents and their young offspring), but many also have some form of extended family (grandparents, uncles, aunts, and cousins). Marriage norms regulate who marries whom. Endogamy restricts group members to marriage within the group; exogamy limits members to marriage outside the group. Monogamy allows one spouse to a man or woman; polygamy allows more than one to a man or woman.

8

THE FAMILY

When the social functions of the family are all lost, affection within the family, and in fact the family itself, will also be lost.

Kingsley Davis*

In eighteenth-century England and America a new religious sect called the Shakers espoused the value of sexual abstinence for all members. Marriage was not allowed and the family did not exist. Even those who joined Shaker colonies as husband and wife lived without sexual activity, as brothers and sisters. Except for the Shakers and other such experimental groups, marriage and the family are found in all human groupings. Why?

BIOLOGICAL ROOTS OF THE FAMILY

The human family is universal because some human biological characteristics are universal. Humans have a long period of dependency after birth. It takes at least 14 years for a human to achieve physical maturity, while most other mammals achieve maturity in no more than a few months. The human animal, with very few instincts to guide behavior, is highly dependent on learning. Humans, therefore, desperately need the help of others to survive and to learn how to continue to survive. There is thus a biological basis for a relatively stable and enduring group to meet the survival needs of the species.

What form the family originally took will never be known. Some sociologists and anthropologists speculate that the earliest family unit was the mother and her offspring.[1] The mother provided the only food the infant could receive and digest. She cared for the child and taught it until it was able to fend for itself. According to this theory, only later in human history did the adult male become a member of the group; thus, the family existed before marriage.

Other sociologists speculate that because the newborn needs constant and intense care, its survival would be in jeopardy if the mother had to leave it alone while she foraged for her own food. Because the mother needs food and

*Kingsley Davis, *Human Society*. New York: Macmillan, 1949.

[1]Robert Briffault, *The Mothers* (New York: The Macmillan Co., 1931).

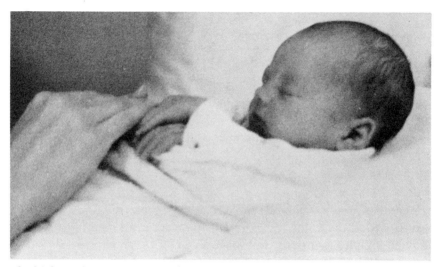

The biological roots of the family made plain: Try to imagine this infant surviving on its own.

because both mother and child need protection during the child's long period of helplessness, another person, the male, was probably part of the original family group. According to this theory, male and female joined together out of sexual attraction and remained together to rear their offspring; marriage came before the family.[2]

The second biological basis of the family is human sexual reproduction, which obviously requires the activity of both sexes. Humans have no "rutting" season (a recurring period of sexual excitement in many animals), and the female does not have to be in heat to mate. There is no human instinct to assure that males and females would pair off during a mating season and remain together afterward. On the contrary, with their unflagging sex drive, males and females would be continuously searching for sexual partners. It is speculated that uncontrolled sexual behavior would have created conflict, jealousy, and disruption. The sexual nature of males and females thus requires some controls such as are provided by marriage and the family.

THE FAMILY AND ITS BASIC SOCIAL FUNCTIONS

In Chapter 3 we noted that all societies face basic problems that must be solved if the group is to survive. Every human society has three common needs: (1) to ensure physical survival, (2) to maintain orderly group living, and (3) to provide

[2]Edward Westermarck, *The History of Human Marriage*, 5th ed. (London: Macmillan & Co., 1921).

for the psychological needs of its members. The family helps to solve these persistent problems through its *functions*.

How the functions of the family are performed is not determined by the family's biological roots but by human creativity and invention. Human creativity also determines the *form* the family will take and the kind of marriage on which it will be based. After clarifying what is meant by *marriage* and *family*, we will look more fully at the functions of the family and at how they are performed in various societies, particularly in our own. We then should be ready to discuss briefly the future of the family in the United States—to ask, "Are marriage and the family really dying institutions, and if so, what will happen to all of us?"

WHAT IS A FAMILY?

Without a modifier, the term *family* is not very precise. *Family* could mean any one of several groups. If a college woman says that she will be spending the holidays with her family, what does she mean? If she is married, she could mean that she, her husband, and their baby will remain on campus; but whether married or single, she could mean that she is going to her parents' home. She may also mean that she, her brothers and sisters, and their spouses and children, aunts, uncles, cousins, and grandparents are all going to gather for a family reunion.

Although it is often apparent from context what is meant by *family*, the social sciences have more precise designations for various types of families. Most basic is the *nuclear family*, a married pair and their immature offspring.[3] Every society recognizes this family form as a distinct grouping. Because the nuclear family is so important in the United States, you may not be impressed that it is universally found. But true *cultural universals* are so rare that it is quite remarkable to find no known exception to this rule: Every society recognizes the nuclear family as a unit distinct from the rest of society. Sometimes it is the only type of family recognized; more often the married pair and their offspring form the *nucleus* of other complex family forms.

In societies like ours people customarily belong to two nuclear families. We are born into a *family of orientation*, the family group that rears us and gives us our basic orientation to life. The family that a married pair begins with the birth of their first child is called their *family of procreation* (which is, of course, also their child's family of orientation).

In 92 out of 192 societies he studied, the anthropologist George P. Murdock found the *extended family*—that is, two or more nuclear families joined by an

[3]George Peter Murdock, *Social Structure* (New York: The Macmillan Co., 1949), p. 2.

213

Depending on the kinship ties of their culture, these people could make up two nuclear families or also an extended family.

extension of the parent–child relationship.[1] The extended family of the ancient Hebrews, for example, contained three generations: an older man and his wife or wives, his unmarried sons and daughters, and his married sons and their wives and children. Typically, all of the members of an extended family live together in a common residence or in nearby dwellings or in some clearly designated compound. People in extended families have closer bonds to fellow members than to their other relatives outside the group.

Societies with extended families distribute some functions of the family throughout the larger family beyond the nucleus. Childrearing, although considered the primary responsibility of the parents, may be shared by other adults, such as grandparents or uncles and aunts. Anthropologists have found that in some extended families roles are strictly assigned. Young sons are disciplined by their fathers and given affection and played with by their uncles; daughters are disciplined by mothers and loved and played with by aunts. Because most parents are also aunts and uncles, they usually play both roles at the same time, but with different children of course.

[1]Murdock, p. 2.

Although the nuclear family is the dominant form in the United States, some sociologists point out that extended family relationships are maintained to some extent. Make a list of all your relatives, and then note how often you have contacts with each of them. Also note the kinds of contacts you have. For example, do you see your grandparents or third cousins on a regular basis or only on special occasions? What is a "special occasion" for your family?

The extended family may be an economic unit in which all its members cooperate in a joint enterprise such as hunting or farming. Various forms of security are provided by the extended family: Older people are assured support and comfort; substitute parents are readily available for children whose parents die; and all members receive some form of aid and affection. Thus, the affectional function of the nuclear family is diluted. Even loyalty to one's spouse is limited by the demands of loyalty to the larger family group.

MARRIAGE: UNIVERSAL BUT VARIED

Marriage is a relationship between two sexually interacting adults, which is sufficiently enduring to provide for the procreation and rearing of children. Marriage is found in all societies, and every society regulates who may marry whom, how marriages are to be formed, and what are the reciprocal rights and duties of spouses. Despite considerable variation in the specific kinds of regulations, every society regulates its marriages and prescribes approved behavior for the spouses.

Every society regulates how many spouses a person can have. Since there are only two sexes, the possible combinations are not endless. The approved form of marriage may be *monogamy*, one man married to one woman. Or it may be *polygamy*, one spouse of either sex having two or more spouses of the opposite sex at the same time. *Polygyny* occurs when one man is married to more than one woman; *polyandry* happens when one woman is married to more than one man. *Group marriage* refers to two or more men married to two or more women. Some observers conclude from our high and rising divorce rate that we are evolving a variation of polygamy called *serial polygamy*, in which each spouse has more than one spouse, but in succession rather than simultaneously. Each basic form of marriage shows considerable variation from society to society. In polygyny the co-wives may be unrelated or they may be sisters, and in either case they may or may not have equal status. In polyandry the co-husbands are usually but not always brothers. Marriage forms also vary as to the roles of the marriage partners, the authority pattern of the family, and how easily the marriage bond can be severed. In almost every primitive society the role of husband includes those tasks that require the most physical strength and absence from the home. The woman, periodically incapacitated by pregnancy and bound to the home to nurse and rear children, is customarily assigned tasks that can be carried out around the home.

Such a division of labor frequently makes the woman dependent upon and subordinate to her husband. This dependency may explain the prevalence of the *patriarchal family,* in which the male has the power and authority. The sociologist Betty Yorburg contends that "Male superiority within the family, in prestige, authority, and privilege, is a fact of life in almost all known societies. No valid instances of true matriarchal societies have been known to exist."[5] In modern, industrialized societies the biological bases for woman's dependency are greatly reduced, and the patriarchal family is more difficult to justify.

RULES FOR MATE SELECTION: WHO MARRIES WHOM

Whatever their marriage form, all societies also regulate who may marry whom. Such rules are generally divided into *endogamous* and *exogamous.* Endogamous rules stipulate that a person must select a mate from *within* a certain group—say, from the same tribe or even from some smaller group within the tribe. Racial and religious endogamy are often found. Until recent decades, certain religious denominations in our society strictly enforced religious endogamy, and racial endogamy is still predominant. Racial and religious endogamy are irrelevant in primitive societies, for members share the same race and religion. Class endogamy is fairly common, even if it means only that the rulers and the ruled should not intermarry.

Exogamous rules stipulate that a person must select a marriage partner from *outside* some designated group. Generally, exogamous rules have a kinship basis; marriage is forbidden between persons related by blood or marriage. All societies have exogamous rules; they never refer only to members of the nuclear family but always define additional relatives as being too closely related to be acceptable marriage partners. Those outside the nuclear family who are prohibited by the exogamous regulations are not necessarily one's closest blood relatives.

Societies do not merely stipulate who are acceptable mates. They also regulate *how* a mate is to be obtained. In many places the marriage is arranged by the

[5]Betty Yorburg, *The Changing Family* (New York: Columbia University Press, 1973), p. 16.

**Why has every society evolved the institution of
marriage and a ceremony for those marrying?**

woman's or man's parents, a go–between, or a special functionary, and some
marriage partners do not meet until their wedding day. Arranged marriage is
no mere oddity of a few primitive societies but has been practiced in such ancient,
highly civilized societies as China, Japan, and India. Throughout history, millions
and millions of marriages have been arranged. The practice is said by some
advocates to result in wiser choices of marriage partners because those who
know the young people try to make reasonable choices without the complications
of passion or romantic love. Whether for this reason or some other, the divorce
rate is lower in societies where arranged marriage prevails.

David and Vera Mace report that in some societies young people, particularly
girls, defend the practice of arranged marriage on the grounds that adolescence
is a more relaxed period if it is uncomplicated by the necessity of attracting
a mate.[6] They see the "free enterprise" mate selection system as one in which

---

[6] David Mace and Vera Mace, *Marriage East and West* (New York: Doubleday and Co., 1960), pp. 144–145.

Do a study on students' attitudes toward marriage and children. Take a sample of students to find out how many see themselves married in the future. Ask if they plan to have children and, if so, how many.

---

there would always be uncertainty and the secret fear that one might be unsuccessful in finding a mate. With arranged marriage, they know that their parents will strive diligently to find them the best possible marriage partner. As we see later, however, the higher incidence of failure among marriages that have not been arranged could result from many factors other than the emphasis on passion or romantic love.

Whether marriages are arranged or the partners choose each other, all societies have a marriage rite or ceremony. It may be a simple ritual, such as publicly exchanging gifts, or a very elaborate affair accompanied by feasting and celebration. In any case, the function of the marriage rite is to announce to the group that the parties are changing their status from single to married and that they are assuming all the responsibilities, rights, and privileges of their new positions.

FUNCTIONS OF THE FAMILY

"To live and to cause to live, to eat food and to beget children, these were the primary wants of men of the past, and they will be the primary wants of men in the future so long as the world lasts."[7] Thus the anthropologist Sir James Frazer explained the prevalent use of magical rites by early humans to regulate the seasons. But his words also describe two basic functions of the family: the economic function—the need to provide food and other goods and services—and the reproductive function. These and the other functions of the family are all essential, and they are tightly intermingled with one another.

THE REPRODUCTIVE FUNCTION: MAKING BABIES

In order to perpetuate itself a society must have offspring. It must therefore endorse the value that reproduction of the species is good, and it must encourage the birth of young. The biology of reproduction does not require marriage, yet all societies have adopted a general norm concerning childbearing: It should occur *in* the family, not *outside* the family. Many societies differ as to how

[7]Sir James G. Frazer, *The New Golden Bough*, ed. Theodor H. Gaster (New York: Criterion Books, 1959), p. 284.

To have its members reproduce is a major goal of every society, for unless new generations succeed old, any society would perish.

they define this norm and adjust it to their own situation. Some societies encourage few children, others many (the infant mortality rate may determine how many births are encouraged). Societies are not equally successful in restricting childbearing to the family, nor equally tolerant when children are born outside the family.

Throughout most of human history population grew very slowly; for this reason societies encouraged couples not only to have children but to have many children. As recently as 1944, the Soviet Union tried to encourage large families by making payments to families ranging from 400 rubles for the third child up to 5000 rubles for the tenth and subsequent children.[8] Honors were also bestowed: a Motherhood Medal to those who had five and six children; the Order of Motherhood Glory to those who had seven, eight, or nine children; Heroine Mother for those who had ten. Much of this drive for a high birth rate can

[8]William F. Kenkel, *The Family in Perspective*, 3rd ed. (New York: Appleton–Century–Crofts, 1973), p, 114.

American families still consider reproduction an important function. But by 2000 the population might be at zero population growth.

be explained by the severe destruction done to the male population by World War II. Still, even before this, in 1936, the Soviets forbade abortion except for serious medical considerations in order to encourage large families.

Today in the Soviet Union abortion is free and easy to obtain, and there are no longer medals for bearing children. We are now accustomed to hearing about overpopulation problems and the effort being spent on encouraging small families. We may need to be reminded that the value of small families is a relatively recent one and that its acceptance is still chiefly in industrialized societies.

The Reproductive Function and the American Family The various measures of fertility and the effects of our fertility habits on the population size are discussed in Chapter 13. Here we take only a quick, statistical look at how the American family is performing its reproductive function. The *crude birth rate*, the number of births per thousand people in the total population, is one measure of the reproductive function. In 1915, the crude birth rate was 25. The rate began to drop in the 1920s and reached a low of 16.7 in the depression year of 1936. Thereafter it began slowly to climb, again reaching 25 after World War II. From 1947 to 1958, the crude birth rate remained at or close to 25. What at first appeared to be a slight decline is now more pronounced. The crude birth rate in 1965 was 19.5 and stands now at about 15.[9]

In 1910 married women between the ages of 45 and 49 (beyond their childbearing years) had an average of 4.74 children during their fertile years. In 1960 women of comparable age had 2.40 children, but it was up to 2.95 for women who completed childbearing in 1971. Over the years, nevertheless, families have indeed been getting smaller.

A society can suffer from a birth rate that is too high as well as from a rate that is too low. In the United States, the small family is back in style, and the number of childless couples is beginning to increase. It is significant, too, that the value of low reproduction is basically accepted. Today couples are not criticized for having no children or for having only one or two. In response to changing conditions, the expression of the reproductive function of the American family has changed—but of course it remains important for the survival of our society.

The social rules of reproduction restrict childbearing to the family. Not all countries keep records on illegitimacy, so it is difficult to determine how our ratio of legitimate to illegitimate childbearing compares to the ratio in other societies. For instance, in 1918 Russia removed all distinctions between legitimate and illegitimate children; it thus legally abolished illegitimacy and stated that "actual descent is regarded as the basis of the family."[10] The name of the father of an illegitimate child could not be used on the birth certificate or school records, and the father was not required to support the child. Although difficult to determine precisely, the number of children born out of wedlock in the Soviet Union is substantial. There is also some evidence of a return to an earlier policy of requiring fathers to support their children born out of wedlock.

Until the mid 1950s, fewer than 4 percent of all births in the United States were illegitimate. Now the figure is about 10 percent—over 300,000 babies a year.[11] In recent years some of the stigma has been removed from illegitimacy, and some women are choosing to have babies outside marriage because they want to be mothers but not wives. Thus, the reproductive function of the family has increasing competition, but not nearly enough to threaten its continued existence.

[9]The number of births and the crude birth rate are reported by U.S. Department of Health, Education and Welfare, *Monthly Vital Statistics Report.*

[10]Kenkel, p. 100.

[11]Number and rates of illegitimate births are reported in U.S. Department of Health, Education and Welfare, *Vital Statistics of the United States* (Washington, D.C.: U.S. Government Printing Office), published annually.

Visit an adoption agency and try to find out what are used as criteria for selecting parents. How do ideal adoptive parents differ from typical natural parents?

THE SOCIALIZATION FUNCTION: TEACHING BABIES

A sufficient crop of infants each year does not in itself assure the survival of a society. Enough of the infants must live to adulthood and must have children of their own who live to adulthood. More than simple physical survival of individuals in needed, however. As we discussed in Chapter 4, all infants must undergo extensive training to acquire the correct personality traits, to internalize the group's values and norms, and to acquire the skills and knowledge necessary for participating in and perpetuating society. No society that wishes to avoid extinction can escape socializing its young. It can, however, determine what is to be included in the socialization process, and who is to do the socializing.

In almost all societies the family is extremely important in socializing the young, and it is usually the first socializing agent. This primacy of contact is significant, for never again will people be as pliable as they are in infancy and early childhood. The learning and experiences of later years will reinforce or contradict what was learned in the home, but later learning must always reckon with the family's early influences on personality development.

The family usually maintains its socializing influence through most of pre-adult life; the repetition and continuity in training and experience assist in establishing basic values and personality traits. Many of the basic values of a society—its fears, superstitions, taboos—first reach the young through the family.

The Family and Socialization: A Changing Role Though it is a major socializing agency, the family is not the only one. Most societies devise other ways to help socialize the young. Modern societies have schools, churches, youth groups, and the like. But even in nonliterate societies, adults outside the family have some part in teaching children the beliefs, values, and practices of the culture. In the Israeli kibbutz, from their birth on, children live separately from their parents in children's houses, where they are reared by specially trained nurses.[12] Children

[12]For a good discussion of kibbutz childrearing practices see Melford E. Spiro, *Children of the Kibbutz* (Cambridge, Mass.: Harvard University Press, 1958); and Rivkah Bar-Yosef, "The Pattern of Early Socialization in the Collective Settlements in Israel," *Human Relations* 12 (1959), 345–360.

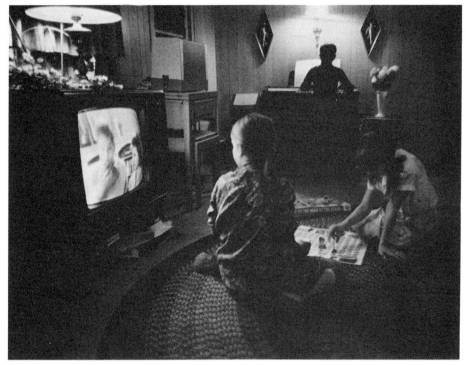

For almost all children in our culture television is an important part of life—and of their socialization.

visit their parents for an hour or two daily, but parents are not the chief agents of socialization. In the kibbutz, the family has a minor role in the socialization of the young.

Long ago the Soviet Union developed day nurseries for children from about two months to about three years of age. These are multifunction institutions, feeding and clothing the children, checking their health, instructing them on many matters, and carefully supervising play activities during the day while the parents work. Although there are not enough places in the day nurseries for most Russian children, millions have been reared in this way. From all indications this sharing of socialization between family and nursery has worked well.[13]

The American family has always had a central role in the socialization of children. Today, however, it shares this function with other agencies much more

[13]For a good discussion of the purposes, types, and functioning of Soviet day nurseries, see Vera Fediaevsky, *Nursery School and Parent Education in Soviet Russia* (New York: E. P. Dutton & Co., 1936).

than it did in earlier times. From age two or three to well beyond puberty, more and more American children come under the influence of socialization forces outside the family, particularly in the schools. Not only do the schools teach academic subjects, but they frequently offer driver training and family life education. In addition, they provide guidance personnel to help youngsters with their plans for adult life. In the schools children learn basic values such as the importance of getting ahead and, paradoxically, the importance of not being too different from other children. Outside the school, commercial agencies and community recreation programs teach children how to swim, to dance, to ride horses, to play tennis, and often reinforce the values learned in school.

Children spend many hours a week, sometimes several hours a day, watching television. It is impossible to determine exactly what children learn from it, but sociologists and most parents know that they learn much. A parent who makes some remark to a child about a circus, a city on the other side of the world, the life of beavers, or any of a million other topics has come to expect the response, "Oh yeah, I saw that on television." The longer years of formal education, the expanded offerings of the schools, television, and the special agencies for teaching children various skills take from the family some of its domination and control over the socialization of children.

When ours was a rural economy, parents taught their children many of the skills needed to be successful adults, but this is no longer true. To become an adult capable of functioning adequately in today's society requires specialized knowledge and skills, which most families cannot provide for their children. Even such skills as dancing and swimming often can be taught more easily and effectively by specialists outside the family. But when it comes to the knowledge and skills needed to make a living in the modern world, specialists outside the family are absolutely essential. While the family has lost its prominence in the socialization function, it is to society's distinct advantage that other agencies share the task of socializing the young.

THE STATUS ASCRIPTION FUNCTION: WHO AM I AND WHO ARE YOU?

To maintain orderly group living, a society must assign status and position to its members. The family plays an important role in this status ascription function, a process that begins when the family gives a name to its newborn child. With its name, the child acquires a position in the family and an answer to the question, "Who am I?"

As children grow older, they learn their various positions. Some people are

---

Interview the parents of children ranging in age from newborn to 7 years. Ask how much time the child spends with its mother or father, playmates, a baby-sitter, at school, watching television, and so on. What do the results of your study suggest about the relative importance of the family in the socialization process?

---

cousins, aunts and uncles, and grandparents; and the child is a grandchild, a cousin, and a nephew or niece. In a primitive society, children learn that they are members of a larger kin grouping, or clan. Children in modern society learn of their family's social class, religion, and race. Although children may eventually change some of these statuses, such as class or religion, their initial placement is made by the family. Through the status ascription function of the family, members of a society learn who they are and how they fit into the larger group.

THE SEXUAL REGULATION FUNCTION: CONTROLLING SEXUAL BEHAVIOR

The family function of regulating sexual behavior helps to solve all three of the basic problems facing any society (physical survival, orderly group living, and the individual's psychological needs). We have seen that sexual behavior must be permitted and encouraged if the group is to perpetuate itself. Sexual behavior also must be regulated to maintain harmonious group living. For the sexual drive is a powerful force, and its uncontrolled expression would disrupt orderly group living. Yet because sex is a strong, basic human drive, any society that attempted to prohibit all sexual behavior would risk serious discontent among its members.

All societies, therefore, must regulate and control the sexual drive while also providing for its expression. In every society the principal source of sexual satisfaction is supposed to be found in marriage. Even while allowing for sexual expression, marriage limits and restricts sexuality. Many primitive societies, for example, have taboos on sexual relations between husband and wife during menstruation, or for some stipulated period before and after the birth of a child, or even before a big hunt or religious festival. Most important, marriage limits sexual expression by stipulating the people with whom one cannot have sexual relations—that is, with those to whom one is not married.

The Universal Incest Taboo One control over sexual behavior found in all societies is the primary *incest taboo,* which forbids sexual relations between

Societies have evolved rules for dating and courtship to regulate the sexual drive.

parent and child and between brother and sister.[14] The primary taboo is always extended to include other relatives. Which other relatives are taboo, whether cousins, uncles and aunts, or grandparents, depends on the society's method of reckoning descent and on the residence rules that affect the family groups that live together.[15]

No natural horror of incest has been proven by investigators. Children are not born with a reluctance to entering into sexual relations with close relatives. Even so, societies everywhere teach their children that such relations are not

[14]Murdock, p. 12.

[15]Murdock has presented an elaborate theory to explain how and why the incest taboo is extended beyond the nuclear family. See Murdock, chap. 10.

appropriate. It has been speculated that the universality of the incest taboo arises from the recognition that to allow sexual relations between close relatives would be extremely disruptive to the family group. Sexual jealousy and conflict would be rampant within the family, and orderly family living would be in peril. The family's status ascription function would be in jeopardy because many confusing relationships would result from such sexual behavior. The female offspring of a father and his daughter would be both the granddaughter and daughter of the father and both the half-sister and daughter of her mother. The socialization function of the family also would be threatened if the typical parental responsibilities of training, controlling behavior, and punishing were intermingled with sexual desire and seduction. The roles of disciplinarian and lover would seem to be difficult to combine.

Sexual Activity Outside Marriage Other restrictions on sexual behavior have a logic similar to that of the incest taboo. They are designed to provide sufficient restraints on who relates sexually with whom so that orderly living within the larger society is not jeopardized. Societies vary considerably as to what controls they believe are necessary and proper. *Extramarital* relations, sexual intercourse between a married person and someone other than his or her spouse, are customarily forbidden. In 120 societies for which information was available, George P. Murdock found only five that freely allowed adultery.[16] Societies are not equally vigilant in preventing such behavior, though; nor are they equally severe in punishing offenders. Death for adultery is surely found, but so are far less severe punishments.

It is with regard to the unmarried, however, that societies show the greatest differences in their sexual values and practices. Some societies, both primitive and modern, attempt to prohibit all sexual intercourse among the unmarried. Premarital chastity may be considered extremely essential and may be preserved, particularly among females, through considerable precautions. In other places, young people are allowed to have premarital intercourse. Murdock found information on premarital sex taboos or their absence in 158 societies. Premarital sex was forbidden in 44 societies, mildly disapproved in 6, conditionally approved in 43, and fully permitted in 65 societies.[17] Societies that approve of premarital intercourse often see it as a prelude to marriage. In societies where premarital sex is defined in this way or otherwise approved by the group, young people have no reason to feel guilt or shame about their sexual behavior.

[16]Murdock, p. 265.

[17]Murdock, p. 263.

Sexual Regulation in the U.S. Because sexual intercourse is usually a private, personal act, it is somewhat surprising how much is actually known about the sexual activity of Americans. Even so, the interpretation of the facts—what they mean with regard to the sex regulation function of the family—remains difficult. It is patently clear that most of the sexual intercourse that takes place in the United States is marital. On a given day, or night, most of the sexual intercourse that takes place is between spouses who are married to each other. What is more, by far most of the sexual intercourse a typical individual experiences throughout his or her lifetime is with his or her spouse.

It thus appears, or can be made to appear, that American society is fulfilling its task of regulating and controlling sexual behavior. Despite appearances, the studies of Alfred Kinsey and his associates, conducted in the late 1940s, demonstrated that much sexual intercourse takes place outside of marriage.[18] Even at that time, half of all women interviewed by Kinsey were not virgins at marriage, and an even larger percentage of men were not. Unfortunately, there has been no comprehensive study of the sexual behavior of Americans since Kinsey's. While the studies that have been conducted are small and sometimes restricted to college samples, they all indicate that sexual behavior outside of marriage has increased, and certainly that sex is more frankly and openly discussed than it was three decades ago.

The statistics on extramarital intercourse reveal considerable departure from the stated norm that sexual relations should be restricted to marriage. Kinsey estimated that at least half of all married men had extramarital intercourse sometime during their married life,[19] and that about one-fourth of the married women had extramarital relations by the time they were 40 years old.[20] These rates are undoubtedly higher today, but by how much it is difficult to tell. It is likely, too, that the double standard, which allowed men more sexual freedom than women, has changed considerably. Men and women are becoming more similar in their attitudes and behavior with regard to sex outside of marriage.[21]

No known society has been able to enforce all of its sexual regulations all of the time, just as none has enforced rules on property rights or other matters with complete success. Too great a discrepancy between what a society says ought to be done and what people actually do opens two courses to the group. It can either make new rules or attempt better enforcement of the old ones.

---

[18]Alfred C. Kinsey, Wardell B. Pomeroy, and Clyde E. Martin, *Sexual Behavior in the Human Male* (Philadelphia: W. B. Saunders, 1948); and Alfred C. Kinsey, Wardell B. Pomeroy, Clyde E. Martin, and Paul H. Gebhard, *Sexual Behavior in the Human Female* (Philadelphia: W. B. Saunders, 1953).

[19]Kinsey, *Male*, p. 585.

[20]Kinsey, *Female*, p. 440.

[21]The double standard has been declining for some time. See Erwin O. Smigel and Rita Seiden, "The Decline and Fall of the Double Standard," *The Annals* 376 (June 1968), 6–17; and Ira L. Reiss, *Premarital Sexual Standards in America* (New York: Free Press, 1960), p. 97.

In every society the family fulfills the need of both children and adults to give and receive love.

The American people, as judged by their actual behavior and their stated beliefs, do not seem to accept the value that sex belongs only in marriage. Pressures to teach this value and to bring about conformity to it do not seem as strong as are the pressures for a more liberal sexual code. The issue, however, is not yet resolved. The resulting ambiguity creates doubts and indecisions for individuals and does not provide an adequate guide for behavior.

THE AFFECTIONAL FUNCTION: MEETING THE NEED FOR LOVE

Researchers in all of the social sciences have recognized the human need for some kind of intimate interaction with other persons. Any society that failed to provide for the satisfaction of this need for love, response, and deep companionship would neglect a critical psychological drive of its members. In all societies the family has some affectional function, and in most societies the family is the major group that meets these affectional needs.

The human need for a warm and loving relationship is evident at infancy. Psychologically and even physiologically, infants fare better when reared by someone who gives them love. Even very young infants seem to need and respond to hugging, cuddling, and soothing talk. Infants reared in orphanages or in similar institutions where they are deprived of physical affection do poorly physically. They become listless and may even suffer permanent damage to their capacity to respond emotionally. In extreme cases, they are said to suffer from *marasmus,* a slow wasting away to death.[22] Fortunately, instances of total deprivation of love are rare, but children who grow up in less than a warm and loving relationship are far from rare. The consequences of such deprivation may be serious—delinquency, unhappy marriages, or other symptoms of a poor ability to relate to people.

The need for affection and intimate response does not end with childhood. Every society recognizes that adults, as well as children, need affection. And most societies expect that adults will satisfy these needs within the family. In some societies marriage and the nuclear family are looked upon as the prime sources of emotional satisfaction. In others, the affectional function may be shared by other groups. The extended family or men's and women's groups, which are sometimes secret and may serve a religious function as well, often serve as a source of emotional gratification for adults. Yet the family always performs *some* affectional function, for it provides an intimate, close relationship in which one receives intense emotional response from others.

The Affectional Function in the American Family The American family is as much a source of affection and companionship for its members as it always was. Among other factors, geographic mobility of nuclear families has deemphasized the extended family. So children must look to the nuclear family for love and security because grandparents, uncles and aunts, and cousins are frequently great distances away. Others may help to train the child and give or withhold praise. But it is in the family that the child is loved unconditionally. For at least a couple of generations, experts have stressed the idea that children need love. It is extremely difficult to determine whether the modern family is performing the affectional function better than the family of the past. By and large, modern parents seem to take this function seriously and try hard to provide their children with love and affection.

To Americans, love and companionship for adults are almost synonymous with marriage, and they are the basic reasons why people marry. A helpmate is really no longer needed economically. Today, society accepts that adults of either sex can find a comfortable way of life without marriage, yet few choose

[22]For a study of this phenomenon and criticisms of the study see Margaret A. Ribble, *The Rights of Infants* (New York: Columbia University Press, 1943); and Samuel R. Pinneau, "A Critique on the Articles by Margaret Ribble," *Child Development* 21 (December 1950), 203-228.

To Americans, love and companionship are almost synonymous with marriage. They are the basic reasons why people marry.

the single life. Most adults seem to need an enduring affectionate relationship with a partner of the other sex, and many adults seek this relationship in marriage.

The strong emphasis on the affectional function of marriage can be a source of strain as well as a source of strength. When the emphasis is on love alone, some people may marry too young, before they are emotionally mature or aware of the obligations of marriage; others choose mates unwisely. Too much may be expected of the affectional and response potential of marriage. To be sure, many find emotional refuge from a cold and uncaring world in the closed circle of their marriage. But it may simply be too much to ask that all the strains and frustrations in the world of work be daily smoothed away in a loving husband–wife relationship.

THE ECONOMIC FUNCTION: MEETING THE NEED FOR CLOTHES, FOOD, AND SHELTER

The part the family plays in producing and distributing goods and services that its members need for survival constitutes the family's *economic function.* For a group to survive, its people must be fed, clothed, and sheltered from the

---

Interview married women who work outside the home and married women who do not have outside jobs. Ask them about the division of household labor with their husbands and also about the sharing of decision-making powers.

---

elements. These basic needs must be met in such a way that the people can live in harmony with one another, without disruptive conflict over scarce resources.

In many primitive societies the family is the basic economic unit. Even at the pioneer stage of our own society the family had a major economic function. Family members built the family home, raised their own food, and made their own clothing. Because there were few surpluses, the family consumed most of what it produced. In preindustrial societies marriage itself almost always has an economic function. Husband and wife usually arrange some division of labor so they and their children obtain needed goods and services. The husband may be expected to hunt and kill animals, the wife to prepare them as food. The wife may plant the corn, the husband grind it, and the wife cook it. Whatever the arrangement, it is customary for marriage and the family to perform some economic function.

In an industrial society the family need not be the major economic unit. There may be better or more efficient ways for a society to perform the economic function. Industrialized societies have consistently reduced the economic function of the family, in particular the family's role as producer of goods and services. Industrialization requires an intricate division of labor and specialization. It brings together people from many families according to their individual skills to produce a great variety of goods. Even the family's economic function as consumer is modified as family members eat their meals and obtain many services away from the home. As with other family functions, the economic function of the family varies considerably from society to society and from time to time.

Few living Americans grew up in a family that was the basic unit of economic production. Even so, quite a number of living Americans remember when all of the baked goods were produced in the home, and when meats were smoked and fruits and vegetables were canned. They remember, too, when jams and preserves were "put up" and when some clothing was made and almost all clothing repaired, cleaned, and altered in the home. This was not the self-sufficient family of pioneer America. But at the turn of the century and even later, it had many productive economic responsibilities. The decline in this family function has been relatively recent and rapid.

IS THE NUCLEAR FAMILY A HAS–BEEN?
WILL THE EXTENDED FAMILY MAKE A COMEBACK?

For some time it has appeared that marriage and the family as we know them are in trouble. Simple monogamy has increasingly turned to serial monogamy, as more and more people divorce and remarry. Not only do more marriages fail today than in times past, however. More people are also expressing distrust of marriage as a social arrangement. Some people are experimenting with marriage contracts that set up in detail the duties and rights of each partner. Many couples have taken to living together without getting married. Those interviewed by sociologists report a greater sense of closeness than they believe they could find in marriage, and a greater sense of personal identity and freedom.

Both marriage contracts and couples living together are still basically monogamous, however. Others are experimenting with marriages on a broader scale—group marriages. Three or more people enter into what are meant to be permanent arrangements. They work out all the problems that couples must—property, duties, and children—but they do it as a unit that includes two or more men or women or both.

Not much sociological research has yet been done on group marriages, mainly because not too many such arrangements yet exist. But what studies have been done tend to show that the children born to group marriages seem to benefit from them. There are more people available to give the children attention and affection; the children develop a greater sense of security; and they benefit from parents who are more relaxed.

Why has monogamous marriage been altered by some and abandoned by others? First, few of those who shun marriage are intent on a life without permanent, intimate bonds with others. But, as you have seen, the social function of the family has narrowed, and a heavier load has been placed on the functions that remain. The family's economic and socializing functions have steadily shrunk. Its affectional function has grown as our society has become increasingly characterized by secondary relations. The gradual liberation of the female and the consequent merging of sex roles have done their share to challenge traditional marriage. Fewer people today believe that happiness or general social harmony can come from a lifelong effort to be everything that one other person needs. And fewer people expect to find all their own needs fulfilled in one other person. So, among the variety of experiments being made, group marriage is growing in popularity as a possible future marital norm.

TABLE 8-1. Employment of Married Women, Husband Present, 1971

Stage in Family Life Cycle	Percentage of Working Wives
Wife under 35, no children under 18	68.4
Wife under 35, child under 6	29.8
Wife under 45, child 6-17	51.2
Wife 45 or older, no children under 18	34.3

Source: U.S. Department of Labor, "Marital and Family Characteristics of the Labor Force, March 1971," p. A-15.

Changing Economic Function of the American Family In today's family, the unit of economic production is the individual. The husband, and increasingly the wife also, contract as individuals to perform some work for a business or firm. In return, they receive a wage that is used to provide for their own needs and for those of the nonproductive family members. Although highly efficient, this system is assuredly different from a common economic venture among family members, in which the family produces and consumes what it needs.

In our society the family's economic function has recently changed most in regard to the rising number of married women employed outside the home. In 1900 only 5.6 percent of married women held jobs. Today about 41 percent of all married women who are living with their husbands work outside the home. It has been estimated that fully 90 percent of American women will be employed at some time during their married life. Although employment rates vary with the presence and age of children in the family, as many as 30 percent of married women with children under six years of age work outside the home, as shown in Table 8-1. The employment rate for this category of women is increasing despite the meagerness of day care facilities for young children.

From the discussion of roles and positions in Chapter 5, we would predict that a major change in the role of wife would affect the counter role of husband. Research has shown that in fact husbands of working wives help out more than do other husbands with such traditionally feminine activities as meal preparation, dishwashing, dusting, and cleaning floors.[23] The working wife is less likely to accept complete responsibility for preparing the husband's breakfast, for washing dishes, and for straightening up the house if company is expected.

Research also shows that shifting economic roles have an impact on family decision-making. While more American couples are working out a system of shared authority and decision-making power, the pattern is particularly notice-able in the middle class and in families in which the wife is employed outside the home. Sociologist Robert Blood concludes that the wife's employment in-

[23]See Robert O. Blood, Jr., "The Effect of the Wife's Employment on the Husband-Wife Relationship," in *Family Roles and Interaction*, ed. Jerold Heiss (Chicago: Rand McNally, 1968), pp. 261-263.

creases her power in decision–making, especially with regard to major economic decisions.[24]

THE FATE OF THE FAMILY

Will marriage and the nuclear family survive in the United States? Should they? These questions are frequently heard today, for in America the family is often blamed for the troubles that beset society. It is predicted that having failed to perform its functions, the family is doomed to extinction.

There is evidence that troubles do beset the institution of marriage and the family. One indication is our divorce rate, the highest in the industrialized world, and still increasing. After the close of the Civil War about 10,000 divorces were granted each year; fifty years later, around 1920, there were over 170,000; and fifty years after that, in 1970, there were 715,000 divorces annually. Today the figure is close to 800,000. Of every 100 marriages performed around 1870, 3 would end in divorce. Of every 100 marriages performed in 1973, we can predict that about 40 will end in divorce.[25]

Millions of couples in the United States (and elsewhere) have had trouble with the institution of marriage and the family. Most will try marriage again, perhaps learning from experience how they can modify and adjust to the institution and make it work for them. But it is difficult to ignore the fact that there is something wrong with the institution itself. And there is more evidence. Communal living, cohabitation without marriage, and homosexual liaisons are of interest to the sociologist because they indicate a discontent with conventional marriage and the family.[26] Some writers in the women's liberation movement, such as Germaine Greer, in *The Female Eunuch*,[27] call for the abolition of the nuclear family on the grounds that it stifles human freedom.

There is evidence, too, that there are considerable strains in the economic function of the family. The nuclear family as a system seems incapable of providing health, education, and sometimes even support for its members, particularly for the old and the young. The economic function of the family can be modified, and probably will be, by state provisions for more medical care, better support for the aged and the poor, day–care centers, increased aid to dependent children, and the like. We can still safely predict, however, that marriage and the nuclear family will survive well beyond this century. The affectional function of the family seems absolutely necessary. Nowhere have people yet been able to delegate

[24]Cited in Blood, p. 267. Gillespie contends, however, that power rests basically with the husband. See Dair L. Gillespie, "Who has the Power?: The Marital Struggle," *Journal of Marriage and the Family* 33 (August 1971), 445–458.

[25]Divorce rates must be interpreted with caution. For a discussion of various rates see Kenkel, pp. 310–314.

[26]See Sara Davidson, "Open Land: Getting Back to the Communal Garden," *Harper's* (June 1970), 91–102.

[27]Germaine Greer, *The Female Eunuch* (New York: McGraw–Hill, 1971).

**With today's divorce rate, should society make
marriage harder, or divorce harder, or neither?**

to nonfamily groups the function of providing completely for the emotional needs of infants and children. In a similar sense, adults have a need for an enduring relationship in which they can obtain emotional gratification. The nuclear family can fulfill this need for most people and even now does so for many.

The important emotional gratification function of the family will, no doubt, continue to dominate other functions. True, there are strains in this function. Many of them can be eliminated and probably will be when, as a society, we work through some of the confusions and contradictions of male–female roles and provide better socialization for marriage. As the sociologist Betty Yorburg puts it, "Marriage and the nuclear family will continue as basic institutions in human societies, functioning imperfectly and inefficiently, and sometimes malevolently, but persevering because it is not possible to come up with anything more workable to provide for the basic emotional needs of human beings—young or old."[28]

[28]Yorburg, p. 194.

Conduct a cross-cultural study of divorce. From the **United Nations Yearbook** or another source determine the divorce rates in a number of societies. Classify the countries according to whether their divorce rate is high, medium, or low. Inspect the countries in the three different categories. Can you explain why the rate is higher in some groups of societies than in others?

We have seen that the family combines in a single institution many of the major social functions. As a socializing agent, it is the first and most important teacher of the values, roles, and norms of a society. Although in advanced industrial societies the economic function of the family has shrunk considerably from its earlier importance, other functions essential to smooth human interaction are still performed by the family—reproduction, sexual regulation, status ascription, and affection. But even in these functions the family in our society has undergone change. There are now many socializing agents besides the family. For decades sexual regulations have been followed by decreasing numbers of people. Couples are living together without marrying, and some women are choosing to be mothers without being wives. Moreover, there is evidence that the heavy stress put on the affectional function of marriage, along with the role conflicts arising from change in values, norms, and roles, is largely responsible for our rising rate of failed marriages.

Although we can predict that the family will survive into the future, it is surely today in the midst of heavy weather, as indeed are all of our institutions, including religion. The religious institution, which was for centuries the major source of values in the societies of Western culture, is the subject of our next chapter. As a socializing agent religion has always claimed to have the force of the supernatural behind it. How are such claims treated today?

SUMMARY POINTS AND QUESTIONS

1. The universality of the family has biological roots in certain characteristics of the human animal. These characteristics are the long dependency periods of humans and the nature of human reproduction.

> *How do these characteristics make the family a necessary institution?*
>
> *What are the functions that have to be performed for the survival of a society?*
>
> *In what ways does the family perform these functions?*

2. The basic form of family is the *nuclear family*, which consists of a married pair and their immature offspring. Another form is the *extended family*, which consists of two or more nuclear families joined by an extension of the parent–child relationship.

> *What factors account for some societies having the nuclear family as the dominant form and others having the extended family?*
>
> *What functions can the extended family perform that are often not performed by the nuclear family?*

3. *Marriage* is a relationship between two sexually associating adults, which is sufficiently enduring to provide for the procreation and rearing of children. While marriage exists in all societies, it is found in various forms such as monogamy, polygyny, polyandry, and group marriage.

> *How does each of these forms of marriage differ from the others?*
>
> *What advantage might one form have over another?*

4. Societies regulate mate selection. *Endogamous* rules stipulate that a person must select his mate from within a specific group, while *exogamous* rules stipulate that one must go outside some designated group when selecting a marriage partner.

> *What functions do these rules have for the stability of the family and the society?*
>
> *Give an example of each type of rule.*

5. All societies have two general norms concerning childbearing: it should occur in families, and it should not occur outside of families. Consequently, the family performs the reproductive function.

> *If the family as an institution did not exist, how would this affect childbearing and childrearing in a society?*
>
> *What changes are taking place in the childbearing function in the United States today?*

6. The family also functions as the primary agent of socialization because it has the first and most extensive contact with the child.

> *What other agents of socialization exist?*
>
> *What is their relative importance compared to that of the family?*
>
> *What changes are taking place in the socialization function of the family today?*

7. A third function performed by the family is the regulation of sexual behavior. This appears necessary to maintain harmony and reduce conflicts in a society.

> *What norms govern sexual behavior in the United States?*
>
> *What might occur if sexual activity were not regulated?*

8. The family also provides affection, love, response, and companionship for the individual on a rather permanent basis.

> *What role does the need for affection play in mate selection in the United States? In other societies?*
>
> *How might the emphasis on companionship and affection be dysfunctional to marriage?*

9. Traditionally, the family has also performed an economic function. For example, in many primitive societies the economic system was centered around the family unit.

How has this changed?

In what ways does industrialization and the division of labor affect both the economic function of the family and the roles of family members?

10. Today in the United States, certain factors indicate change in the institution of marriage and the family. Among these factors are the high divorce rate, alternative forms of social organization, such as communal living and cohabitation without marriage, and criticisms of marriage as a repressive institution.

What changes do you foresee might take place in the institution of marriage and the family?

What marriage and family functions can other types of groups perform as well as or better than the family? Are there any functions that new, non-marriage groups cannot perform as well as marriage?

SUGGESTED READINGS

Billingsley, Andrew. *Black Families in White America.* Englewood Cliffs, N.J.: Prentice-Hall, 1968. A structural-functional approach to the problems of American black families.

Chafety, Janet Saltzman. *Masculine/Feminine or Human?* Itasca, Ill.: F. E. Peacock Publishers, 1974. An excellent treatment of the sociology of sex roles, how roles are learned, and how they affect male-female interaction.

Farber, Bernard. *Kinship and Class.* New York: Basic Books, 1971. A sociological study of kinship relations in two midwestern cities.

Fullerton, Gail Putney. *Survival in Marriage.* New York: Holt, Rinehart and Winston, 1972. A view of the family in modern mass society. The emphasis is on factors that lead to family conflict and breakdown.

Hsu, Francis L., ed. *Kinship and Culture.* Chicago: Aldine, 1971. A reader on family structure and parental roles in a wide range of cultures.

Kenkel, William F. *The Family in Perspective.* 3rd ed. New York: Appleton-Century-Crofts, 1973. A basic text in family sociology. Deals with the family in other cultures and provides various approaches to the study of the family.

O'Neill, Nena and George O'Neill. *Open Marriage.* New York: M. Evans & Co., 1972. Describes the advantages of a life style for couples that could allow them to escape the boredom and entrapment of traditional marriage.

Reeves, Nancy. *Womankind: Beyond the Stereo-Types.* Chicago: Aldine, 1971. The book is divided into three parts. The first two deal with images about women and relationships of women. The third part is a collection of essays on the role of women.

Centuries ago you would have gone to a clergyman for help with the salvation of your soul. The clergyman knew best the ways of God and what beliefs and behavior would guarantee that you could spend the afterlife in the right place. Would you go to a clergyman for the same reasons today? For many people the clergyman's role is now less well defined. To those people who are interested, however, religions continue to offer beliefs and practices that help them in their struggle with the ultimate problems of human life. Are we a religious people? Sociologists aren't yet certain. Religious belief is a complex thing to define and measure. Our society further complicates the issue by separating church and state. Nevertheless, sociologists have found connections among religious affiliation, social class, and social behavior.

9

RELIGION AND SOCIETY

Blessed be Balmer, who gave us our wavelengths.
Blessed be Bohr, who brought us understanding.

Blessed be long-radio waves, which oscillate slowly.
Blessed be broadcast waves, for which we thank Hertz.

Blessed be X-rays, sacred to Roentgen, the prober within.

We give thanks for Planck. We give thanks for Einstein.
We give thanks in the highest for Maxwell.
In the strength of the spectrum, the quantum, and the
    holy angstrom, peace!

This quotation is not from an irreverent parody of the beatitudes of the Christian religion. It is from "The Electromagnetic Litany," a prayer uttered sincerely, devoutly, and humbly by the Vorsters, a science-fiction people who inhabit the earth and other planets in the twenty-first and twenty-second centuries.[1] The atom is their God, but they recognize a stronger force, which controls their fates and which can grant them immortality. Despite extreme population pressures and other problems of unimaginable proportions, they have faith. They pray before the Blue Flame and worship in chapels where a cobalt-60 cube adorns the altar.

Out of context these rituals and practices may sound like the worst of science (and possibly the worst of fiction as well). Yet in this novel one point is clear: To understand the Vorsters' way of life, the problems that beset them, their concern with genetic research, and many other features of their society, one must try to understand their religion. To do otherwise would be to miss the meaning of their existence, their highest values, and their ultimate concerns.

In Chapter 3 we noted that the culture of every society contains three broad elements: (1) ideas for physical survival, (2) ideas for living together in an orderly

[1]Robert Silverberg, *To Open The Sky* (New York: Ballantine Books, 1967), reprinted by permission of the author and his agents, Scott Meredith Literary Agency, Inc., 580 Fifth Avenue, New York, N.Y. 10036.

way, and (3) ideas for meeting the psychological needs of the society's members. In this chapter we explore how, as a basic social institution, religion is related to these universals of culture, and particularly how religion gives meaning to the various ways humans have invented to meet their needs. Were sociologists to ignore religion they would deprive themselves of valuable insights into human interaction and human groups.

We could begin this chapter by trying to present a terse definition of religion. It would, of course, have to be sufficiently broad to encompass such modern movements as the Jesus Freaks and Mahara Ji followers of the 1970s in the United States, the ancient religions of Buddhism and Christianity, and all else that we tend to think of as religion in primitive and modern societies. Rather than attempting a formal definition of religion at this point, let us approach the subject in a more relaxed manner. Settle down, then, and read about some of the problems with which scholars have wrestled in their attempts to distinguish religion from related phenomena.

We first examine the interrelationship of magic, religion, and science, the three systems humanity has developed to give meaning to its problems. Then we should be better able to explain what we mean by *religion,* and to discuss how sociologists study religion to expand their understanding of human social interaction.

MAGIC, RELIGION, AND SCIENCE

Throughout the ages humankind has stood in awe of the forces of nature. Men and women have found these forces bewildering, frightening, enchanting, fascinating, and inspiring. Most of all, they have realized that their lives and destinies are affected by the forces that they observe or believe to exist. Disease and death, famines and floods are as real in the world of today as they were in the dim past. Fears of an avalanche or a nuclear holocaust acknowledge that frightening forces can be unleashed with disastrous results. Plagues that wipe out entire groups and fears of the effects of overcrowding are but opposite sides of the same population coin. It is no wonder that humanity has sought to understand and manipulate natural forces to satisfy its wants and to escape from harm.

In 1890 Sir James George Frazer published *The Golden Bough,* a classic study of magic and religion that linked our ancient taboos, rituals, superstitions, and beliefs with our perennial problems and wants.[2] Frazer concluded that the needs and wants of men and women everywhere are basically the same, but that

---

[2]Sir James G. Frazer, *The New Golden Bough,* ed. Theodor H. Gaster (New York: Criterion Books, 1959).

In all religions, the gods, immensely powerful beings, are able to control nature. Is there a necessary clash here with scientific dogma?

throughout the centuries different modes of seeking solutions have been used. As Frazer saw it, humanity has progressed from magic to religion to science in its unending search for control of the forces of nature. Magic assumes a certain order to nature, which humans by their own means can control to suit their needs. When early humans, as Frazer saw it, discovered that their powers to control nature were imaginary, they threw themselves on the mercy of invisible beings, or gods, to whom they ascribed the powers they once thought themselves to have. Gradually, magic was superseded by religion. (The distinction between magic and religion will be explored shortly.) The gods of primitive religion were thought to be vastly more powerful than humans and to have the ability to control the forces of nature. But this concept assumes an irregular and variable universe, one that is controlled by the whims or capriciousness of the gods.

Frazer theorized that in time humans became impressed with the order of natural events. They came to realize that, if understood properly, such events could be predicted with some degree of accuracy and acted upon accordingly. As Frazer put it, "In short, religion as an explanation of nature, is displaced by science."[3] Interestingly, Frazer did not consider science the final stage in the sequence of humanity's attempt to understand and deal with nature, but only the current stage. According to Frazer, ". . . as science has supplanted its predecessors, so it may hereafter be itself superseded by some more perfect hypothesis, perhaps by some totally different way of looking at the phenomena—of registering the shadows on the screen—of which we in this generation can form no idea."[4]

Modern sociologists do not actually devote much attention to the origin of religion, not because it is unimportant, but because it is felt that the quest is futile. For the most part, religion is accepted as a given, an ancient and universal institution that continues to have profound effects on societies and their members. Even while the search for origins has been abandoned and while the orderly, progressive sequence of magic, religion, and science has been rejected, there remains the tantalizing thought that there is *some* connection among these three systems. What is magic, and how does it differ from religion? Is there actually a conflict between science and religion? And what is the relationship among these three modes of thought?

MAGIC AND RELIGION

It is not easy to make a rigid distinction between magic and religion. Both systems of belief assume that there is a supernatural or unknown world, and both assume that there is power in this supernatural world that can affect life in the natural world. The supernatural is what is beyond the world of the senses, what we can see, hear, or touch. It is scientifically unknowable and incapable of proof or disproof.

Although the rituals of magic and religion shade into one another, several features are more common to what sociologists and anthropologists refer to as magic, and others are more common to religion. Keeping in mind that it is not entirely possible to distinguish magic from religion, we can nevertheless discuss how religion and magic can be compared and contrasted. Their differences are as follow: (1) the assumptions each system makes about the supernatural; (2) the ends or goals pursued; (3) the means used to seek those ends; and (4) the effects of the systems on society and the individual. Because the bulk of this chapter deals with these attributes as they relate to religion, in the section that follows we pay close attention to magic.

[3]Frazer, p. 649.
[4]Frazer, pp. 649–650.

Assumptions about the Supernatural Characteristically, religions include a belief that the power that influences the unknown world is a being or beings of some sort. These beings may have the physical form or other characteristics of humans. While it may seem to be stretching the matter to say that the wind, the sun, or a mountain has animate power, these too should be included, for power is sometimes ascribed to this type of "being." In what is called *animate power,* the source of power is given a definite location, equivalent to a person or personality.

Magic, by contrast, is more frequently characterized by a belief in inanimate rather than animate power. The unknown world of the supernatural contains forces that can be manipulated by those who understand them. This type of power can be compared to modern man's conception of electricity. It is just there. He who has the knowledge can use it, for good or evil. So if two different groups were seeking the same results—say, rain to end a drought, or someone's return to health—and one group believed in magic and the other religion, they might both use ritual. However, the religious ritual would be directed to an invisible *person* with power over rain or health, whereas the magic ritual would be used to directly tap invisible, impersonal *forces* that control rain or health.

The Goals of Magic and Religion In magic, the goal relates to the observable world, is usually desired immediately, and is usually personal. A man might consult a magician to assure the fertility of his field, or for that matter of his wife. A witch doctor may be sought to heal a sore or cure a disease. These are personal goals, and the results are anticipated almost immediately. The magician is consulted because it is felt that he has learned the secrets that enable him to tap the power in the unknown world.

Goals pursued by religious means also can be practical and personal. One may pray for health or success, for the life of a loved one, or for rain for his crops. Often the ends, though personal, are expressed differently by the religious person than by the magic-oriented person. A Christian may pray for guidance to cope with life's problems, or for the strength to endure what cannot be cured. There is no formula for such ends in any system of magic. Yet the major distinction between the goals of magic and religion is that usually the important goals of religion are not practical, whereas the basic goal of magic is the solution of life's immediate problems. Religion offers a philosophy of life and addresses itself to ultimate values; magic generally does not.

Magical and Religious Rituals Magic and religion also differ in the means used by each to reach the desired goal. Sometimes their rituals, whether bodily movements, incantations, or the offering of a sacrifice, appear similar. But if one investigates the symbolic *meanings* of the behavior and the *spirit* and *attitudes*

Magic, like this voodoo ritual in Haiti, pursues immediate, practical goals in this life, can this usually be said of religion?

accompanying the behavior, striking differences can be noted. Magic is a businesslike affair, with the magician performing his rites in an impersonal manner. A contractual relationship is established between the practitioner of magic and his customer. When a witch doctor is consulted to break a spell, his superior skill is recognized, but he is not considered a superior being. The magician or witch doctor is not beseeched or entreated. He is simply hired if it is decided that he can do the job at hand. Behind the religious ritual, on the other hand, is the tacit recognition that an appeal is being made to a vastly superior being (the god), who is approached with deference, awe, and piety. There is thus a difference—admittedly sometimes subtle—in the behavior and accompanying attitudes of the participants in a religious as opposed to a magical ritual.

Social and Personal Consequences Magic is both similar to and different from religion in its social and personal effects. By almost any definition, magic can be considered beneficial. Millions of people have been cured by witch doctors, and millions more have experienced great emotional relief to learn that an evil spell has been broken. Magic has also been used to cast evil spells, to bring about the death of an enemy, or to gain another's property illegally. Such black magic is not only harmful to the victim but may be harmful to the society as well. It may force individuals to use life's precious moments engaging in counter-magic or guarding their hair or nail clippings so they cannot be used by a wicked enemy. To be sure, religion can do and has done both good and harm to individuals and societies, and we deal with this later. Generally, however, religion has not been used to achieve ends contrary to the group's own goals, while magic has been.

Again, it is not easy to make a rigid distinction between magic and religion. As a further complication, the two systems can coexist within a society, and either or both can coexist with science.

SCIENCE AND RELIGION: COMPETITION AND COEXISTENCE

As we have seen, religion deals with the supernatural. Its system of beliefs, accepted on faith, seeks to determine the values and to describe the forces that in some ultimate sense affect human destiny. By definition, then, religion deals with the extraordinary, with phenomena that are not knowable in an ordinary way. There is a profound and essential difference between the questions "Is there a heaven?" and "How many people believe there is a heaven?" Science cannot tell us that there is or is not a heaven. A scientific survey showing that belief in an afterlife is declining might make people question their beliefs, but the findings could not be construed as challenging the belief itself or providing evidence contrary to it. Why, then, is there any problem? If science and religion use different methods and deal with different phenomena, how can there possibly be a conflict?

Part of the problem is that the distinction between the knowable and the unknowable is not clear-cut. Sometimes it cannot definitely be said that a certain phenomenon is incapable of being studied by scientific means. It may be true today, but not tomorrow. Not too many years ago science could tell us nothing about the origin of human life on earth; when, where, and how life began were unknowable by scientific means. Christianity, as well as other religions, had strong beliefs about these matters. Questions about the origin of human life were considered to be in the realm of religion, and just about every religion had long ago offered answers with its own account of creation.

Over the years, people came to believe that to seek knowledge about the origin of their species was legitimately within the scope of science. Beginning in the Renaissance, questions on the origin of human life were transferred from the domain of religion to that of science. But as late as 1929 the contest was

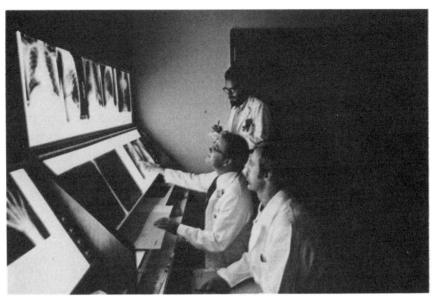

We now learn of the physical world—both visible and invisible—through science. Must religion and science therefore be enemies?

still alive. It was so alive, in fact, that John Scopes was convicted at the famous "monkey trial" in Tennessee for teaching Darwin's theory of evolution in a public school, in violation of state law. For a considerable time, then, religion and science were in conflict on this issue. One cannot accept both a literal interpretation of Biblical creation and the biological theory of evolution.

Other examples of the impermanence of the boundary between science and religion, between the knowable and the unknowable, are not difficult to find. The Copernican theory that the earth and other planets revolved around the sun was once considered heresy, for it conflicted with the official belief of the Church that the universe is earth-centered. Galileo first gave and then withdrew his public support of the Copernican theory. He was treading on the shifting boundary between religion and science. Even though he had confirmed Copernican theory with his telescope, under the threat of excommunication and death at the stake, he cast his lot with religion. Ultimately, the battle was won for science, for the Christian denominations now consider it legitimate for scientists to study the moon, the stars, and the planets objectively and to report their findings factually, be they what they may. The proper source of knowledge of the physical world has shifted from religion to science.

It may appear that religion has been forced again and again to surrender to science. Often, however, it has not been a total surrender. By reinterpreting its views or by shifting the issue to a more philosophical and less literal plane, religion has erased the contradictions between religious beliefs and scientific facts. Thus, Christians can believe that the earth and its inhabitants have a special place in the eyes of their God, so much so that He sent His son to dwell here and sacrifice himself for human salvation. But they can also accept the scientific fact that the universe is not earth-centered. Discovery of intelligent life on another planet could also be reconciled with religious beliefs. Could not this be what Jesus meant when He said, "Other sheep I have who are not of this fold"? As science has advanced, people have looked to it for answers to more and more questions. Yet questions remain about ultimate causes, the meaning of human existence, and human destiny, and these questions cannot—yet—be answered by science.

THE NATURE OF RELIGION

Perhaps in a chapter on religion it is not too much to ask the reader for a little faith, not unquestioning belief in a specific dogma, but rather faith that we will soon show why understanding religion is important to the sociologist. But first a formal definition of religion will enable us to agree on just what is important and consequential.

Following the sociologist J. Milton Yinger, we will define religion as "a system of beliefs and practices by means of which a group of people struggle with [the] ultimate problems of human life."[5] Charles Glock and Rodney Stark, other authorities in the sociology of religion, define religion as ". . . one variety of value. orientations, those institutionalized systems of beliefs, symbols, values, and practices that provide groups of men with solutions to their questions of ultimate meaning."[6] Let us examine these definitions and see what they include and exclude.

ULTIMATE MEANINGS

Probably the most abstract but most significant aspect of both definitions is the idea that religion deals with ultimate meanings. We noted in our discussion of magic and religion that humans have always been concerned with a reality beyond experience. A system of ultimate meanings describes this reality, gives the reasons for human existence, and defines the nature of humanity: its origins,

[5] J. Milton Yinger, *Religion, Society and the Individual* (New York: Macmillan, 1957), p. 9.

[6] Charles Y. Glock and Rodney Stark, *Religion and Society in Tension* (Chicago: Rand McNally & Co., 1965), p. 17.

its purpose, its relationship to the natural world, and its eventual fate. A system of ultimate meanings allows one to answer, even if tentatively, the universal and pervasive question, "What am I doing on this earth?"

Not so many years ago almost any group gathered around a campfire or at a "song fest" would sooner or later get around to the song:

> Tell me why the stars do shine;
> Tell me why the ivy twines;
> Tell me why the skys are blue;
> And I will tell you why I love you.

The next stanza answers that God is the cause of all such things.[7] This song is a light-hearted echo of concerns that have occupied humanity for as long as we have a record, concerns that have found expression through our poets. A well-known example of such questionings is "The Tiger" by William Blake:

> Tiger! Tiger! burning bright
> In the forests of the night,
> What immortal hand or eye
> Could frame thy fearful symmetry?
>
> When the stars threw down their spears,
> And watered heaven with their tears,
> Did he smile his work to see?
> Did he who made the Lamb make thee?
>
> Tiger! Tiger! burning bright
> In the forests of the night,
> What immortal hand or eye
> Dare frame thy fearful symmetry?

Each of these, the campfire song and the poem, asks in its own way questions that express a search for the final causes of life.

It would be next to impossible to find agreement on some listing of the ultimate human concerns. The following, however, are among the problems to which human societies and individuals have sought answers through their religions:

> What is the purpose of life?
>
> What is death, and what is beyond it?
>
> Is there a central meaning to life which can help us understand life's disappointments, sufferings, and tragedies?
>
> Can interpersonal and intergroup hates and hostilities be controlled or even neutralized?

---

[7]Rejecting God as the responsible agent, a student at M.I.T. supplied a rationalistic substitute for the second verse:

> Nuclear fusion makes the stars to shine;
> Tropisms make the ivy twine;
> Rayleigh scattering makes skies so blue;
> Testicular hormones is why I love you.

If we believe in ultimate meanings above but within our lives, we have some protection from life's pain and uncertainties.

Religion cannot supply scientifically testable answers to these and other fundamental questions. It can furnish a system of *beliefs* about these ultimate concerns.

BELIEFS

The essence of any belief is the conviction that an idea is correct. What is believed is accepted as being true; empirical or logical proof is not required. To the sociologist it does not really matter whether a religious belief is true. The essential thing is to ascertain and to understand what it is that a group believes.

Every religion contains a set of beliefs. These beliefs relate to the ultimate meanings we discussed. Emile Durkheim's definition of religion, in his classic work *The Elementary Forms of Religious Life,* provides a starting point for a fuller appreciation of religious beliefs:

> All known religious beliefs, whether simple or complex, present one common characteristic; they presuppose a classification of all things, real and ideal, of which men think, into two classes or opposed groups, generally designated by two distinct terms which are translated well enough by the words *profane* and *sacred.*[8]

[8]Emile Durkheim, *Elementary Forms of Religious Life* (New York: Macmillan, 1926), p. 36.

What is regarded as *sacred* or *holy* is set apart from the *ordinary*, the *secular*, or in Durkheim's words, the *profane*. Sacredness is in the minds of believers. People define what is sacred, and people develop and display attitudes of awe, respect, and reverence toward what they consider sacred, whether it is in the supernatural or the natural world.

In the great religions of the world, much of what is defined as sacred deals with the supernatural, that which is beyond the world we can see, hear, or touch. Belief in an existence beyond the grave or in a power that manifests itself in the universe, belief in gods, angels, eternal reward or damnation—all these are extraordinary or supernatural matters that groups have defined as sacred. Within the supernatural, specific personages—such as the Holy Spirit of Christian religions, Allah and Mohammed his Prophet, Zeus, or Jupiter—may also be considered sacred.

Sacredness is also attributed to objects in the natural, material world. To Moslems, the Black Stone of the Kaaba is sacred. To Jews the Ark of the Covenant is sacred. And to Christians the cross is sacred. Books, prayer wheels, candles, cows, rosary beads, ikons, fire, and water have all been considered sacred. These and many other objects are not sacred because of built-in natural qualities, but because they have symbolic connection with a group's beliefs about the supernatural.

Religious beliefs, whether about the natural or the supernatural realm, may be highly articulated and specific, as in the Nicene Creed, which recites the fundamental articles of Christian faith; or they may be implicit in a systematic and intricately organized theology. In any case, religious beliefs define for the believers what is sacred and what is not. More than this, the beliefs relate the sacred to the nonsacred. They specify, in other words, how the unseen and the unknowable are related to the observable world. Although beliefs themselves rest in the mind, they have a bearing on behavior, at the very least on the behavior known as religious practices or rituals.

RITUAL

Sociologists use the term *religion* to include certain kinds of behavior. Religious groups prescribe behavior and practices that relate to the supernatural or to the sacred objects that symbolize their beliefs. Such practices are called *religious rituals*. This ritualistic element is what distinguishes religion from a philosophy of life, which is closest to religion in containing beliefs about the nature of the universe or about the ultimate meanings of human existence. A philosophy of life would undoubtedly influence its holder's day-to-day behavior, yet it would have no prescribed rites or rituals. Some religions have elaborate rituals; others

Women praying in Kashmir characterize the faith of all religious people. They call upon their god for help in times of stress, or give thanksgiving for his compassion.

have simple ones. Some expect frequent performance of rituals. (Five times a day the Moslem faces Mecca and prays; each week he is expected to join in the noon prayers at the mosque; during Ramadan, the ninth month of the Moslem year, he is expected to fast; and at least once during his lifetime he is expected to make the pilgrimage to Mecca.) Other religions have less demanding rituals, but all religions have some.

Almost every type of behavior has at one time been used as a religious ritual: fasting and feasting, kneeling and standing, singing and shouting, lighting fires, immersing oneself in certain waters, offering human sacrifices, taking drugs, and many specific movements of the head, hands, or body. Sacred objects are manipulated and sacred words are spoken. Special articles of clothing are worn, such as tie-dye vestments, ermine cloaks, or skull caps. The list is almost limitless, and the variety of behavior is staggering.

A Moslem observing a Roman Catholic walking to a church altar and accepting a wafer of unleavened bread would not see the act as self-evidently religious, nor would the Catholic recognize the religious significance of the Moslem's walking seven times around the Kaaba and kissing the Black Stone in its wall.

Visit several types of religious services such as a baptism, a confirmation, a wedding, and a funeral. What functions do each of these services perform? For whom?

Both have been taught that their behavior is religious. They have learned that seemingly ordinary actions are extraordinary and have special meaning or symbolism. Rituals, then, provide people with a way of relating to the unseen, supernatural world. Rituals can also serve as a reminder of an event in the group's history. This function can be observed in the Christian's reverence for the cross or in the breaking of a wine glass during a Jewish marriage ceremony in memory of the destruction of Jerusalem and its temple.

FUNCTIONS OF RELIGION

As found in Chapter 1, the functionalist theory holds that all behavior within an institution has some effect on the larger social system. Sometimes it maintains the on-going society; at other times it changes it and creates disorder. At times the functions or their consequences may either be *manifest* (intended and recognized) or *latent* (unintended and not generally recognized). In discussing the functions of religion, then, we must study its consequences for society.

The distinction between individual and social functions is sometimes arbitrary. As we discussed in Chapter 3, every society must seek to satisfy its members' deep-seated psychological needs. If religion helps to satisfy some of these needs, it simultaneously affects the well-being of individuals and the well-being of the society. Not all of the functions of religion for the individual can be related to its social functions, but even so we may presume that some effect on the group will result from the effect on individuals. We should not assume, however, that all the consequences of religion are beneficial for the individual or the society. We will find that at times religion contributes neither to the stability of the individual nor to the maintenance of the group.

FUNCTIONS FOR THE INDIVIDUAL

People everywhere experience frustrations, crises, tragedies, and disappointments. The young person may dream of the future only to awaken in middle age to the stark realization that those dreams never will come true. Anyone reasonably sensitive to the plight of humanity realizes that many people are

Which do you think fares better by the matador's faith—his psychological or his physical well-being?

living in poverty and deprivation. Injustices abound in almost any society and can produce discomfort and agony not only for the victims but also for the witnesses. Why are some people oppressed and others free? Why are the good and the just not always rewarded in this world while wrong–doers often escape punishment? Why does a family already besieged with more than its share of life's problems suffer yet another tragedy? There are sometimes rational, scientific answers to these questions, but often they are not fully satisfying. A historian or psychologist can explain Stalin's murder of thousands or Hitler's execution of millions by describing the totalitarian mentality. But no one can scientifically explain why the world is the kind of place in which such mentality and cruelty can exist and gain power.

We are thinking, but also feeling, creatures. Intellectually, parents might understand the medical explanation of why one of their children was born blind and another is mentally retarded. Still, the nagging, unanswerable question remains: "Why did it have to happen to us?" Variations of this question are uttered earnestly if hopelessly by those who lose their homes by flood or fire, who are stricken with painful disabilities, who are fired from their jobs, and so on through the distressing list of crises and tragedies that beset us all. Religion offers many people an interpretation for such events, and in doing so provides solace and peace of mind. People are able to live with their sorrows because they believe in a guiding force, a final cause, a God who in His wisdom, which we may not understand, permits such things to happen.

Sooner or later we experience the loss through death of a relative or close friend, and sooner or later we must come to grips with the meaning of our own death. For many people death is the ultimate mystery, the event which more than all others transcends human control. Because everyone will die, all societies must develop a means of allowing their members to understand and cope with death. Partly through its consoling rituals, but more importantly through its system of beliefs, religion sometimes performs this function. It is not surprising that most religions of the world contain a belief in immortality. With the poet, many people find genuine comfort in the belief that "dust thou art to dust returnest, was not spoken of the soul."[9]

Benefits and Costs for the Individual Research findings generally support the idea that religion can have positive effects on the happiness and serenity of practitioners. In a national study, *Americans View Their Mental Health,* it was found that both Catholics and Protestants who attended church regularly reported a better self-concept, less general distress, and more happiness on the job than those who did not attend church.[10] The most striking finding, however, was the relationship between church attendance and marital happiness. Those who reported extreme unhappiness in their marriages were the Protestants who never attended church and the Catholics who attended church only a few times each year.[11] Those who professed no religion were not included in the analysis, but it is probable that many such people are happy in their jobs and in their personal lives. Although studying church attendance may tell us little about what is helpful to people in religion, it seems that many people find in religion an inner contentment that keeps them at peace with their fellow humans and happy in their marriages.

[9]Henry Wadsworth Longfellow, *A Psalm of Life.*

[10]Gerald Gurin, Joseph Veroff, and Sheila Feld, *Americans View Their Mental Health* (New York: Basic Books, 1960), p. 245.

[11]Gurin, Veroff, and Feld, p. 241.

Because everyone must die, and experience the deaths of loved ones, in every society there are rituals for coping with death.

But modern-day religions have also proved damaging to the well-being of some individuals. A few examples should suffice. Each year children die because their Christian Scientist parents could not in conscience allow them to receive a blood transfusion or undergo surgery. In parts of Kentucky and West Virginia, some religious sects hold a literal interpretation of the New Testament passage "They shall take up serpents; and if they drink any deadly thing, it shall not hurt them" (Mark 16:17–18). Part of the religious rituals of these sects requires the handling of poisonous snakes, and though most believers remain unscathed, now and then a person is bitten and dies. During the war between West Pakistan and East Pakistan, out of which came the new state of Bangladesh in 1972, approximately 200,000 Moslem women were reported to have been raped by West Pakistan occupation forces. According to Moslem customs the victimized women were considered unclean and were therefore deserted by their husbands.

The examples so far have shown the damage that can come from the prescribed beliefs and rituals of organized religions. In addition, some individuals make their own interpretations of religious belief and suffer terror or guilt, or they may become what are generally called religious fanatics. Far from strengthening marriages and helping individuals, such religious beliefs can bring about psychological and physical suffering.

Religion and Individual Identity As we have seen, religion is a group experience. An individual's sense of belonging to a group of fellow believers and participants in rituals should have a positive function. Indeed, membership in a community of believers may be what gives members their inner security and sense of well-being. Because not all religious groups seem to offer an equal sense of community, and because this aspect of organized religion appears to be changing, how strong a sense of identity community members can draw from their religion is worth exploring.

In Chapter 1 we referred to Emile Durkheim's study, *Suicide.* As part of that study, Durkheim attempted to explain why the suicide rate was lower for Roman Catholics than for Protestants. The relevant belief systems of the two groups were similar. Both considered suicide sinful, and both held that in the next life man would be punished for his sins. Durkheim noted, however, that Catholics had a stronger attachment to their religious groups and participated more in their group-centered activities than did Protestants. The greater individualism of Protestants and their lower reliance on group participation, according to Durkheim, accounted for their higher suicide rate.

There is much sociological evidence that human beings derive great satisfaction from associations with others and that most people require warm primary group associations. Yet religion has often failed to provide meaningful groups to which the members of a society could anchor themselves. What is more, it has been suggested that modern religious groups in the United States are failing in this respect at the very time when more of us are living in the impersonal anonymity of urban areas.[12] Individuals are now satisfying their need for group identification in a variety of functionally equivalent groups, some clearly secular, others with religious overtones.

Symptoms of Contemporary Religious Failure A fascinating development in the United States is the interest in the occult, which expresses itself most vividly in Satanism and witchcraft. Few people practice witchcraft singly; almost all witchcraft practices are group activities. Some of the rituals, such as the double-spiral dance performed in the nude or the ritualistic sexual intercourse practiced in some covens, suggest a need among the practitioners to gather with fellow worshipers who share beliefs about the mystery of the unknown world. One interpretation of the growing interest in the occult is that people have a deep-

---

[12]Thomas F. O'Dea, *Sociology and the Study of Religion* (New York: Basic Books, 1970), p. 261.

By a simple questionnaire see if you can find differences between generations regarding the importance of religion. Phrase questions such as, "Do you think our country would be better off if more people took religion seriously?" or "All things considered, do you think religion has done more harm or good in the world?"

seated need for *myth* (stories that express values and beliefs in emotionally expressive ways) and a strong desire to relate to the unseen world, neither of which are being met by organized religious groups.

We have reviewed some of the functions that religion serves for the individual. For many people in our own and other societies religion has no place, however. They do not seem to need or to miss the religious experience. To the sociologist the behavior of such people is neither laudable nor blameworthy; it simply must be taken into account as we attempt to develop a full picture of the consequences religion has for the individual.

SOCIAL FUNCTIONS OF RELIGION

As we discuss the social functions of religion, two points must be remembered. First, sociologists do not endorse functions of religion; they do not hold that religion should have particular consequences. Second, it is often difficult to evaluate the consequences of religion, even by the group's own value system. For instance, religion may give its believers a strong sense of stability that the group values. Yet this very stability may make the group tradition–bound and unable to keep pace with the developing world. On the other hand, the group may value some functions of their religion but not others, or it may value certain consequences in the present but at a later time consider them dysfunctions. For example, Catholics in Latin America value many features of their religion today but may later consider the Church's stand on contraception as dysfunctional.

Most sociologists of religion consider religion's most valuable social function to be the integrative function. Kingsley Davis goes so far as to say that religion makes an "indispensable contribution to the social integration."[13] Any on–going group is somewhat integrated if its members perform specialized but interrelated activities and are therefore dependent on one another. Religion often produces a special kind of group unity and a strong social cohesion. It can supply the bond or force that holds members of a group in interaction, and it can give them strong, positive feelings toward the group.

[13]Kingsley Davis, *Human Society* (New York: Macmillan, 1950), p. 529.

You've heard of sacred cows. In overpopulated India, with millions starving, the Hindu religion makes these cows safe from becoming food.

Supernatural Endorsement of Society's Values Religion can contribute to group integration in different ways. Probably the most significant of these for society is that religion can forcefully help to legitimize the group's most cherished values. When religion justifies and affirms a system of values, a compelling dimension is added to the value system. The values are then seen not merely as good, but rather as the morally correct system. We need look no further than our Declaration of Independence for an example. It does not state that a handful of intelligent men, borrowing liberally from the thinking of past philosophers, put together an attractive list of norms for judging the rightness and wrongness of things. It states instead that people were endowed by their Creator with certain inalienable rights. What higher appeal can be made? The value statements are not only legitimized, they are sanctified. Guides to action and standards for judging one's own and others' behavior in the natural world are infused with beliefs about the supernatural. So by offering the highest-order explanation for group values, religion can persuade members to agree with and accept the group norms and goals. Sacred objects and sacred symbols provide tangible references to the sacred values, and religious rituals provide a means for expressing and reinforcing the beliefs of the group. In these ways religion can contribute to social integration.

Religious Resistance to Change However, religion also can have disruptive effects on a group: It can be dysfunctional as well as functional. Those who emphasize the dysfunctions of religion frequently seize upon its justification of the status quo and its resistance to necessary change.

It is not difficult to understand why religion is often resistant to change. Those who stress the supernatural can easily be indifferent or even opposed to worldly progress and accomplishments. Then, too, the major world religions lean heavily on the past by holding as sacred the beliefs of their founders or the form of their ancient rituals. As Gerhard Lenski has pointed out, "Creeds formulated fifteen hundred and more years ago are still accepted as definitive statements of faith by major groups. Scriptures originating two and three thousand years ago continue to be regarded as sacred documents."[14]

Instances abound of religious support for the status quo and inhibition of social change. The gross inequalities of the caste system of India received justification from the Hindu religion. The higher castes felt morally justified in their greater privileges, for these privileges were signs that in previous existences they had led moral and pious lives. Lower caste members accepted their fates, believing that by performing their humble tasks ungrudgingly they would be better off in a future existence. The Russian Orthodox Church, to take another example, supported what we now consider the harsh subjugation of women, likening the father of the family to God and giving him the moral right to beat his wife and children. In Christian European countries, Jews were for centuries treated as outcasts and forbidden to pursue certain occupations or to own land. These beliefs and actions were considered right by the religious standards of the times. With some notable exceptions, clergymen in the United States found religious justification for slavery. These historical examples show that religion's resistance to change and its support of what can be considered unworthy conditions are not new.

Religion as an Agent of Change Religion also has been a force behind social change. Long before the Peace Corps and United Nations technical assistance programs, Christian missionaries were serving as agents of change in Africa, Asia, Latin America, and elsewhere. They built and operated hospitals and schools, taught the latest agricultural techniques, and took other deliberate steps to foster social change. Recently the Catholic clergy in Chile, Brazil, and other Latin American countries have engaged in socioeconomic reform through such means as distributing church lands to peasants and operating technical training institutes.[15] Today in the United States many religious denominations are seeking

[14]Gerhard Lenski, *The Religious Factor*, rev. ed. (Garden City, N.Y.: Doubleday & Co., 1963), p. 355.

[15]Ivan Vallier, "Religious Elites in Latin America: Catholicism, Leadership and Social Change" (Unpublished manuscript, 1965). See also, Vallier, "Church, Society, and Labor Resources," *American Journal of Sociology* 68 (July 1962), 21–33.

Christian missionaries are the classic example of how religion promotes cultural and social change.

to produce change in inner–city ghettos and to improve the lot of the rural poor, the worker, and the minority–group member.

Of course, religious support for change can be judged differently by different value systems. Is it right or wrong to attempt to win converts to Christianity, even if the effort is accompanied by measures to improve their health and welfare? Was it right or wrong for many Protestant denominations to seek to change the way of life in America by vigorously supporting national prohibition (of alcoholic beverages)? Were Protestant and Catholic clergy who resisted the status quo by teaching civil disobedience in civil rights matters or by thwarting the military draft system behaving rightly or wrongly? Regardless of one's evaluation, such activities illustrate that religion has been for change as well as against it.

RELIGION IN THE UNITED STATES

We hope our study of religion and its individual and social functions has persuaded you that this institution is both important and complicated. As we turn now to a sociological treatment of religion in the United States, you should recognize that we present a mere overview of this complex and changing institution.

SEPARATION OF CHURCH AND STATE

One feature of organized religion in the United States, separation of church and state, is so generally accepted by Americans that we may forget how unique it is now and how radical an idea it was at the time of its inception. It is only partly a joke to say that the early settlers came to these shores to practice their religion—and make everybody else do likewise. In some colonies religious differences were not tolerated. Rhode Island was founded by religious fugitives from Massachusetts; and in Virginia the Church of England was in essence the established church of the colony. At the same time the seeds of religious freedom were being firmly planted. While Maryland is often thought to have been a Catholic settlement, the original charter clearly provided for religious freedom. And other colonies that attempted to have an established church also rapidly changed.

For centuries in most European countries, one Christian denomination or another either was the established church or was definitely intertwined with the political order. The rulers presumably felt that a cohesive social system could best be maintained by loyalty to a single religion. The radical idea that developed during the colonial period was that a social order could exist without compulsory allegiance to a common religion. By the time the colonies gained their independence this new idea was widely, although not completely, accepted. Consequently, the First Amendment to the Constitution specified that "Congress shall make no law respecting an establishment of religion, or prohibiting the free exercise thereof." Its drafters and ratifiers meant that there should be no one official denomination, and that the government should not support any religious denomination, financially or otherwise. All people should be free to worship in the religion of their choice, or not to worship, without penalty or harassment.

Separation: An Elusive Concept For two hundred years we have lived with the idea of separation of church and state, and if anything, the principle is more strongly endorsed today than ever before. Even so, almost from the beginning the principle has been periodically violated. The wave of immigrants from Catholic countries aroused anti–Catholic feelings. The Know–Nothing party maintained that no one who owed allegiance to "any foreign prince or potentate" (the Pope) should be a candidate for public office. The Mormons, whose religion endorsed polygamy, were persecuted until they fled to the territories where United States law did not yet hold.

Even today many norms and values of the larger, secular American society often come into conflict with religious norms and values, producing lengthy court battles between the government and a religious sect. Only after considerable litigation did members of the Native American Church win the right to use peyote, an otherwise illegal hallucinogen, in their religious ceremonies. The Amish have only recently won the right not to violate their religious convictions by sending their children to school beyond the eighth grade. Mennonites do not have to wear legally required safety helmets on construction jobs, for such a requirement violates their clothing taboos. Jehovah's Witnesses and others are at best mistrusted and at worst persecuted because they believe it idolatrous to salute the flag.

Not only do secular and religious norms sometimes conflict, but many controversies have raged over the exact extent and intent of the First Amendment in matters of religion. Probably the greatest controversy followed the Supreme Court decision several years ago that mandatory prayers in schools and other public assemblies were unconstitutional. Some people feel that there is nothing wrong with providing transportation or books for children attending a parochial school, but others feel it is a gross violation of the First Amendment. Some feel we are compromising our principles by not levying taxes on church property, while others feel that to do so would constitute governmental harassment by making it difficult for people to freely practice their religion.

Despite these and other conflicts and controversies, separation of church and state appears to be relatively functional for our society. In a society of many religious denominations, with no single one having political sanction, controversies seem inevitable.

DENOMINATIONAL PLURALISM

Although most of us are accustomed to thinking of the religious variety in our society as threefold—Protestant, Catholic, and Jewish—our religious spectrum is far more diverse than that. There are almost 250 Protestant denominations; there are small Catholic groups, such as the Polish National Church of America and the Old Catholic Church; and there are Orthodox, Conservative, and Reformed Jewish congregations.[16] But there are also about 100,000 Americans in the Buddhist

---

[16]For membership and other data on religious bodies in the United States see *Yearbook of American Churches,* (New York: National Council of Churches of Christ in the United States), published annually.

Eighty percent of our society is Protestant, Catholic, or Jewish. But other groups, like the Hare Krishna, have become visible in recent years.

Churches of America, and over 2 million people belong to other religious groups that cannot be classified as Protestant, Catholic, or Jewish.

Nevertheless, about 60 percent of the population is affiliated with one of three broad Christian denominations: Catholic, Baptist, or Methodist. If we add four more religious bodies—Lutheran, Presbyterian, Episcopalian, and Jewish—we account for 80 percent of the population. Each of the Protestant denominations, however, has several subgroups that can be considered separate denominations. Members of the Lutheran Church, Missouri Synod, usually make it clear that they are not merely Lutheran, as Southern Baptists make it clear that they are not merely Baptist. The diversity within broad denominations, the numerous small religious bodies, and the seemingly endless formation of splinter groups and new sects are all part of the denominational pluralism that is a prominent feature of religion in the United States.

ECUMENISM: THE DESIRE FOR UNITY

Another characteristic of religion in the United States, but one that is neither new nor unique to our society, is ecumenism. The goal of ecumenism is the universal integration and unity of all Christian bodies. Landmarks in the move-

---

Visit a Catholic, Protestant, and a Jewish religious service. Compare what takes place during the services. Is the emphasis on sacraments or the sermon? What is the importance of the rituals, the music, and so forth? To what extent does the congregation actually participate?

---

ment include the international conference in Edinburgh in 1910 and the formation of the World Council of Churches in 1948. In the United States, however, Christian unity is receiving more attention and effort than it previously had.

The impact of the ecumenical movement in the United States is difficult to assess. As a goal it seems to have considerable support, and some, but not an impressive number, of denominations have merged. Bridges have been built between Protestant bodies and the Catholic Church. Under some circumstances, clergymen of both faiths can officiate at a mixed marriage involving a Catholic and a Protestant. Recently the Catholic Church stipulated that Protestants can participate in the Catholic communion service, again under certain circumstances.

HOW RELIGIOUS ARE AMERICANS?

No sociologist who begins a research project by asking, "How religious are Americans?" is going to achieve a single, final, definitive answer. Religious preference can be measured, as can official church membership and actual church attendance. Some sociologists even use a scale of five dimensions, which we examine below, for determining religiosity.

Religious preference is the denomination, if any, with which an individual identifies or to which he or she claims some sort of allegiance. It is the answer a person gives when asked his or her religion. "Protestant" has become a catchall category for an unmeasurable number of Americans who know they are neither Catholic nor Jewish but feel they should indicate some religion. Partly for this reason the number of religious people we arrive at by using stated religious preference is quite large. Very few Americans—less than 10 percent of all adults—claim that they are atheists, agnostics, or otherwise have no religion.

Official membership in a church gives us a different picture of the religious nature of Americans. Even though these figures are at best misleading—for the records of most churches are incomplete and out of date—we come up with far fewer religious people by using church membership rolls than by using stated preference. Records for the very early years of our country are sketchy and of questionable validity, but some contend that in 1800 only about 10 percent of the population belonged to a church, and that it was the large mass of un-

How can religiosity be measured? Can all of these communicants be considered equally religious because of their participation?

churched people that led to the great revivals.[17] Whether caused by the waves of revivalism or not, by 1900 about 43 percent of the population belonged to some church. Church membership increased steadily, so that by 1970 almost two-thirds of the people were church members.

You can claim to be a Protestant and you can hold membership in a specific Methodist church, but are you either a Protestant or a Methodist if you never attend church? *Church attendance* is thus another way of describing how religious Americans are. In 1971 about 40 percent of all Americans reported attending church in a typical week. Church attendance varies among the major denominations: 57 percent of Catholics, 37 percent of Protestants, and 19 percent of Jews attend weekly.[18] (Jews and Protestants are encouraged by their clergy to attend services, but Catholics who do not obey church law by attending Mass on Sunday commit a sin.) Church attenders are more likely to be women than men, and more church-goers are found among the college educated, the wealthy, and in the rural segments of society.

[17]See Yinger, p. 437.

[18]George Gallup, Jr. and John O. Davies III, *The Gallup Opinion Index* (Princeton, N.J.: Gallup International, 1971), p. 8.

TABLE 9-1. Proportion of Adults Attending Church During Typical Week

Year	Percent
1940	37
1950	39
1955	49
1960	47
1965	44
1970	42
1971	40

Source: Gallup Polls for respective years.

During the last 30 years, as shown in Table 9-1, church attendance in the United States first increased and then declined. The high point was the middle to late 1950s. Although the rate today is declining, it is still higher than it was in the 1940s. The current attendance rate of adults under 30 years of age is particularly noteworthy. About half of the Catholics between the ages of 21 and 29 attend weekly, while 70 percent of those over 30 go to church once a week. The comparable rates for Protestants are 32 percent and 45 percent.

A Model for Precise Measurement Individual acceptance of religious beliefs, participation in rituals, and understanding of religious dogma also affect social behavior. Because a person can "be religious" in different ways, considerable research effort has been spent developing concepts of "religiosity" and scales to measure how religious people are and in what ways. Sociologists now commonly refer to different *dimensions of religiosity,* such as those developed by Charles Glock and Rodney Stark, who distinguish five dimensions:[19]

1. The *experiential dimension:* the religious emotions and feelings expressed by an individual.

2. The *ideological dimension:* the religious beliefs of an individual; how many of the basic principles of the particular religion are accepted, and how strongly.

3. The *ritualistic dimension:* the extent to which a person engages in the rituals and practices of his or her religion.

4. The *intellectual dimension:* how much a person knows about the basic tenets of his or her faith—its origin, history, and literature.

5. The *consequential dimensions:* secular effects of the first four dimensions; the degree to which religious principles are acted out in daily life.

[19]Glock and Stark, Ch. 2.

We might expect some overlapping among the five dimensions of religiosity, but not that much is found. People can score considerably higher in one dimension than in another. In other words, people can be more religious in some aspects than in others. More refinements are needed in such scales of religiosity, for if religious commitment has significant behavioral consequences, we must be able to measure it with some precision.

THE CONSEQUENCES OF RELIGIOUS BEHAVIOR

Sociologists have long known that when Americans are categorized by their religious affiliations, major differences become apparent among them. Sociological research, therefore, often uses religion as a variable to explain a variety of human behavior. For example, while sociologists are not yet able to give precise reasons for the relationship, it has become apparent that religion is intertwined with the class system in America.[20] Studies repeatedly find that different denominations draw the bulk of their memberships from different levels of society. People of higher social status tend to be concentrated in the Episcopal, Presbyterian, and Congregational Churches. The churches of the middle class tend to be the Methodist, the Lutheran, and the Disciples of Christ, while lower class people are over-represented in the Baptist, Holiness, and Pentecostal congregations. The Catholic Church draws its membership disproportionately from the lower and middle classes, in that order.

Unfortunately, most of the research relating social class and religion has been more descriptive than explanatory, giving statistics but venturing no firm conclusions. But Gerhard Lenski's study, *The Religious Factor,* stands as a landmark of research that went beyond a description.[21] By studying a Detroit-area sample of Jews, Catholics, and white and black Protestants, Lenski sought to discover how religious belief and practice affected family life, economic behavior, political involvement, and so on. Lenski's treatment of the interrelationship of these variables is notable. To take but one example, he found that Catholics generally are more closely attached to their family and kinship groups than are Protestants. This difference is shown by visiting patterns, the influence of the family on voting behavior, and the migration pattern of the groups. The attachment to family and relatives—particularly as shown by an unwillingness to move geo-

---

[20]National studies of religious identification of people of different occupational and educational levels have had consistent findings. See *National Data Program for the Social Sciences, Spring 1972* (Chicago: National Opinion Research Center); see also Lenski, pp. 79–81.

[21]Lenski.

graphically—is seen as a partial explanation of why Catholics are less likely than Protestants to achieve upward social mobility.[22] By its effects on the institution of the family, religion affects the class system in America as well.

Lenski summarizes a few of his findings as follows:

> Depending on the socio-religious group to which a person belongs, the probabilities are increased or decreased that he will enjoy his occupation, indulge in installment buying, save to achieve objectives far in the future, believe in the American Dream, vote Republican, favor the welfare state, take a liberal view on the issue of freedom of speech, oppose racial integration in the schools, migrate to another community, maintain close ties with his family, develop a commitment to the principle of intellectual autonomy, have a large family, complete a given unit of education, or rise in the class system.[23]

Extrapolating from his study, Lenski traces the growth of our industrial state to the predominance of Protestants in American society and speculates on the consequences that religion has for economic development elsewhere: "In view of the social heritage of contemporary Catholicism, it seems unlikely that in the foreseeable future any devoutly Catholic state will become a leading industrial nation. . . . Catholicism seems to contain too many elements which are incompatible with such a role."[24] We have not, to be sure, done justice to Lenski's wealth of research findings, his detailed analyses, and the theoretical arguments that are based on his research. But we have tried to illustrate the kind of sociological work that can enable us to understand the many and far-reaching consequences of religion, and to speculate on the future of such an influential force in our society.

THE FUTURE OF RELIGION IN THE UNITED STATES

The facts gathered in recent years by sociologists indicate that religion is still a living institution in the United States. After all, less than 10 percent of the population claims no religious affiliation; and even though church attendance

[22]One study concluded that Catholics and Protestants had similar rates of social mobility, but re-analysis of the data by Lenski led him to conclude that the findings were not accurately stated. See Raymond Mack et al., "The Protestant Ethic, Level of Aspiration, and Social Mobility," *American Sociological Review* 21 (June 1956), 295–300; and Lenski, p. 83.

[23]Lenski, p. 349.

[24]Lenski, p. 320.

is low, about 40 percent of Americans attend church during a typical week. This percentage equals Canadian attendance and is about twice that of Great Britain, Australia, and some other countries. Of course, as we have seen, church attendance is not synonymous with religiosity, but it is still difficult to conclude from data on participation that organized religion is in the throes of death and is merely awaiting a decent (Christian?) burial.

Curiously, other data show that Americans are increasingly questioning the influence of religion on our norms and values. For example, three-fourths of the people responding to a public opinion poll in 1970 felt that religion was losing its influence on American life, while in 1957 only 14 percent felt this way. The editors of the Gallup Index consider this change "one of the most dramatic reversals in opinion in the history of polling."[25] Interestingly, the Gallup Poll also found that about 60 percent of ministers, priests, and rabbis felt that religion is less influential in our daily lives than it once was.

As polls so often do, these results leave a number of questions unanswered, particularly those that would shed light on the fate of organized religion. Presumably religious leaders look with displeasure on the declining impact of religion, but what about society in general? It makes a difference whether most people think of such a decline as a liberation from the shackles of organized religion or as a disturbing loss of a potent force in their lives. It would also be helpful to know what Americans think has caused this loss of religious influence. Is it thought that the churches are hopelessly irrelevant for today's world, and that other social forces are shaping moral values and guiding behavior? Perhaps Americans are not truly disenchanted with religion but simply feel that our major social problems today are secular problems and should be dealt with by secular institutions. Or perhaps the presumed disenchantment with religion indicates that Americans are generally dissatisfied with our present way of life and with the ability of our institutions to deal with our problems.

THE YOUNG: A MAJOR UNKNOWN FOR RELIGION

The older adults who make pronouncements on our churches and schools will not be around much longer. Wherever they are going, they will be followed with discomforting swiftness by those in their middle years. It makes sense, then, to look to the behavior and attitudes of young people for some insights into the future of religion in our society.

We have already noted that far fewer people under 30 years of age attend church than do those over 30. In addition, more younger than older people profess

[25]Gallup and Davies, p. 45.

Are the Jesus Freaks to be short-lived or long-lived, a blow to established religion, a sustenance, or neither? How will religion fare with the young?

no religious affiliation. To the Gallup Poll question, asked of a cross section of college students, "Is organized religion a relevant part of your life at the present time, or not?" 58 percent responded that it was not relevant.[26] The students were more evenly split on the question of whether religion can answer all or most of today's problems or whether it is largely out of date. Unfortunately, we lack comparable data for the younger adults who are not college students, and who are the majority of the younger generation. Then, too, are we witnessing a lasting change or simply a difference between generations? That is, as the younger adults grow older, will they become more like their parents in religious participation and attitudes? To add to the complexity of the prediction problem, many young people are part of the Jesus Freak movement or otherwise show a deep concern for religious experiences.

[26]Gallup and Davies, p. 18.

IS THE DEVIL A SOCIALIZING AGENT?

Is Satan alive and well and living inside of all of us? These being troubled times, perhaps he (or—let's be fair—she) is. Far fewer people believe in the Devil than believe in God. And many people think that widespread belief in Satan ended when the age of science took hold of society. Certainly psychology has no place for the Devil, except as a mythical character who plays a role in the delusions of some disturbed persons.

Yet even in our supposedly enlightened society it has been found that belief in the Devil rises and falls according to how things are going. Hard times of strife and unrest raise the popularity of the Devil as the evildoer behind all our problems. But "out of sight, out of mind": When things are going fairly smoothly the Devil is not given his due, and fewer people believe in him. Right now, however, his stock is one of the few that are running high.

The truth or falseness of any religious belief is beyond the professional concerns of the sociologist. But in the last few years there has been ample stimulus for investigations of witchcraft, devil worship, and the occult as social phenomena.

In our society more and more people in each succeeding decade have obtained college educations. At the same time, colleges have given increasing prominence to the social sciences. Government at all levels, but especially the federal government, has also placed greater reliance on the knowledge and methods of the social sciences in establishing public policy (with the recent exceptions noted in the issue to Chapter 1). The scientific method has achieved prominence among people of most political persuasions as the best source of knowledge about ourselves and our society.

Why, then, this rather abrupt turnabout? Why the resurgence of medieval witchcraft and belief in the Devil? Why did so many youths who turned away from drugs embrace a fundamentalist Bible religion instead of the established religions that were trying to reach them? Can it be that those who reject the God of organized religion and side with his or her enemy share something in common with those who choose God but reject the established churches?

Is a world made intelligible by scientific methods somehow too impersonal for the psychological needs of some people? Or is society itself simply too complex, too impersonal, too much a collection of secondary groupings and relationships? And has organized religion gone the same way? Has it outgrown the ability to serve individuals in need of intimate touch with the supernatural and with each other?

Develop a list of courses in the area of religion (e.g., sociology of religion) taught at your own or at a nearby college. Find out what have been the enrollment trends in the courses for the last ten years. How do the instructors explain the increasing (or decreasing) popularity of the courses?

By now it should be clear that we cannot predict with any certainty the future of organized religion in the United States. Religion will continue to change of course. In the immediate future, we will probably see the churches attempting to address themselves to relevant social issues without compromising theological principles. For the thoroughly disillusioned, these efforts will seem to be in vain. Some already see organized religion not as an agency for dealing with modern problems, but as part of the problem. We must not forget, however, that religion includes a lot more than church attendance, liturgy, and changing emphases on social issues. So long as people have ultimate concerns incapable of being answered by the best of their science, and so long as people seek rescue from their cosmic loneliness, they will need religion. It is safe to predict that these conditions will continue for a long, long time.

The religious institution generally comes closer than any other social institution to dealing exclusively with beliefs, values, norms, and other aspects of nonmaterial culture. The place of religion in our society is complicated by the fact that although our society is secular, and is kept so by our Constitution, most of our social values come from a long history in which church and state intimately shared the guiding role and were for centuries virtually inseparable.

The power of the religious institution depends on how many members of a society choose to share its stated beliefs and values. Because religion is a voluntary institution—that is, having only members who choose to join or to remain—it has perhaps not suffered strains quite as severe as other institutions have in recent years. The institution we examine in the next chapter, education, also deals with the nonmaterial elements of culture. But education is today suffering from unprecedented stresses and conflicts. This is partly because in our society participation in the institution is compulsory, and partly because changes in the other institutions have had a variety of confusing consequences for the schools, their goals, and their methods.

SUMMARY POINTS AND QUESTIONS

1. Religion and magic, although in some ways similar, differ in terms of the assumptions each makes about the supernatural, the goals pursued by its adherents, the means used to achieve these goals, and the effects each has on society and on the individual.

> *Specifically, how do these two systems differ in terms of assumptions, ends, means, and effects?*
>
> *How are they similar?*

2. While religion deals with the supernatural, science deals with the natural. During different historical periods, the boundaries between the supernatural and the natural have been ambiguous, resulting in conflict between these two systems.

> *What are some historical issues over which science and religion have come into conflict?*
>
> *One contention is that the more that is explained by science, the less importance religion will have. Do you agree?*

3. Religion can be defined as an institutionalized system of beliefs, symbols, rituals, values, and practices that deal with ultimate meanings.

> *What questions does religion attempt to answer?*
>
> *What are some experiences, other than religion, in which man searches for ultimate meanings?*

4. Religion functions for the individual by providing meaning for tragedy and death and by providing meaningful group experiences.

> *What religious beliefs and practices serve these functions?*
>
> *Besides religion, what other institutions or groups also serve to fulfill these functions?*

5. Religion functions for society by producing and maintaining the integration of the society. This might be dysfunctional when it inhibits needed social change.

> *What are some examples of the ways in which religion has inhibited social change to the detriment of a society?*
>
> *When has religion been an impetus to change?*

6. The separation of church and state, denominational pluralism, and ecumenism have all been associated with religion in the United States.

> *How do issues such as aid to religious schools, tax-exempt religious property, and prayers in public schools relate to the above factors?*

7. The religiosity of Americans might be indicated by religious preference, official membership in a church, and by church attendance. While less than 10 percent of Americans indicate they have no religious preference, only 42 percent of Americans attend church weekly.

> *How do you account for this discrepancy?*

> *Does it indicate a failure of religious institutions to meet the needs of individuals?*

8. Religious affiliation and participation appear to be related to numerous variables such as family attachment, political attitudes, views on educational importance, and relationship to the economic system.

> *How do you think being Protestant, Catholic, or Jewish would affect the above mentioned variables?*

9. It appears that religious participation is becoming less important to the lives of many Americans.

> *How do you account for this?*

> *Do you think this is a short-term trend? Why or why not?*

SUGGESTED READINGS

Berger, Peter L. *The Sacred Canopy: Elements of a Sociological Theory of Religion.* Garden City, N.Y.: Doubleday & Co., 1967. Applies a theoretical perspective derived from the sociology of knowledge to the phenomenon of religion. Shows how religion functions in the construction of a world view and how the process of secularization affects this world view.

Carrier, Herve. *The Sociology of Religious Belongings.* New York: Herder and Herder, 1965. Deals with the need for people to belong to meaningful groups. The author holds that the religious group experience is a source of identification for people, provides a self-image, and integrates the individual into secure social community.

Durkheim, Emile. *The Elementary Forms of the Religious Life.* New York: The Free Press, 1965. Originally published in 1915. A classic in the area of the sociology of religion. It contends that the function of religion is to integrate persons into the society, and that this is accomplished by rituals, sacrifice, and beliefs.

Freud, Sigmund. *The Future of an Illusion.* Garden City, N.Y.: Doubleday & Co., 1964. Originally published in Vienna in 1927. Argues that religious ideas are born out of the need to make tolerable one's feelings of helplessness, which stem from one's memories of the helplessness of childhood.

Greeley, Andrew M. *Unsecular Man: The Persistence of Religion.* New York: Schocken Books, 1972. Presents the thesis that there are basic human religious needs, that these needs have not changed historically, and that the modern unsecular mood is only temporary.

Herberg, Will. *Protestant-Catholic-Jew.* Garden City, N.Y.: Doubleday & Co., 1960. An historical treatise on the rise of three religious communities in the United States.

Seligmann, Kurt. *Magic, Supernaturalism, and Religion.* New York: Grosset and Dunlap, 1968. A history of magic and its influence on Western civilization.

Weber, Max. *The Sociology of Religion.* Boston: Beacon Press, 1964. Originally published in Germany in 1922. A classical work on the sociology of religion. Weber deals with the difference between religion and magic, offers classical definitions of the prophet, the priest, and the magician; and discusses asceticism, mysticism, and salvation religion.

Yinger, J. Milton. *Sociology Looks at Religion.* New York: Macmillan, 1961. Deals with the relationship of religion to social change from a structural–functional point of view. The author also has a chapter on the areas of research for the sociology of religion.

What's the difference between socialization and education? None, really: Education is a form of socialization. In the early generations of our society, all a person had to learn to become a Christian farmer or tradesman was how to read the Bible, how to do essential bookkeeping sums, and how to write occasional letters. Today our society is far more complex and demands transmission of more knowledge before a person can be economically and politically productive. Also, our culture values equality of opportunity. And education, whatever its failings, is considered a means to that end. The failure to meet that goal is a sore issue today. In fact, few people are now pleased with school systems. Many say that educational goals are poorly defined; that those which are defined are not achieved; and moreover that the goals are not suited to today's and tomorrow's society.

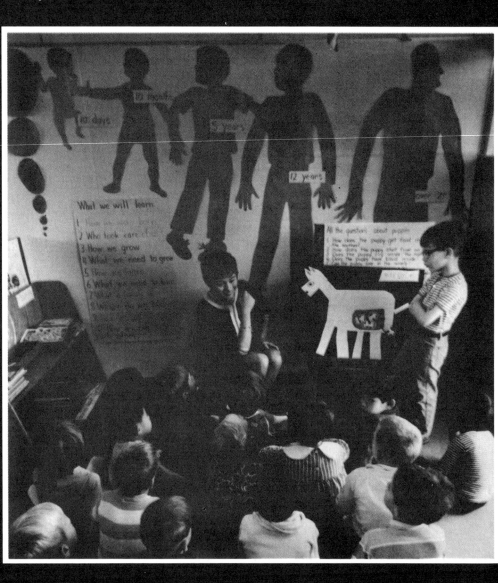

EDUCATION AND SOCIETY

School . . . is the major component of the system of consumer production that is becoming more complex and specialized and bureaucratized. Schooling is necessary to produce the habits and expectations of the managed consumer society. Inevitably it produces institutional dependence and ranking in spite of any effort by the teacher to the contrary.

Ivan Illich*

The saddest disappointment of the Scarecrow in the Land of Oz was that he could not think because he had no brain. The Wizard of Oz led him to see that he was really just as smart as anyone else, and that he simply lacked a certification of his intelligence. The Wizard then awarded him the degree Doctor of Thinkology. The Scarecrow's problems were solved and the Wizard showed that he was indeed a wizard.

Everywhere outside the Land of Oz there is more to learning and being educated than a certificate—at least there should be. In its broadest meaning, education is the same as socialization, for no society stops its socialization with the early years of childhood when the family is still the primary socializing agent. All societies educate their pre–adults to enable them to participate in their society and to assume the occupations and other roles required by the group. In simpler societies, education is largely informal, even though not all the teachers may be the child's parents. One mark of an advanced and complex society is its tremendous store of knowledge and its consequent dependence on the printed word. The growth in knowledge, coupled with the great diversity of adult roles, has led all but the simplest societies to formalize education, to assign that function to organizations whose primary function is to educate.

THE FUNCTIONS OF EDUCATION

In this chapter we investigate what the educational institution does to and for society. We look at the major functions of this institution and their applications in our own society. We examine what goes into the organizations that embody the institution and what we receive in return for the resources devoted to them.

You all know much about our schools from your own experiences in them. A sociological study of the educational system should add a different dimension to your knowledge, one that shows how the schools fit into the broader social

---

*Ivan Illich, "Education Without School: How It Can Be Done," *New York Review of Books,* January 7, 1971. Reprinted with permission from New York Review of Books. Copyright 1971, NYREV.

system. A sociological study should also be interesting, maddening, challenging, upsetting, and possibly action-provoking.[1] This is a big order. Read on.

TRANSMISSION OF KNOWLEDGE

If people were asked why we have schools and did not think the question too absurd to merit an answer, most would probably say that we have schools so that children can learn. True: One of the major functions of our formal education system is to transmit knowledge. But to fulfill this function is not as simple as it may first appear.

For all practical purposes we can consider that knowledge is infinite. There is no end to what we can learn about ourselves, our world in all its dimensions, and the universe. Thus—and this is sometimes overlooked—some selection must be made. Of all the knowledge that has been accumulated by and about past and present cultures, of all the languages both living and dead, of all the information that we have about biology, optics, chemistry, and so on, and of all the mental and physical skills that can be taught to humans, we must select what knowledge and skills should be taught.

In the early generations of our society there appeared to be much agreement on what sorts of knowledge were important enough to transmit to the next generation through formal education. Children were expected to spend several years in school learning how to read and write and do arithmetic. These skills were felt necessary to prepare children for life in the kind of world in which their elders thought they would live. Once educated, they could read the Bible, engage in commerce, and participate in the budding democracy. These were highly utilitarian educational goals, for they were related to living and working in the real world. To be sure, there were institutions of higher learning, here and abroad, for those few who wanted to study the classics or to prepare themselves for the professions, particularly the ministry. In time, more years of public education were provided, and eventually compulsory attendance laws were enacted. Private and public colleges sprang up all over the nation. As a society we seemed to be saying that more of the infinite storehouse of knowledge should be transmitted to more people. We now have the same educational institution as we had in colonial days, but the way in which it must perform its function has changed drastically. Herein lies one of our problems. We nod our heads vigorously, and sometimes woefully, whenever we hear mention of the "knowledge explosion," but sometimes we act as if we do not understand its profound implications. What knowledge should be transmitted to whom? Why? Think about it. Later in the chapter we look into the problems of what we sometimes glibly call the transmission of knowledge.

[1]For an overview of the sociology of education see Donald Hansen and Joel Gerstl, eds., *Society and Education* (Boston: Allyn & Bacon, 1967); and Patricia Sexton, *The American School: A Sociological Analysis* (Englewood Cliffs, N.J.: Prentice-Hall, 1967).

EQUALITY OF OPPORTUNITY

We discussed in Chapter 7 that the rewards of our society are not distributed equally: Some get more than others. The difference in financial rewards is due mostly to the fact that some occupations pay more than others. Education, in turn, either directly or indirectly affects the type of work a person will pursue.

An important stated function of our school system is to provide *equality of opportunity:* education for all who want it and are mentally able to profit from it. Presumably, most people in our society feel that income and the good things of life should not be distributed equally, but rather that every one of us should have a chance to do what we want to do and reap the rewards according to our ability, motivation, and personal desires. Some would end up richer than others, some would be in more prestigious occupations than others, and some would have more knowledge and skills than others. But the chances for success should be equal even though the result would be inequality of rewards.

The value of equal opportunity means that our chances for success should depend not on how well we chose the family we were born into but on what we ourselves want to do and are able to do. Success would not be guaranteed to anyone, but everyone would be offered the same opportunities for it. Society should gain from such a value system. Important positions would be filled by those who best used the opportunities that were offered them. The reservoir of talent from which we could draw would be broad, for the abilities of people from all backgrounds would be used.

The value of equal educational opportunities places a tremendous burden on the school system. Whether or not the school system can actually provide equal opportunities is a question being widely explored today. There is more agreement that the schools are not providing equality of opportunity than there is agreement on the reasons for failure. One side claims culture and environment are the problem; the other claims inherited differences are the cause. Let us assume, first, that the conclusions of Arthur Jensen are correct, and that intelligence is substantially influenced by genetic factors.[2] Equality of opportunity could be assured by giving all children the chance to be educated to the limits of their ability to learn. Innately superior children, regardless of race, family background, or finances, would be educated in such a manner that they would have an equal chance to attend college and professional schools if they wished. Some compensatory educational programs, like Headstart, might be necessary to make up for the absence of preschool learning for intelligent children of humble birth, thus equalizing their chances of profiting from formal education.

But what if intelligence is culturally and environmentally determined, and

---

[2]Arthur Jensen, "How Much Can We Boost IQ and Scholastic Achievement?" *Harvard Educational Review* 39 (Winter–Summer 1969), 1–123. The role of IQ in perpetuating inequalities in American society is a complicated and emotionally charged area. See the discussion and many references cited in Christopher Jencks and others, *Inequality: A Reassessment of the Effect of Family and Schooling in America* (New York: Basic Books, 1972), Ch. 3.

The schools have been assigned many tasks, among them equality of opportunity. Why have they generally failed in this as in other tasks?

early childhood socialization and the presence or absence of a stimulating home environment radically affect the preschooler's ability to learn? Then more individual attention to children from disadvantaged homes would fail to produce equality of opportunity, for strong countervailing forces would still be operating to stifle the child's intellectual motivation and ability to learn. And what if intelligence is partially genetic but strongly influenced by early childhood socialization? Finally, what can, or should, the schools do with children who have the ability to learn but are not motivated to do so, or with those who are motivated but apparently lack the ability?

Our educational system continues to have the manifest function of providing equal opportunities for all to attain academic success and ultimately success in life. In a later section we investigate how, and how well, this function, so basic in the American value system, actually is being achieved.

CREATION OF NEW KNOWLEDGE

Another function of education is to discover new knowledge. In most universities this function is defined explicitly: The university professor has the responsibility to conduct research as well as to teach. Whether the field is marine biology, physics, English literature, animal science, or sociology, the collective efforts of researchers should generate new facts, new explanations for phenomena, or new solutions to problems. As a result of these efforts we should find out more and more about humanity, society, the physical world, and so on.

New knowledge is not sought or discovered only in universities. Private enterprise spends large sums for research and development, and a high value is placed on new knowledge throughout our entire educational system. In elementary school, for example, students learn about classical inventions and discoveries, and science fairs encourage students to apply the basic principles of the scientific method. In high school, students gain more practical experience in conducting experiments in various fields. Implicitly at least, children are taught both the value of new knowledge and one method by which it can be developed. Students are supposedly taught to think for themselves. That is, they should become able to generate new knowledge, new ideas, and fresh ways of looking at familiar problems.

If students learn these lessons well, the educational system should be an instrument of change. Many people are able to accept this consequence in some areas of knowledge but not in others. The development of safer automobiles, of new anti–pollution devices, of cheaper methods of producing energy all require the willingness and the ability to consider new ideas. But when students who have been taught to think for themselves apply their innovative skills to other areas, their efforts are not always applauded. Investigating new methods of taxation, better ways of caring for the poor, or more humanitarian methods of providing economically for those unable to do so for themselves often lead to ideas that challenge the status quo or conflict with cherished traditions. Our society is clearly beset with many "people problems," and social innovations of various kinds are sorely needed. One of the functions of the educational system is to encourage innovative thought and new knowledge, which in turn could lead to rational, humanitarian change. Paradoxically, we are often threatened when our schools work this way and critical when they do not.

PLACEMENT

Still another function of our educational system is *placement,* or sorting. Throughout our school careers we are tested and evaluated as to how well we are doing and what course of study we should be encouraged to pursue. Whether or not labels such as "slow learner" or "college material" are used, children are steered along different paths according to evaluations of their performance.[3] Indeed, if placement tests and course prerequisites are part of the system, the term "steer" is too gentle.

The placement function would at first seem to be socially useful, for every society must be sure that the necessary work is done. In a complex society with many adult roles, it would seem logical to have some kind of a sifting and sorting process, based on reasonable criteria, that would place people in jobs for which they are best suited. But there are problems with this function and the way in which it is actually performed.

The validity of placement criteria has been seriously questioned. What do test scores and similar measures really tell us about what children can, or should, do with their own lives? The evaluation devices sometimes appear logical: For example, repeated failure in high school math indicates pretty well that a person will not be able to pursue a successful career in engineering. This logic sounds reasonable until we venture into the touchy area of what kind of mathematics courses were offered, how they were taught, and how it was determined that some children had real ability and others little talent in this area. The problem is magnified when we look at the overall placement function rather than at individual performance. Each year thousands of students drop out of school, others switch into vocational programs or trade schools, while still others remain on the so-called academic track. This variation brings us to another aspect of the placement function; that is, the schools not only place children, but they also teach them their place.

The methods used to convince children where they belong are not subtle. Testing and grading are the most prominent means, and children are usually convinced that such evaluative devices are legitimate. If these evaluations are accepted, repeated failures or low scores or the recognition that they are near the bottom of the class can be powerful devices to persuade children to drop out of the academic program. Children learn their place, even if they suffer loss of self-esteem in the process.

Many bright students are turned off by the whole educational process; not so bright ones have career aspirations beyond their abilities; and many others seriously mismatch their chosen careers with their true interests and abilities. Perhaps in simpler societies there are gentler and more humane ways of encouraging people to prepare for and accept the necessary adult roles. No society can ignore this function. In our own and other complex societies, this function is administered by the educational bureaucracy.

[3]For an account of how this works at the junior college level, see Burton R. Clark, "The 'Cooling-Out' Function in Higher Education," *American Journal of Sociology* 65 (May 1960), 569–576.

.From the schools' placement function, children learn their place, even if they suffer loss of self-esteem in the process.

OTHER EDUCATIONAL FUNCTIONS

Our system of formal education performs still other functions, both manifest and latent. Schools perform a *custodial* function; they keep children out of the home a good many hours a day, five days a week. This function should not be viewed lightly. Many women go back into the labor force once their youngest child is in school, and recently much demand has been expressed for day care centers that would allow mothers of preschool children to work outside the home. Apparently we need or want responsible agencies to keep children out of the home. If this function makes the schools seem like some kind of an isolation ward, a world apart from the real world where children and youth can be kept until they are cleansed of the awful stain of youthfulness, consider that almost all jobs in our society are for people of adult years, and that this fact is not likely to change. If we did not have schools, we would have to invent something very much like them to give our young people something to do.

Schools also allow young people to be socializing agents for one another.[4] This function works more dramatically if the students come from different backgrounds than if there is segregation by class or race. Through their interaction, children can learn both important and trivial information from each other: the lives and hobbies of their peers, the different jobs held by their parents, the differing political or religious convictions of their parents. Perhaps most important of all, they can learn that such differences exist. Of course, children also teach one another how to blow bubble gum, how to whistle through their fingers, how to smoke cigarettes or pot, how to run underground newspapers, and the like.

The schools, finally, provide the child with an ongoing experience in a hierarchical bureaucratic organization.[5] They see that test grades and attendance records are kept, that memoranda regularly flow from the principal to the teachers, that they need proper identification before they can borrow a book from the library, and that they need "hall passes" if they are not to get in trouble for being out of the classroom. Just as surely, they learn that there are ways to beat the system, to get by without conforming to the rules, and that for every rule there seems to be a bewildering array of exceptions. They learn, too, that there is a ranking system of authority and prestige within the school and, if they are at all perceptive, that the real power and prestige do not always fit with the formal system. All this, and more, teaches them how things work in the bureaucracies they will meet beyond the school.

EDUCATION IN THE UNITED STATES

Education in the United States is an enormous enterprise, with all the merits and imperfections of a big business. In 1972 there were about 120,000 schools from elementary to college level, with about 56 million students.[6] On a typical day over 3 million children were in kindergarten and 1.5 million in nursery

[4]Coleman's study of 10 high schools contains a wealth of information on adolescent behaviors, attitudes, and values. See James S. Coleman, *The Adolescent Society* (New York: Free Press, 1961).

[5]For an interesting account of "red tape" in the schools, see Bel Kaufman, *Up the Down Staircase* (Englewood Cliffs, N.J.: Prentice-Hall, 1964). See also James Herndon, *How to Survive in Your Native Land* (New York: Bantam Books, 1972). For a provocative piece on how the schools put students down, see Jerry Farber, *The Student as Nigger* (New York: Pocket Books, 1970).

[6]Enrollments, percentage increases, and number of teachers assembled from and computed from U.S. Bureau of the Census, *Statistical Abstract of the United States: 1971* (Washington, D.C.: U.S. Government Printing Office, 1971) and U.S. Bureau of the Census, *Current Population Reports*, Series P-20 (February 1973).

Do a functional analysis of course grades. In what ways are grades functional and dysfunctional to education? Which of the functions and dysfunctions are manifest and which latent?

---

schools, bringing the total to over 60 million students in schools at all levels. When trade and business schools, training schools operated by industries, and correspondence schools are included, the best estimate is that on a typical day almost one–third of our population is attending some type of school.

Education in the United States is expanding, as Table 10–1 and Figure 10–1 show. Though sometimes difficult to grasp, sheer numbers are both a measure of our success and a part of our problem. Between 1950 and 1972 the number of students in kindergarten increased by almost 2 million, those in elementary school by over 11 million, in high school by almost 9 million, and in college by almost 6 million. The total number of students at all levels thus doubled from about 30 million to over 60 million in 22 years. A couple of decades can be an excruciatingly short time for any society to create places in its schools for over 30 million additional students. But we did it, at the same time that we were building homes and cars, feeding a growing number of people, getting men on the moon, and engaging in two wars.

Percentage increases are equally impressive. The steepest increases in school enrollment have been at the college and the kindergarten levels. From 1950 to 1972, college enrollments increased 213 percent, kindergarten 167 percent, high school 135 percent, and grade school 53 percent. In this time, by comparison, the total population of the United States grew only 37 percent.

More students require more teachers. In 1970 there were over 2 million teachers in the nation's public elementary and high schools, more than double their number in 1950. Actually, the combined teaching staffs at these levels increased by a higher percentage than school enrollments, and employment in education rose faster than general employment. From 1950 to 1970 combined enrollments in public grade and high schools jumped 100 percent; total employment in the United States rose 20 percent; while the number of elementary and high school teachers combined climbed 125 percent.

Millions of other workers are toiling less visibly in the educational vineyard. Architects design school buildings, service workers keep them clean and repaired, and others make the furniture, publish the books, and make and maintain our schools' machines and equipment. The list could go on and on.

Another indication of the vastness of our expanding educational enterprise is the amount of money our society devotes to education. Scarcely 9 billion

TABLE 10-1.   U.S. School Enrollments, 1930–1972

Year	Kindergarten	Elementary	High School	College	Total
1972	3,135,000	32,242,000	15,169,000	8,313,000	60,142,000
1970	3,183,000	33,950,000	14,715,000	7,413,000	59,261,000
1960	2,293,000	30,119,000	9,600,000	3,216,000	45,228,000
1950	1,175,000	21,032,000	6,453,000	2,659,000	31,319,000
1940	661,000	20,466,000	7,130,000	1,494,000	29,751,000
1930	786,000	22,953,000	4,812,000	1,101,000	26,652,000

Source: *Statistical Abstracts,* 1971 and *Current Population Reports* P-20, No. 247, February, 1973.

dollars was spent for education in 1950.[7] In 1973 about 90 billion dollars was spent. About 97 percent of this was for public schools at all levels. Even allowing for inflation, there has been a tremendous growth in school expenditures over the two decades. The cost of education rose almost 925 percent in the 20 years, significantly more than the increase in the number of teachers or the number of students. In 1973, 8 percent of our gross national product went for public education, as compared with 3 percent in 1950.

What is our society getting for the money and other resources it devotes to education? The question is crucial, but unfortunately there are no easy answers. Perhaps the easiest approach to an answer—although not necessarily the one that addresses the fundamental issue—is quantitative: the percent of the population in the appropriate age groups who are in school, retention rates, degrees awarded, and the like.

In 1970, practically every child between the ages of seven and thirteen, and over 90 percent of those between fourteen and seventeen years of age was enrolled in school. The schools thus reach most of the clientele that they should be reaching.

The school retention rates and their changes over the years give another view of the payoff we receive for our educational dollars. Out of every 1000 students who entered the fifth grade in 1926, 400 entered the twelfth grade and 333, or exactly a third, actually graduated from high school. Out of the original 1000, 129 went on to enroll in college (but this does not mean they graduated). But look at a more recent picture, the high school class of 1972. Of each 1000 children who entered the fifth grade in 1964, 75 percent graduated from high school and almost half of the original group of fifth graders enrolled in college. The increase from one-third to three-fourths graduating from high school is impressive.

The data on those who completed college round out the picture on the educational achievements of our society's students.[8] In recent years, over a million

[7]Expenditures for education from U.S. Bureau of the Census, *Statistical Abstract of the United States: 1973* (Washington, D.C.: U.S. Government Printing Office, 1973), p. 107.

[8]U.S. Office of Education, *Earned Degrees Conferred* (Washington, D.C.: U.S. Government Printing Office), published annually.

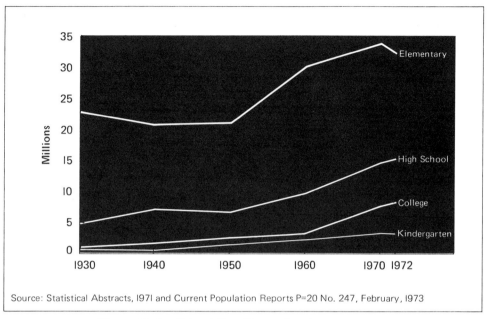

Figure 10-1. *School Enrollment Levels, 1930–1972*

college degrees have been awarded annually. The increase in the number of college degrees has been fantastic. In the ten years from 1960 to 1970, the number of bachelor's degrees awarded jumped by 111 percent, master's degrees by 179 percent, and doctorates by 200 percent. Another way of looking at the growth in college degrees awarded is to see how it has affected the proportion of our population of young adults that have one or more college degrees. In 1940, 6 percent of the people between the ages of 25 and 29 had completed four or more years of college. The comparable figures for 1950, 1960, and 1970 are 8 percent, 11 percent, and 16 percent.

These pages of figures about what our society puts into our educational system and what we get out of it do not reveal what most people would consider issues in education: Do those who are enrolled in schools attend regularly? Do those who attend learn anything? Do retention rates mean the students have learned whatever it is they are supposed to be learning at one level before being promoted to the next, or are they just being moved along through the system? Among those who are learning—and surely there must be some—what are they learning? Is it what they should be learning? Are our total educational dollars spent in such a way to provide the same quality of education for all children, or do some receive a bigger slice of the educational pie than others? These are blunt and perhaps unpleasant questions, but they are persistently raised. Straight answers can be equally unpleasant.

MAJOR ISSUES IN AMERICAN EDUCATION

The concerns that Americans have about their schools are many and varied, ranging from the serious to the trivial. We have hinted at only a few of them. We can discuss these concerns by looking again at the major functions of our educational system, this time concentrating on how well they are being performed.

PROBLEMS CONCERNING THE TRANSMISSION OF KNOWLEDGE

Presumably, no one would deny that one function of our schools should be to transmit knowledge. But as we mentioned earlier, serious questions can be raised about what knowledge should be transmitted to whom and for what purpose. Rational humans should be able to develop logical guidelines for determining what knowledge is sufficiently important to transmit to the next generation through formal education. In other words, we should have sound educational goals.

If any general statement can be made, it is simply that educational goals have become less related to working and living than they were in the past. Today it is charged that the main purpose of the early years of grade school is to prepare students for the later years; the purpose of the later years is to prepare students for high school; and an important goal of our high schools is to prepare students for college. Then what? The basic problem does not seem to lie in the function of transmitting knowledge but in the educational goals that serve as guidelines for this transmission.

Three major criticisms are commonly made of today's educational goals. First, our goals are poorly defined. Second, our goals, however poorly defined, are not being achieved, at least not enough to justify the vast time and money spent. Third and most devastating of all, our educational goals are bad, or—less bluntly—are ill-suited for the present and emerging social condition.

Poor Definition of Educational Goals It is possible to find general statements of educational goals, but these are often vague. Such vagueness makes it almost impossible to evaluate a given course of action. Take, for example, the question of how much choice students should have in selecting their high school courses. Should it be much or little? Should we have several different "tracks," or should all students basically meet the same requirements? These questions can be answered meaningfully only if we can agree on the purpose of high school education.

For another example, sex education was rapidly introduced into our grade and high schools, presumably because "somebody" thought it desirable. But in some communities it was just as swiftly withdrawn when groups strongly objected to the way it was handled.[9] On what grounds can we evaluate either the introduction or the removal?

Why are modern foreign languages taught? If children should learn a foreign language, why are they not taught one in grade schools? Studies have shown that young children learn another language more easily than do older children. Should archery instruction be part of the physical education program?

These and many other questions are continually answered in the form of decisions on what should or shouldn't be done in the schools. Many have an uneasy feeling that important decisions may not be guided by well–formulated goals. It has been said that if you don't know where you're going any path will get you there. For a leisurely hike in the woods, perhaps it makes no difference which path you take or which destination you reach. There would seem much to be gained, however, by making our educational goals as explicit as possible. At the very least, it would allow us to see where the many paths are taking our children, and all of us.

Educational Goals Not Being Achieved Even though it would be foolish to make a blanket indictment of the entire nation's school system, there is ample evidence that schools are failing to reach their own goals, however poorly these may be defined. Most Americans have read about the terrible conditions in large city schools, where teachers claim to be chiefly disciplinarians but from all reports are not succeeding too well even in that role.[10] Knifings, muggings, extortion, and physical attacks on teachers are now so common that only the most blatant cases draw the attention of the press. Not much could possibly be taught or learned in what appear to be poorly run detention centers. Even the schools in smaller cities and in the suburbs have their share of discipline problems. It is not uncommon, but still a little frightening, to see security guards, with walkie–talkies on their hips, patrolling the halls and playgrounds of elementary and high schools.

Nationally, our literacy rate is high, but anyone who has gone through our grade and high schools knows that a certain proportion of pupils did not learn what they were supposed to learn and were nevertheless passed through the grades. The present system of "social promotion" may be more humane than

[9]See Luther G. Baker, Jr., "The Rising Furor Over Sex Education," *The Family Coordinator* 18 (July 1969), 210–217; and Mary S. Calderone, "Special Report: Siecus in 1969," *Journal of Marriage and the Family* 31 (November 1969), 674–676.

[10]James Herndon, *The Way It Spozed To Be* (New York: Bantam Books, 1969).

the older system of keeping the students back. But at least the older practice implied that students were supposed to be learning something, and those who did not learn it had to repeat the grade until they did. In the practice of passing non-learners, there is the cynical suggestion that teaching and learning may not be important functions of our educational system at all.

College instructors are notorious for their complaints that many of their students have come to college poorly prepared in logical reasoning, have trouble reading and writing their native language, and lack mathematical skills. The blame can be passed to the high schools, and then to the elementary schools, where it can be returned to the college professors who taught the teachers. Wherever the blame lies, our educational system is failing in what presumably is one of its major functions—to educate.

The Question of Relevancy Many students have speculated that the real problem is not the failure to meet educational goals but the irrelevance of the goals themselves. They claim that the schools, or certain courses of study, are simply not relevant to contemporary life. We can dismiss such complaints as idle prattle of the immature, or we can admit that just possibly those who are supposed to be profiting from the system have discovered a serious flaw in it.

Formal education, as part of the broad socialization process, should be future-oriented. Ideally, it should prepare children to live in the world they will find when they become adults. But neither parents nor educators can possibly know for certain what tomorrow will be like. The best we can do is to equip the adults of the future so they will be able to build and rebuild it for themselves. Nevertheless, critics contend that our schools are attempting to prepare our children to live in a world that no longer exists.

In a 1939 satire on education, *The Sabre-Tooth Curriculum*,[11] a mythical paleolithic society was described in which the elders insisted that children be taught how to kill sabre-tooth tigers long after the tigers were all but extinct. Children were also expected to learn how to club the wooly horse even though the little wooly horses had deserted the area. Educators were not addressing themselves to the real problems of the day: the fierce glacial bears who migrated to the area and whose threat to it could not be dealt with by the same tactics used on tigers. To teach antelope snaring was somewhat subversive, even though the antelope had replaced the wooly horse and clubbing would not capture antelopes, whose skins and meat were sorely needed by the group. Many of today's students could quickly see parallels to the present and would assert that today's school is seriously out of phase with their own and with society's real needs.

[11] J. Abner Peddiwell, *The Sabre-Tooth Curriculum* (New York: McGraw-Hill, 1939).

What, then, should be taught in the schools? Sociologists are not specialists in curriculum development. They look at the society and try to relate our institutionalized system of learning to what they know about the society. Ours is a society of onrushing change. Routine assembly-line work is rapidly disappearing and will continue to do so. Within the lifetime of individuals now graduating from high school, whole career lines will fold and new ones will open up, forcing many to change careers perhaps several times if they wish to stay employed. Many other changes will occur. In this type of society, as George Leonard puts it, "the schools may best serve society by serving the individual capacity to keep learning, to keep changing, to keep creating."[12] The rapid pace of change will require individuals who are able to cope with it. Increasingly greater abilities to judge and to make choices, to be imaginative and creative, and to be adaptable will be required in the post-industrial society (a society in which the production of services is more important than the production of goods). If our physical climate were changing drastically because a new ice age was approaching, and we did not change our institutions to enable individuals to deal with the change, the survival chances of our society would be low. In a similar sense, to serve society, our educational system must alter its goals to respond to the profound social, economic, and political changes of today and tomorrow.

PROBLEMS WITH EQUALITY OF OPPORTUNITY

When evaluating the function of providing equality of opportunity, we must keep in mind that this is actually two functions: equality *in* the school system, and equality *through* the school system. First, are children treated equally and otherwise given equal chances of succeeding in school? Second, how well do the schools provide all children with equal chances for success in life? If the educational experience is in any way related to success in later life, the two aspects of equality of opportunity should be related. Nevertheless, they are not identical.

One way of evaluating how well the schools are providing equality of opportunity is to use the familiar input-output model: We look first at the various resources that go into different types of schools, and then we look at the extent to which students of different backgrounds are receiving equally good education and equal chances for success in life. Finally, we should look briefly at the long-term output to see whether there are systematic differences in actual success in life, particularly with respect to lifetime occupation and income.

[12]George B. Leonard, *The Man and Woman Thing* (New York: Dell, 1964), p. 104.

Black and other minority youth have usually gotten the short end of educational inputs—their schools lack programs, supplies, personnel.

SCHOOL INPUTS

One measure of inputs into our schools is the amount of money spent per pupil. Nationally, we spent about $930 in 1972 for each student in our public elementary and high schools. New York spent $1466 per pupil, and Connecticut, Michigan, and Minnesota each spent over $1100. By contrast, Mississippi spent $634 per pupil, Alabama $543, while the average for the eight East and West South Central states was $699. Thus, there are gross inequalities among the various states. In addition, large inequalities exist within states. In general, schools in wealthy suburbs spend about twice as much per pupil as do inner city schools.[13] Wealthy suburbs have a predominantly white population, whereas inner city populations are mainly black. There is, then, both a systematic racial and social class bias in the funds that schools receive.

Numerous other indicators of inequalities among schools show that the poor

[13]James S. Coleman et al., *Equality of Educational Opportunity* (Washington, D.C.: U.S. Government Printing Office, 1966).

Select a community in which there are at least six elementary schools. In what ways are the schools different in facilities? Does each serve a different social class of students? Try to find out the per pupil budget in the different schools.

---

and the blacks are receiving less than their share of educational inputs.[14] As a group, black pupils are less likely to attend accredited secondary schools with an accelerated program, a debating team, a school newspaper, or speech impairment classes. Fewer blacks than whites attend schools that have a physics laboratory or a shop equipped with power tools. Blacks are more likely to attend secondary schools that do not provide free textbooks, have few library books per pupil, and no full-time librarian. These facts apply to the nation as a whole. Within some sections of the country, the inequalities among schools are extremely great, although some school systems have made valiant efforts to equalize inputs. There are, however, two major points to remember: (1) in the United States there has long been a great disparity among schools in the amount of financial resources per pupil; and (2) the differential has not been random, but systematic; that is, the poor, the blacks, and other minority groups are much more likely to be attending inferior schools than are the whites and the more affluent.

One of the main reasons for these differences in financial input is related to how school funds are obtained. Basically, money to run the schools is obtained partly from the state and partly from local taxes. Although the proportion derived from the state varies with each state, so long as local property taxes are used to finance local schools, those who live in more expensive homes pay more property taxes and can afford better schools in their areas. Theoretically, a state could develop a formula that would yield more state aid to poorer school districts than to richer ones, thus equalizing the total amount of money available for each school. States have indeed attempted to do this but apparently not with much success. In some states it has become a legal issue. In 1972 Michigan's Supreme Court ruled that the formula for state aid did not, in fact, equalize the money available to school districts and was therefore unconstitutional.[15] Equalizing the amount of money available per pupil within a state would not solve the problems either. We would still have the state-by-state variations. Is it fair that $543 is spent per pupil in Alabama but $1175 in Michigan?

[14]Coleman et al., *Equality of Educational Opportunity.* This report contains considerable data bearing on inequalities in the schools, including those cited in this chapter.

[15]*State Government News* 16 (Lexington, Kentucky: Council of State Governments, January 1973).

There is still the unresolved problem of equality and racially segregated schools. Twenty years ago the United States Supreme Court ruled that separate educational facilities for the races are inherently unequal. Even if teachers' salaries, library facilities, lunch programs, and all else were identical in white and black schools, the mere act of separating the races, it was reasoned, generates a feeling of inferiority on the part of blacks. And this deprives them of an educational experience equal to the majority of students. Following the Court's decision, efforts were made, sometimes peacefully, sometimes under protest, to integrate the races in the schools.

As late as 1965, however, a national study by the federal government found that racially segregated schools were still very much with us.[16] The study found, among other things, that over two-thirds of all black pupils in the first grade were attending schools that were between 90 and 100 percent black; eighty-seven percent of all black first graders were in schools where fifty percent or more of the students were black. White children were found to be the most segregated in the nation as a whole, with almost 80 percent in the first and twelfth grades attending schools where 90 to 100 percent of the students were white.

In some parts of the country there are so few blacks or other minorities that most white children would necessarily attend predominantly white schools. But segregated schools are especially prevalent where blacks form a significant proportion of the population. In short, the vast majority of American students were attending schools where almost all of their fellow students were of the same racial background. Following the Supreme Court's definition of racially segregated schools as inherently unequal, we can say that inequality still exists in American schools.

It is by no means easy to remove the inequality in American education resulting from segregated schools. Busing students around the city has been tried with varying degrees of success, but it is a controversial measure and disfavored by most politicians. School districts have been redrawn, but at times with such ingenuity that racial integration was prevented rather than achieved. Accepting the harsh reality that true integration is not soon to be achieved, some blacks now prefer segregated but otherwise equal schools for their children. Other people, both blacks and whites, view this as a sorry surrender. As scientists, sociologists are supposed to report their findings without judging; yet it can be reported that if one function of our system is to provide equality of opportunity in the system, the schools have failed rather dismally in performing this function. This is true both of the various economic inputs and of the subtler inequality resulting from racial segregation.

[16]Coleman et al., *Equality of Educational Opportunity.*

Busing has proved to be a controversial solution to problems of racial segregation. If, as it seems, it has failed, why?

EDUCATIONAL OUTPUTS

One could argue that whether or not school facilities and the like are equal, the critical question is how good an education—the output of our school system—children from different backgrounds are receiving. Such output can be measured in many ways, some dealing more with quantity of education than with quality, but each telling us something a little different about what happens to our children in the schools.

If years of school completed are compared, white and nonwhite groups under 30 years of age differ considerably, as shown in Table 10-2. In 1972 over 22 percent more whites than blacks had completed high school, 72 percent more whites had completed four or more years of college and, conversely, blacks were more likely than whites to have had less than five years of elementary school. But this disparity is less than it was years ago: In 1940, 29 percent more whites than blacks completed high school, while 24 percent more blacks than whites

TABLE 10–2. Percent of Persons, by Race, 25–29 Completing Specified Years of School[a]

	WHITE		
	Less Than 5 Years of Elementary School	4 Years of High School	4 or More Years of College	Median School Years Completed
1972	1	82	20	13
1970	1	78	17	13
1960	2	64	12	12
1950	3	55	8	12
1940	3	41	6	11
	NONWHITE		
	Less Than 5 Years of Elementary School	4 Years of High School	4 or More Years of College	Median School Years Completed
1972	1	67	12	12
1970	2	58	10	12
1960	7	39	5	11
1950	15	23	3	9
1940	27	12	2	7

[a]Percentages may not total exactly 100 because each percent is rounded to nearest value; that is, 64.4 becomes 64, while 64.5 becomes 65.

Source: U.S. Department of Health, Education, and Welfare, *Digest of Educational Statistics, 1972* (Washington, D.C.: U.S. Government Printing Office, 1973).

completed less than five years of elementary school. Blacks are better educated today than in the past, but even in the "enlightened" 1970s the amount of formal education is still related to race.

School dropouts are those persons of roughly school age who are not enrolled in school and who are not high school graduates. Here, again, we note a systematic difference by race. As Table 10–3 shows, in 1970, 7 percent of all white males and 16 percent of all black males were school dropouts. Among females the corresponding rates are 8 percent of whites and 13 percent of blacks.[17] The odds are distinctly greater that a black will be a school dropout than that a white will be one.

What can we say about the *quality* of education received by different groups within our society? Have all high school graduates received equal intellectual payoff from their 12 years spent in school? In 1965 the federal government made a detailed study of the school system that included analyzing the achievement test scores of students at grades 1, 3, 6, 9, and 12.[18] Standardized achievement tests are used on the assumption that students are supposed to be acquiring

[17]U.S. Bureau of the Census, *Current Population Reports* (Washington, D.C.: Government Printing Office, 1971), series P–23, no. 38.

[18]Coleman et al., *Equality of Educational Opportunity.*

TABLE 10-3. Percent of High School Dropouts by Race and Sex, 1970

Age	Black		White	
	Male	Female	Male	Female
Total, 14 to 19 years old	15.9%	13.3%	6.7%	8.1%
14 years old	0.9	2.9	1.4	1.1
15 years old	3.3	2.7	2.0	2.4
16 years old	10.9	11.1	5.0	6.7
17 years old	16.0	13.7	7.6	10.2
18 years old	29.8	27.8	13.6	14.1
19 years old	44.1	25.8	12.9	15.7

Source: U.S. Bureau of the Census, *Current Population Reports*, series P-23, no. 38.

such intellectual skills as reading, writing, calculating, and problem solving. The tests show how much of such skills they are actually acquiring during their school years.

Achievement tests do not take into account that some children come from homes that have encyclopedias and others do not, or that some children receive more intellectual stimulation and encouragement than do others. The reasoning behind achievement tests is simply that certain skills, abilities, and general information are necessary for obtaining a job and for participating fully in our society. The higher your achievement, the better are your chances of finding a good job. Also greater, it would seem, are your chances for continuing your education beyond high school, securing promotions in your career field, and even changing careers. To simplify the voluminous details of the nationally administered achievement tests, only median scores are reported and these only for first and twelfth grade students.

The figures in Table 10-4 make distressingly clear that some are getting more out of our schools than others. In the fall of their first year of school, black children were already behind white children in both verbal and nonverbal achievement. For whatever reasons, the two races start school unequally in these skills. But in the twelfth grade, half of the blacks scored below 41, whereas half of the whites scored below 52. After 12 years in school, blacks and whites show a greater difference in achievement than when they started school. Recall, too, that the dropout rate is higher among blacks than whites. Assuming that those who are doing the least well are most likely to drop out, by twelfth grade the group of blacks should be somewhat overweighted with better achievers. Even those blacks who stick it out for twelve years in the schools end up receiving less of what the schools are supposed to be providing than do whites, Oriental Americans, and Mexican Americans.

TABLE 10-4. Nationwide Median Achievement Test Scores

| Test | Racial or ethnic group | | | |
	Mexican Americans	Oriental Americans	Black	White
1st grade				
Nonverbal	50.1	56.6	43.4	54.1
Verbal	46.5	51.6	45.4	53.2
12th grade				
Nonverbal	45.0	51.6	40.9	52.0
Verbal	43.8	49.6	40.9	52.1
General Information	43.3	49.0	40.6	52.2

Source: Adapted from James S. Coleman and others, *Equality of Educational Opportunity* (Washington, D.C.: U.S. Government Printing Office, 1966), p. 20. Data are for 1965.

One of the goals of formal education is to prepare people to be productive, participating, and successful members of society. There are many ways of defining these terms. Whatever else is included, to have a job is one measure of productivity and success. While it may be true that the best things in life are free, the next best often cost money. Income, then, is another measure of success even if it is sometimes overrated and overemphasized.

Many interesting facts and relationships can be discovered from the data in Table 10-5. First, the more years of formal education you have had, the better are your chances of being employed in a white collar occupation. Although that relationship is the focus of our present discussion, two other points are noteworthy: (1) Among males with comparable education, blacks are less likely than whites to hold a white collar job, but are more likely to be service workers; (2) women at the same educational levels as men are more likely to be engaged in service jobs but are also more likely to be in white collar jobs. One could also compare black women with white women, black men with black women, and so forth. Nevertheless, education indeed affects the kind of work you will do. When you think of the hours per day and the years per lifetime spent on the job, the effects of formal education on your life are almost incalculable.

Because occupation and income are related, the more years of school you completed, the higher will be your yearly and lifetime income. The differences in lifetime income are particularly revealing. The average person with four or more years of college earns $586,000 over the course of his or her life. This is $236,000 more than what is earned by a high school graduate and $328,000 more than a grade school graduate.[19]

[19]U.S. Bureau of the Census, *Current Population Reports*, Series P-60, no. 74 and U.S. Bureau of the Census, *Statistical Abstract of the United States: 1972* (Washington, D.C.: U.S. Government Printing Office, 1972), p. 114.

TABLE 10-5. Percent of Persons in Occupational Groups by Race and Years of School Completed

| | 1972 Employed Males | | | |
| | White | | Black and Other | |
Percent, by Occupation	Less Than 4 Years of High School	4 Years of High School or More	Less Than 4 Years of High School	4 Years of High School or More
White collar	17	55	8	38
Blue Collar	66	37	67	45
Service, including private household workers	9	6	18	15
Farm	8	3	7	2
	Employed Females			
	White		Black and Other	
Percent, by Occupation	Less Than 4 Years of High School	4 Years of High School or More	Less Than 4 Years of High School	4 Years of High School or More
White collar	30	77	11	59
Blue collar	34	9	22	14
Service, including private household workers	33	14	66	26
Farm	3	1	2	0.3

Source: U.S. Bureau of the Census, *Statistical Abstracts of the United States: 1973* (Washington, D.C.: U.S. Government Printing Office, 1973), p. 115.

Cynics claim that it is not how much you know that counts but whether or not you have the proper credentials, the right piece of paper, the diploma. There is some truth in this. The lifetime earnings of those who have had some high school are considerably less than the earnings of those who graduated, and persons with some college earn much less than college graduates. Apparently, completion of a given level of education affects the kind of job you can find and thus your potential earnings.

SCHOOLS AND CULTURAL BIAS

We have seen that there are systematic differences in how far a person will progress through the school system and how this, in turn, will have profound effects on his or her life. It would take an unscrupulous wizard, fast with rhetoric but loose with facts and logic, to maintain that the schools are performing their

Some cynics claim that today's college degree really has no more value than the high school diploma had a generation ago. Do you agree?

function of providing equal opportunity. But what has gone wrong? To explain why some people continue in school longer than others and achieve more than others, we must look at the schools, the students, and the interaction between the two.

Studies have shown that the inequality of resources that go into our schools accounts for some, but not much, of the difference in achievement test scores.[20] As we discussed in Chapter 7, the public school system is basically a middle class institution, reflecting and instilling middle class virtues and values. An obvious bias favors those who are obedient, who will learn by rote when it is demanded, who learn how to take tests, and who, in short, catch on to the rules of the educational game and are willing to play by them.[21] The child who has or acquires these personality traits will get along without too much difficulty in our present day schools.

[20]Coleman et al., *Equality of Educational Opportunity,* p. 8.

[21]Students who do not accept the middle class values are often defined as troublemakers. See Arthur L. Stinchcombe, *Rebellion in a High School* (Chicago: Quadrangle Books, 1969).

One nationwide study found that attitudes and beliefs are highly related to achievement in school. People who believe that they can control their lives and environments will do far better in school than people who feel that fate, luck, or the facts of life are in control. Life has taught some children, cruelly but with certainty, that what middle class people would term an unduly fatalistic attitude is basically correct. Groups that are discriminated against do not have much control over what happens to them. In addition, while some children learn good grammar at home merely by hearing it spoken, or have reading and reference materials in their home, or have parents who praise schooling and defend its competitiveness and reward system, other children are what is euphemistically called "culturally deprived." They lack these conditions for success in school, obviously not through the fault of the schools. Perhaps the schools cannot be expected to perform the function of providing equal opportunities until or unless some basic social changes are made.

CONTROL OF THE SCHOOLS

In the United States, the public schools are supposed to be controlled by the people who live in each school district. The state may set minimums in curriculum standards or in length of school sessions, but the local boards of education implement these standards. The local boards have more direct control over the schools than do the states since the boards hire superintendents and teachers and approve educational programs. Although this system of local control through boards has long been part of our educational tradition, it has begun to receive criticisms of its philosophy and practice.

School boards have been severely criticized for not actually representing "the people." It is typically charged that most of the members of most school boards are power figures in the community, such as bankers, clergymen, and business leaders. Although extremely unpopular individuals can be removed at the next election, this takes time and organization, and people are often afraid that the new members will be no better than those they replaced. Minority group members and the poor are rarely found on school boards.

One problem is that there is no such thing as "the people"; the phrase is rhetoric meant to suggest that some vague, undefinable group has greater legitimacy than others. Not only is such a claim for greater legitimacy not true in law, but also each of us is of "the people." So to say without qualification that the boards should represent the people is almost meaningless. As we shall see, every group that claims to be, or to represent, the people excludes other groups that have equally legitimate claims.

Control by the people sometimes means that the parents of those children now in school should have the most influence on how the schools are run. Suggestions

---

Attend a school board meeting in your community. How many ordinary citizens were in attendance? Observe and record the interaction that takes place. Who controlled the meeting? Were any controversial issues taken up? Was there any indication that some issues had been practically settled before the open meeting?

---

have been made for giving such parents more direct control, and one method proposed has come to be called the "voucher system." Under this arrangement, parents of a school–age child would be given a certificate worth so many dollars to spend on education. Then they could shop around and enroll their child in the public or private school most to their liking. The theory is that competition would be brought into the education system and would improve it. Schools would have to shape up to the demands of parents or close their doors.

The utter administrative confusion that the voucher system would presumably create is not the most serious complaint against it. If schools shape the minds of students who, in turn, will shape and reshape society, should not the unmarried, the childless couples, and those whose children are out of school also have some control over the schools? Not only do these people pay taxes that fund the schools, but they too can be genuinely concerned about the schools and the impact that educational policies will have for the present and future of our society.

Control by the people sometimes means neighborhood control. In some large cities, blacks, Mexican Americans, Puerto Rican Americans, or other minority groups have sought control over schools so they could initiate programs and courses of study suitable to their needs.[22] Such arrangements would make the schools less of a white middle class institution and more responsive to the particular needs of certain minority groups.

Professional educators, the teachers and administrators who daily interact with the students, have a different point of view. They claim that their training as well as the demands of their roles should enable them to make major decisions about what is taught and how the schools should be run. However, students too are people. How much control should students have over what is taught to them, by whom it is taught, or how educational dollars should be spent? Students are not likely to let us forget them entirely. Having heard participatory democracy praised for many years they might well want to practice it in the schools that taught it to them.

[22]Diane Divoky, "New York's Mini-Schools: Small Miracles, Big Troubles," *Saturday Review* (December 19, 1971), 60–68; and Ronald Gross and Beatrice Gross, eds., *Radical School Reform* (Hinsdale, Ill.: Dryden Press, 1970).

304

CAN'T READ, JOHNNY? SO SUE THE TEACHER

The functions of a given institution may come and go. Changes in these functions can produce social confusion and discomfort. But what happens to a society when an institution is simply failing in its functions? The number of schools and students that are failing is large enough to have made the schools targets of intense criticism for some time now. Year after year school boards and school districts are embarrassed by the declining level of achievement in their schools. Is the failure in ourselves as students or in the schools? Many seem to have decided that the schools have failed the students, and have talked of taking the schools to court to force them to shape up.

In late 1972 the San Francisco Unified School District was made the plaintiff in an action brought against it by Peter Doe. Peter Doe is the fictitious name of an actual 18-year-old white male high school graduate. After 13 years in San Francisco public schools, Peter Doe, who has a normal IQ, had average grades, kept good attendance, and was not a disciplinary problem, was found to have fifth-grade reading abilities. Private tutoring—after high school graduation—significantly improved his reading. Throughout his school years his parents had told teachers that they were concerned about Peter's apparent difficulty in reading. But they were assured he was an average reader. The schools that Peter Doe attended are being charged with negligence, false representations, and violation of various statutes.

The courts have been used before against the schools. The historic **Brown vs. Board of Education of Topeka (1954)** prohibited racial segregation in schools. Other decisions have required equal public educational facilities for all, regardless of community financial resources. The latest efforts are based on changing the legal status of education from a privilege to a right. Even so, can the courts be made to settle the complex matters of learning? One advocate of educational reform, Gary Saretsky, attended a conference on legal strategies for accomplishing such reform. He was impressed with the legal sophistication of the strategists, but he was appalled at the strategists' ignorance and their simplemindedness about the theories and practice of education. Could taking the schools to court produce, as Saretsky fears, a cure worse than the present illness of bad performance? Can the complicated, elusive functions of an entire social institution be defined and made enforceable by lawyers and judges?

Much that has been said about the public schools applies also to colleges and universities. To be sure, institutions of higher learning allow much academic freedom. Controversial ideas can be explored without penalty, and research findings can be released without fear of reprisals from groups with vested interests. Although colleges and universities are relatively free in these respects, they are only as free as those who control them allow them to be. Boards of trustees are not noted for their civil libertarian views. Funds to run colleges and universities must come from state legislatures, private endowments, or sometimes cities. In any case, we have the familiar problem of how much control those who hold the purse strings should be allowed to have. College faculties can be counted on to take a strong stand for academic freedom and to seek some control of their institutions. Student control is a more intensely sought goal than at the high school level, possibly because college students are more sophisticated and because they or their parents are paying tuition in addition to taxes.[23] Between the high school and the college, the question of whether students should control the system or the system should control the students differs only in degree.

The power struggle for control of schools at all levels is likely to continue. Although it indicates a dissatisfaction with how things are presently being done, it at least shows that people care enough about education to be willing to fight about it.

DISENCHANTMENT WITH THE SCHOOLS

Schools throughout the United States are in trouble. School bond issues are voted down. Legislatures are more concerned than ever with how much money should be devoted to education. Many have even suggested that not a single additional dollar should be spent on education until there is proof that the public is getting its money's worth. The disenchantment with education shows up in other ways, such as the serious questioning by middle class youth of whether or not they should go to college. They can afford to go, but they wonder whether what they will learn will have any real impact on their lives, or at least on the kind of lives they wish to live. The Golden Age of education, during which we believed that more education for more people would solve all our problems, is, depending on your point of view, either threatened or over.

Our system of education, from kindergarten to professional schools, has been compared to a mutated octopus that has grown more and more tentacles while

[23]See "Students Protest" *AAUP Bulletin* (Autumn 1969), 309–326; and The Cox Commission, *Crisis at Columbia* (New York: Vintage Books, 1968).

Disenchantment with the schools shows up in many ways—from the voting down of bond issues to dropout rates.

retaining its miniscule brain. The system also can be likened to the Minotaur in Greek mythology, a creature partly human but mostly bull. The Minotaur was fed seven young boys and girls a year. Ours has a larger appetite.

The analogy to a mutated octopus may not be inappropriate, although certainly the idea could be expressed more delicately. The growth of the system itself seems to be matched only by the growth of conflicting views about what the schools should be doing. The educational functions are obviously in conflict. How can any system simultaneously educate the masses, prepare everyone for jobs, give quality academic education to the few destined for graduate and professional schools, prepare all groups for life in general, smooth out racial and ethnic inequalities, and come down hard on sex stereotyping? Perhaps we are doomed to disappointment if we expect the schools, as presently structured, to be all things for all people.

The current disenchantment with the nation's schools should not be taken lightly. In some cities parents have pulled out of the system and are operating "free schools" or store front schools that reject most of the goals and traditions of the established educational system. None of these schools has been open long enough for us to know whether they will do a good job of preparing children for life. Such efforts nevertheless demonstrate an extreme degree of dissatisfaction, a magnified version of the disenchantment felt by many. Still, the schools are not about to close their doors, nor has our faith in education been so badly shattered that there will be great pressure for them to do so. In the years ahead we will see creative and even radical changes in our educational system. For the good of our children and our society, we can only hope that these years will be as productive as they promise to be exciting.

EDUCATION AND THE TWO CHIEF SOCIOLOGICAL MODELS

Our examination of the American institution of education in the United States has probably made it clear that while decades ago structural–functionalism seemed the best model, today the conflict model seems more apt. In the early days of our history, the family was a far more dominant socializing and economic force than it is today. And although official church membership was lower than in our own century, the religious values of Protestantism also played a major socializing role. Despite separation of church and state, religious values were more explicitly at work in our culture. For these combined reasons education played a much narrower role in the socializing process. Schools were expected to teach little more than the basic utilitarian skills of reading, writing, and arithmetic.

Throughout the second half of the nineteenth century and the entire twentieth, however, the institution of education has undergone several major changes. It became compulsory by law for every child to attend school, and school curricula expanded over the decades. Meanwhile, our society was becoming more complex in many ways. The economic institution was growing in complexity and creating more and more jobs requiring hitherto unneeded kinds of mental training and

Is it wrong for teachers to strike even though other groups have found that striking effectively focuses attention on their problems?

skills. City dwellers were becoming an ever larger percentage of the total population. At the same time, the cities were becoming areas of ethnic diversity as our growing economy, combined with famines and political unrest throughout Europe, sent waves of immigrants to this country.

In the early decades of this century education was feeling not only these pressures from outside but also internal pressures. New theories of education and educational psychology strove for dominance within the institution. The traditionalists allowed education only the role of teaching the basic skills mentioned before plus other subjects: geography, history, geometry, and the like. The progressives sought chiefly to develop the whole person, to socialize children in such a way that they could participate most effectively as adults in a democratic society. Education today is still wavering uncertainly between these two poles.

As if everything we've mentioned so far weren't enough to tear the institution apart, the racial and ethnic minorities struggling to achieve equality and end discrimination began to realize the importance that contemporary society places upon education. They began at the same time to see that the schools had their own built-in modes of discrimination. They viewed the schools as extensions of the white, Protestant, middle class culture into the area of learning. Hence the demands first for integration and then for community control.

The schools have thus become arenas for social conflict. There is conflict over what functions education itself should perform; conflict over what kind of society we should have and how large a role education should play in achieving it. There is conflict over why the schools are generally failing in even the traditional role of teaching basic skills. In recent years, there has even been conflict among many social scientists and parents about what value other social institutions should be allowed to place on educational achievement. Many now claim that the young should have a meaningful choice between vocational training with early entry into the job market, on the one hand, and academic high school preparation for college, on the other. They believe that college and even high school diplomas should be required for fewer occupational positions in the economy than they now are. We see that, in the present at least, the functions of education are inseparable from the economic and political institutions, where material well-being and power ultimately come from. These two institutions are the subject of the next chapter.

SUMMARY POINTS AND QUESTIONS

1. Formal education is an extension of socialization. In simple societies, education is largely informal and almost identical to socialization. In modern societies, because of the complexity of knowledge, education is institutionalized and conducted by specific organizations.

> *In modern society, what are some ways other than formal education by which individuals become educated?*

2. Four major functions of education are the transmission of knowledge, the provision of equal educational opportunities, the creation of new knowledge, and the placement or sorting of persons into socially functional roles.

> *What specific practices can be found in educational systems that fulfill each of these functions?*
>
> *Do these functions ever come into conflict with each other? How?*

3. Other functions provided by educational institutions are the custodial function, informal socialization by peers, and an on-going experience in a hierarchical bureaucratic organization.

> *How would you assess the importance of these functions compared to the four major functions?*

4. Education in the United States has gone through a period of rapid expansion. This is indicated by the number of facilities, the enrollment of students, the amount of money spent on education, and the number of degrees rewarded. Spiro Agnew stated that we are becoming an overeducated society.

> *What did he mean by this statement?*
>
> *Do you agree?*

5. One set of criticisms of education in the United States is that goals are poorly defined, that they are not being achieved, and that the content of our education is irrelevant to living in the modern world.

> *What are the goals of our educational system? What are your personal goals?*
>
> *Does the educational system allow you to fullfill your own goals?*
>
> *What educational practices are irrelevant to you and your goals?*

6. Another issue in American education is the equality of opportunity. This idea is used in two senses: equality *in* the school system and equality *through* the school system.

> *How are these two ideas different from one another?*
>
> *Can the educational system provide equality of opportunity in the school system but not through it?*

7. One way of evaluating whether or not the educational system is providing equality of opportunity is by the use of the input–output model.

What are some examples of inputs? Outputs?

Using these examples, can you assess the success of the educational system in providing equality of opportunity?

8. Another educational issue is, "Who should control the schools?"

What groups are interested in controlling a local school system?

In what ways might their interests come into conflict?

9. A final indicator of the many problems that American education is experiencing is the disenchantment with the schools by both parents and students.

What are some indicators of this disenchantment?

To what alternatives are disenchanted persons turning?

SUGGESTED READINGS

Coles, Robert. *Children of Crisis: A Study of Courage and Fear.* New York: Dell Publishing Co., 1964. Shows the effect that racial strife has on children. Also deals with the feelings of parents, teachers, civil rights workers, and segregationists in a racially tense situation.

Conant, James B. *Slums and Suburbs.* New York: McGraw-Hill, 1961. Examines the difference in the financing, quality, and success of education between white suburban school systems and non-white city school systems.

Kozol, Jonathan. *Death at an Early Age.* Boston: Houghton Mifflin, 1967. An analysis and critique of the educational policies and methods in the Boston public school system, particularly how these policies negatively affect poor children.

_____. *Free Schools.* Boston: Houghton Mifflin, 1972. Examines the dissatisfaction of parents with the public school system, and the "free school" movement that grew out of this dissatisfaction.

Machlup, Fritz. *The Production and Distribution of Knowledge in the United States.* Princeton, N.J.: Princeton University Press, 1962. Views education as a knowledge industry. Essentially a source of statistical information in the form of the input–output model.

O'Neill, William F., ed. *Selected Educational Heresies.* Glenview, Ill.: Scott, Foresman, 1969. Essays on education by well known authors such as Orwell, Huxley, Rogers, Skinner, Maslow, and Mead. Good discussions of autonomy, alienation, relevancy, and educational values and goals.

Rosenthal, Robert and Lenore Jacobs. *Pygmalion in the Classroom*. New York: Holt, Rinehart and Winston, 1968. An interesting discussion of the educational system in relation to the lower class child. It centers around the problems of cultural deprivation and teachers' expectations.

Silberman, Charles E., ed. *The Open Classroom Reader*. New York: Random House, 1973. Essays on the open classroom, the role of the teacher, the curriculum, and the aims of education. An attempt to present alternatives for making education relevant.

Wolff, Robert P. *The Ideal of the University*. Boston: Beacon Press, 1969. Constructs four models of higher education in terms of purpose and then analyzes the type and quality of education which results. Contains interesting chapters on relevancy, value-neutrality, grading, and the governance of the university.

How is passing the peace pipe at a tribal council like passing a bill in a legislature? Both are political acts. What does an Eskimo hunting an Arctic seal share with a General Motors chairman at a board meeting? Both are engaged in economic acts. Clearly in two different societies the same institution will take on very different forms. But its functions remain the same. Ours is a mass society, and our politics and economics reflect this fact. We have mass participation in both institutions. Almost everyone over 18 has the right to vote, and almost every adult is an economic producer and consumer. If large, impersonal government and economic bureaucracies dominate our lives, what holds us together? Surely in the long run even the government's power and effectiveness at social control is not sufficient by itself. Most of us share the same political and economic ideologies: We believe in our form of government and our way of distributing goods and services.

11

GOVERNMENT AND ECONOMY: DISTRIBUTING GOODS AND POWER

> The history of modern society may readily be understood as the story of the enlargement and the centralization of the means of power—in economic, in political, and in military institutions. The rise of industrial society has involved these developments in the means of economic production. The rise of the nation–state has involved similar developments in the means of violence and in those of political administration.
>
> C. Wright Mills

Having read this far, you now know that there is more to society and culture than most people realize. You know, too, that in their attempt to understand society, sociologists use scientific concepts and methodology, and have access to superior information. In this and the preceding three chapters the central concept has been the institution, a cluster of norms centering on one or more major functions of society. Scientific methodology, discussed in Chapter 2, does not merely provide the means of collecting data. It enables the sociologist to separate truth and fiction, to give order to the facts that have been collected, to trace associations among events, and to project trends.

Although concepts and methodology are essential, the sociologist's main advantage lies in having large amounts of reliable information. Vast quantities of data are generated by the discipline of sociology, and the sociologist is fortunate in being able to draw on many other sources as well. History, anthropology, political science, and economics, to name just the most useful fields, all contribute to the sociological understanding of political and economic institutions.

Anthropologists and historians provide the sociologist with valuable information about the immense variety of political and economic institutions. They discourage us from conceiving of our forms of these institutions as the *only* forms, or as necessarily the *best* forms. In hunting Polar bear or Arctic seal, the Eskimo is participating in an economic system, even though it bears little resemblance to our own mass consumption economy. Likewise, the passing of the peace pipe in a tribal council is no less a political ritual than is the casting of ballots in our elections.

315

THE FUNCTIONS OF POLITICAL AND ECONOMIC INSTITUTIONS

As we saw in Chapter 3, three universal problems establish broad functional needs, which institutions try to satisfy in all societies. These are the needs to (1) ensure physical survival, (2) maintain order within the group, and (3) provide for the individual's psychological well-being. The first need may seem to be the function of the economy, and the second to be the function of government. But in fact both government and the economy function in all three areas of need. For example, through military defense, our government promotes physical survival of the people and the nation, and democracy generates psychological satisfaction by its ego-building stress on equality. In a similar sense, capitalism has social control functions; for by permitting property accumulation, it creates vested interests that usually favor order. To the extent that the pursuit of economic self-interest can be a source of pleasure, capitalism also gives psychological comfort.

Like the other social institutions, the political–economic institutions not only work to fulfill each of the three social functions, they attempt to solve a given need in more than one way. A government may promote social order by means of political socialization, ceremonies calling for a display of allegiance, a police force and legal system, military diplomacy and war, and so on. But more intriguing than these rather manifest devices of social control are the political elements that function latently to promote order. Consider the welfare system, which reduces discontent among the unemployed; or consider the similarity of the two major parties, which discourages major ideological fights.

Just as institutions have universal functions, they also have fairly general structural elements. Among these structural elements are activities of group members, organizational structures, norms and beliefs, and leadership. These four structural elements—mass participation, bureaucracy, ideology, and power—form the major subdivisions of this chapter. Each institutional element is discussed, as is the institution as a whole.

DYSFUNCTION: THE FLY IN THE OINTMENT

Any study of the functions of government and the economy must consider their dysfunctional activities as well, which the advocates of the structural–functional approach are tempted to neglect. The pursuit of military defense, for instance, seems to be one source of the recurring "brush" wars in Southeast Asia and the Near East. Moreover, the arms race has been dysfunctional for the physical survival of many people and someday may be so for entire nations, should nuclear holocaust occur. In the meantime, the threat of worldwide destruction hardly promotes a sense of psychological well-being.

Structural and functional *conflicts* also must not be overlooked. In the electronic age, some citizens feel threatened by the government's quest for social order through the tapping of telephones and the maintenance of computerized data banks. Structurally, the irrefutable political influence of a few businessmen seems to be in conflict with the theory of democracy. These examples are but a small reminder that a model of politics and the economy must also take into account dysfunctions and conflicts.

MASS SOCIETY—WHAT IT IS AND WHERE IT CAME FROM

Sociologists define our contemporary society as a *mass society.* A mass society is one characterized by impersonal and contractual relations, specialization and division of labor, mass production and mass consumption, large-scale organizations, and preference for change. Individuals experience mass society as one composed of secondary group relations, high mobility, and alienation. Although this description is grossly oversimplified, you can see that our political and economic systems cannot be completely comprehended without a broader understanding of mass society and its origins. By explaining the roots of our mass society, historians also aid our understanding of contemporary political and economic institutions.[1]

Of the many sources of mass society, four deserve special mention: the rise of the nation-state, the Industrial Revolution, technology, and significant growth in population. The modern nation, first established in Europe around 1500, is one of the older roots of mass society. In earlier societies the political authority of the feudal lord, the king, or other ruler, was considered limited by the superior authority of the emperor, the parallel authority of the church, and the authority of natural law. The idea that within a definite geographic area the political unit has supreme and exclusive authority is thus not very old. But the idea grew and with it the notion that the authority of a nation-state, whether a monarchy or a republic, should be centrally controlled. The development of separate and sovereign nation-states, each with its centrally controlled bodies for making and enforcing laws and maintaining order, is therefore one of the early roots of mass society.

As these political units grew in number and size, they were driven to impersonal and contractual treatment of the citizenry, and they created some of the first bureaucratic organizations. Economically, the modern nation gave support to mercantilism, colonialism, and later to industrialism.

Like the nation, the Industrial Revolution, beginning in Europe in the late 1700s and in America in the 1800s, contributed to the rise of bureaucracy. With

---

[1]Almost any survey text in European history can provide the historical details. For example, see Jerome Blum et al., *A History: The European World* (Boston: Little, Brown, 1966), Chs. 2, 4, 15, 23, and 27.

The mass society is experienced by the individual chiefly as a collection of secondary relationships. Should it be surprising that alienation is common?

the development of national transportation systems and later the assembly line came mass production and consumption, and big business and unions demanded contractual relations enforced by government. Technology, by providing basic inventions, gave much push to the Industrial Revolution. By the twentieth century, the revolution had become self-sustaining. Through research and development, it was actively seeking new inventions and techniques to improve efficiency and generate new products. In the process, technology furthered specialization, mechanized bureaucracy, and encouraged consolidation. In the form of the computer, it epitomized impersonality. Governments fell under technology's influence, too, as a glance at a military bomber, a police car, or a utility bill immediately verifies.

The modern state, industrialism, and technology, then, are the three major roots of our mass society and its institutions. A major characteristic of the mass society is mass participation in the economic and political functions. We shall see, however, that political participation can be purely symbolic in some societies. And in all societies economic participation is unequal.

MASS PARTICIPATION: THE PEOPLE IN POLITICS AND ECONOMICS

Everyone can name some obvious ways of participating in politics and the economy: holding a job and consuming goods, casting ballots and being kept safe from violence. On close consideration, however, broad questions about participation crop up: In how many ways does the political system function to promote the welfare of individuals? How do individuals function to benefit the system? What is the distribution of the goods and services, and how much is given in exchange? In the world context, which nations receive most and which give most?

ECONOMIC PRODUCTION: FUNCTIONS AND DYSFUNCTIONS

Economic production and consumption are basic human activities, functioning for the physical, social, and psychological welfare of people and nations. The economy is the institution in which such production and consumption are conducted. Goods and services are produced and consumed, either by the producer or by another. We obtain goods we have not produced by exchanging other goods and services or their equivalent value in money.

In both production and consumption, distribution is unequal. Many of the world's four billion people labor not for surplus but instead for bare survival. Much of the struggle for survival is an uphill agrarian battle fought with a minimum of tools and technology. But in America farmers are only about 5 percent of the labor force, trailing far behind service laborers (10 percent), blue collar workers (35 percent), and white collar workers (50 percent).[2] With automation, most workers will be producing services instead of goods, and white collar workers will become more dominant. In time, more of them are also likely to work for the government.

While escaping the uncertainties of agrarian life, laborers in more industrialized nations still have many complaints. Blue collar assembly-line work involves relentless drudgery; layoffs or work reductions threaten income; and the chances of promotion virtually cease after a few years. Despite more pleasant physical conditions on the job, the white collar worker faces bureaucratic intrigue, status anxiety, and pressure to sell self and soul to the corporation.

We must be careful not to generalize too much about alienation, however. Some workers enjoy the struggle with the land, factory work, or the opportunities of bureaucracy. Work remains a necessary element of their self-definition. For

[2]The Statistical Abstract of the United States for 1970 (Washington, D.C.: U.S. Census Bureau, 1971), p. 220.

them, work is the great contest of life, one of the few arenas in society where a person has a chance to win the game.

For minorities, though, the chances of winning the game are more remote. Indeed, minority group members are often not even allowed on the field. Unemployment among ghetto blacks usually runs three to four times the national average, and blacks hold perhaps 60 percent of the menial jobs. Their social class and ethnic background hinder them from succeeding in school, acquiring the traits of the dominant culture, and making appropriate social contacts, all so valuable in white, middle class professions. Women, too—despite their rise from 30 to 40 percent of the labor force in twenty years—are prevented by stereotypes from full participation in the job market. Among the prejudices are that their occupational place is in the secretarial pool (97 percent female), around the store counter (73 percent female), or behind the teacher's desk (70 percent female).[3]

American labor unions, 88 percent white and 80 percent male in 1972, do not appear to offer a solution to the employment problems of minorities, and some job-related problems of other groups receive little aid. Some unions are hesitant to open apprenticeships to blacks and Chicanos. Women, in their rush to fill newly opened job categories, often have been willing to forego unionization and even some legislative protection. For many reasons, white collar workers have opposed unionization, although this norm is beginning to change. Finally, for the blue collar worker, unions seldom deal with the most obvious irritation, the assembly line and other sources of tedium, or a more ominous one, automation. By the mid-1970s, organized labor claimed only 20 percent of the American working force, down considerably from its peak two decades earlier.[4]

ECONOMIC CONSUMPTION: FUNCTIONS AND DYSFUNCTIONS

Naturally, we produce to consume. The Eskimo hunter, the Mekong Delta rice farmer, the Detroit autoworker, the Washington lawyer, and the rest of us all must consume to survive. And insofar as we survive, the economic institution is fulfilling its function. But is it really that simple? Consider that a fourth of the world goes to bed hungry every night. This fact is symbolic of the great and growing inequity between the poor and rich nations of the world. By contrast, America, with about 6 percent of the earth's population, consumes more than 40 percent of the earth's produce, almost as much as the other 94 percent of the world's people use.

Although one of the leaders in per capita income, America also has some of the greater extremes of wealth and poverty of major industrialized nations.

[3]U.S. Department of Labor Statistics, cited in U.S. News & World Report, 14 January 1974, pp. 69–70.

[4]U.S. Department of Labor Statistics, cited in U.S. News & World Report, 18 December 1972, p. 98.

The top fifth of the families received 41.4 percent of the nation's income before taxes in 1972, and the bottom fifth had 5.4 percent. To cite a more extreme case, the top 5 percent received about three times as much income as did the lowest 20 percent! During two-thirds of a century, the federal income tax did not significantly redistribute wealth.

It is not uncommon to be poor in America. The 1972 Census figure for persons living in poverty was 12 percent, down from 22 percent in 1959.[5] However, some critics place the current figure at 20 percent, and they claim it has not changed much since World War II. If those persons existing just above the poverty line—most of whom would be driven into poverty by recession or lasting inflation—are included, the percentage of those living in poverty in America becomes vastly larger.

Minorities hold a special disadvantage in income. In 1972 in this country, a nonwhite family's annual income averaged 60 percent of a white family's. Even though one-ninth of whites are poor one-third of blacks are, and a fifth of Americans over 65 must end their lives in poverty.[6] No matter what their age, American women typically earn 60 percent of what men make in many job categories.

Only now are Americans facing serious inflation and shortages, two problems which many of the world's poor have suffered for decades. Both trends, which promise to be enduring, hurt the poor more than the rich because the poor must spend a greater portion of their income for necessities, not luxuries.

PATTERNS OF CONSUMPTION: BAD NEWS FOR THE FUTURE?

The flawed quality of many American goods and services is not always a matter of chance. American business often designs products to look obsolete or engineers into them varying rates of self-destruction, thereby helping to maintain consumption levels. Obsolescence is planned into products as varied as toys and weapons. Also, inferior products are not evenly distributed by class. Poor people tend to get less for their dollar at the grocery store. The general merchandise stores they shop at may have cheaper initial prices for a given category of goods, but these goods may have a much shorter life-span than the somewhat higher priced version that the rich tend to buy.

Despite our irritation about inferior products, a tremendous rate of production and consumption is a matter of national pride for many Americans. For the producers, however, it has been a problem.

The productive glut is so great in America that a variety of strategies must be employed to avoid a massive surplus of nonessential products. Among these

[5]Figures from the Council of Economic Advisors, cited in *Time*, 11 February 1974, p. 71.

[6]U.S. Census Bureau statistics, cited in *Time*, 3 September 1973, p. 75.

American business often designs products to look obsolete or engineers into them varying rates of self-destruction, thereby helping to maintain consumption levels.

strategies, advertising—a major industry in itself—is used to convince people that luxuries are really necessities, and that one's social success may depend on choosing the proper anti-perspirant. Planned obsolescence is another tactic aimed at convincing Americans to buy what they don't really need. Automobiles, kitchen appliances, and other products are frequently changed in minor and superficial ways with no other purpose than to make previous models appear out-dated. And finally, products that could be designed to provide many years of dependable service are intentionally made to wear out after a brief period. In fairness, however, American business is not alone in these practices, although it was among the first to raise the practice of planned overconsumption to a science.

Flawed products and wasteful consumption have done much to keep industrial economies functional in the past. But this wastefulness is becoming dysfunctional today, not only for manufacturers and consumers, but also in a larger social sense. Wasteful consumption eats up large sums of income that might be spent creating a better quality of life for all of us. Again, it is the poor who suffer most in a society of inferior goods and conspicuous consumption. We are all

---

Make a grocery shopping list. Price the items on your list at food markets in upper, lower, and middle class neighborhoods. Do people in different social classes pay the same price for the same product?

---

socialized to the same values and goals, especially today in the age of mass media. So the poor overreach themselves in an effort to keep up, or they end up feeling deprived when they cannot buy what they think they should have. In addition, we all consume at the expense of the natural environment, from which resources are taken in large quantities and replaced with large quantities of waste. Finally, excessive consumption is an international problem. America and other industrialized nations take a disproportionate amount of resources of the world that cannot be replaced and that one day will disappear.

GOVERNMENT: A SYSTEM OF GIVE AND TAKE

Much as the people participate in the economy as consumers and producers, so they receive the services of government and fulfill certain obligations in return. This functional relationship between citizen and state is ancient, but in the modern world it is widening, both in industrial and agrarian nations. Governments are giving more but also asking more. Many services of government affect the welfare of the people and the nation. Among these are national defense, economic regulation, education, transportation, health, citizen rights, social control, and environmental protection. Other services are directed at specific groups, such as poor people, farmers, businesses, and unions, although the functions of these services may have much to do with general and national well-being.

America is among the leaders of the developed nations in expenditures on defense and education, but it trails behind in the areas of health and welfare. It is also in the first rank in overall prosperity and violent crime. This sketch means little for the question of quality of life, although a closer look at the government's concern with national defense, public welfare, and social control will give us more insight.

Defense Expenditures Of the major nations, only Russia spends more than America on national defense, be it in absolute dollars, percentage of government budget, or fraction of gross national product (GNP). While the percentage trend generally has been downward over the last two decades, 30 to 35 percent of the federal budget still goes to defense. When other military spending categories are added, such as the space budget or interest on the largely war-incurred national debt, the government may use as much as half of its income for defense spending.[7] Put in a favorable light, these tens of billions of dollars keep democracy safe and provide for about three million civilian jobs. But they also mean support for highly inefficient businesses, extreme lobbying pressure on the political system, and immense neglect of social services.

Welfare Expenditures As with defense, America spends huge sums on welfare. In fact, it spends more than any other nation in absolute dollars. Unlike defense spending, welfare spending causes loud complaint in America, even though it amounts to only about 6.5 percent of the GNP as compared with European expenditures of 10 to 15 percent of their GNP. About 15 million Americans (7 percent) received some kind of welfare aid in 1973, although much of the 6.5 percent of the GNP expended on welfare went for administrative costs.[8] With some justice, the opponents of welfare spending point out that the programs are not curing poverty and frequently may even be perpetuating it. On the other hand, most people on welfare are unable to help themselves, and many people not on welfare are eligible for it.

Critics also point out that the nation provides "welfare" for the rich. Defense and other federal spending means profit for the wealthy, as do subsidies to businesses and farmers. In 1970, moreover, 22 percent of the families making over $25,000 annually received some form of direct aid such as social security payments.[9] A multitude of tax loopholes allows several hundred American families with six-figure incomes to pay no income tax, and legislation in both domestic and foreign affairs may indirectly protect or enlarge wealth.

Social Control Expenditures Because legislation for special interest groups may protect the status quo, it is a reminder that governments generally seek to maintain social order. The importance of social control in the American political mind can be seen in dollars and cents. At the federal level, both the FBI and the National Guard spend millions to discourage social disorder; local governments use a large portion of their income for police forces. In 1972, federal and local governments spent 10.5 billion dollars in their effort to maintain social order.[10] Other nations may spend a greater fraction of their GNP on social control, yet any comparison is somewhat misleading because, as we shall see, much of social control cannot be measured in dollars and cents.

[7]*The Budget of the United States Government, Fiscal Year 1973* (Washington, D.C.: U.S. Government Printing Office), p. 73.

[8]Figures from the U.S. Department of Health, Education and Welfare, cited in *U.S. News & World Report*, 12 November 1973, p. 90.

[9]See *Time*, 11 February 1974, p. 71.

[10]*U.S. News & World Report*, 20 August 1973, p. 63.

The government gives and the government takes. From our taxes come defense and exploratory funds.

Such expenditures do not fully indicate the government's preoccupation with order. Legislation, speeches, ceremonies, and statements of ideology may encourage public conformity. In promoting domestic order, governments are functioning for the benefit of the people or for the benefit of special interests; further, they are protecting their own legitimacy and reasserting their right to use violence. The advocacy of civil order is both an effort to uphold the laws and an opposition to any revolution that might threaten government legitimacy.

Finally, notice that governments are able to define by legislation what is orderly behavior. In so doing, they may discriminate for and against various groups. For example, during the 1960s, the possession or sale of small amounts of marijuana was a felony in many states, although in most of them it has since been reduced to a misdemeanor. As another indication, laws regarding white collar crime are few in number and vague in definition, making capture and conviction difficult.

Much more clear is the legislation on crimes against private property, most of which is owned by the upper classes. However, we must be careful about drawing conclusions about class favoritism in the law. For the sake of perspective, notice too that social control is the work of all institutions, not just government. By the time most citizens are adults, they function as their own best policeman.

THE FUNCTIONS OF THE CITIZEN

To keep the political system operating, governments require material and non-material support of the people; in America we give our votes. But probably governments prefer unqualified emotional attachment rather than critical, intellectual concern. America may not be too different from other countries in the balance of emotional and intellectual patriotism, except that we are often more open about dissent. Americans have access to more information about their society than citizens of many nations, yet a social scientist might doubt that they take much advantage of it, either in acquiring facts or in analyzing them. Indeed, there seems to be a popular tendency in the love-it-or-leave-it mentality to equate patriotism with authoritarianism. Despite pessimistic speculation about the decline of patriotism, unrest is perhaps better interpreted as a desire to become part of the American establishment.

Citizens help maintain government with their taxes, too. About a dozen major nations ask more than the United States does in taxes. Whereas the United States receives about 28 percent of its GNP from taxes, Denmark gets 44 percent of its GNP through taxation.[11] Despite our so-called progressive income tax, when taxes of all kinds are included, our tax system is "regressive"; that is, the poor pay a somewhat greater percentage of their income in local, state, and federal taxes than do the rich, by some estimates.[12]

It is not only in taxation that America takes a disproportionately large share from its poor. We require that the poor give their lives as well as their money. This comes about because most lower class people in the armed services are enlisted personnel, the "foot soldiers" who have the most face-to-face contact with the enemy. Also, with a declining job market, unskilled lower class men are often drawn to the military as their only source of employment. For these two reasons, it has been the lower classes which have paid most heavily to make the world "safe for democracy." When you realize that our nation has been at war for about twelve years out of the last thirty, this inequity in the loss of human life is no small matter.

[11]Statistics from Organization for Economic Cooperation and Development, cited in *U.S. News & World Report,* 10 December 1973, p. 110.

[12]For a more precise but not the most extreme breakdown, see Philip M. Stern, *The Rape of the Taxpayer* (New York: Random House, 1973), pp. 24–25.

Do a power study in your community. Select a major decision that has been made. Ask 25 people, of different ages and class backgrounds, who they think was responsible for making that decision. How much similarity did you find?

A WIDER PERSPECTIVE ON MASS PARTICIPATION

By now it is clear that mass politics and mass economics are related. There are direct correlations between job chances, income, voting patterns, and military service in America. Obvious, too, is the broader correlation of political–economic characteristics with education, class, divorce rate, and mental health.

With time, modern political–economic systems have come to resemble "total institutions," encompassing the individual by taking over functions once belonging to other institutions. For instance, the church was once a chief source of formal education, and the family functioned as the primary unit of economic production, but no more. As a result, in mass society the functioning of political-economic systems has become immeasurably complex. How well they function for the individual or for the society as a whole is a difficult but worthwhile question.

No formula neatly measures how much an individual uses and is used, or how much he or she consumes and produces in the political–economic system. Nor can such measurements be made for social classes or nations, except in the crudest way. The quality of what is given and received is impossible to balance out without making highly debatable assumptions. True, America consumes huge amounts of raw materials, but does it give back more in technology than it receives in resources? Upper classes enjoy a life that is materially and culturally richer than the lives of the poor, but does their leadership in the nation count for more? What of a blue collar worker, his life distorted by alienation: Is his contribution worth nothing better? Is it fair that the unemployed person is denied the good life because he does not seem to function productively? The answers depend on which values are held, not on simple matters of fact.

Whatever the inequities and their justness (or unjustness), some means must exist to maintain the day-to-day functioning of mass society. Bureaucracy, a complex organization of people and activities, carries this burden in a wide variety of circumstances.

BUREAUCRACY: DAY–TO–DAY DECISIONS AND SERVICES

Although it was far rarer in the distant past than today, bureaucracy is almost as ancient as China. In the modern world, however, almost no social activity escapes its influence. NATO, General Motors, and NBC have bureaucracies, and the Pentagon is one too. Methodists, Teamsters, and Boy Scouts depend on them. From *capomafia* to enforcer, even the Mafia families have bureaucrats—perhaps the most efficient ones of all.

We saw in Chapter 6 that a bureaucracy has a formal structure, including division of labor, chain of command, and coordination of activities. We saw also that it has other structural elements, among them an informal structure based on personal relations and primary groups. Likewise, the bureaucracy has both manifest and latent functions, intended by neither the organization nor its members. Bureaucracy certainly must be reckoned with, but it is too varied and complex to be grasped by a simple description, as a survey of political and economic bureaucracies will illustrate.

POLITICAL AND ECONOMIC BUREAUCRACIES

In recent years, bureaucracies in many nations have undergone significant changes.[13] First, some bureaucrats seem to be less authoritarian. Even some of President Nixon's top bureaucrats were willing to disagree publicly with each other and with the President about the economy and energy and the future of these. Second, in contrast to punishment–centered control, there is a shift to "representative" bureaucracy, in which more persons are at least superficially included in the decision process. Third, to manage a new society, many highly specialized bureaucratic roles have emerged, often leaving the person at the top with only a faint idea of what his or her subordinates are doing. Whatever effect this specialization has had on the validity of decisions, the authority of elected officials and conventional business leaders has diminished in the process. Fourth, the computer—which does routine jobs without delay, supplies facts impartially, makes cold and calculated decisions, and even gives orders without a conscience—is a major new force, probably more than offsetting bureaucratic authoritarianism. More broadly, the computer revolution has remade the face although not the soul of bureaucracy.

Political and economic bureaucracies have changed in more obvious ways than those just mentioned. They have grown in number and size: America now

[13]These trends are stated in Peter M. Blau and Marshall W. Meyer, *Bureaucracy in Modern Society* (New York: Random House, 1971), pp. 139ff.

Bureaucracy in action: the Pentagon in Washington, D.C., is the world's largest office building; it employs 30,000 people in offices that occupy 3,707,745 square feet.

has 1.4 million corporations, most of which have bureaucratic hierarchies. The bureaucracy of the largest branch of government, the Executive, has 11 Cabinet departments, 50 agencies, and 1800 bureaus, branches, corporations, administrations, commissions, and so on. Altogether, the federal bureaucracy employs almost three million persons and has a payroll of 29 billion dollars. In vertical rank, as well as in number and size, bureaucracies have enlarged: A political bureaucracy may extend from raw Army recruit to Commander-in-Chief of the Armed Forces, with hundreds of positions (and of course many thousands of occupants) in between. An economic bureaucracy may range from apprentice seaman aboard a tanker in the Persian Gulf to the chairman of the board of Standard Oil.

Taken all together, these factors—informal structures and dysfunctioning bureaucrats, technocrats and powerful computers, endless numbers and vast size—suggest an overwhelming complexity. It is difficult to imagine what goes on and what results when all of these internal elements interact or even when bureaucracies interact with one another. Consider, for example, that the regulation of our environment is divided among more than 60 federal agencies, with little coordination among them. Suppose that each of the agencies—in a spirit of cooperation—sought to contact every other one at the same moment. At least 3600 phones would try to ring! Then there are the links among the local, state, and federal government systems, in all about 80,000 separate political units.[14] And the complexity is compounded by ties between political and economic bureaucracies.

POLITICAL AND ECONOMIC BUREAUCRACIES TODAY AND TOMORROW

Not only has the scope of the bureaucracy of any single institution increased, but so has the influence of political and economic bureaucracies on each other. The clearest indication is the increasing governmental regulation of the economy, which in a mass society means more bureaucratic interrelationships. In addition to growth in number, linkages are changing in kind. For one, computers are now signaling each other from bureaucracy to bureaucracy. Such trends suggest that bureaucracy will become a larger force both in institutions and in mass society as a whole.

For many reasons, not the least of which is the rising influence of bureaucracy in mass society, an enduring fashion is to denounce bureaucracy and bureaucrats, so long as we are not talking about ourselves. Yet, for the time being, bureaucracy is both inescapable and essential, producing goods and services that we value highly. It produces cars on assemly lines, stacks groceries on supermarket shelves, provides instruction in schools, watches out for national security, and so on without end. Despite its serious deficiencies, bureaucracy is one of the more effective structures in mass society. It is only one means of maintaining a functional society, however, as a look at ideology and power will demonstrate.

IDEOLOGIES: PERCEPTIONS OF GOVERNMENT AND ECONOMY

There are Republican and Democratic views of politics, capitalistic and socialistic economic positions, and reactionary and radical attitudes, all of which are *ideologies*. In crude terms, an ideology is "the way we look at things." A sociologist would prefer to think of ideology as a set of commonly accepted beliefs and attitudes about social reality. Although this definition suggests to some sociologists that an ideology is a distorted view of reality, an ideology is not necessarily or totally false.

[14]Jack Anderson and Carl Kalvelage, *American Government . . . Like It Is* (Morristown, N.J.: General Learning Corporation, 1972), p. 60.

Why does George Wallace, once painted as a racist, now draw many votes from Southern blacks? Whose ideas changed?

That an ideology is a popularly accepted view tells us something of its origin. As you have seen in previous chapters, beliefs and attitudes are embedded in the whole culture and make up a significant part of its nonmaterial aspect. Even though ideologies are deeply rooted, they are not necessarily unchangeable or beyond deliberate manipulation. Organizations of all sorts and sizes present their view of whatever aspect of reality concerns them. To cite two examples, the leadership of General Motors at one time proclaimed that what is good for GM is good for the country; and many members of the John Birch Society, an ultraconservative organization, are certain that the Communist overthrow of America is at hand. Just as the manipulation of ideology is a group process, so is it an individual process: People are continually remodeling their ideas, making them more agreeable to those of others.

Individuals and groups not only have specific descriptions of social reality, but they also have general attitudes about it. Two of these attitudes are labeled conservative and liberal, and what chiefly divides them is their outlook on the

---

Construct a questionnaire that focuses on political and economic attitudes. Ask each of the persons to whom you give the questionnaire to rate himself or herself as liberal or conservative in both politics and economics. Are the attitudes expressed by your informants consistent with their self-ratings?

---

status quo.[15] By and large, the conservative is more happy than the liberal is with "things as they are"—or more properly in these times, with things as they once *were*. Although the conservative may admit that some change is an essential part of the contemporary world, the conservative does not encourage change as much as the liberal does, and he or she may even seek to slow the pace. As we find later, liberals and conservatives also divide on particular issues, such as human nature, the distribution of wealth, and the justice system.

On the far extremes of liberalism and conservatism are the radical and reactionary groups. Their willingness to support rapid changes, even revolutionary changes, sets them apart from both conservatives and liberals. Despite a common discontent with present circumstances, radicals and reactionaries are fundamentally opponents. The reactionary wants to escape the present by restoring aspects of the past, whereas the radical earnestly works for a new future.

These four labels must be used carefully and sparingly, for several reasons. First, their meanings have changed historically. What a Republican believes today might be liberal if not radical by Republican standards of the last century. Second, an individual may hold one attitude in some areas of life and different attitudes in others. For instance, some Americans are radical in economics, favoring socialism, and reactionary in marital affairs, rejecting women's liberation and demanding a return to older family structures. Third, such attitudes may shift as a matter of expediency, making temporary allies of enemies. In Oklahoma just before Prohibition, some members of the Anti-Saloon League and bootleggers became temporary allies because both favored the end of legal alcohol. Finally, it is a mistake to believe that the reactionary, conservative, liberal, or radical always has a clear view of his or her beliefs. People happily attach these labels to themselves without knowing fully and precisely what they mean. Just as a Christian may know little theology or a Democrat may not know the party platform, so any of the four positions may be more a matter of emotion than intellect.

Even though ideologies sometimes have little clear meaning for their supporters, they still have a definite function. As we have hinted, the label alone may pro-

---

[15]For a lively essay on the subject see Reo M. Christenson, *Heresies Right and Left: Some Political Assumptions Reexamined* (New York: Harper & Row, 1973), Ch. 4.

vide some psychological satisfaction for the individual, while the whole set of beliefs gives order, value, and manageability to social reality. Vaguely understood or not, ideologies may be forces for social control, as Karl Marx and Friedrich Nietzsche argued. Marx saw Christianity and other religions as opiates, discouraging unrest by promising the poor their just reward in heaven. In upholding respect for equality, democracy hinders the powerful from abusing the weak, the philosopher Nietzsche claimed (disapprovingly, it might be added).

POLITICAL IDEOLOGIES

There are many ways of classifying political systems and their ideologies. The philosopher Plato, 2500 years ago, classified political systems on the basis of how much power was granted the populace. To name a few, *tyranny* was rule by one person; *aristocracy*, rule by the few "best" people; and *democracy*, rule by the masses. As might be guessed, Plato believed the first and last to be inferior ideologies. The amount of power possessed and exercised by the state—and its opposite, the amount of freedom allowed the citizen—is another measure of ideology. The two extremes are *anarchism*, in which the state is virtually powerless or even nonexistent, and *totalitarianism*, an ideology of total state control of the individual; both of these ideologies are relatively recent.

Of popular ideologies, communism and democracy have been the most influential in Western cultures. Some early forms of communism were basically economic doctrines, concerned with the common holding of property, as the name suggetsts. *Marxian communism*, prevalent now, is primarily a political doctrine drawn up by Karl Marx in the last century. Although it has many specific doctrines, such as economic determinism (economic arrangements control society and history), class struggle, and revolution, the long-term goal is the change of the communist state from its present totalitarian form (the so-called "dictatorship of the proletariat") to a future condition of anarchy (the "withering away" of the state). In this stateless utopia, Marx believed, people will voluntarily and wisely order their actions so political coercion will be unnecessary.

Interestingly enough, the democratic ideology also makes optimistic assumptions about human nature. In its classical sense, democracy considered the individual to be of fundamental value, unlike ideologies such as fascism, which place a higher value on the state. (Of course, democracy may socialize the individual to sacrifice himself "voluntarily" for the state.) Under democracy, freedom is considered essential, along with responsibility, although the limits of each depend on one's conservative or liberal slant. That the average citizen is rational is another democratic belief, especially in liberal versions of the ideology. Belief in the equality of all people is also part of the democratic ideology; here disputes arise about whether people are equal, or should be, in origin, in opportunity, or in fact.

Our electoral process supposes that we citizens are rational and make wise choices. Is this an ideological assumption?

Additional assumptions are part of democratic ideology, but enough has been stated to point up three difficulties. First, there is serious disagreement on the meaning of some of these terms, as noted in the case of equality. Second, different people holding the same ideology place different degrees of importance on each value within it, such as on the relative worth of the individual and the state. Finally, there is some question about how well democratic assumptions fit the facts. For example, human rationality has been seriously doubted by psychologists ever since the rise of Freudianism, which stresses the domination of the individual by unconscious and irrational inner forces. In addition, although Marx did not originate the concept of ideology, his lasting mark on almost everyone's thought is that *any* ideological framework prejudges events and other ideologies.

Many supporters of democracy seem to neglect or deny the third problem and, instead, preoccupy themselves with the first two. Disagreements over the meaning and value of basic democratic assumptions are largely responsible for making some people Republicans and others Democrats. In a loose sense, Republicans (and conservatives) place less value on the individual, on freedom, on the rationality of the populace, and on equality; in fairness, however, we must note that these terms also mean something a little different to them than to Democrats. Democrats and Republicans also manage to be opponents on other issues, from foreign policy to economics. Since the list of issues is long, and since the two parties have traded positions back and forth in the past, the details of their platforms are better discussed in a government text or in a course in political sociology.[16]

ECONOMIC IDEOLOGIES

Economic ideologies are as numerous as political ones, but in the contemporary world two stand out: socialism and capitalism.[17] They differ basically on the issue of private property. Socialism professes government ownership of the major means of both production and distribution of goods and services. When socialism is associated with democratic ideology, as it often is, the people are the owners (although such collective ownership is not to be confused with private ownership). Traditionally, capitalism denies government the right to property ownership for purposes of production or distribution, with minor exceptions such as the postal service or public utilities.

Socialism and capitalism differ also on the critical question of government regulation of property. Socialism has allowed government unlimited power to regulate property, whereas capitalist ideology has shifted historically on the issue. *Laissez–faire* capitalism, an ideology popular a century ago, permitted government little role in the private economy. If some people grew too rich and powerful, government did not have the right to restrict them. If others were unemployed or hungry because of recession, government could not aid them. Practice and ideology never did match perfectly, but this version of capitalism dominated American thinking until the Democrats' New Deal of the 1930s.

Since the 1930s, both Democrats and Republicans have come to accept a capitalistic ideology that allows considerable government control of private property and participation in the general economy. How much regulation and participation is needed and for what purposes remains a matter of debate between them. Liberals argue for a welfare capitalism that will ensure each individual at least minimum economic comforts and health. Conservatives seem more concerned with a regulatory capitalism to protect the stability of the economy as a whole, leaving the individual to fend for her– or himself in a general atmosphere of prosperity.

[16]See Jerry Tucker, *The Experience of Politics* (San Francisco: Canfield Press, 1974).

[17]A book-length study is William N. Loucks' *Comparative Economic Systems*, 7th ed. (New York: Harper & Row, 1965).

IDEOLOGY AND THE WHOLE CULTURE

We have looked at ideologies narrowly, almost as though they existed in isolation from each other and from other elements of culture. A brief survey of Max Weber's ideas about the ideological connection of Christianity and capitalism will free us from such an error. Weber defended the hypothesis that one version of Christian ideology, Calvinistic theology and its Protestant ethic, was a major stimulus to the rise of Western capitalism in the centuries after 1500.[18]

The Protestant ethic, not entirely the result of Calvinist theology, is a code of conduct for Christians. It preaches hard work, thrift, sobriety, obedience, and the doctrine of the calling, among other norms. Only a little thought is required to see how such norms would be functional in an economy of rising capitalism. Hard work is a useful trait for the owner of an expanding business, and for the worker, especially from the owner's viewpoint. Thrift is necessary in a period of rapid business growth because it encourages efficient operation and the accumulation of capital. It is less functional in America's current stage of capitalism, which demands less money for investment and more consumer spending to keep the economy going. Coupled with the norm of thrift is that of reinvestment of savings, the rationale being that money ultimately belongs to God, and the Christian has the obligation to see God's Kingdom grow. Sobriety and obedience of the workers promote economic growth and make the owner's life simpler. Finally, the doctrine of the calling, a Lutheran notion, holds that God calls people to all occupations, not just to medicine or the mission field; thus, religious incentive is added to the labors of the "butcher, baker, and candlestick maker."

Such were the norms that the influential Calvinist sect provided the culture for the development of capitalism. But these norms might not have had such a great force without some motivating beliefs. Much of that force came from belief in *predestination,* the doctrine that membership in Heaven or Hell is decided by God alone. People are predestined to one place or the other, and their efforts, prayers, and money cannot change the outcome. Indeed, they cannot even be certain of the outcome until the next life. In the centuries after the Reformation in 1519, good Calvinists felt the need for an immediate sign of their future life, which they found by rather ingenious reasoning. They argued that God would send morally good people to Heaven, although not all such people would be guaranteed a place there. Moreover, they affirmed the doctrine of immediate rewards, which states that God punishes and rewards behavior in this life by material and other means. From these beliefs they concluded that moral people would be rewarded with wordly success and immoral ones would

---

[18]Max Weber, *The Protestant Ethic and the Spirit of Capitalism* (New York: Charles Scribner's Sons, 1958). For an evaluation of the Weber thesis see Kurt Samuelsson, *Religion and Economic Activity: A Critique of Max Weber* (New York: Harper & Row, 1961).

fail. So, success in this life was a possible sign of eternal life in Heaven, and failure was an even more certain assurance of Hell. In part because many Calvinists desperately wanted to arrive in Heaven, they were obsessed with economic gain and worldly success.

Weber's hypothesis has been attacked with some success. Furthermore, our view omitted its dysfunctional aspects and other inadequacies. Yet Weber's hypothesis does suggest the wider functional connections between economic ideologies and other beliefs.

POWER: PEOPLE AND GROUPS IN CHARGE

In everyday terms, power, is "what you're big enough to get away with," although for most persons this amounts to not much, either in a free society or in a totalitarian state. Economic power basically involves control over resources, production, distribution, or even consumption. Political power is concerned with the security and social control of the people and the survival of the state. Sociologists generally define *power* as the ability to make and carry out—or have carried out—decisions despite opposition.

The concept of power has a long and varied history, often having been used interchangeably with such terms as *authority, legitimacy,* and *influence.* Today, some sociologists use these three terms for selected aspects of the broader concept of power. Thus, *authority* is the means used to gain obedience from others, and *legitimacy* is power recognized by people as justifiable and deserving respect. *Influence* is informal power, lacking clearly defined norms or organizations to support it.

The concept of power can be better understood by studying its aspects, such as type, amount, means, scope, and distribution. *Types* of power include political, economic, psychological, educational–propaganda, technological, and so on. The power of technology is accelerating today to the point that critics like Jacques Ellul see technology as being out of human control. Propaganda is radically altered, too, now tending toward a one-way channel with a few speakers at one end and many listeners—you and me and most people—at the other.

As seen previously, the *amount* of power can range politically from a society in which the state has none (anarchism) to one in which the state has near limitless power (totalitarianism). Economically, power ranges from *laissez-faire* capitalism to complete state socialism. Among the *means* to gaining or maintaining power are persuasion, bargaining, and revolution. The *scope* of power refers to who or what is affected by it, humans, the environment, or whatever. Finally, power has varying degrees of *distribution* among its different holders, as we explore next.

POLITICAL ELITES AND PLURALITIES

Almost every public school student has been told that all Americans have an equal voice in government. But political scientists and sociologists have long debated among themselves whether the nation is controlled and run by a fairly unified elite or by a disunited plurality of pressure groups.[19] C. Wright Mills and others see America dominated by a military, industrial, political group, the "power elite." Despite some differences, this elite interacts on a personal basis and has a sense of social and psychological oneness; their interaction is not a conspiracy but a matter of common outlook. They own much of the corporate economy and may be somewhat invisible, influencing events but not always sitting in the seats of power. By helping to finance both major political parties, they minimize political issues and differences that might otherwise create conflict and unrest and that might produce significant change. They also use the media to divert the public with entertainment and to maintain the appearance of democracy. Even though they do not control everything, the elite exerts great influence on crucial areas, such as foreign policy and the economy. In the past, elites have encouraged heavy defense spending and protection of big business and wealth.[20]

The advocates of pluralism, such as Arnold Rose, claim that the reality of power is closer to the democratic idea. Power is divided among diverse groups—including parties, unions, businesses, governments, and bureaucracies—with none dominating all the time. They usually interact, behind the scenes, through competitive bargaining. So long as these pressure groups must appeal to the public for support, the people have some power. Most commonly, the public may sometimes change the character of parties and governments but seldom their bureaucratic organization.[21]

From both the power elite and the pluralist views, change tends to be slow and small. Political principles and ideals have little part in the decision–making process. Expediency seems to be the overriding concern. The people and their interests are at best a secondary concern and influence.

---

[19]For a brief but somewhat dated view of the debate, see William Kornhauser, "Power Elite or Veto Groups?" in S. M. Lipset and Leo Lowenthal, eds., *Culture and Social Character* (New York: Free Press, 1961), pp. 252–267.

[20]The seminal study is C. Wright Mills, *The Power Elite* (New York: Oxford University Press, 1956). A slightly different view is given by G. William Domhoff, *The Higher Circles* (New York: Random House, 1970).

[21]Arnold M. Rose, *The Power Structure* (New York: Oxford University Press, 1967); and Robert A. Dahl, *Pluralist Democracy in the United States* (Chicago: Rand McNally, 1967).

How close really are government and big industry? How real is the military-industrial complex? Is there a unified "power elite"?

PEOPLE POWER

Are the people not to be reckoned with politically? Let us look at two ways in which they can and do participate: mass movements and ritualism.

In a manner similar to the social movements processes described in Chapter 6, the public may force change by a mass movement in politics. Such a movement is commonly emotional, moralistic, and issue-centered. By the standards of those in power, its ideology may be politically extreme. As in the antiwar and civil rights protests of the 1960s, unconventional techniques may be used to gain attention and power, such as mass rallies, marches, and violence. Established governments, democratic or not, tend to fear or respect such a movement's potential. Rarely do the governments help or allow the movement to gain its ends. They usually move to weaken or divert it, to give it the appearance of victory without the substance, and to hope it will disappear. The seeming indifference or opposition of governments faced by mass movements arises in part

In the '60s and early '70s the U.S. waged a war that made those of all ideologies in some way unhappy.

from rational factors, such as ideological disagreement, and in part from less rational ones, such as the inertia of bureaucracy.

More often than not, the people in a political system do not rise up in great numbers. They play the game, if allowed at all, in ritualized conforming and dissenting ways. According to Mills, the political party game leaves the people powerless to score. Rose, on the other hand, finds some worth in party politics. The typical American, however, may feel a sense of futility, because political candidates seem not to be of his or her choosing. They may also seem to differ little in theory, and to be unresponsive once they are in office. In addition, the citizen may fear the consequences of political activity because such involve-

---

Who has power in your college? Find out who sits on the Board of Trustees. Ascertain their backgrounds and their connections with corporations or their political structure. What outside interests do they serve?

---

ment can threaten friendships, occupational security, or ego satisfaction. Finally, politics may seem to lack a sense of urgency because the subject matter is not compelling or because success in participation meets few immediate needs.[22]

These democratic realities surely help explain voter characteristics. In our national elections of recent years, about 60 percent of the eligible voters turned out, a rather low percentage by European standards. Moreover, the typical citizen, voter or not, is almost always poorly informed, either through being denied access to political facts or through apathy. The average voter is likely to be a white male, in his mid-thirties, rather educated and settled, and above average in wealth and influence in the community.[23] If participation is equated with something more than occasional voting, then perhaps 10 percent of the American electorate is active.[24]

POLITICAL SOCIALIZATION

Much of our political outlook and behavior—our political *culture*—comes from our political socialization. In a nondemocratic society, people may learn the norms and rationale of one-party or no-party politics. This learning may be done by family pressure, under a teacher's manipulation, by peer prodding, or through media suggestion. The young may be drilled in political beliefs, particularly if a totalitarian government pretends to be a "people's" democracy. Or they may receive, instead, no explicit education in beliefs or in methods of political participation. However, even such a conspiracy of silence and inaction teaches a great deal. Just as in some societies people learn to be involved in specific ways, in other societies people learn not to participate at all.

The process is not much different in a democratic system.[25] If anything, it

[22]Morris Rosenberg, "Some Determinants of Political Apathy," *Public Opinion Quarterly* 18 (1954), 349–366.

[23]A book-length study is Lester M. Milbrath's *Political Participation: How and Why Do People Get Involved in Politics?* (Chicago: Rand McNally, 1965).

[24]R. E. Agger and V. A. Ostrom, "Political Participation in a Small Community," in Heinz Eulau *et al.* eds., *Political Behavior* (New York: Free Press, 1956).

[25]Recent book-length studies of the subject include Richard E. Dawson and Kenneth Prewitt, *Political Socialization* (Boston: Little, Brown, 1969); and Kenneth Langton, *Political Socialization* (New York: Oxford University Press, 1969).

is less carefully regulated and more varied. At a very early age, we learn our basic political affiliation from the family. Thereafter we may hold as dogmatically to our political party as did primitive people to their totems (their family emblems). The public schools give significant instruction in at least two ways. Outwardly, they teach the democratic myth, which affirms that individuals are of about equal power in politics. In actuality, the schools tend to encourage an uncritical authoritarianism, an acceptance of the decisions and policies of those in power.

Other pressures add variety and complexity to the outcome of political socialization. As youth acquire an increasingly distinctive subculture, the peer group may counter earlier family and school socialization. The generation gap, such as it is, may extend to politics. As seen in the protest movements of the 1960s, many young radicals were products of middle class homes. College, too, can be an ambivalent force. Whereas in the last decade it was a major center of political activism, in this decade the campus is somewhat more quiet, as student interest in careers seems to have gained in relative importance.

The experiences of recent years have taught us that political socialization of minorities is a complex process. What appear to be similar backgrounds may produce an advocate of women's liberation or a quiet housewife. "Uncle Toms," content with the status quo, and black militants are produced in the same community, school, and family. Much as in nondemocratic countries, then, Americans learn to participate politically in limited and often ineffective ways. Is it surprising that, as elsewhere, many learn not to participate at all?

ECONOMIC POWER

Much older than the debate between power elitists and pluralists is the argument over monopoly and free enterprise. As an historian would confirm, big business has long been a major fact of economic life, sometimes restricting free competition in the marketplace. Equality of size and total freedom of competition no longer are capitalistic realities in many sectors of the market, as big business has come to find unplanned competition too uncertain. Much as in noncapitalistic systems, some American businesses seek to survive by controlling their sectors of the economy, beginning with the collection of raw materials and ending with the final sale of the product. A chief difference between the two economies is that the *obvious* aid and influence of government is missing in capitalism.[26]

What little is left of the free enterprise debate today must distinguish between *monopoly,* domination of a given economic activity by one concern or a cooperative group, and *oligopoly,* power in the market divided among a handful of large companies. By 1960, in each of seven major product areas, only four manufacturers dominated the markets. In all, 150 manufacturers produced about 50

[26]John Kenneth Galbraith, *The New Industrial State* (Boston: Houghton Mifflin, 1967), pp. 22–34.

The sheer size of this machine (a strip-mining shovel) can symbolize the power of the technostructure. Has big business superseded ideology?

percent of our nation's output by then, and apparently consolidation has since increased.[27] Such consolidation exists not only in manufacturing but also in distribution and in the financial world. The financial world, a common resource for businesses of all types, is not only itself highly consolidated, but also directly holds much stock in competing businesses. For example, 49 banks in the nation own 600 billion dollars worth of stock.[28] At the least, oligopoly is a fact of life in America, as it is elsewhere. Such ties as personal friendships, connections with the political establishment, common financial sources, and interlocking directorates make informal monopoly easily imaginable, too.

Many claim that what does more to keep big business in check than competition is the countervailing power, not within an industry, but among business, labor, and government. But given what we have seen of political power, even this theory deserves skepticism. If political power is divided, as the pluralist contends, then consolidated business may still tip the balance in its favor. Even when

[27]A. A. Berle, "Economic Power and the Free Society," in Andrew Hacker, ed., *The Corporation Take-Over* (New York: Harper & Row, 1964), pp. 101–102; A. A. Berle, *The American Economic Republic* (New York: Harcourt Brace Jovanovich, 1963), p. 150.

[28]Morton Mintz and Jerry S. Cohen, *America, Inc.: Who Owns and Operates the United States* (New York: Dial Press, 1971), p. 42.

Supposedly there is a growing trend to international corporatism. Select a major corporation and find out in what countries it is located, where it has subsidiaries, and where it markets its products.

---

they are united, political powers are sometimes dwarfed by the sheer size of business. The budgets of General Motors and Standard Oil are each larger than that of any of the 50 states. Finally, there are some who doubt that even unions are countering forces to business interests.[29] Unions and businesses may divide on wages and working conditions, but they often unite on other matters. Bigger markets for business—say, a lucrative government contract to build airplanes—mean more union jobs in certain industries. And shrunken or lost markets, as automobile makers suffered with their large cars during the fuel crisis of 1973–1974, hurt workers as well as business.

A newer element of economic power is found in the *technostructure* of big business.[30] Increasingly, technicians, and their methods and machines are influencing economic decisions around the world, with little regard for ideology. How they arrive at their decisions is often beyond the grasp of the corporate head, the government, and the public. These technocrats are invading an older base of economic power and shaping decisions in ways that business leaders and others may be helpless to control.

Are the people economically powerless and dependent on the good will of business owners, technicians, and bureaucrats? As consumers, people occasionally rise up *en masse* to win change, or they may form people's lobbies or present class action suits in court. But such movements are rare and their effects small. Although stock ownership is widespread in America, for the typical stockholder it is not a means of influencing the corporation. Unions may aid their members by seeking salary increases, but this is not necessarily an inconvenience for business because increases can be passed along to the consumer without requiring changes in the business structure. Frequently the people remain powerless and indifferent or quietly dissatisfied. Could it be that we are socialized to our economic culture much as we are to the political culture?

Many situations suggest that there are close ties between political and economic powers: lobbyists' activities and the funding of political campaigns by big business; the government acting as both consumer and regulator in the marketplace; the interactions of political, military, and economic groups. Especially indicative

[29]Galbraith, p. 281.

[30]Galbraith, pp. 60–71.

HAS THE THROW-AWAY CULTURE
THROWN AWAY ITS FUTURE?

Are we acting out the fable of the grasshoppers and the ants on a grand, suicidal scale, living for today without planning for tomorrow? If we are, then in our reenactment we are all grasshoppers; there are no ants. When the fuel shortage supposedly created by the Arab oil embargo ended in early 1974, things returned to what they had been before. The oil crisis was only a brief intermission in our high standard of living—our high levels of consumption and waste.

To anyone concerned about energy waste, our large, thirsty cars and power-hungry appliances are only the tip of the iceberg. Our entire economy and way of life use far more energy per capita than any other advanced industrial nation: from our stereos, TVs, electric toothbrushes, knives, and can openers, to our precooked, prepackaged convenience foods.

The shortages provoked by the oil embargo sparked great controversy about the autonomy of the large oil companies (their freedom from government regulation). Are they obsessed with maximizing profits through monopoly and restriction of supplies? Is there any authoritative government agency to monitor their activities and bring them under control? The issue is a maze of confusion, contradictions, accusations, and counteraccusations.

What most people have ignored or forgotten is that the earth's supply of fossil fuels is limited. It will someday run out completely—deep wells and mines, shale oil and strip coal, everything. Long before it finally runs out, though, we will experience severe shortages as energy-consuming nations compete for fuel sold on the international market. Meanwhile our consumption rate continues to increase annually.

The evidence is clear to scientists that we should have begun long ago to retool our economy. We should have been researching and developing alternate energy sources: from the sun, from the heat within the earth, from fusion and fission. Changing to these sources will itself consume enormous quantities of our traditional fuels.

The question is: In our society, with its values of individual liberties, limited governmental control, operation of the economy by market demand rather than planning, how can we be made to change? The federal government has so far taken few steps to educate us or give us moral leadership in meeting the crisis ahead. Will our values have proven dysfunctional in an environment that punishes waste? Will our socialized belief in progress—the belief that most change is for the better—be painfully exploded?

Design and building of military weapons is handled by private corporations. How can this interdependence of government and industry be limited?

of these ties, however, are two contemporary conditions, the military–industrial complex and the multinational corporation.

Multinational companies are an old idea and practice, as any student of colonial expansion and imperialism knows; yet today they are new in scope and power.[31] ITT, one of the larger multinational companies, has 200,000 employees in about 50 nations. As noted earlier, the budgets of several American corporations are larger than those of most nations. Because the power of multinational concerns is not stopped by national boundaries, they tend to be a law unto themselves. Their strength seems to have grown faster than the ability or willingness of governments to control them, and they now seem to constitute a new kind of imperialism. Some countries believe this permits the United States to practice political as well as economic imperialism, with the government using the multinational corporations to help dominate the host country. Certainly no foreign powers drew comfort from revelations that in 1970 ITT, to protect its business operations in Chile, requested CIA interference in the Chilean elections to prevent the Marxist Allende from coming to power. Whatever the variety of forms it now takes, the connection of political and economic power at the world level is growing.

By now, hardly anyone is willing to believe that the phrase "military–industrial complex" is totally meaningless, especially since the majority of prime defense

[31]A recent study is Louis Turner's *Invisible Empires: Multinational Companies and the Modern World* (New York: Harcourt Brace Jovanovich, 1971).

contracts have gone to only 100 corporations in recent years.[32] Whether the Pentagon is master or servant, however, is difficult to tell. It has a sizable lobbying force in Congress, and several thousand retired officers of high rank are employed by defense contractors. With several million military and civilian employees and a budget in the billions, it is larger than many nations, making it an influential force at the world level as well as domestically. This military–industrial complex is also an instance of the broader political–economic ties with other institutions. In one respect, military–industrial–educational complex is a more accurate description because the Pentagon has long contracted research with the universities. In another respect, military–industrial–union complex would be more accurate because defense contracts support heavily unionized industries.

A BALANCED VIEW OF POWER

Representative government and free enterprise, in their classical definition, fail to fit the facts of American life. Political and military leaders, business and union directors, technocrats and bureaucrats, and even the people help make our system less than perfectly democratic and capitalistic. Yet we must be careful not to reject these labels, not to substitute other inaccurate descriptions, and not to be too quickly disillusioned.

Corporate and state power in America are not absolute. Certain ideologies and norms are boundaries that even the most powerful may hesitate to change or cross, although the Watergate participants produced numerous exceptions to the rule, as did monopolists like Commodore Vanderbilt long ago. In some nations, the media may act as a guardian and conscience of public morality, Watergate again being a case in point. Also, there is still enough division of power, as even C. Wright Mills admitted, to make a would-be dictator or corporate head think twice before acting capriciously. The people have a fraction of that power. Much of their power lies in the fear that an unpredictable public inspires in its leaders, no matter what kind of state or economy. Ultimately, such counter-power or the threat of it may be the only way of keeping established power in check.

That the people are usually powerless is not necessarily dysfunctional, not even in a democratic, capitalistic society. Whatever its structure or label, a system may still serve the interests of the society as a whole or the people individually. In America, some critics overlook the fact that a less than representative system has in fact provided the people with some benefits and reforms. And we see in the part that follows, beginning with Chapter 12 on social change, that as uncertain as our evaluation of the present may be, the future promises more uncertainty still about our economic, political, and other institutions.

[32]For a collection of essays, see Carroll W. Pursell, Jr., ed., *The Military-Industrial Complex* (New York: Harper & Row, 1972).

SUMMARY POINTS AND QUESTIONS

1. The sociologist has several intellectual tools that permit a sophisticated study of political and economic institutions.

> *How do sociological concepts, the scientific method, and other disciplines aid the study of these institutions?*
>
> *What is the historian's special contribution, and why is it important?*

2. Governments and economies serve the three universal needs of culture. On close inspection, such functioning of political–economic institutions turns out to be complicated, as shown by a few examples.

> *In which ways are the three universal needs complex, demanding in turn complex economic and political activity?*
>
> *Why is it important to consider the concepts of dysfunction and conflict in doing a structural–functional study of these institutions?*

3. The people are important in the functioning of the economy, chiefly as producers and consumers. Whatever functional benefits this provides for the whole economy, the people may see their mass participation as dysfunctional for themselves.

> *By which specific activities do people help the economy function?*
>
> *In which ways is the economy a problem for them, both as producers and consumers?*

4. A government may function for the sake of the individual, the whole society, and itself. At the same time, it demands much of the citizenry.

> *How many actions of government can you describe that primarily benefit the people, and how many are primarily self-serving?*
>
> *What is asked of the people in exchange for services provided by government?*

5. Modern political and economic institutions cannot be understood without a grasp of bureaucracy, both as a concept and in specific modern forms.

> *What are some trends in present-day bureaucracies?*
>
> *What do you see as the significance of the interconnections of different types of bureaucracies?*

6. Ideologies are the beliefs and attitudes through which we see and relate to social reality. In the modern world, their number has multiplied, causing considerable confusion and creating functional problems as well as benefits.

> *What are the basic distinctions between reactionary, conservative, liberal, and radical positions?*
>
> *How many of the assumptions of democracy and capitalism can you explain?*
>
> *What are two major varieties of capitalism and their relation to socialism?*
>
> *What relation did Weber find between Christianity and capitalism?*

7. Sociologists generally agree that the American people have little or no real power, but they are divided as to how concentrated the power is.

> How do the power elite and pluralist views differ?

> How does political socialization help to explain the willingness of people to accept a rather powerless position?

8. The consolidation of economic power raises doubts about free competition in America, while the growing alliance between business and government hardly appears to favor capitalism or democracy.

> What are some contemporary trends in economic power?

> What do you see as the role of the military–industrial complex or the multinational corporation?

SUGGESTED READINGS

Blau, Peter M. and Marshall W. Meyer. *Bureaucracy in Modern Society*. New York: Random House, 1971. A recent work on the subject by leading scholars of the field.

Christenson, Reo M. et al. *Ideologies and Modern Politics*. New York: Dodd, Mead, 1971. A comprehensive account of contemporary ideologies.

Dahl, Robert A. *Pluralist Democracy in the United States*. Chicago: Rand McNally, 1967. Dahl's is a major work arguing for the pluralist view of power.

Daly, Herman E., ed. *Toward a Steady-State Economy*. San Francisco: W. H. Freeman and Co., 1973. A collection of essays critical of growth-oriented economies.

Dawson, Richard E. and Kenneth Prewitt. *Political Socialization*. Boston: Little, Brown, 1969. A good survey of the subject of political socialization.

Domhoff, G. William. *The Higher Circles*. New York: Random House, 1970. An elitist view that sees economic interests as the dominant force in political life.

Galbraith, John K. *The New Industrial State*. Boston: Houghton Mifflin, 1967. A broad survey of contemporary economic life by a leading liberal scholar.

Harrington, Michael. *The Other America: Poverty in the United States*. Baltimore: Penguin Books, 1962. The work that did much to make Americans recognize the existence of poverty in their land.

Marcson, Simon. *Automation, Alienation, and Anomie*. New York: Harper & Row, 1970. A discussion of the problems of the worker in industrial and bureaucratic society.

Mills, C. Wright. *The Power Elite*. New York: Oxford University Press, 1956. The classic statement of the elitist position on power.

Mintz, Morton and Jerry S. Cohen. *America, Inc.: Who Owns and Operates the United States*. New York: Dial, 1971. A critical exploration of the influence of big business in American life.

Pursell, Carroll W., Jr., ed. *The Military-Industrial Complex*. New York: Harper & Row, 1972. The sources, characteristics, and problems of the complex as discussed by outstanding scholars.

IV

UNDERSTANDING CONFLICT AND CHANGE

We found much earlier that all cultures change. By invention or discovery within a culture or by diffusion among cultures, new objects, beliefs, or needs are introduced. As you read especially in the previous part of this book, change is very much with us today. Our study of social institutions also gave us some idea of the role that conflict plays in contemporary social life. In the following part we see that conflict is all around us, and within many of us as well.

Despite the long service the structural–functional model has given many sociologists, they are hard–put today to defend it as a scientific description of how societies operate. On the other hand, as you saw in Chapter 1, many sociologists cannot accept the conflict model as adequate by itself. In the absence of a third comprehensive theory, sociologists have had to make eclectic use of what strike them as the sound elements of the rival major theories. In this part of the book we use the eclectic view—stressing elements of the conflict model as the more useful—to study several areas of contemporary social conflict and change.

One kind of sociologist, the social demographer, takes change as his or her subject. Demographers study the growth, decrease, and distribution of populations—on a worldwide scale or in a specific society or community. Birth rates, mortality rates, and migration rates may seem to have little interest except as curiosities for people fascinated by large numbers, but they do indeed have immense scientific value. They have value not only as a description of the present condition of a population, but also as a sign of what the future will bring.

In addition, demographers can lead other sociologists to pursue answers to questions that otherwise might not have been asked. Demographers have shown that general fertility rates (births per 1000 women aged 15 to 44) become higher as you descend the social strata of our society. Other sociologists, picking up the clue, asked themselves why this was so. At first, they thought that the lower class probably had different values from those of the classes above it, values that lead lower class people to want larger families. This is a hypothesis for testing. Sample surveys and questionnaires failed to prove the hypothesis correct. Sociologists ultimately discovered that the desired family size is pretty much the same in each socioeconomic class. The difference was that birth control information was not uniformly accessible or sought out, owing partly to financial resources and partly to attitudes toward discussing sexual matters with others.

Demographers also study migration, and internal migration (from one state to another or from one part of a state to another) has become a marked characteristic of our society. In addition, it was migration that long ago began enlarging our cities. In 100 years we've been transformed from a predominantly rural to an overwhelmingly urban people. More than three-quarters of our population lives in urban areas (in 1800, 6 percent did; in 1900, 40 percent).

Why, then, are the cities in trouble? Because the central or inner city is only one part of an urban area. The suburbs must be included as well. The suburbs are not a new feature of our cities, but their phenomenal growth after World War II dwarfs their previous size. This rapid growth has had a devastating effect on the cities because the suburbs have filled up with white, middle class, well-off families. Such families could have provided a sound tax base from which cities could draw their operating revenues. Furthermore, cities were needing more and more revenues because as the middle classes were migrating to the suburbs, the white and nonwhite poor were migrating from rural areas to the cities in search of better jobs and an improved standard of living. The poor by necessity rely more heavily than the well-off on public services: health care, transportation, housing, and the like.

Some white, middle class people continue to live in the central city. And whites of the lower middle and working classes are even more numerous in the cities. So nonwhite and ethnic minorities have invariably been forced to live in certain areas of the inner cities. Virtually every American city has slums—decayed, high-crime areas where the white poor and some of the nonwhite poor live. But most of the nonwhite poor live in ghettos. Although slums and ghettos look very much alike, they are significantly different. Slums are places that people can pass through on their way up the socioeconomic ladder. But ghettos are places that most nonwhite groups are virtually forced to live in. Slums are created by poverty, ghettos by discrimination.

You well know that racism is as old as the history of this nation. Slavery was an established part of our economic institution when we were still a collection of colonies. American Indians seem to have been victims of ethnocentrism more than of racism. However, the distinction between these two "isms" is nonexistent in relation to how subordinate groups are treated. The reservations are the American Indian's ghettos, and those who live "off the reservation" frequently live in urban ghettos.

Using the work of biologists and physical anthropologists, sociologists have been able to confirm that racism has social rather than biological roots. The apparent built-in differences among races have been traced to cultural and social class differences. A few people still seek to prove that blacks are inherently less intelligent than whites. But the overwhelming evidence of research is that the only true biological differences among races are the superficial ones of skin color, hair texture, shape of the eyes, average height, characteristic muscle tone, and a few others.

Racism may be built on a myth, but its social consequences are very real. Most nonwhites are "ghettoized" not only in where they live but in just about every other detail of their lives. Compared to whites, their infant mortality rates are higher; their life expectancies are shorter; their family life is less stable; and their economic chances are poorer. Despite the commitment of the federal government and the energetic efforts of many minority groups in past years, progress toward social equality and improved life chances has been tortoise-slow.

Racism and discrimination may one day be behind us, but one element that promises to be with us always is social deviancy. Certain acts, like murder, incest, and theft, are considered deviant by almost all societies. Nevertheless, societies vary widely in what other kinds of behavior are considered intolerable. In our society various violent and nonviolent acts that have victims are crimes: rape, murder, extortion, burglary. Yet so are some acts that have no victims (unless you choose to think of the actor as his or her own victim). Use of certain drugs is a crime, and to some thinkers a symptom of mental or emotional illness. Homosexual acts are almost everywhere in our society a crime, although, again, many consider them expressions of sickness. (Many others, most homosexuals included, consider homosexuality neither a crime nor a sickness, but rather an alternative form of behavior.)

Sociologists have not come up with entirely promising theories to explain the group basis of deviant behavior. Of the three major theories in use, each can explain why certain forms of deviancy may occur, but none of the theories truly explains why some people and not others become deviants of various kinds. Perhaps the core of the problem is that much more work must be done to distinguish among the kinds of deviancy. In our society both habitual criminals and homosexuals are considered deviants. Even so, they have not necessarily become deviants by the same processes or for the same reasons. In addition, society may have different reasons for considering the two kinds of behavior deviant. Before sociologists produce a better theory of deviancy, they will probably have to explore far back into the past of our Western culture.

How do you feel about changes in our culture and society? You probably accept some and not others. But are you surprised that changes happen? Probably not, because constant, rapid change has become part of our lives. Few changes fail to produce other changes, so the source of change is often difficult to trace. Yet almost all changes seem to begin either in our material culture (our tools and techniques) or in our nonmaterial culture (our values and beliefs). Later these changes are reflected in our institutions as norms, positions, and roles change. Do changes occur smoothly? Often, no. Cultural lag—the failure of values to keep up with techniques—is common in most societies. To an increasing degree social change has come about through collective behavior, when crowds, movements, or publics make their demands heard by force of numbers.

12

SOCIAL AND CULTURAL CHANGE

We, in the Twentieth Century, are concluding an era of mankind five
thousand years in length. . . . We open our eyes like prehistoric men;
we see a world totally new.

Kurt Marek[1]

In the several months before this book went to press, there were changes of
government—either by legal means or by revolution—in England, the United
States, Cyprus, Chile, Israel, Argentina, and other countries. Americans have
survived their first winter of fuel shortages since World War II, and we are
now coming to take for granted the increasing shortages and rising costs of such
essentials as food and energy. Something is going on, and we may or may not
know what it is. Regardless of our knowledge or ignorance, the fact remains
that we are living in a period of vastly accelerating human and environmental
evolution. This situation is not simply a matter of change—things have always
changed—but of the *rate* at which change is occurring. So let us put things within
an evolutionary context.

Current estimates place the age of the earth at about 4.5 billion years. The
fossil record begins about 1 billion years ago, but *homo sapiens* doesn't arrive
on the scene until almost a thousand million years after that. Further, recorded
human history takes us back only 10,000 years. So you can see that within this
evolutionary context, we are relative newcomers to the planet. Even so, the
changes we have gone through during our brief residence here have been nothing
short of fantastic.

Consider transportation. If we wanted to travel from one place to another,
say in 6000 B.C., about the best we could do would be to hitch a ride on a
camel: 8 miles per hour. It took more than 4000 years to improve on this mode
of transportation. The chariot, invented about 1600 B.C., made travel at up to

---

[1]Cited in Don Fabun, *Dynamics of Change* (Englewood Cliffs, N.J.: Prentice-Hall, 1967), p. 2.

20 miles per hour possible. Thirty-five hundred years later, the steam locomotive came along, boosting that top speed to 100 m.p.h. Then a mere 60 years after that, we invented the airplane, capable of speeds up to 400 m.p.h. Today, about half a century since the first working airplane, we have rockets whose speeds exceed 4000 miles per hour.

Communication? Prior to 3500 B.C., information was stored in human brains and transmitted by speech. The first use of external memory banks and retrieval systems came about 5000 years ago with the Sumerian invention of cuneiform writing on clay tablets. The invention of papyrus and then of paper reduced bulk and facilitated transportation of written messages, but no really significant changes occurred until 500 years ago with the invention of movable type for printing. By 1850, the telegraph was operational; 25 years after that we had the telephone. By 1920 the radio had been invented, followed in another 25 years by television. Now satellites, lasers, holography, and electronic computers create a vast mechanism for communication.

What is most significant about these changes is the steadily decreasing time period between each new development. The same accelerating growth is evident in virtually all technological fields, in population growth, in the generation of new information, and in our ability to control the environment.

What all this amounts to is an acceleration in the process of evolutionary change. Unlike the other species with whom we share this planet, human evolution is not predominantly *autoplastic*.[2] That is, what changes is not the human body, but the functions we are capable of performing with the technology we have invented. It took the reptiles millions of years to develop wings, and once they had them they were stuck with them. We, on the other hand, invented the airplane, giving us a birdlike capacity for flight without the sacrifice of physiological flexibility. With the airplane, in effect, we put on and take off our wings whenever we want to. This is very convenient if we want to go swimming, or run fast, or use our hands for delicate tasks.

Clearly, change is occurring more rapidly now than it has in the past. But there is more to it than that. As our ability to bring about change grows in efficiency and power, the effect that we have on the larger social and ecological systems enormously increases. By now, it is a commonplace observation that our understanding of these larger systems has not kept pace with our ability to change them. True, we can build high-rise apartment houses, but do we understand how these affect the people who live in them and the cities where they are built? The invention of the automobile was a boon to modern transportation. Yet who could have foreseen the effects: air pollution, the network of roads and highways that destroy arable land, the monumental waste of ir-

---

[2]The term *autoplastic,* referring to an organism's own body, comes from Weston La Barre, *The Human Animal* (Chicago: University of Chicago Press, 1954), p. 90.

Today in much of the world people, like these Egyptian farmers, sustain themselves by methods that go back into prehistory.

replaceable natural resources, and even the changes in the dating behavior of American teen-agers?

Buckminster Fuller has characterized our present situation as one in which we are faced with a choice between Utopia or oblivion.[3] We have at our disposal the know-how and technological tools to transform the planet into a garden or a wasteland. If we don't incorporate the appropriate changes into our societies, life styles, ecology, and way of thinking, we shall surely die off, just as many species before us have. If we are to survive, the kinds of changes we must bring about will be so extreme and so fundamental that they will constitute a new evolutionary development in human beings.

For one thing, we shall have to achieve social organization, cooperation, and communication on a global level, a situation unprecedented in the history of our species. We shall have to restructure international relations and economic practices to bring them in line with what we know of ecological processes. Our concepts of normality and morality will have to be radically reconsidered. In short, there is no aspect of our contemporary life that will escape transformation.

[3]Buckminster Fuller, *Utopia or Oblivion* (New York: Bantam Books, 1969).

SOCIAL CHANGE: THEORIES AND CONCEPTS

Change is a fact of life. It has always occurred and, as you have seen, it is occurring faster now than ever before. The sociologist is not just interested in the fact that change happens. He or she is also interested in why and how it happens. Many theories have been put forth to account for social change. None of these is entirely satisfactory, but each sheds some light on the process. So before going into detail about the changes currently sweeping over our society, it will be useful to survey some of the theories and concepts used by sociologists in their attempts to understand social change.

THEORIES OF SOCIAL CHANGE

Evolutionary Theory We discussed in Chapter 1 that the early sociologists assumed quite confidently that society was an evolutionary system. Auguste Comte assumed that it evolved in stages, and that these stages could be characterized by how people thought about the world. First, the world is seen as a playing field of supernatural forces, then as an arena of human–created abstractions, and finally as a "positive" creation of scientific principles. Herbert Spencer and Karl Marx were also evolutionists. Spencer saw society evolving by the same laws that operate in biological evolution. He thought that society, like any living organism, would become perfect through the struggle for survival and the survival of the fittest. To Marx, history had its laws, and they were carried out in human society. Evolution occurred through the resolution of the internal contradictions present in each state of society. In turn, each resolution had its own self-contradictions, and so on until the final stage—the classless society, the end of history.

Structural-Functional Theory The structural-functionalist maintains that change occurs at least partly because people learn from experience. They retain these lessons and apply them in later situations and pass them on to their young, who in turn will probably learn new techniques and knowledge. Also, all societies seem to discover that division of labor is more efficient than the performance of all tasks by everyone. With increasing specialization, more integration is mandatory, for a person performing only some of the necessary tasks is dependent on others, and vice versa. A natural result of these developments, according to the structural-functionalist, is greater social complexity.

Conflict Theory Conflict theorists, you will recall, see society as composed of group pitted against group. Clashes of interest abound and contending forces struggle either to maintain power or to grasp it. From the struggle comes change that is not only inevitable but meritable. A society in conflict must be dynamic. The struggle for power results in a redistribution of power that, temporarily at least, better reflects the interests of society's members. But the struggle continues, and with each realignment of power the society changes.

Which, if any, of these and the many other theories of social change is correct has neither been agreed upon by sociologists nor settled by the evidence. Each seems to touch at least partly upon a feature of change, but none answers all the questions. Recall, too, that sociologists have given considerable attention to diffusion of ideas from society to society, to invention, and to other elements of cultural change.

VALUES AND BELIEFS

No material cultural innovation is known to have had an effect on a society unless the nonmaterial aspects of the culture were receptive to it. If an invention or discovery is entirely hostile, or simply irrelevant, to the values and beliefs of a society, it will be rejected or neglected, either permanently or temporarily. We saw in Chapter 3 that the eleventh-century discovery by the Scandinavians of what they called Vinland—the North American continent—was little used by them. Their material culture and their values and beliefs simply did not motivate them to attempt any major colonization; it would have given them no benefit. If you reflect on your response to that fact, you will probably see more clearly the vast difference between our values and theirs. The Scandinavians were a vigorous, active, inquisitive people (their discovery of Vinland, so far from home, attests to that), yet they made no use of what to us would have been an exciting discovery. But we live in an age partly created by cultures that have increasingly developed the *value of change*. In significant and trivial ways, we have come to consider change not merely a fact of life but a value, something to be desired and sought after.

The evidence is everywhere around us, although chiefly in the material realm of our culture. Our economy depends in part on our acceptance of change. A simple example is when many people change their present car for a new one as often as they can afford to. It has been common knowledge for years that

That our values of consumption and progress conflict with our environment promises us future troubles.

car makers introduce cosmetic design changes to encourage rapid turnover, and that most cars and many other machines and appliances have built-in, planned obsolescence that limits their useful life.

CULTURAL LAG

Curiously enough, while change itself has become one of our values, we change values themselves slowly and with great reluctance. This paradox seems to relate to another value of ours—one that is more refined in the United States than in any other society in the world—the value of *materialism*. Most of us are more receptive to and curious about new things than we are about new ideas. This cautiousness seems to be a basic human trait and is the chief cause of *cultural lag*, the disparity between our material culture and our values and beliefs. To cite a familiar example of such lag, we should consider the generous size and natural abundance of this continent in relation to the libertarian social and political values that took shape early in our history. These elements have produced a complex set of norms and folkways expressing our values of individual freedom and privacy. In the last decade or so, however, it has become abundantly clear that we are polluting our environment, destroying its natural beauties, and rapidly exhausting its finite supplies of many resources. And even though we saw in the last chapter that the *political* liberties guaranteed by the Constitution are not universally esteemed in our society, our personal right to be wasteful of resources by perpetuating "the throw-away culture" is being firmly maintained against the facts. Among commuters, for instance, car pools are a rarity. The network of mass commuter transit was allowed to wither in the years after World War II, and the idea of reviving this network and of improving it with technical advances has generally met with either resistance or neglect.

We have long believed, more so than any other technologically advanced society, that the human mastery of nature is a fact and a right—a *value*. The disparity between our environmental circumstances and our values, which worsen the crisis while resisting its remedies, is a painful example of cultural lag. Many scientists and ecologists maintain that unless we voluntarily change our values and norms that relate to the environment, the environment will change them for us—and by them, many add, it may be too late to avert catastrophe.

TECHNOLOGY AND SOCIAL CHANGE

The role of technology in social change may be most vividly seen if once again we go back tens of thousands of years in human history. When prehistoric humans had learned to make and use tools, to use fire, and had developed a language, a vast range of activities opened up to them. With fire they could protect themselves from cold, from wild animals, and from each other. With better tools they could hunt more effectively. With their language they could transmit all that they had learned to their young. For thousands of years they gradually became better and better equipped to cope with their environment. Building on the past, they developed ever better ways to shelter themselves from the elements, to gather food, and to protect themselves from enemies. Still, these fundamental necessities occupied most of their time.

Then, only about 6000 to 7000 years ago, humans learned how to raise food and then to domesticate animals. Food became more abundant, and the chances for survival increased dramatically. People could dwell in one place, for no longer was it necessary to roam long distances in search of food. With more available food and food that could be stored, hunters, fishermen, and food-gatherers were released for other activities. They began to smelt and work metals,

Fire, tools, and language have been immensely important in the development of human cultures. By these essentials the modern-day Tasaday survive.

the wheel was invented, writing was developed, and small cities arose. Within a thousand years after this change, the rudiments of civilization as we now think of it were established. For a long time thereafter, although only gradual technological changes took place, our nonmaterial culture began to undergo vast changes.

The third great technological change occurred only recently, in the mid-eighteenth century: the Industrial Revolution. Even though there had been industry before this time, hand-powered looms had prevailed, and various arts and crafts were practiced in the home or in small shops. Steam power called for radical changes in industry as well as in the home. Steam proved to be quite efficient and relatively cheap, but steam must be used close to where it is produced. So the workers were collected in a large place where the steam-powered machines were. From this change, the factory system was born.

Over this span of thousands of years, from the first use of tools, fire, and language, human life has changed immensely in every way. Not only has our technology, the material aspect of our culture, vastly improved over its primitive beginnings, but our nonmaterial culture and our social institutions have changed as well. We still have the same five basic institutions because the human needs they fill appear to be permanent. But within these institutions, the changes in roles and the addition of roles and positions appear to be enormous.

TECHNOLOGY: PEOPLE AMPLIFIERS

We referred above to the fact that human evolution is not, for the most part, autoplastic. We change our tools, not our bodies. Instead of growing wings, we use airplanes. Our teeth and nails can remain short (allowing us to use our mouths for talking and our hands for writing) because we have knives for cutting food and bullets for killing each other. This much is fairly obvious. What is perhaps less obvious is the extent to which technologies function as actual *extensions* of our bodies.[4]

Human beings are basically capable of performing three distinctly different kinds of functions: (1) We receive information through our senses; (2) we process this information in our central nervous system; and (3) we act on this information by using our muscles. Virtually all technologies extend or amplify one or more of these functions. Every time you watch television, read a book or newspaper, or listen to the radio, you are receiving information through your eyes or ears, information that would not be available to you without the technologies of printing and electronics. Each time you use a calculating device—whether an abacus, a pocket calculator, or a giant computer—you are amplifying the power of your brain, increasing its speed and accuracy. Moreover, if you had to depend on your muscles to perform the functions now accomplished by technology, you would have to walk instead of ride, build fires for light instead of pushing a button. And you would have to kill your enemies with your bare hands (or teeth) instead of exterminating them at a distance with bombs and such.

It is important to recognize, however, that technology not only makes some things simpler or faster or more efficient. It also makes the impossible possible. A telescope, for example, extends our vision and gives us a better view of the moon than we have with the naked eye. Yet a telescope also allows us to see objects that, with the naked eye, would be invisible and whose existence we never would have suspected. The same is true of computers. They allow us to calculate more quickly as well as to do things that would be impossible without them. True, the record-keeping and calculating done by most computers in education, business, and research probably could be accomplished—although far

---

[4]The idea of technologies as extensions of physiological functions is developed by Marshall McLuhan, *Understanding Media* (New York: McGraw-Hill, 1965).

Much of human evolution has been outside our skins. To fly we build wings rather than growing them.

less efficiently—by people. But even the best mathematicians in the world, working together, could not have substituted for the computers that put us on the moon. The reason for this is simple. The computer can receive information from an in–flight space craft, process it, and alter the course of the craft in a matter of seconds. No mathematician or team of mathematicians can do this task. There is just too much data and too little time.

What, you may ask, have these high–powered telescopes and computers got to do with me? Quite a lot, actually, when you stop to realize that the same technological know–how that goes into them also goes into eyeglasses, hearing aids, telephones, and pacemakers. In medicine, technology is helping those who have suffered the loss or impairment of some faculty. Eyeglasses and hearing aids are only the most obvious examples. Heart pacemakers and kidney dialysis machines are the result of far more sophisticated technologies. And then there are prosthetic devices, which substitute man–made limbs and organs for their

---

What functions are amplified or extended by the telephone? Live without using telephones for one week. Can you do it? If so, what difference does it make in your social interaction?

---

malfunctioning natural counterparts. We've come a long way from the pirate's hook and wooden leg. Writing more than five years ago, the science writer Gordon Taylor described the "man-amplifiers" being developed by the Navy and Air Force:

> Like a lobster, which carries its skeleton outside its flesh, not inside as we do, the amplified man wears a steel "exoskeleton" powered by hydraulic motors instead of muscles. Inside it he wears a light framework equipped with sensors which sense his every movement and cause the exoskeleton to repeat or follow it instantaneously. Preliminary designs called for the man-amplifier to be able to support a load of 1000 lb. (half a ton) on either hand.[5]

There is a currently popular television show called "The Six Million Dollar Man." Its hero, who is capable of superhuman tasks, is part flesh and part machinery. In view of the research being carried out today, we may well wonder whether this is science fiction or science fact.

CHEMICAL TECHNOLOGIES

If you were asked to name in one minute as many examples of modern technology as you could think of, you would probably rattle off objects made of steel, aluminum, plastic, and so on: television, automobiles, airplanes, perhaps electric toothbrushes and can-openers. All of these objects have grown out of our knowledge of physics and the engineering based on physics. Much more recent, however, are the technologies based on chemistry. The patent medicine industry, which does billions of dollars worth of business each year, is one example of an industry based on our knowledge of chemistry. Each time you take an aspirin, or brush your teeth with toothpaste, or put antiseptic on a cut, you are making use of modern chemical technology. Then there is the synthetic fertilizer industry, whose production of nitrogen fertilizers has allowed farmers to increase their per-acre yield of grains many times over. And of course the coal, oil, and gas on which we rely for most of our energy are the result of a highly sophisticated petrochemical technology. There are many other examples: the preservatives

[5]Gordon Rattray Taylor, *The Biological Time Bomb* (New York: New American Library, 1968), pp. 82-83.

and additives found in almost all of our food, the insecticides that we use in our homes and on our fields, the detergents with which we wash our clothes. There are serious questions about many of these technologies, about how good they are for us and our environment. We deal with some of these questions later in this chapter. Now, however, we consider two examples of how chemical technology can affect both individuals and their social interactions.

The Pill In the opening section of this chapter, we noted that change is occurring so rapidly that all aspects of our lives will be radically altered. This alteration has already begun. In the 1960s, we began to hear talk about the "sexual revolution" and the "new morality." Sexual relationships outside of marriage became more common, and more people—especially women—freely admitted to engaging in extra-marital intercourse. The double standard in sexual behavior, which allows sexual freedom to men while denying it to women, was on its way out.

The revolution in sexual morality did not "just happen." It was helped considerably by a sophisticated contraceptive technology, and especially by the invention of "the pill." The pill not only made birth control a relatively simple and dependable process, but it turned responsibility for contraception over to the women. It is always difficult to say what would have been if . . ., but it seems unlikely that the sexual freedom of today would have been possible without the pill.

It is difficult (and usually an over-simplification) to attribute a large social movement to a single cause. Yet the women's movement, which is in the process of effecting radical change in all our institutions and modes of interaction, was surely greatly aided by the pill. To understand this situation, it is important to recognize that technologies do not simply make life easier. They also change people and restructure the ways in which people interact. The pill, by providing women with unprecedented control over their own bodies and futures, gave to them a new sense of responsibility and independence. While certainly not the only factor, the pill was surely an important one in giving impetus to the liberation movement.

Mind Expansion Psychedelic (mind-altering) substances have been with us for a long time. Peyote, mescaline, opium, and marijuana grow freely in many parts of the world and have been used by many primitive (and civilized) peoples in their religious rituals.[6] Even so, it was only about 10 years ago, in the mid-1960s, that psychedelic technology came to the United States.

There is probably no social problem in our country that has received so much attention as the problem of drug abuse. Drugs have been cited as a major cause of crime in our large cities. They have been blamed for destroying lives and

[6]See Peter T. Furst, ed., *Flesh of the Gods* (New York: Praeger, 1972).

If the women's liberation movement can be traced to one chief cause, is it technological ("the pill")? Or is this oversimple?

breaking up families. All of this, no doubt, is true: Drug abuse is a major problem. However, if you have been alive for the last 10 years, watching television, reading newspapers, talking to friends, you probably know about this side of the story. What most people have not given much thought to, though, is that there is a difference between drug abuse and drug use. It is true that many people abuse drugs, thus creating problems both for themselves and for society, but it is also true that drugs (even psychedelics) can be used in constructive ways. In Canada, for example, where legal access to psychedelics is less restricted than it is in the United States, doctors have achieved good success in using LSD to treat alcoholism. Even in our country, LSD has occasionally been used to prepare terminally ill people to meet their death with acceptance rather than fear.

The major impact of LSD and the other psychedelics on our society has not come through controlled medical research. Rather, it has come through the individual, unauthorized, and illegal experimentation by millions of young peo-

Timothy Leary led those who believed LSD would bring us to truth—through the confusions and contradictions of social life. Where are they now?

ple. Whatever you may think of the morality of engaging in illegal acts, the fact remains that psychedelic drugs have made a profound impact on life in this country.

Like the women's liberation movement, which was given impetus by the availability of the contraceptive pill, the hippie movement, which swept America in the mid–1960s, would probably never have happened without the assistance of two powerful technologies: the technique of electronic sound amplification, and the chemical technology that created LSD.

The hippie movement is now long over, but its effects are still with us: in our hair styles, our clothing, our music, and even in some of our styles of interaction. The social smoking of hashish or marijuana, for example, gave rise to a new kind of interaction among people, called *rapping*. Free–associating under the influence of the drug, marijuana smokers frequently engaged in conversations that had no point and no object. One person might pick up on something said by someone else and "trip out on it," creating a verbal fantasy that others could share and add to. Today, *rapping*—to the extent that the word is used at all—has many different meanings. Originally, though, it referred to a conversation composed entirely of digressions. It was communication for the fun of it.[7]

The human potential movement, which flourished at the same time as the hippie movement, is still very much with us. Encounter groups, T-groups, sensitivity training, consciousness-raising groups, massage, and various meditation techniques reflect the need felt by many people to change their normal consciousness by getting in touch with their bodies, with other people, or with the cosmos. For many, involvement in such groups or activities, especially meditation, comes after experience with a psychedelic drug has convinced them that they can "change their heads."

Mystics, yogis, and shamans, at all times and in all societies, have known that the normal state of consciousness is not the only kind possible. Sometimes with drugs and sometimes without them, these people have attempted to change their consciousness and to teach others to do the same. Today, these ancient techniques in conjunction with the new psychedelic technologies have transformed the lives of many Americans.

Many who wanted to explore the inner space of their own minds have decided that psychedelic drugs are not a final solution. Nevertheless they have been used to open the door and give some people a glimpse of what's there.[8] Like the Apollo space program, which demonstrated what can be done in outer space, LSD and the other psychedelics have revealed to some the equally novel domain of inner space. It was once thought by many that the individual and social consequences of such exploration might far exceed the effects of our space program:

> The revolution in the study of mind is at hand. *The Varieties of Psychedelic Experience* may suggest that that revolution can effect an *evolution* of mind also. For we doubt that extensive work in this area can fail to result in pushing human consciousness beyond its present limitations and on towards capacities not yet realized and perhaps undreamed of.[9]

Clearly in the 1960s it was expected that psychedelics would reveal to us profound truths that were simply buried too deep for our conscious minds to grasp. Such drugs are now seen, however, chiefly as tools with definite but limited use in scientific exploration of how the brain operates and of how consciousness is constituted.

---

[7]For a detailed discussion of rapping, see Marc Rosenberg, "Rapping," *Journal of Popular Culture* (Summer 1974).

[8]See, for example, Aldous Huxley, *The Doors of Perception and Heaven and Hell* (New York: Harper & Row, 1954).

[9]R. E. L. Masters and Jean Housten, *The Varieties of Psychedelic Experience* (New York: Holt, Rinehart and Winston, 1966), pp. 315–316.

TELEVISION: THE ELECTRONIC GIANT

If you look at Figure 12-1, you will notice that it can be seen either as a vase or as two profiles. When you see it as a vase, the maroon profiles become background. When you pay attention to the profiles, you no longer see the vase.

Very good. But did you notice that the entire figure—vase and profiles—is itself set against a background consisting of a page in this book? Or that the book itself can be seen as a figure set against the background of your desk or table? This "figure-ground phenomenon" is one of the most fundamental characteristics of perception. We *select* from our environment objects or events to which we want to attend. This selection process is just as true of hearing as it is of vision. We can listen to one voice out of a hubbub of background noise, or we can ignore the ticking of a clock. In any case, the figure is what we notice. The background against which the figure is situated is taken for granted, almost invisible.

TELEVISION PROGRAMING

In television, what is the figure and what is the ground? There is no one way to answer this question. Just as the vase and profiles alternate as figure and ground and are together a single figure against the ground of the page, so does television consist of a series of embedded figures and grounds.

First of all, there is the most obvious content of television, the programing. This is what becomes listed in *TV Guide* and in your local newspapers: news programs, soap operas, sports events, documentaries, drama, and so forth. It is this content of television that most people refer to when they say that television is good or bad. Is there too much violence on television? Not enough in–depth news coverage? Too little intelligent programing for children (and adults)? Are soap operas juvenile and game shows inane? All of these questions have to do with programing content. And they are key questions, for it is estimated that the average American spends five and a half hours each day watching television.[10]

The importance of program content as a socializing force cannot be overemphasized. As children grow up with television, they learn values and roles. They identify with heroes, and often they base their fantasies and expectations on what they have seen on television. Are women always portrayed as housewives, or can they be seen as executives, artists, lawyers, and doctors? Do minorities appear only as menial laborers, or are they shown in professional roles?

---

[10]Michael Shamberg and Raindance Corporation, *Guerrilla Television* (New York: Holt, Rinehart and Winston, 1971), p. 1.

Figure 12-1. Is the image of a vase or of two profiles?

Television programs present Americans with an image of themselves. This image may be true or false, realistic or fanciful. Even though it is difficult to measure the actual *effect* that television has on people, it is probably safe to assume that such a pervasive medium of communication does affect the way that we—and especially children—think about ourselves and our world.

COMMERCIALS

What is the background against which we perceive the programing content of television? In what kind of context is the television program embedded? The answer is obvious: commercials. Many educated and literate people claim that commercials are the most interesting things on television, and they may well be right. Because of the high cost of television time, commercials must be brief and well-made. They must present a compelling image of the product and a message that will persuade people to buy it, all within the space of, say, 30 seconds.

It you ask people how they feel about commercials, many will say that they are a necessary evil, that we have to put up with them, and that most of us don't pay attention to them anyway. Indeed, it has been said that during prime-time television shows or Sunday afternoon football games, refrigerator doors open and toilets flush in perfect synchrony with the commercial breaks. Never-

As hard as it is to measure, the effect of TV on people's self-image, and on their relation to their culture, seems pervasive.

theless, since market research studies show a clear relationship between television advertising and consumer purchasing behavior, many people must indeed watch commercials.

However, the real importance and impact of television commercials may not have to do so much with the message of the commercial, which, in one form or another, is always "Buy this." The message, we must remember, is the content or figure of the commercial. Just as commercials are the background of television programing, so commercials themselves are divided into figure and ground. The background of commercials is that almost invisible setting in which the message is placed.

Look at almost any detergent commercial. Typically, we see a woman faced with some monumentally dirty piece of clothing (role stereotype). Often, we are given the distinct impression that if she fails to clean it, she will have failed in her duties as wife and mother. (What values are suggested by this?) And then, of course, there is the actual physical environment in which this drama takes place. The house is usually suburban ranch–style. The kitchen is all–electric and sparkling clean. The woman, though perhaps distraught by the challenge facing her, is well-dressed, well-groomed, and comfortable in a nice, middle class way.

Now, all this background may be invisible enough if the viewer is the same kind of person as the woman portrayed in the commercial. Yet what if the viewer is a Mexican American with three children and no husband? She sees a life that is different from and more comfortable than her own. She may or may not want the particular product being sold. Even so, how do you think she feels about the all-electric kitchen, the house in the suburbs, in short, the entire life style suggested by the commercial? The *intention* of commercials may be to sell a certain product, but in fact what commercials sell most effectively is Madison Avenue's idea of the American Dream.

ELECTRONIC INFORMATION

Cut. Fade. Zoom in. Zoom out. Pan. Negative image. Multiple projection. Special effects. Television bombards us with information, both visual and auditory. It's all there, and we have only to sit back, look, and listen. It's an easy, relatively painless, and passive way of receiving information. For most American children, it's the first way they learn. Even before he or she can speak, the young child can recognize images on television.

Is it any wonder, then, that so many children have so much difficulty in learning how to read? First of all, they must consciously learn the alphabet. They must learn the sounds associated with each letter. They must learn how letters are put together—often in totally illogical ways—to form words that often don't sound the way they look. Having learned all this, the child must read, one word at a time, one sentence after another. It is a slow, often painful process. After struggling through two or three paragraphs of print, the child may have as much information as would be conveyed in a few seconds of television time.

Television and print are different *media* of communication. They organize information and present it in different ways. The skills required to watch television are easily and unconsciously learned, whereas those required for reading must be consciously learned during years of formal education. There has been considerable debate on the social and psychological consequences of these differences. Marshall McLuhan, the media analyst and social historian, claims that with television we have moved from a print-oriented society to one based on electronc communication.[11] McLuhan believes that many modes of social organization are simply reflections of the dominant communication medium of a society. Although McLuhan's arguments are fascinating and provocative, they are too complex to discuss in detail. Nevertheless, it is clear that television has had, and will continue to have, a major role in our changing society.

[11]See McLuhan.

Watch five television commercials. Pay particular attention to the roles portrayed and the values to which the commercials appeal. Note also the background of the commercials. Pool your observations with those of your classmates. What kinds of generalizations can you make?

TELEVISION AND SOCIAL MOVEMENTS

Let us focus for a moment on just one function of the various communication media: presenting the news. Traditionally, newscasting has been the primary function of newspapers. News magazines and radio also perform this function. But none of these media presents the news in such an immediate and evocative way as does television. During the Vietnam war, for example, the print and radio media reported events: battles won and lost, number of casualties, and so on. Three hundred people died today; a village was destroyed by napalm; a helicopter was shot down, killing five American advisors. We read about such things in our newspapers; we heard about them on radio. Eventually, some of us came to take it all for granted. However, what we could not so easily take for granted were the vivid pictures displayed on our television screens.

It is one thing to hear about hundreds of people dying: Numbers soon lose their meaning. It is quite another thing to see one man actually writhing in agony with a leg blown off. It is one thing to hear or read that a village has been destroyed by napalm—a regrettable but somewhat abstract fact. Yet that abstraction quickly becomes concrete and very real when we see a young Vietnamese girl running in terror, fleeing the pain engulfing her body. The image of a baby, its face forever disfigured by napalm burns, is more compelling, more real, than all the facts and figures, all the *words,* conveyed to us by newspaper and radio.

From its beginnings with a few so–called "radical" protesters to its development into a sweeping social movement, the protest against the war in Vietnam disrupted, divided, and confused American society. Over time, many supporters of the war became "radicalized" and sided with the protest movement. Young men, rather than fight in a war that they believed to be unjust, accepted exile or prison. Finally, after years of death and protest and internal strife, the war was brought to an end. What role did television play in all this? Would resistance to the war have been so intense and so prolonged if the reality of the war had not been brought into our homes each night at dinner time, displayed on screens in our living rooms for all to see?

Compare the difficulty of learning to read with the ease of being entertained or informed by TV. Does this make TV superior to printed matter?

THE OTHER TELEVISION

So far, we have discussed television only as a medium of mass communication. Nevertheless, television and its related technologies can be used on a much smaller scale. Many stores and almost all banks now use closed circuit television systems for security and surveillance. In Mount Vernon, New York, television cameras are mounted on street lights, from which they scan the streets and relay information back to police headquarters.

In education, television has so far been used mainly as a one-way medium. That is, pre-packaged "educational" programs can be selected from a school's videotape library and shown to students. For the most part, though, educators have been slow to realize that the most valuable use of television may lie in allowing students to use the equipment. What little work has been done in this area suggests that even very young children can be taught to handle video equipment and that, if left on their own, often will come up with interesting and creative results. Most educators, however, having been brought up and

Most educators, raised and educated in a world of print, tend to use TV in education as a one-way medium, like books.

educated in a world dominated by print, naturally tend to use video just as they use books. Their failure to recognize that television is an effective *interactive* medium gives some support to the theory of cultural lag.

Before concluding this section on television, something should be said about the use of video as a research tool. It is often difficult to observe human interaction in a systematic way. People move and talk faster than an observer can take notes. Often, the small pieces of behavior, such as gestures and tone of voice, go unnoticed. With videotape, though, the student of human interaction can tape people interacting and then look at the tape over and over again. Unlike film, the videotape can be viewed immediately, and then it can be re-used, erased and re-recorded. For sociologists, anthropologists, psychologists, and others who are interested in face-to-face interaction among people, videotape is an indispensable research tool.

COLLECTIVE BEHAVIOR: PEOPLE AS AGENTS OF CHANGE AND ACTORS IN CHANGE

To fully appreciate the impact of technology on social change, it would make an interesting assignment to try to deliberately exaggerate the importance of, say, electronic technology for social change in modern America. Try it; it will probably prove more difficult than you first imagine. What areas of life are untouched and unaffected by electronic technology? Do television and radio affect our religious behavior? The many religious broadcasts and appeals for greater adherence to religious values suggest that they do. Does the computer affect our vacation activities? For some it does, because computers are used to determine vacancies in our national parks and to reserve campsites.

But we must not forget the people. Sociologists have studied how and under what circumstances numbers of people acting together can achieve some objective or take social action. Concern with the role of collectivities in social change is not difficult to understand. After all, don't we often hear such expressions as "an aroused public" or "enlightened public opinion," which imply that masses of people will take some action or will help to bring about some change?

The 1960s saw many repeated examples of numbers of people responding to a common influence; race riots in Watts, Detroit, Newark, Harlem, and elsewhere; the riots at the 1968 Democratic National Convention in Chicago, the mass protests against the Vietnam war, and so on. Sociologists use the concept *collective behavior* to refer to such unstructured, spontaneous reactions of numbers of people. Collective behavior is impossible to define precisely because the concept encompasses such a broad range of social interaction, from social movements (which are loose-knit but directed to a purpose or goal) to a rioting mob at a huge open-air rock concert.

How does collective behavior affect social change? Sociologists are particularly interested in that form of collective behavior called the *crowd* and how the crowd can respond to social change or help to bring about change. While it is the *active crowd,* as we shall see, that is intent upon some action or objective, other types of crowds can become active ones. It is useful, therefore, to distinguish among several types of crowds. We can then discuss how active crowds develop and how much impact they have on social change.

CROWDS

The sociologist defines the crowd as a collection of people who are gathered together for a single purpose or to respond to a single stimulus. Such a definition

Whether gathered for violence or only symbolic action, a group of protesters is called an active crowd, like this one in Rome.

would include the rock concert audience, a church congregation, a protest rally, and a riot. A crowd like that at a rock concert is an *expressive* crowd; the people have gathered to experience the performance and to participate in it by expressing the feelings generated by it. Collections of people at a protest or a riot are an *active* crowd; they have gathered for action, whether violent or symbolic. That is, rioters protest conditions or express their feelings by violating norms, while often protesters gather peacefully in hopes of showing by their numbers the force of public opinion behind their position. Frequently a riot will spring from what is known as a *casual* crowd, a crowd that gathers spontaneously to witness some incident, such as a traffic accident or an arrest. So long as the crowd is passive, simply watching events unfold, it remains casual; it can disperse without producing any incidents of its own. But if, as we see below, a *precipitating factor* occurs, the casual crowd may become an *active* crowd.

Sociologist Neil Smelser theorizes six preconditions, each one building on the others, that are conducive to potentially explosive collective behavior in a society.[12] Let us apply them to racial riots.

[12]Neil Smelser, *Theory of Collective Behavior* (New York: Free Press, 1963).

1. *Structural Conduciveness.* The sheer density of population in large cities makes life in them impersonal and anonymous. Secondary rather than primary relationships predominate. Cities also gather people diversified by race, religion, income, status, and so on. Some areas of the city gather different ethnic and racial groups, which can prevent common bonds from developing among people living there. Other areas are segregated according to race, nationality, and the like. Many of these are ghettos, where people share the common experiences of racial discrimination and poverty. The racial riots of the 1960s all occurred or began in ghettos.

2. *Structural Strain.* Particularly in large cities, extreme contrasts in wealth are evident, to both rich and poor. This coexistence of wealth and poverty makes the poor far more conscious of their poverty than if they lived a great distance from the wealthy. It is not difficult to understand why minority groups begin to think of themselves as victims of social injustice. Feelings of relative deprivation and social injustice set the stage for potentially explosive collective behavior.

3. *Growth and Spread of a Generalized Belief.* After years of quiet acceptance of discrimination and poverty or of trying to bring about social change nonviolently, many blacks felt that they were no better off then they had been years ago. They still felt deprived by white supremacy; their wages were still too low; they still could not get a good job or a good education; and they saw no signs of change in the near future. They had been deprived for hundreds of years, and they were tired of waiting for the white man to give them their fair share. Many began to hold the idea that something had to be done—and soon—even if it meant bloodshed.

4. *Precipitating Factors.* Each of the riots of the mid–1960s was triggered by what ghetto dwellers considered police harassment or brutality. Sociologists often use the concept of *selective perception* to explain what can happen in a tense situation: Members of a crowd of witnesses, who have become emotionally involved in the events, react to an ambiguous incident as if its meaning were absolutely clear. Say that someone is resisting arrest and the police become involved in pushing and shoving. An emotionally involved crowd is capable of viewing this activity as police brutality. They will have noticed the behavior of the police and ignored or interpreted favorably the resistance of the arrestee. The concept of selective perception appears to be sound. But it has limited usefulness. After all, the sources of the sociologist's information on a riot, or indeed the sociologist's own experiences, are just as capable of selective perception as is the crowd. The ability to perceive selectively is a human one, not merely the property of the crowds. Nevertheless, since relations between police and many ghetto dwellers are uncomfortable at best, the grounds for selective perception and the potential for precipitating factors are both quite strong.

5. *Mobilization for Action.* Once a precipitating factor has activated the crowd, a particular quality of crowds becomes evident: In a crowd everyone is anonymous; many people cease to be controlled by the norms that ordinarily guide their behavior, and they may do many things that they would otherwise never have considered doing.

6. *Traditional Social Controls Are Ineffective.* The normal modes of external social control become as ineffective as the crowd member's norms. The police are greatly outnumbered and on the defensive. They must either retreat or call for reinforcements. But the last alternative is usually ineffective if the crowd has already reached the fifth stage. The police then find themselves surrounded by a normless vacuum.

PUBLIC OPINION

Active crowds can initiate social change or speed up change already underway. A crowd of angry shoppers protesting at a supermarket may spearhead a consumer movement. Many of the civil rights demonstrations in the 1960s made it difficult for communities to continue more blatant forms of discrimination. Active crowds can also have an indirect and partial influence on social change by affecting *public opinion.* Publics and public opinion are forms of collective behavior rather than of group interaction because they are neither gathered in a crowd nor bound by other modes of group interaction. A public is spread out—how broadly depends on the issue in which members share an interest. The particular issue is what defines a public; for to have created a public its members must have made those in power over whatever is the focus of interest *aware* of this interest. By *interest,* of course, we do not mean mere attention or curiosity; interest is generated in members of a public by their belief that they will be affected by the outcome of whatever is at issue.

Thus, *public opinion* refers to the attitudes and judgments held by a public on a given issue, such as race riots, the Vietnam war, the environment, or whatever. Public opinion need not be unanimous; it can be divided or fragmented into many positions. Public opinion of rioters may take the form of sympathy for the rioters based on the belief that ghetto life is intolerable and an assault on the person. But despite this sympathy, public opinion also may include an insistence on lawful means of self-expression and a rejection of the rioters' methods.

Public opinion is measured by polls, surveys made of samples of a society's members. It also may be measured by comparing the balance of opinions expressed in letters and telegrams to local or national politicians.

Many riots, while having particular fuses, seem to have history as their explosive, coming as they do from prolonged injustice and discrimination.

We have seen that technology has in turn changed our world and how we respond to it. Our machines, instruments, and vehicles have altered the appearance of the earth and have changed our relationship to outer space as well. But just as our improved ability to move around has made the world seem to shrink, our increased knowledge and immediate perceptions of the world, thanks to technology, have made the world seem to expand. These changes have had the combined effect of inviting us, and sometimes forcing us, to develop new ideas and ways of thinking.

NEW IDEAS FOR NEW TIMES

Computer scientists often find it useful to distinguish between "hardware" technology and "software" technology. Hardware refers to machinery of various kinds, and software includes the programs and other information fed into the machines. People, of course, create the programs and run the machines. So far in this chapter, we have talked almost exclusively about hardware; about machines and chemicals—about things and how they affect change. We have talked also about crowds and how they can facilitate change by creating public awareness of the need for change, or by influencing public opinion.

But the changes in society are not just related to our invention of new things, or to the activities of concerned collectivities. They are also related to new ways of thinking and to new ideas.[13] These new ways of thinking can be considered our software technology. They are the ideas that we run through our brains as we attempt to make sense out of our world and decide how to act in it.

FLIP-FLOP

It will be useful if you take a moment now to look at Figure 12-2. The figure is called the "Necker Isometric Cube." If you look at it steadily for a few seconds, it will appear to flip-flop. With a little practice, you can make it change back and forth at will. Once you've done this little experiment, consider the following question: Where is the difference? The cube appears to change, but obviously it does not. No matter how you see the cube, the lines on the paper remain the same. What must be changing, then, is the way in which you look at the cube, your point of view. For those of you who believe that there is an "objective" world "out there" and that all sane people must agree on what it's like, this experiment should cause you to stop and think again. For the cube demonstrates quite clearly that the same thing can be perceived in very different ways.

Probably all of us have experienced similar examples of this same phenomenon. A peanut butter sandwich can seem like a feast if you're hungry, but after a full meal it will arouse no interest at all. A ringing telephone can be a source of joy or fear, depending on our expectations. It is necessary to stress that these are not just trivial examples. Because our behavior is geared to our perceptions, the way we see things will affect the way we act. Imagine that you're going to a job interview and that you feel insecure and lacking in self-confidence. Your perception of yourself will be reflected in your behavior and—since you're likely to make a poor impression—in the behavior of your potential employer as well. On another day, though, you may be feeling better about yourself. Who you are and what you can do have not changed, but now you exude self-confidence and assurance. You make a better impression, and you have a better chance of getting that job.

These examples can serve as a model for the kinds of changes now occurring in our ways of thinking. The laws of nature and society have not changed, but our ways of thinking about them have changed. We have already talked about some of these changes, and later we talk about others. Right now, however, we explore some new ideas and their effects on society and on human interaction.

[13]For a brilliant exposition of these new ways of thinking, see Gregory Bateson, *Steps To An Ecology Of Mind* (New York: Ballantine Books, 1972).

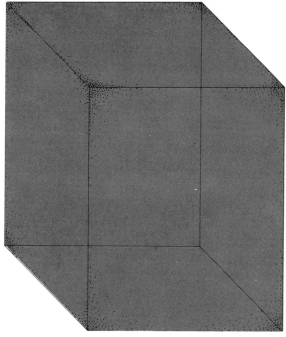

Figure 12-2. Necker Isometric Cube: Where's the difference?

MAKING DISTINCTIONS: WHERE TO DRAW THE LINE

All of us make distinctions. We mark off events and physical objects with boundaries of some kind. These boundary markers may be quite simple and obvious, like the frame around a picture or the bell that ends a class period. Distinctions also may be extremely subtle and difficult to explain. Here's another experiment that you can try. First, work up some saliva in your mouth, and then swallow it. No problem. Now do the same thing, but instead of swallowing the saliva, spit it into a cup or glass. Now drink it. If you're like most people, you will experience these two acts as different. But why and how they are different is not easy to explain.

We break our world up into pieces, and then we give names to these pieces. Yet the world itself is not fragmented. It is we who divide it up and label it for our own convenience. Moreover, how we divide up the world varies from one society to another and is learned during the process of socialization. The conventional distinctions that we make are well learned and almost universally shared by other members of our society. As a result, it may be difficult to believe that these distinctions are relatively arbitrary, that they have to do more with how we think than with the actual organization of the world.[14] Nonetheless,

[14]See, for example, Benjamin Lee Whorf, *Language, Thought, and Reality,* John B. Carroll, ed. (Cambridge, Mass.: The M.I.T. Press, 1956); see also Dorothy Lee, *Freedom and Culture* (Englewood Cliffs, N.J.: Prentice-Hall, 1959).

this is true, and the remainder of this section is devoted to exploring some of the implications of how and where we draw our lines.

SPECIALIST AND GENERALIST

Since this is a textbook in sociology and since you are reading it, it is likely that you are enrolled in a sociology course in a college or university. Your course is probably one of many such courses offered by the sociology department. You probably are taking other courses as well—perhaps in history, English, mathematics, chemistry, and so on. Again, each of these courses is given by a particular department. Each department has its own faculty and its own field of study. As a beginning student, you are allowed—perhaps even required—to take courses in many different areas. Later, you will have to specialize. If you choose to specialize in sociology, then most of your courses will be in that area. You may "round out" your studies with some work in psychology, history, or anthropology, but it is unlikely that you will take advanced courses in, say, biology, physics, or literature. As you continue your education, perhaps into graduate school, you will specialize more and more. As a sociologist, you might choose to specialize in marriage and the family, or in race relations, or in demography. In short, you will become an expert, knowing more and more about less and less.

To some extent, this kind of specialization is both necessary and useful. The world needs people with detailed and specialized knowledge. Only quite recently, however, have we recognized the need to go in the other direction as well, to educate *generalists* as well as specialists. During the Renaissance, it was quite common for educated people to be generalists. In fact the term *Renaissance man* refers to someone with expertise in a variety of different areas. Sir Philip Sidney was both a professional soldier and a poet. Leonardo da Vinci combined poetry, art, and engineering. John Donne was an ambassador as well as a clergyman and a poet.

The explosion of knowledge and the development of the scientific method, both of which began in the Renaissance, gave rise to the kind of specialization that today you can see in the departmental organization of your college. Indeed, specialization is so much a part of our lives that we have several derogatory terms to describe those who refuse to specialize. We call such people *dilettantes*, suggesting that they dabble in different areas but that their knowledge is superficial. Or we say of someone that he is a "jack of all trades but master of none."

It was only about twenty-five years ago, in the early 1950s, that an opposite trend got under way. At the conferences sponsored by the Josiah Macy Foundation, biologists, engineers, communication theorists, anthropologists, and others stepped outside the boundaries of their formal training and began to talk to each other.[15] They discovered that although they were concerned with very

[15]The Josiah Macy, Jr. Foundation, *A Review of Activities: 1930–1955* (New York: Josiah Macy, Jr. Foundation, 1955).

Where are the lines drawn in your classroom? Between teacher and students? Between students? Who talks to whom? In many classes, the teacher talks to the students, and the students ask questions. In some classes, the students are encouraged to talk to each other. In a few classes, students and teacher may actually talk together. What difference do these differences make? Refer to your own experience or ask others.

---

different things, the questions they were asking were quite similar. They found, too, that the knowledge gained in one field of specialization could be put to good use in other fields.

The results of this new trend are evident today in a number of different areas. First of all, there are the so-called "hyphenated sciences": psychobiology, ethnolinguistics, biophysics, and the like. Then, too, we are beginning to see multidisciplinary curricula in some of our colleges and universities. Unlike traditional curricula, which require students to specialize in a specific field of study, these new programs are "problem-oriented." They allow the student to select some issue in which he or she is interested, and to take whatever courses are relevant to the problem. Say, for example, that you are interested in perception. In a multidisciplinary program, you would probably take courses in psychology, physiology, anthropology, philosophy, art history, and so forth. In other words, your course of study would be determined by what was relevant to your interests rather than by the need to specialize in any one discipline.

There is a great need today for people whose knowledge and thinking goes beyond the lines drawn by traditional academic disciplines. As we learn more and more about subjects like ecology, sociology, and chemistry, we find that these areas of study often overlap. In planning a housing project, for example, we need architects to design the buildings as well as social scientists to tell us how human interaction is affected by the architectural spaces. We need sociologists and city planners who know something about how such projects relate to the cities in which they are built—how they affect the city and are affected by it. As another example, the chemist who develops a new kind of detergent no longer can be satisfied with understanding the effect that it has on dirt. The chemist should also know something about marine biology, so that he or she can predict what the effect will be when the detergent runs off into streams, rivers, and oceans.

There is just too much knowledge in the world for any one person to know everything about everything. But there is no excuse for educated people to develop "tunnel vision," which blinds them to everything outside their own narrow field of specialization. At the very least, we need people who can talk to, and learn from, people whose knowledge is different from their own. We need people who can see the whole picture.

CHANGE AND THE FUTURE

Throughout this chapter, we have discussed social change as it relates to technology, mass movements, new ideas and values, and the media of communication. We have given only passing consideration to whether the changes that we are now experiencing are good or bad. In some ways, this emphasis is appropriate, for it is the sociologist's business to seek the facts about society, not to make value judgments.

Even so, the sociologist is necessarily a part of the system that he or she studies—at least, a citizen of a nation; at most, a citizen of the world. Also, it is a basic premise of sociological thought that a society, like an organism, must adapt to its environment, and that if it fails to adapt, it will not survive. So when the sociologist sees a society heading inevitably toward extinction, he or she may be excused for shedding the cloak of scientific detachment and engaging in a bit of impassioned rhetoric.

THE LIMITS TO GROWTH

There are probably few Americans who have not seen a photograph of the earth taken from outer space. The impact of this new vision may differ from person to person. But at the very least it makes one fact abundantly clear: our planet is a finite, spherically shaped object. Because it is finite, it has only so much space and so many resources. Now, the space and resources that we have may be large, but they are not infinite. If we keep using them up, they will eventually run out. The faster we use them up, the sooner they will run out. And we are now using up both our space and our resources very quickly indeed. For how much longer can we continue in our present patterns of growth and consumption before something breaks down? There is no clear answer to this question, but the authors of *The Limits to Growth* think it may be as little as 100 years:

1. If the present growth trends in world population, industrialization, pollution, food production, and resource depletion continue unchanged, the limits to growth on this planet will be reached sometime within the next one hundred years. The most probable result will be a rather sudden and uncontrollable decline in both population and industrial capacity.

2. It is possible to alter these growth trends and to establish a condition of ecological and economic stability that is sustainable far into the future. The state of global equilibrium could be designed so that the basic material needs of each person on earth are satisfied and each person has an equal opportunity to realize his individual human potential.

WOMEN—OFF THE PEDESTAL
AND INTO THE PRESIDENCY?

In 1923 a resolution was presented to Congress. It proposed an amendment giving equal rights to women. Forty-nine years later, in 1972, it passed both houses and began its journey around the United States for ratification by the states. The Equal Rights Amendment (ERA) says only: "Equality of rights under the law shall not be denied or abridged by the United States or by any State on account of sex."

Why is such an amendment needed in an egalitarian society like ours? This is of course a naive question. Throughout the land inequalities are written into our laws and built into our behavior in every social institution. Why? Chiefly because women are thought of, by most men and by many women themselves, as the weaker sex both physically and mentally. The ERA would vastly simplify and quicken women's attainment of equal legal rights everywhere in society.

Women are now both discriminated against and overprotected. If they do the same work as men, they are almost always paid less. State work laws require rest breaks for working women and prevent them from working overtime or lifting loads of more than a specified weight. In most states women are legally prevented from conducting business transactions on their own or from maintaining their own credit. And considering that women make up about half our population, they are even more under-represented in political offices than are racial and ethnic minorities.

With ratification of the ERA all of this would begin to change. Many women are impatient to begin assuming the roles and exercising the rights that have long been denied them, either on legal or traditional grounds. Certainly the rate of change would be an accelerating one, for as we have seen, change produces change.

Men who fear the ERA should realize that it frees them as well as women from discrimination. In divorce cases, alimony no longer could be automatically extracted from the man to support the woman. It could go either way, as could custody of children. It would encourage parents to share the child-rearing role more equally without fear of social stigma. More men would be able to take turns occupying the income-earner and home-maker roles without thinking of themselves, or being thought of by others, as weird. In short, the ERA should have profound effects on our society over coming decades.

3. If the world's people decide to strive for this second outcome rather than the first, the sooner they begin working on it, the greater will be their chances of success.[16]

THE MYTH OF PROGRESS

Americans have been called "waste-makers" and "conspicuous consumers." It has been said that ours is a "throw-away culture." Unpleasant as it may be to face up to these charges, they are borne out by the facts. With less than 6 percent of the world's population, America accounts for 30 percent of the world's consumption of raw materials.[17] We build gas-guzzling cars, which we trade in every two or three years. Those that can't be resold are allowed to rust in junkyards, where their valuable steel turns into useless iron oxide. We are told—and judging by our buying patterns, apparently believe—that paper and plastic cups are more convenient than glass. What we are not told is that plastic must be made from petroleum, and that to make paper we must decimate forests. Nor are we told about the lethal hydrocarbons released into the air when our disposable plastics are burned in incinerators or garbage dumps. Indeed, as regards our use of natural resources, we behave as if there were no tomorrow. If we continue in this way, we may just prove ourselves correct.

To understand the origins of this suicidal behavior, we must go back in history and regard the matter in relation to the cultural lag example presented earlier in this chapter. Until recently, most people believed that the "golden age" of humanity existed some time in the past. We can find this belief in Greek mythology and even in the Bible with its account of the Garden of Eden. The idea of *progress*—that we are moving forward to a better life—was invented in the Renaissance and reached its peak around the time of the Industrial Revolution.

During the early years of our nation, the idea of progress was particularly appealing. Here was a vast, unspoiled continent, with apparently limitless resources and possibilities. There were few people, much land, and the chance of a marvelous future for those with the strength and ingenuity to make it work. (Of course, the Indians were pesky, but that was a minor nuisance. And besides, they weren't even white.)

Today, we still have many of the same values that were developed in America during the eighteenth and nineteenth centuries. But the situation has changed. We are now a highly advanced, industrialized nation of some 215 million people. Thus, we need to ask ourselves whether the values that were required to build a nation are the same as those needed to maintain it. The economist, Kenneth Boulding, thinks they are not:

[16]Donella H. Meadows et al., *The Limits to Growth* (New York: Universe Books, 1972), pp. 23–24.

[17]Paul R. Ehrlich and Anne H. Ehrlich, *Population, Resources, Environment* (San Francisco: W. H. Freeman, 1970), p. 72.

The closed earth of the future requires economic principles which are somewhat different from those of the open earth of the past. For the sake of picturesqueness, I am tempted to call the open economy the "cowboy economy," the cowboy being symbolic of the illimitable plains and also associated with reckless, exploitive, romantic, and violent behavior, which is characteristic of open societies. The closed economy of the future might similarly be called the "spaceman" economy, in which the earth has become a single spaceship, without unlimited reservoirs of anything, either for extraction or for pollution, and in which, therefore, man must find his place in a cyclical ecological system which is capable of continuous reproduction of material form even though it cannot escape having inputs of energy.[18]

It will not be easy for a society that values growth and progress to engage in a massive re-evaluation of its beliefs, attitudes, and behavior. It may be somewhat easier, though, if we realize that improvement does not necessarily mean producing and consuming more *things*. It is worth noting that there is only one living organism that engages in growth for its own sake: the cancer cell.

In this chapter we have seen that all societies change. Sociologists, whether they subscribe to structural-functional theory, conflict theory, or some other general theory, attempt to explain social change. To deal with what is unique in the human experience—the rapidity of change in modern society—we had to investigate how technology has penetrated our lives. Another element of social change is important enough to devote a full chapter to—the population of our society. Social demography, the topic of the next chapter, deals with changes in the population size and how these changes affect and are affected by social interaction.

SUMMARY POINTS AND QUESTIONS

1. A long view of human history makes it clear that the rate of social change has accelerated. All societies have changed. What is new is how rapidly our society is changing and will continue to change.

> *Illustrate the acceleration of change in the areas of transportation and communication.*
>
> *How can the rapidity of change we are able to produce have consequences for which we are unprepared?*

[18]Kenneth Boulding, "Economics of the Coming Spaceship Earth," in *The Environmental Handbook*, ed. Garrett De Bell (New York: Ballantine Books, 1970), p. 96.

2. While change itself is one of the values of our society, our willingness to accept new ideas falls behind our willingness to accept new elements of material culture. This phenomenon is called culture lag.

> *Illustrate how our ideas and values on individual freedom interfere with the solution of environmental problems.*
>
> *What values would have to change more rapidly if we are to live more in harmony with our environment?*

3. Some of our technological developments serve to extend the functions of our bodies, amplifying our ability to receive, process, and act on information.

> *Show how many technologies improve our ability to receive information.*
>
> *Illustrate how some technologies not only improve our abilities but allow us to do things we could not do at all without them.*

4. The impact of chemical technologies is sometimes not taken notice of. But developments in medicine, farm chemicals, and petrochemistry have profound effects on our lives and social interaction.

> *How has the chemical contraception of the pill helped to produce changes in sexual morality and in the role of the sexes?*
>
> *How has psychedelic technology affected our lives?*

5. Television is an important and far-reaching teaching device. Through its programs and commercials it affects our ideas on social roles, our values, and the way we think about ourselves and the world.

> *Show how television programs can affect the aspirations of children. Do the same for television commercials.*
>
> *In what ways can television affect the self-image and satisfaction of adults?*

6. From a print-oriented society we are moving to one dominated by electronic communication.

> *Show how electronic communication, itself a product of change, can continue to produce change.*
>
> *Did television speed up the Vietnam war resistance movement? How?*

7. Collective behavior is unstructured behavior of people responding to a common influence. One form is the crowd, a collection of people gathered together for a single purpose. Crowds have at times called attention to change, at other times have reacted to it, and have influenced public opinion regarding it.

> *Give an example of a casual crowd, an expressive crowd, and an active crowd.*
>
> *Describe the six preconditions that allow a casual crowd to become an active, explosive crowd.*
>
> *Illustrate how crowds can affect social change by influencing public opinion.*

8. A new idea that is beginning to have an influence on social change is that there is an absolute limit to growth in production and consumption. This means that new values are needed to maintain our society rather than to keep building and expanding it.

> Describe the social and environmental conditions that led to the value that growth and expansion are good.
> Develop an extensive list of attitudes and values that would have to change if the main objective of our society was to maintain the nation rather than to expand it.

SUGGESTED READINGS

Agel, Jerome. *Is Today Tomorrow?* New York: Ballantine, 1972. An imaginatively put together collage of ideas concerning the future and possible alternatives.

Albertson, Peter and Margery Barnett. *Managing the Planet.* Englewood Cliffs, N.J.: Prentice-Hall, 1972. A collection of essays by both physical and social scientists on the necessity of planning for the future to ensure a high quality of life for the world community.

Applebaum, Richard P. *Theories of Social Change.* Chicago: Markham, 1970. Classifies and presents the major theoretical frameworks used to account for social change. These include evolutionary theory, equilibrium theory, conflict theory, and rise and fall theories.

Etzioni, Amitai. *Studies in Social Change.* New York: Holt, Rinehart and Winston, 1966. A short book dealing with strategies and theories of social change. It also includes a number of case studies of social change.

McPherson, William, ed. *Ideology and Change.* Palo Alto, Calif.: National Press, 1973. A reader on social thought, radicalism, fundamentalism, ideology and propaganda and the effects of these systems of thought on social change.

Moore, Wilbert E. *Order and Change: Essays in Comparative Sociology.* New York: John Wiley, 1967. Focuses on order and change in various societies and the effects of modernization on these processes.

Schneider, Kenneth R. *Destiny of Change.* New York: Holt, Rinehart and Winston, 1968. An analysis of the effect on industrialization, urbanization, and bureaucratization on the personality of the individual.

Smelser, Neil J. *Theory of Collective Behavior.* New York: Free Press, 1963. Develops a paradigm for the analysis of collective behavior, specifically such phenomena as the panic, the craze, the hostile outbursts, and the social movement.

Theobald, Robert, ed. *Futures Conditional.* New York: Bobbs-Merrill, 1972. A collection of readings from sociology to science fiction designed to orient the student to possible futures.

Toffler, Alvin. *Future Shock.* New York: Random House, 1970. A fascinating work on social change in modern society. Argues that the lack of permanence of both products and social institutions is psychologically disorienting to the individual.

Isn't social demography simply a numbers game? After all, demographers count male and female, young and old, married and unmarried, black and white, and so on. What use can statistics be? Plenty. Demographers can help a society in many ways to plan for the future. For example, knowing how many 4-year-olds are in your community tells you how many classrooms will be needed in 2 years. But demographers do more than help us to make intelligent plans. Their studies, conducted with census data, vital records (births, deaths, marriages, divorces), and population sample surveys, enrich our knowledge of society. Demographers tell us how social class, religion, and race affect—and are in turn affected by—fertility and mortality rates and migration. In short, they tell us how population characteristics affect society and how society affects population.

13

SOCIAL DEMOGRAPHY

While you are reading these words four people will have died from starvation. Most of them children.

Paul R. Ehrlich

We have been God-like in our planned breeding of our domesticated plants and animals but we have been rabbit-like in our unplanned breeding of ourselves.

Arnold Toynbee

In November 1970, a giant tidal wave swept the Bay of Bengal and killed 300,000 Pakistanis. But within 15 days, 300,000 babies were born in Pakistan, bringing the population of that country back to where it had been before the catastrophe. Almost a year later another tidal wave hit the coast of India and killed an estimated 15,000 persons, slightly fewer people than are born there in six hours. It is tragic and frightening to realize that nature can unleash its fury and instantly destroy huge numbers of people. Of course, the tragedy that touched the millions of families in India and Pakistan cannot be measured by a death count. Yet when the deaths are related to births, we find a dramatic illustration of the population explosion in these countries. This, too, is frightening—and even tragic.

World population has risen from about 1 billion in 1950 to over 4 billion in 1975. In the United States there are now over 100 million more people than there were a mere 50 years ago. Why? (The answer is not as simple as you might think.) What would happen if our own and the world's rate of growth continue as they are? Or what would happen if somehow we could achieve zero population growth here and throughout the world? It would be foolish to promise answers to these questions, as important as they are. The best we can promise is to describe in this chapter how sociologists who specialize in demography seek answers to these and other serious questions, and how they obtain information on the population of societies.

One of the crucial problems facing the United States, and indeed humanity worldwide, is how to deal with a surging growth in population. The population time bomb and the fury it can unleash cannot be ignored, and we consider such concerns later in the chapter. But first we need some intellectual tools, facts, and basic concepts before we can deal meaningfully with serious population issues. Demographers study much more than "the population explosion." In this chapter we discover (1) what phenomena social demographers study, (2) the framework and some of the methods of their research, (3) the findings of such research, and (4) the implications of the findings, particularly for our own society and its population pressures.[1]

THE SOCIAL DEMOGRAPHER'S GOALS AND METHODS

Perhaps the easiest way to begin our many-faceted task is to imagine a hypothetical community and ask what kind of information the demographer would like to collect about the individuals in it.[2] Ideally, the demographer would like to know the age, sex, and physical location of each person, and often the marital status and race of the individuals. Information on these individual characteristics are gathered for two purposes. First, the information permits a description of the social system under study. If the data were complete, we would know how many people live in the community, the proportion of males and females, the number of children or old people, and so forth. Second, we would obtain a fuller description of the community if we studied different combinations of these factors, such as age and sex, or age, sex, and marital status. By such analyses we could give a more meaningful statistical description of the community than by knowing merely that, say, 50,000 people lived in it.

A demographic description of a community can be extremely valuable, even without knowing how the community evolved to its present state or where it is heading. For example, assuming no out-migration (no one is moving away), if we found that there were many more 4-year-olds than 6-year-olds, we would know that more schoolrooms would be needed, not just 2 years from now but for the next 12 years. Again, knowing how many people will soon become 18 years old tells us how many jobs or places in college are needed. Or suppose that we wanted to know how many young people should be encouraged to leave the community. We would first find out how many young people actually leave the community. This can be done by analyzing two time periods and comparing

[1]The presentation in this chapter follows that of Ford and Dejong. See Thomas R. Ford and Gordon F. Dejong, eds., *Social Demography* (Englewood Cliffs, N.J.: Prentice-Hall, 1970).

[2]Ford and Dejong, pp. 7–8.

Some claim that rich nations unfairly push birth control on poor nations. But can't the quality of life and health be affected by population size?

how many persons were between 15 and 19 years old at the first period with how many were between 20 and 24 years old five years later. We could further determine whether more males than females left the community or more unmarried than married persons left. To take a different example, a simple count of the number of people over age 65 would indicate what kinds of social services, homes, recreational facilities, and hospitals are needed.

These and many other analyses describe certain features of the people in a community. The descriptive demographic profile may suggest that the community has problems, now or in the near future, and the community can be studied to see how it will meet these problems and how it will change. Demographic description also prompts one to seek explanations for the discovered statistical facts. How did the community come to have its particular demographic profile? Will it keep this profile? What will happen to it if it does, or if it does not?

THE INTERPLAY OF SOCIAL AND DEMOGRAPHIC FACTORS

Social demographers, therefore, go beyond a merely descriptive analysis of a community, a nation, or any other social system. In sociological and social psychological studies, basic demographic factors are used in two different ways. On the one hand, the demographic factors are treated as the *independent variables* (those that produce change), and the social and cultural factors are treated as *dependent variables* (those that are changed or that show change). The analyst seeks to discover how the demographic factors affect the society. For example, will the changing age structure make the community politically more conservative? Will the present growth rate add to problems of pollution and overcrowding? What are the effects of the current death rate? Perhaps the deaths of older people give younger ones a feeling that there are ample opportunities for them to assume leadership roles and affect changes in the community. Questions such as these clearly suggest that demographic factors have an effect, for good or for ill, on the society.

Social demographers also look at the reverse situation, that is, how various features of a society affect the population structure and demographic processes. In such analyses the social and cultural characteristics are considered the independent variables, while the demographic factors are the dependent variables. Demographers may examine how the level of industrialization affects the migration rate, or how a group's aspirations for a higher standard of living influence the number of children married couples choose to have. One could also study how health knowledge or the availability of medical services affect the death rate, perhaps for persons in a particular age group or social class.

Although treating demographic factors as either independent or dependent variables is useful for conducting studies, it often oversimplifies the matter. Social and cultural variables and demographic factors often interact in far more complex ways, both being simultaneously producers and products of change. Consider the following hypothetical situation: Because a demographic survey revealed that a certain community had a potential labor force of young women, a light industry that usually employs women to assemble small electronic components decided to locate in the community. If the employment opportunities encouraged unmarried women to postpone marriage and married ones to postpone having a child or another child, the birth rate would be reduced. A continued decline in the birth rate would eventually produce an unbalanced population with too few people of working age, which in turn could encourage migration into the community, perhaps changing its ethnic, racial, or religious composition. Thus,

Many small communities have deteriorated or even died because their young people have migrated to cities. What forces have impelled them there?

two or three decades after the initial demographic survey, we might find a very changed community, both culturally and demographically, which would have evolved through a complex interplay of demographic and social factors.

To study the characteristics of a population and the possible effects of population change and growth, demographers use three basic concepts, usually considered the fundamental demographic processes: fertility, mortality, and migration. In order to study these processes, we must first look briefly at the methods used by demographers.

GATHERING DEMOGRAPHIC DATA

Basic demographic statistics are gathered in three different ways: by censuses; by registration of certain events, such as births and deaths, when they occur; and by surveys of a population sample or by studies of special groups within the population.

CENSUS DATA: HEAD COUNTS AND MORE

A census counts the number of individuals in the population of a given area, such as a nation or a state, at a certain time. According to the Constitution, a census must be taken every ten years so seats in the House of Representatives can be apportioned among the states on the basis of their population size. But over the years the scope of these censuses has been greatly enlarged to gain considerably more information. A partial list of the kinds of information reported in censuses is presented in Table 13-1.

Many informative analyses could be made that would describe the population at the time of the census and indicate how it has changed between censuses. For instance, a women's liberation group could study the trend in the number of years of school completed by each sex. They could discover whether proportionately more or fewer women earn higher degrees than in the recent past. Moreover, the median incomes of female and male workers could be compared. To cite another example, studies of median family income would reveal whether poverty was decreasing or increasing. If age, geographic location, and other data were included in the study of poverty, we would have a better understanding of the poverty in our midst and would be better equipped to pinpoint selected groups for social action. As a final example, the number of children born to mothers of specified ages is an important indication of what to expect by way of continued population growth.

Because census data are gathered by counting people and asking them questions, they are not always as accurate as one might think.[3] For example, a recent census in Hungary, a Roman Catholic country, discovered considerably more married women than married men, an obvious impossibility. Apparently, divorced men reported themselves divorced. But divorced women, apparently considering their marriages not truly dissolved because the Church does not grant divorces, reported themselves married.

Other types of errors have been discovered. Entire households may be missed in a census. Frequently, black male adults have been undercounted, for many are not permanently attached to a household or are living in apartments that have no registered addresses. Sometimes ages are misstated; very old people tend to exaggerate their ages, and many people round off their ages, saying, for example, that they are 30 when in fact they are 28 or 31.

Even totally objective data must be interpreted. The same facts, whether they deal with the number of children under five years of age, housing conditions,

[3]See Mortimer Spiegelman, *Introduction to Demography*, rev. ed. (Cambridge, Mass.: Harvard University Press, 1968), p. 59.

TABLE 13–1   Types of Data Reported in Population Census and Special Studies[a]

Personal Characteristics
    Age
    Sex
    Marital Status
    Race
Economic Characteristics
    Employment in major industrial groups
    Employment in major occupational groups
    Employment by sex and marital status
    Number of hours worked
    Unemployment
    Family income
    Per capita income
    Characteristics of low income families
Family and Fertility
    Number of families
    Size of family households
    Number of children born
Educational Characteristics
    Total enrollment in schools
    Highest grade in school completed
    College degrees awarded
Residential Characteristics
    Distribution of population in regions
    Rural–urban distribution
    Population in urbanized areas
    Characteristics of farm population
    In- and out–migration
    Condition of housing
    Plumbing facilities available

---

[a]Listing is incomplete. A better idea of the scope of the reports and studies of the Bureau of the Census can be obtained by consulting a library card catalog under *U.S. Bureau of the Census.*

per capita income, or what have you, can be used in different ways. They may support one person's basic satisfaction with the "American Way of Life," another's pessimistic outlook, and still another's ingrained feeling that a total revolution is needed to correct a dismal situation.

REGISTRATION DATA: LIFE STORIES IN BRIEF

Demographic data are also obtained from registrations of important life events. These data are called *vital statistics,* for the events are births, marriages, divorces, and deaths. Such data are collected when the event occurs, and so the information differs from what we get from a census. When a marriage is performed, the

Census data yield more than head counts. They can show change—such as how many women graduate from college.

date of the marriage is recorded, as well as the age and previous marital status of the spouses. We can tabulate all the marriages that occurred in a given month or year or in a given place, and by comparing this information with records for previous years, we could discover whether the marriage rate is going up or down. When a census is taken, we obtain information on everyone who has the status "married" at the time the enumeration is made. But some were married the day before the census taker called, some five or 25 years ago, and so on. Still, the census gives us a record of the proportion of the population that is married, and we could determine whether this proportion changed between censuses and how. Each source of data—statistics, records, and censuses—is useful for different kinds of studies.

For a long time governments have recorded vital statistics.[4] Apparently the

[4]Spiegelman, pp. 2-3.

Incas of Peru had a system for counting their births and deaths. In the sixteenth century, Henry VIII ordered the clergy throughout England and Wales to record baptisms, marriages, and deaths. In the United States, beginning in 1842, Massachusetts required that births, marriages, and deaths be recorded.

But not until 1900 did the federal government annually collect national death statistics, and not until 1915 did it annually collect national birth statistics. Today, information in addition to the vital event itself is usually obtained and recorded. With births, for example, it is common to record the mother's and father's ages and races, and also whether it is the mother's first, second, third, or later child. Most states record the mother's marital status, allowing for compilations of illegitimate births. These facts can be cross–tabulated and analyzed. We can determine the birth rate for specific racial groups or determine which age group of women contributes most of the illegitimate births.

Despite laws that require the recording and reporting of vital events, the records are not actually complete. Through error or oversight marriages are sometimes simply not reported. The marital status of mothers can be falsified. Many births have been unrecorded, particularly in the past when more births took place in the home and without the assistance of a physician. The large proportion of births now taking place in hospitals has led to a far more complete registration of births. It has been estimated that over 99 percent of all white births and about 97 percent of all nonwhite births currently are reported.

SURVEYS AND SPECIAL STUDIES

Each month the Bureau of the Census conducts a population survey to gather some of the same kinds of information obtained in a dicennial census. The surveys allow us to keep up with changes in the size and makeup of the population. Results are published under the title, *Current Population Reports,* and each report usually deals with a quite specific topic, such as the number and types of families, the number of families who have or have not moved within the past year, and the marital status of the population. In these surveys a sample of the population, up to 50,000 households, are selected for interviewing. The findings thus vary slightly from what is obtained when a full census is made.

In addition to these surveys, the Bureau of the Census conducts many special analyses of demographic data. One such recent study dealt with the probability of marriages by age and race and the probability of divorce by number of years married. Another special study was devoted to the social and economic status of blacks. These special studies are quite valuable. They often use data collected in the special surveys, but because they consist of detailed analyses rather than a mere report of head counts, they sometimes are not issued until several years after the survey was taken.

Demographic data must be interpreted. The story that emerges might be influenced by the perspective of the interpreter.

THE DEMOGRAPHIC PROCESSES

Earlier we referred to the basic demographic processes of fertility, mortality, and migration. Age and sex strongly influence each of the three processes, as the processes themselves profoundly influence the characteristics of the population. We look into these processes in detail, explaining common methods used for studying them. And we report some of the findings, particularly as they relate to the United States.

FERTILITY

Fertility, the number of births within a group in a given period, has a profound effect on a group's destiny. Without enough births, a group would die out. Today, many fear that there are too many births and that our society and our planet are in as much trouble as we would be with too few births. But terms like *too few* and *too many* are vague. For not only can births be counted, we can also determine how rapidly or slowly the birth rate is changing. Social demographers indicate how fertility affects society—other than its obvious effect on population size—and how social factors affect fertility. First, let us see how fertility is measured.

A simple measure of fertility is to count how many births occur within a specific time for a specific group. As you can see in Table 13-2, in recent years about 3 million babies were born each year in the United States. We can look back, say to 1957, and note that the sheer number of births per year has been dropping. Turning to 1971, we could compare 3.5 million births with the number in other countries. In India during 1971 there were 24 million births; in the People's Republic of China over 25 million, and in Sweden about 110,000.

Sheer numbers are both fascinating and full of useful information. They can tell us whether our society will need more or fewer diapers, diphtheria shots, or baby sheets, and they can tell us whether there are more Indians than Americans born each year. The number of births over a period of time can suggest the rate at which a society is growing. We can note, for example, that the over 4 million babies born in the United States in 1957 will reach marriageable age (18–21) between 1975 and 1978 and will begin to have babies of their own.

THE CRUDE BIRTH RATE

Whether we look at our own society at different times or compare different societies, the sheer number of births does not tell us enough about the fertility pattern of the group. Demographers have other measures as well. The *crude birth rate* measures the number of births at a given time against the number of people in the society at the same time; it is expressed as the number of births per 1000 persons in the group. The crude birth rate of the United States is available as far back as 1910. For many countries of the world it is available as far back as at least a quarter of a century ago.

A look at the United States data makes it clear that since 1910 the crude birth rate first declined, reaching a low point during the depression years of the 1930s, then began to rise steadily. (Not shown in Table 13-2 is a dip in 1944 and 1945 when many men were out of the country fighting in World War II.) The rise continued until 1957 when it was 25.3; thereafter it began again to decline, with a slight upsurge for a couple of years. The present crude birth rate, 15.0, is the lowest it has been in our history.

That the crude birth rate is calculated from the total population of a society is one of its limitations, for only women between certain ages can have babies. Thus, two societies with identical population sizes, or the same society at two different periods of time, could have widely different crude birth rates, depending on their age and sex compositions. Because crude birth rate is based on total population, a higher proportion of women at childbearing ages will create a

TABLE 13-2. Number of Live Births, Birth Rates, and Fertility Rates (United States, 1910-1971)

Year	Number of Births	Crude Birth Rate	Fertility Rate
1910	2,777,000	—	126.8
1920	2,950,000	27.7	117.9
1930	2,618,000	21.3	89.2
1940	2,559,000	19.4	79.9
1950	3,632,000	24.1	106.2
1951	3,823,000	24.9	111.5
1952	3,913,000	25.1	113.9
1953	3,965,000	25.1	115.2
1954	4,078,000	25.3	118.1
1955	4,104,000	25.0	118.5
1956	4,218,000	25.2	121.2
1957	4,308,000	25.3	122.9
1958	4,255,000	24.5	120.2
1959	4,295,000	24.3	118.0
1960	4,257,850	23.7	117.2
1961	4,268,326	23.3	112.2
1962	4,167,362	22.4	108.5
1963	4,098,020	21.7	105.0
1964	4,027,490	21.0	96.6
1965	3,760,358	19.4	91.3
1966	3,606,274	18.4	87.6
1967	3,533,000	17.8	85.1
1968	3,470,000	17.5	85.5
1969	3,539,000	17.7	87.6
1970	3,718,000	18.2	87.6
1971	3,559,000	17.3	82.3
1972	3,256,000	15.6	73.4
1973	3,141,000	15.0	69.3

Source: U.S. Department of Health, Education, and Welfare, *Vital Statistics of the United States*, 1966, vol. 1 (Washington, D.C.: U.S. Government Printing Office, 1967); and *Monthly Vital Statistic Report*, various issues.

higher crude birth rate, other things being equal. But, alas, other things are seldom equal. What we need, then, is a measure of the actual reproductive performance of women.

THE GENERAL FERTILITY RATE

The *general fertility rate* is the number of births in a year per 1000 women aged 15 to 44. Fertility rates also can be computed for narrower age groups, say women 15 to 19 years of age, 20 to 24, and so on. (Fertility rates for such narrower age spans are not called *general* fertility rates.) For example, in the depression year 1932, the general fertility rate was 81.7, while in 1960 it was 118, and in 1970 it was 87.6. The greater number of births in 1960 and 1970, therefore, was mostly because more women were within their reproductive years, but also partly because they were having more babies. What does all this tell us about the future?

Sheer numbers of babies provide useful information, but we need to know more than numbers to understand the fertility patterns of groups.

Fertility rates in the United States are highest for women between 20 and 29 years of age. In 1975 there were 18.2 million women in this age group. By 1980 this number will increase to almost 20 million, and by 1985 to about 20.5 million. Our marriage rate continues to be high, so we can assume that most of these women will marry. Obviously, when 20 million married couples go to bed each night, more conceptions are likely to occur than when a couple of a million fewer do so. Yet will there actually be more conceptions and births? Although the general fertility rate has been dropping rapidly, there still may be more births in 1980 than in recent years, thus making a larger base of potential mothers in the year 2000 and after. Whether potential mothers, now and in the future, actually bear children, and at what rate they do so, depends in large part on the social factors that affect fertility.

SOCIAL FACTORS AFFECTING FERTILITY

Fertility is so obviously biological—intercourse, conception, development of the fetus, birth—that it can be amazing to discover that social factors do influence fertility. For example, the number of births varies with the seasons. According to a study lasting more than 10 years, one researcher found that the peak months for births are August and September, and the low months are in the spring, usually April and May.[5] Folk belief has been that during the cold winter months husbands and wives engage in sexual intercourse more frequently, and during the hot, sticky months less frequently. This would account for there being more births in August and September and fewer in April and May. Although the many air-conditioned bedrooms might be expected to have erased the seasonal variation, they seem not to have done so.

Because so many couples in the United States use birth control methods, however, it could be that there is no seasonal variation in coitus, but only a seasonal variation in conceptions as more couples decide at one time of the year than at others that the wife will "go off the pill." If so, we must ask why parents seem to prefer to have their children more at certain times in the year than at others. Since the seasonal variation in births is not large, and since a high proportion of all births are first births and thus first conceptions, perhaps the seasonal peak in births is related to the seasonal peak in marriages. Whatever the final answer, social factors, such as the time of the year when people marry, can affect the birth rate.

SOCIOECONOMIC STATUS

Sociologists have long known that social class and fertility are strongly related. Whether we describe social class by income, educational level, or occupation, the conclusion is the same: the higher the social class, the smaller the family. This relationship existed before widespread birth control information was available, and certainly before Margaret Sanger opened her first birth control clinic in 1916. For example, the New York State Census of 1865 showed that wives of unskilled laborers had the most children, wives of skilled laborers had fewer, and wives of white collar workers had the fewest.[6] Even at this early date, then, higher socioeconomic couples somehow were able to control their fertility, and they continued to do so until 1940. Between 1940 and 1952, however, the fertility difference between classes narrowed. As economic conditions improved after the depression years, higher socioeconomic couples began to have more children than previously, thus bringing their fertility closer to that of lower socioeconomic couples.

Class differences in fertility continue to narrow, but only slowly. Today for every 100 births to women with less than eight years of schooling, college edu-

[5]The seasonal variation in births has been noted by others, but surprisingly little work has been on the subject. See Benjamin Pasamanick, Simon Dinitz, and Hilda Knobloch, "Geographic and Seasonal Variations in Births," *Public Health Reports* 74 (April 1959), 285–286.

[6]Wendell H. Bash, "Differential Fertility in Madison County, New York; 1865," *Milbank Memorial Fund Quarterly* 33 (April 1955), 161–186.

Social class and education affect fertility. How many of these people would have been married parents at their ages, say, 20 years ago?

cated women have 53 births, while a few years ago they had only 44. In turn, for every 100 births to wives of unskilled workers, wives of professional workers have about 70 births, while wives in families with incomes of $10,000 or more have about 62 births. Thus, education, occupation, and income are related to fertility in our society.

VALUES, KNOWLEDGE, AND FERTILITY

Such a relationship between socioeconomic status and fertility does not provide its own explanation. The numerous studies that have been conducted to explain this relationship are roughly of two kinds: first, those that concentrate on values, attitudes, and other social psychological characteristics of people; and second, those that focus on differences in contraceptive knowledge.[7] Studies of the first type hypothesize that working class people have their own outlook on family

[7] For a concise treatment of the relationship between social class and fertility see Kenkel and the sources cited therein. William F. Kenkel, *The Family in Perspective,* 3rd ed. (New York: Appleton-Century-Crofts, 1973), pp. 198–206. See also Julian L. Simon, *The Effects of Income on Fertility* (Chapel Hill, N.C.: Carolina Population Center, 1974).

size, either wanting many children, or not really caring about how many they have. It was also hypothesized that their fertility values are influenced by their having been raised in large families or having migrated from rural areas where fertility has traditionally been high. But recent studies indicate that attitudes toward desirable family size do not differ as much by social class as once was supposed.[8]

It may be difficult to believe that despite the efforts of groups like Planned Parenthood, despite the contraceptive advertisements in women's magazines, and despite the contraceptive devices often displayed and always available at the corner drugstore, lower socioeconomic people still do not know how to control conception. No one appears to be trying to keep contraceptive knowledge from them—quite the contrary. Even so, information and the ability to make choices are not the same thing. Lacking money, the poor are less able to consult private doctors, or to change doctors, or in other ways to become able to choose knowledgeably among contraceptive alternatives. And because the less educated communicate less effectively, they are not likely to understand fully what they hear or read about contraception. Also, because lower class husbands and wives generally do not like to talk about sexual matters with one another, they are less likely to discuss possible ways of limiting family size by a mutually acceptable, effective method. The continued inverse relationship between socioeconomic class and fertility, and the various explanations for it, clearly indicate how social factors affect fertility. We can treat only briefly other social factors than class that affect fertility.

OUR RURAL BACKGROUND

Rural families have traditionally been larger than urban families. In the past, the more children that rural parents had, the more help they could expect in the fields and in the home. In addition, because farms were more isolated and family farms were economically important, the young farm boys and girls working for their families were preparing themselves for adult roles on a farm. Today, much of this pattern has changed. With greater mechanization, fewer hands are needed, and those few must be trained adults and not children. Proper management is essential to successful farming, again requiring educated and experienced adults, not children. And because the farm is no longer isolated from the mainstream of life, farm children have an extensive life away from home. As the number of farms shrinks, many children born on the farm will spend their adult lives living and working in a city.

If it makes little sense for farmers to have more children than city people have, why do they? For one thing, many couples seem to have families of the

[8]Pascal K. Whelpton et al., *Fertility and Family Planning in the United States* (Princeton, N.J.: Princeton University Press, 1966), p. 99.

Visit a Planned Parenthood Clinic and report on this organization's efforts to provide birth control information and services. How many and what kinds of people does it serve each year? Try to estimate of the number of potential clients who are not being reached and why this is so.

---

same size as their families of orientation. Apparently the idea of the "right" number of children to have is learned early and dies hard. But it is dying. Rural-urban differences in fertility have been narrowing consistently over the years. In 1940 urban families were about two thirds as large as farm families. By 1969 non-farm families were about 72 percent as large as farm families. Today, non-farm women bear about 84 percent as many children as farm women.

RELIGION AND FERTILITY

Catholics, Mormons, and Southern Baptists have more children than people of other religions. An obvious explanation for Catholics is the official prohibition of any form of "artificial" birth control: mechanical, chemical or hormonal devices. But what seems obvious is not necessarily true; at least two-thirds of all Catholic couples in the United States practice some form of family limitation.[9] Catholic families average about 11 percent more children than most Protestant families, not as large a difference as might be expected. Because Southern Baptists number more rural and working class people than do, say, Episcopalians or Congregationalists, the higher Southern Baptist fertility rate may not be due to religion itself but to residence and social class factors. Mormons place great emphasis on strong families, and traditionally this has meant large families. Thus, Mormon family size is less likely a matter of religious prescription than a social value toward family life that encourages high fertility.

Internationally, the relationship between religion and fertility is not clear-cut. Throughout Latin America we find high fertility and the predominance of Catholicism. Nevertheless, the high fertility regions of Asia and Africa are predominantly not Christian, nor do the native religions expressly forbid birth control practices. Finally, when 11 Roman Catholic European countries were compared with 15 non-Roman Catholic countries, the fertility rates were very much the same.[10] Although in the United States religion itself, particularly Catholicism, does influence family size, the differences clearly traceable to religion are small.

[9]Ronald Freedman et al., *Family Planning, Sterility and Population Growth* (New York: McGraw-Hill, 1959), p. 104. See also Basil G. Zimmer and Calvin Goldscheider, "A Further Look at Catholic Fertility," *Demography* 3 (1966), 462–469.

[10]"Do Roman Catholic Countries Have the Highest Birth Rates?" *Population Profile* (Washington, D.C.: Population Reference Bureau, Inc., July 1968), 3.

RACE AND FERTILITY

For as far back as adequate records go, blacks have had higher birth rates than whites.[11] The difference had seemed to be directly related to race because it was found at various class levels, and rural blacks have higher fertility rates than rural whites. But recently, college educated black women, on the average, are bearing somewhat fewer children than college educated white women. Even though blacks traditionally either accepted or espoused larger families than whites, their tendencies seem to be changing.

Whatever the factor used for comparison—class, rural–urban residence, religion, or race—differences in family size are narrowing. Nevertheless, for the present these social factors are related to childbearing performance. Although it is intriguing that social rather than biological factors allow us to predict fertility in different categories of the population, no less intriguing are the social factors that affect deaths, the topic to which we now turn.

MORTALITY

Through the ages humanity has applied its intelligence and skills to preserving life, to preventing and curing its diseases and ailments. Throughout most of human history, though, attempts to obtain a low death rate were not too successful. It has been estimated that in the Early Stone Age the death rate—the number of deaths per 1000 people in one year—was 49.7, while the birth rate was 50. This difference is about as close to zero population growth as one could hope—or fear—to come. In some places in the world today, such as most of Africa, the death rate is still high, in some countries as high as 26 per 1000 population.[12] In the United States, the crude death rate has dropped from 17.0 in 1900 to 9.4 in 1973. Our current death rate is one of the lowest in the world.[13]

Since all people are mortal, social and cultural factors do not determine *whether* a person will die, but they have a clear influence on *how* and *when*. A society's ability to prevent famine, to control epidemics and communicable diseases, to learn and practice proper nutrition and sanitation, and to avoid wars or minimize their effects all have profound effects on when its members will die and how.

---

[11]See Wilson H. Grabill et al., *The Fertility of American Women* (New York: John Wiley & Sons, 1958), chs. 4–6.

[12]For births, deaths, total population estimates, and other data for 160 countries, see *World Population Data Sheet* (Washington, D.C.: Population Reference Bureau, Inc., yearly).

[13]For U.S. data see U.S. Department of Health, Education, and Welfare, *Vital Statistics of the United States* (Washington, D.C.: U.S. Government Printing Office, yearly).

SOCIAL FACTORS AND MORTALITY RATES

In the United States the death rate is lower among the upper classes, in part because they can afford better and more frequent medical attention, more nourishing food, and their education enables them to act in ways that preserve their health.[14] Mortality is also affected by another social characteristic, marital status; the unmarried and the divorced have higher death rates than the married.

The death rate is consistently lower for women than for men. This difference could be either a social factor or a biological indication of the natural superiority of women. It could be argued that because men have traditionally engaged in hazardous occupations, the difference is social. In the past men hunted wild animals or made sea voyages that subjected them to scurvy. Today they work in mines where they daily risk accidents and eventually ruin their lungs. They suffer more farm accidents than women, they go off to war, are employed in heavy construction work, and do more occupational travelling than women do.

Giving birth is a hazardous occupation, so the role of women has also been fraught with danger, although less today than in the past. As early as 1900, however, the death rate for females was 16.5, compared with 17.9 for males. A biological explanation for the lower death rate of females is suggested by the fact that fewer females are miscarried or die in infancy. But the female mortality rate has declined much more rapidly than the male's; in a mere 50 years, from 1900 to 1950, the death rate of women was cut in half, surely too short a time for nature to improve on presumed biological superiority. In the same period the death rate of males dropped from 17.9 to 11.1. Even today it is only 10.8, the rate achieved by women in the late 1920s. All things considered, it would appear that the female is the more durable of the species, although the biological edge is narrow. Social factors, such as our ability to deal effectively with a once-common cause of female deaths, that is, deaths of mothers during childbearing, add to the advantage that women already have.

INFANT MORTALITY RATE

The death rate of a society can tell us much about the group, its standard of living, its knowledge, and whether its priorities reflect humanistic or materialistic values. Particularly revealing is the infant mortality rate, the number of deaths within the first year of life per 1000 live births a year.[15] The human infant, weak, helpless, and susceptible to many diseases, has had a very high mortality

---

[14]For a discussion of various social factors related to the death rate, see Spiegelman, pp. 89–94.

[15]See Spiegelman, pp. 84–85.

In a mere 50 years, from 1900 to 1950, the death rate of women was halved, surely too short a time for nature to improve on presumed biological superiority.

rate throughout history; had there not also been many births the species could not have survived. As recently as about 150 years ago, one-third of European children died in infancy.

In the United States, the infant mortality rate has dropped sharply from almost 100 in 1915 to less than 18 in 1974. To understand the social importance of this change, consider what would have happened had the 1915 infant mortality rate continued: From then until now, 10 million fewer infants would have survived. Or imagine that today's infant mortality rate had prevailed from 1915 to the present day. Three to four million more babies would have survived their first year, a predictable number of them would have lived until adulthood, had children of their own, who in turn would have had children of their own, and so on. Our population would be many millions larger than it is now.

The infant mortality rate has other, more subtle effects on society. Before medicine demonstrated that something could be done to prevent infant deaths, societies with high infant mortality rates had to accept them as a tragic fact of life and encourage a high birth rate to sustain society's need for new members.

This need for a high birth rate became so ingrained in some societies that they have failed to respond to new conditions by adopting family planning. In India, for example, many families fail to realize that they no longer need as many children to ensure that a certain number will survive to adulthood.

The same social factors that affect the death rate in general also affect the infant mortality rate: knowledge of medical and nutritional rules, the availability of doctors and hospitals, and related to these, standards of living and education. One might suppose that the United States, with its affluence, its gleaming hospitals, and the funds spent for medical research, would have the lowest infant death rate in the world. But we have not, and according to the best data available we stand in about thirteenth place, behind such countries as Sweden, Finland, the Netherlands, Iceland, Norway, Switzerland, Denmark, New Zealand, Australia, and England.[16]

Though not the lowest, the infant death rate in the United States is low and has been dropping. Perhaps the likeliest reason why it has not been as low as in some other countries is that in our society you receive the medical services you can afford. Again, income and education chiefly determine whether mother and child have the proper nutrition. The cards are stacked against the poor and the blacks. In every state the infant mortality rate of nonwhites is higher than that of whites. In some states, such as Mississippi and Florida, the nonwhite rate is twice that for whites.[17] The rate varies among regions, with the Southern states generally the highest, sometimes 50 percent higher than the national average. There is thus ample evidence that social factors affect the infant death rate, and more than this, affect different social groups unequally. It is painfully obvious that the chances of living through the first year of life are not equal.

LIFE SPAN AND LIFE EXPECTANCY

Life span is the length of time that members of a species have the biological capacity for living. This period varies considerably among the species of the animal kingdom, from a few hours for the fruit fly, to hundreds of years for the giant tortoise. Barring accident or disease, members of a species could anticipate living out their full biological span of time. The life span of the human species undoubtedly is somewhat more than the Biblical "four score and ten." It is probably about 100 years, although a few people have lived to far more advanced ages than 100. Possibly our earliest ancestors had a shorter span of life, but there is no indication that the human life span has changed for a long, long time.

[16]See *Vital Statistics of the United States.*

[17]Various data on differences in the infant mortality rate can be found in *Vital Statistics of the United States.*

LIFE EXPECTANCY: THE ODDS AGAINST US

Life expectancy is an entirely different matter. It is the average number of years that a group of persons born at a given time *will* live under present circumstances, not how long they *can* live. Of all of the people born in a given year, a certain predictable number will die in infancy, some will die each year thereafter, and a few will live out the life span of the species. If we knew the number that die at each age, we could calculate the average life expectancy at birth for the group. Life expectancy averages can be calculated for groups at any given age, and not just at birth. In such cases, they would refer to the average number of additional years persons of the same age would live.

In many places in the world today the average life expectancy at birth is exceedingly low. In several African nations it is 35 years or less, in India, Burma, Vietnam, and Pakistan it is no more than 45 years, while worldwide it averages somewhat over 50 years. In the United States at the turn of the century, life expectancy at birth was 48 years for males and 51 years for females. Today it is 67 and 74, respectively. The sharp increase in life expectancy is largely due to the decline in the death rate of infants and children. It does *not* mean that on the average people live to older ages than did their parents or grandparents. For example, males who had reached age 65 in 1900 had a life expectancy of 11.5 years; today males who reach 65 have a life expectancy of about 13 additional years. Death control, in other words, has so far been much more effective for younger than for older people.

MIGRATION

A part of us seems to yearn for stability, to put down roots and to remain where we are, but another part is restless, seeking to be on the move. As we saw in Chapter 3, two of the four basic human wishes are contradictory in the behavior they demand, the wishes for security and for new experience. Of course, individuals, groups, and sometimes entire populations have had to move whether they wanted to or not, fleeing political or religious persecution or torture or death. Thus, from curiosity and from necessity, millions of people have moved from continent to continent, from nation to nation, and from place to place within a nation.

Studies of migration, the third major demographic process, deal with the number of migrants, their social and personal characteristics, where they came from and where they are going, the reasons for migrating or for not migrating, the effects of migration on the community the migrants left, and the effects of migration on the receiving community. This partial list should indicate the

Symbolic of migration everywhere, women and children in South Sudan trek across the Aluma plateau. Do you think more migration is born of curiosity or of necessity?

kind of knowledge sought by social demographers specializing in migration studies.

Our nation came into being through migration. What started as a trickle of Europeans to our shores took on larger and larger proportions. The influx did not end with the colonial period or the early days of the Republic; from 1820 to 1970 over 45 million migrated to the United States, about 80 percent from Europe and about 6 percent from Africa. (In the early years, of course, the Africans did not come by their own choice.) In the decade from 1960 to 1970, between 300,000 and 400,000 people migrated to the United States each year. Although such numbers contribute only a fraction of a percent to our population growth, they help to keep alive the cultural variety within our social system.

INTERNAL MIGRATION

Internal migration is migration within a society. Demographers who study internal migration are interested in why and how the people redistribute themselves, and the results of their movements. People who leave a community are *out-migrants*, while people who enter a community are *in-migrants*. (Clearly, just about every out–migrant becomes an in–migrant somewhere else.) The distinction between in– and out–migrants is useful, for the terms relate the migrating individuals to groups or communities. If the number of people moving into a community equaled the number who left, a community would remain stable in size. But if the rates of in– and out–migration were uneven, or were even but were also substantial, the community would likely be unstable, for its class, age, or ethnic composition could change drastically.

The net migration of a region, state, or community for a given period of time is obtained by determining the population change for the period and then subtracting the births and adding the deaths that occurred during the same period. For example, if from the census we found that a population increased by 1000 people in a year, we would subtract the 500 births during that year and add the 300 deaths: There was a net in–migration of 800 people during the year. (Perhaps there were actually more in–migrants, but the additional ones were offset by the number of out–migrants.)

Internal migration is not random or haphazard. In general, the streams of migration in the United States run from South to North, from East to West, from areas with poor employment opportunities to those with good opportunities, and from rural to urban areas, although usually a few people are also moving in the opposite directions. Migration figures show that rural areas, the South, and places with poor employment opportunities have lost population. Also, young adults, men, and the better educated are more likely to migrate. Furthermore, people who move once are more likely to move again.

The extent of migration is significant in the United States.[18] In March 1971, for example, about 36 million Americans were not living in the same house in which they had lived the previous March. About 7 million people had crossed state lines in their moves, and another 6 million crossed county lines. Near or far, between 18 and 20 percent of the population move each year. (Some of these are repeaters, so the number of different individuals or families who move annually is not quite as large as the percentage indicates.)

When about 13 million migrants annually cross county or state lines, the effects of migration can be staggering. The effects on the counties or regions from which there is a net out–migration can be as devastating. Letcher County, in the Appalachian area of Kentucky, had a total population of about 40,000 in 1950, 30,000 in 1960 and 23,000 in 1970.[19] Between 1950 and 1960 the county experienced a net out–migration of almost 17,000 people, and between 1960 and 1970 a net out–migration of over 10,000. The excess of births over deaths between 1960 and 1970 was less than half what it was in the previous decade. This

[18]Mobility data for the United States can be found in U.S. Bureau of the Census, *Statistical Abstract of the United States* (Washington, D.C.: U.S. Government Printing office, yearly).

[19]Ralph Ramsey, *Population Change in Kentucky Counties: 1950, 1960 and 1970* (Lexington, Kentucky: Department of Sociology, University of Kentucky, 1971), p. 7.

Make two demographic maps of your community, one which shows the present density of the population (number of people per square mile) and one which shows the density of the population 10 years earlier. Which areas experienced the most change? Why?

---

phenomenon confirms what special studies in Appalachia and other areas have discovered.[20] It is the young people, the potential parents, who are leaving Appalachia. Counties like Letcher thus spend thousands of dollars educating children only to have them leave when they are at an age when they could make a contribution to the economy of the area. Meanwhile, the age composition of the county changes, with the consequent need for more hospitals and nursing homes but fewer schools. Who is going to pay for the nursing homes and hospitals if there has been a net out-migration of those of working age? The lack of economic opportunities in Appalachia encourages out-migration, while the out-migration aggravates the problems of the region. Once again we see how demographic factors are affected by, and, in turn, affect the social characteristics of a community.

WORLD POPULATION GROWTH

Although almost everyone today knows there is a world population problem, many people are confused by the problem. This confusion arises partly because of the problem's complexity, and partly, too, because intermingled with current growth rates are projections and estimates based on the assumption that current rates will continue. We should say immediately that the future population of the world cannot be *predicted* (that is, foretold with certainty). Any book or tract that claims otherwise should be swiftly and unceremoniously transferred from the science to the fiction section of your library. Yet population *projections* are both valuable and necessary.

Projections are based on observed facts, such as current population sizes, birth rates, and death rates. These facts are then subjected to the most sophisticated statistical techniques, which use what is known about how the rates themselves are changing and what the effects will be on the natural increase of the population. Why, then, are population predictions fictions? First, we do not know with any certainty how many people there are on earth; second, and

---

[20]For a good treatment of the out-migration and in-migration streams in Appalachia, see Harry K. Schwarzweller, James S. Brown, Joseph J. Mangalam, *Mountain Families in Transition* (University Park, Penna.: The Pennsylvania State University Press, 1971).

Every year people move into new houses as they migrate to new neighborhoods or cities, but some families prefer to take their old home with them.

the main problem, the rates that affect natural increase may change in unexpected ways. Moreover, the "self-defeating prophecy," which we discussed in Chapter 2, might come into play. That is, precisely because some predictions for the future are *made,* they are bound not to come true. If people believe the predictions and take their implications seriously, and if they evaluate such implications negatively and have the proper knowledge, they can take corrective action. The original prophecy will be false precisely because it could have been true! Note the number of *ifs;* there is no assurance that once the facts are known people will quickly modify their behavior to relieve the world's population pressure. But let us look at the world population facts, as best we know them.

Despite a high birth rate, a high death rate throughout most of its history slowed humanity's growth rate. In 6000 B.C. there were no more than a few million people on the entire earth. It took the 6000 years from then to the time of Christ for the world's population to increase tenfold, to about 250 million—not too many more people than now live in the United States. It then took more than 1600 years to double from what it was at the time of Christ, reaching about 500 million by the year 1650. Then in only 200 years it doubled once again, bringing world population close to an even billion by 1850. In 80 years it doubled again to about 2 billion in 1930. In 1971 the world's population stood at 3.7 billion, representing a "doubling time" of about 46 years. If the current rate of growth continues, it will take 35 years for the population to double once more, leading to a projected 7 billion people on earth before the year 2000.

While it once took 1600 years for 250 million people to double their population, now it takes 35 years for 3.7 billion to double their numbers. Because of the enormous number of people, an annual growth rate of two percent, which sounds low, is actually so high that babies born today will see the population of the world double before they are even middle aged, and many will live long enough to see it double *twice*—if all rates (birth, death, and fertility) remain what they now are. We have indeed had a world population explosion, as the slope of the graph in Figure 13-1 depicts. We are on a collision course with disaster and our only hope is to alter the course. But how? Understanding how we got on the course should help us to answer the question or at least to appreciate the bewildering complexity of it.

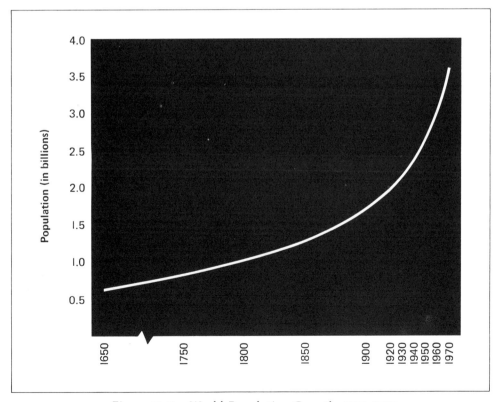

Figure 13-1. World Population Growth, 1650-1970

THE REASONS FOR ACCELERATED GROWTH

Since 1650 numerous events have combined to put us on our collision course, and to transform the Western world from agrarian to urban and industrial societies. Agriculture expanded greatly; more land was used, and better soil fertilizers and improved techniques increased farm productivity per farm worker. At the same time that improved techniques and new machines were reducing the number of workers needed on farms, machines were *increasing* the number of workers needed in the cities for manufacturing. The development of the steam engine and its use in factory after factory to drive gigantic quantities of machinery greatly reduced the costs of production and created cheap, mass-market goods. Cities grew; trade grew as division of labor and its necessary consequence, interdependence, grew; and naturally bureaucracies grew as trade became broader and more complex, involving distant markets, shopping, and so on.[21]

In addition, there has been an equally impressive revolution in the treatment and prevention of diseases. As we noted earlier, the crude death rate, and particularly the infant mortality rate, responded to the advances in medicine and dropped to all-time lows in Western countries. In these countries the crude birth rate was also falling—not always steadily or everywhere alike, but more or less parallel to the declining death rate. So long as there are more births than deaths the population will increase. The Western countries, therefore, continued to grow, but not as rapidly as the world average. Western Europe, for example, has an annual growth rate of six-tenths of one percent, the United States an increase of 1.1 percent, and Eastern Europe eight-tenths of one percent, all considerably below the world average of 2 percent. The inability of Western countries to bring their birth rates closer to the reduced death rate is part of the reason for the world's population growth.

GOOD NEWS AND BAD NEWS: FEWER DEATHS
AND TOO MANY BIRTHS

In underdeveloped countries the picture has been quite different. This situation is dramatically illustrated in Figure 13-2, which shows a sharp reduction in the death rate but only a slight reduction in the birth rate. Unlike the Western countries, these countries are not yet reducing their birth rates as their death rates are reduced. Timing explains the difference: Death control, deliberately introduced into the countries of Africa, Asia, and Latin America, is readily accepted, requires little initiative from the people, and often is relatively inexpensive. For example, DDT sprayed from airplanes rapidly reduces malaria, at one time probably the world's most potent cause of sickness and death. Agricultural

---

[21]Population Reference Bureau, Inc., "Man's Population Predicament," *Population Bulletin* 27 (April 1971), 9-10.

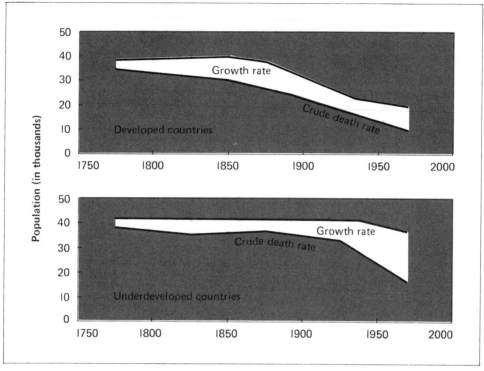

Figure 13-2. Estimated Birth and Death Rates, 1770-1970. Source: United Nations, A Concise Summary of the World Population Situation in 1970 (New York: United Nations, 1971).

and industrial advances have also been made. But birth control has been introduced into the underdeveloped countries with little effect. It is not as popular as death control, it does require initiative and cooperation of the people, and on a mass basis it can be expensive.

The countries of the West underwent a *demographic transition,* gradually but significantly lowering their birth rates and death rates.[22] As the decline in deaths increased the population, first the better-educated, urban people lowered their fertility, and later others did, as they too realized that many children were a liability in the kind of industrialized, urbanized society that was developing.

The underdeveloped countries, by contrast, have not experienced a demographic transition. Their fertility rates remain higher than the world average, even while their death rates approach the world average and probably will continue to decline. And so the population of the world grows and grows. More effective fertility control obviously is necessary if the underdeveloped countries are to

[22]Donald O. Cowgill, "Transition Theory as General Population Theory," *Social Forces* 41 (March 1963), 270-274.

A high rate of death control can create much real suffering if the rate of birth control doesn't also rise.

contribute less to world population growth. Better fertility control undoubtedly will come; the question is whether it will come soon enough. Already the under-developed countries have gigantic problems in feeding and housing more and more people. The picture is bleak, and it could worsen.

UNITED STATES POPULATION GROWTH

Just as we cannot forecast world population growth, we cannot forecast the size of the United States population for any future year. Earlier generations of husbands and wives demonstrated vividly that they could drastically restrict their family sizes. Recall the sharp drop in births reflected in the birth rates of 1930 and 1940, as shown in Table 13-2. As economic conditions improved, later husbands and wives showed that they could have, on the average, more than three children, largely because they wanted to.

As we discussed earlier, there are now or will be in the immediate future more potential mothers than ever before. If each of these women averages slightly over three children, our population will be 320 million by 2000, 440 million by 2020, and 600 million by 2050. But if couples were to begin tomorrow to restrict themselves to an average of two children, we would have 266 million people by 2000 and about 300 million by 2020. Which will it be?

There is evidence that three or more children are no longer the norm. Two children seems to be becoming the norm, particularly among the recently married. As a society, though, we have not reduced average family size to *replacement level*—that is, just enough births each year to balance deaths and keep our population size stable. We can safely predict that our population will grow to about 300 million by 2000; and even if this prediction is high, we would reach that number soon after 2000. We will have to watch the 1970s and 1980s carefully, for if the fertility rate remains above the replacement level we not only will have more births, we also may have an *echo effect*. That is, more births mean still more potential mothers and thus a still higher birth rate about 20 years later. If we go down to replacement level, this will not just slow our present growth but will reduce the number of potential mothers in the future.

OPTIMUM VERSUS MAXIMUM POPULATION SIZE

A distinction should be made between maximum and optimum population size. The *maximum* is the largest number of people who somehow could be fed, clothed, housed, and otherwise cared for at approximately a subsistence level of living by a community, a society, or the planet. The *optimum* is the ideal population size, the size that would permit the society to provide a good life for its members. Although neither maximum nor optimum size is precisely measurable, the distinction remains useful. For example, many middle class families could support a maximum family of, say, ten children. They would have a house, food on the table, and clothing. But obviously most middle class families do not consider this the optimum family size. Housing would be so crowded there would be little or no privacy or freedom of movement, so tensions and irritations would be constantly high. The time demanded of parents to rear so many children and to manage the home would allow little or no individual attention for each child. With the constant financial drain on such a family, time or money for leisure activities or vacations would be rare or nonexistent.

Choose one country from each continent and compare the birth and mortality rates. What factors account for any differences you find?

The family probably could not support any of the children beyond high school age. Such a family could survive, but most people would agree they would not be living the "good life."

If you extend this example to the scope of a community, a society, a continent, or the entire planet, you can see that maximum and optimum populations make for important differences in living. Although there is room for disagreement, our society probably could support a population of 300 million or more, even if this figure were reached within a few decades. There is no danger that in the immediate future we will smother ourselves to death with sheer numbers of bodies or take to eating seaweed in order to survive. But would such greatly increased numbers be in the best interests of the people?

The signs are that we have enough problems coping with 215 million people. Crowds are everywhere; it takes longer to commute to and from work; supermarket lines are longer; recreation areas are overcrowded; and each year more and more of the countryside is used for factories and homes. We are polluting our environment and using up our natural resources (and those of many other countries) at an alarming rate. The list, which could be continued, is not very pretty, even if we somehow managed to adjust to the conditions. What does it profit us to gain a few years in life expectancy only to spend them commuting to work or driving long distances "to get away from it all"? Some people, such as Stewart Udall, former Secretary of the Interior, believe that if we judge by the destruction of our environment, we have already passed the optimum population level in this country.[23] Others see not the sheer number of people, but our high standard of living and our mismanagements as responsible for pollution, destruction of the environment, and overcrowding. Even people of this persuasion admit that we are unable or unwilling to provide the "good life" for our present 215 million. How, then, can we do so for 300 million? Since there seems to be general agreement that our fertility patterns of recent years have adversely affected society, the optimum population growth would seem to be as near replacement level as possible for the immediate future. This rate would at least give us time to catch up with various unsolved problems and to plan for the future.

[23]Quoted in Leslie A. Westoff and Charles F. Westoff, *From Now to Zero* (Boston: Little, Brown, 1971), p. 345.

"Human pollution" in recreation areas, such as on the Rogue River in California when the salmon run, is one saddening result of overcrowding.

ACHIEVING REPLACEMENT LEVEL FERTILITY

For the most part, the social factors that affect fertility have not yet been the result of a deliberate policy. Because social factors do affect fertility, however, our growth rate could be changed—or, put more bluntly, manipulated. Testifying at the Hearings of the President's Commission on Population Growth, Rufus E. Miles, Jr. urged the drafting and passage of a Population Policy Act that "would establish national objectives and a continuing means of evaluating our progress in meeting those objectives. . . . It should establish the clear-cut principle that our national interest requires a 'no-growth population objective' within the foreseeable future." If such a policy were adopted, after all sectors of our society had been sounded for their points of view, it could be implemented in many ways. Some would work better than others; some would be more acceptable than others; and probably the best that should be expected is that they would direct us toward our population objectives rather than immediately achieving the goal. The means suggested range from methods of persuasion to methods of coercion, complete with legal penalties for violations of norms.

Education Part of the school curriculum for every child in the nation would include information on the society's population objectives and the individual's responsibility for meeting them. Public service messages in the mass media would assure continued exposure of these objectives and responsibilities. No one can say how effective such persuasive educational means would be, particularly because better educated people would presumably respond best to this technique, and they already have the fewest children.

More Family Planning Centers Many more centers where people could receive counseling and advice on family planning and birth control methods might help to achieve the national objective chiefly by reducing the number of unwanted children. About 80 percent of all children born are wanted, though; so reducing unwanted births does not have much affect on total population size.

Encouragement of New Roles for Women More and more women accept the notion that marriage and motherhood are not the only careers open to them. But because the proper role of women has traditionally been that of wife and mother, many girls and young women are unable to make a full commitment to an occupation outside the home. Such a full commitment would include pursuing an education in the field of her choice, making long-term career plans, and the like. One way to encourage women to make such a full commitment would be government subsidy of higher education and technical training, like the subsidy now received by men in the Armed Forces. Another form of encouragement would be a guarantee of good employment opportunities for qualified women.

Incentives and Penalties The methods so far listed have included information, persuasion, and encouragement. Yet if such methods are not sufficiently effective, a variety of penalties and incentives could be introduced to encourage couples to have fewer children. In fact, certain steps will have to be taken, such as withdrawing income tax deductions for children, or the economic structure will be defeating the purpose of the methods already mentioned. Reversing the tax benefits to reward childless couples, cash bonuses for "proper" child spacing, and similar bonuses for voluntary sterilization would be a few such measures to augment other methods of persuasion. These and similar proposals that smacked of economic coercion might be unpopular even if the populace agreed that a stationary population was desirable. On the other hand, in recent years increasing numbers of single people and childless couples have been expressing discontent with tax discriminations against them.

OVERPOPULATION AND MISERY—IS THE EXCEPTION ABOUT TO PROVE THE RULE?

What country has a population with a 4 percent growth rate, with a doubling time of less than 35 years—the highest growth rate in the world? Where are the people found with the lowest death rate in the world? In what country will you find that the women of ages 40 through 44 have a higher fertility rate than French, Swedish, and British women in their maximum fertility years of 20 through 29? The answer to all these questions is the United States.

To be sure, not the entire population of the United States, but a tiny percentage of it—the Hutterites. Although they are now less than one-third of one percent of our population, if their growth rate remains constant and the present overall growth rate of the United States remains constant, then in 100 years the Hutterites will make up about 15 percent of our total population.

Who are these superfertile people? The Hutterites are a strongly religious, communal farming people found in South Dakota, Montana, and parts of Canada. They emigrated from Russia about 100 years ago, 440 persons in number. They now number around 20,000. Why have they grown so rapidly? They are strict followers of the Bible. In Genesis it is said, "Be fruitful and multiply." So well do they follow this command that some social scientists suspect that the Hutterites have actually inbred a superfertility.

Fertility rates not even as high as that of the Hutterites have been among the chief causes of economic and social distress in India, most of South America, and parts of Africa. But so far the Hutterites have been blessed for following the Bible. Because the Hutterites use labor-saving machinery, they have no need for large numbers of workers. Their communities are prosperous even though members can retire from work at the age of 45. Because they are prosperous, when a "colony" reaches a certain size—say 150 people for 4000 acres—they buy more land and begin a new colony.

Even so, the Hutterites may be in for hard times. Their neighbors have sought to prevent the sale of land to them. The Hutterites are disliked because they are "communists"; because they shun nearby communities and educate their own children; because they buy their supplies wholesale in cities rather than in nearby towns; and because their large land purchases "disrupt rural patterns of business and livelihood." The Hutterites have maintained tight-knit, stable communities by controlling the size of each. If they become unable to expand, their future may become a grim forecast of what awaits the rest of us. How their values change, or fail to change, in response to conditions that make them dysfunctional will perhaps be a rich source of sociological knowledge.

> Conduct an attitude survey on family size by using a sample with females and males, college students, and people of the same age but not in college. Ask each person "How many children would you like to have?" and "How many children do you actually expect to have?" Tabulate the answers. Are there differences between groups? Differences in answers to the two questions?

More Stringent Methods for Population Control Economic incentives may *seem* coercive, but other means of controlling population growth are blatantly coercive. For instance, temporary sterilizing agents could be added to certain foods or to the water supply so practically no one could bear a child during a given period. Licenses for childbearing could be required, with severe penalties for having a child without a license. Men and women could be required to submit to sterilization after they have had a specified number of children, in much the same way that certain vaccinations are required by law for the common good. The social unrest and the personal tragedies that could result from such coercive measures may not be pleasant to think about, but neither are the consequences of drastic overpopulation.

EFFECTS OF A STATIONARY POPULATION

Throughout this chapter we have seen how the social demographer alternately studies the demographic effects on the group, and the social effects on the basic demographic processes. It seems fitting therefore, to conclude the chapter with a few remarks on the social consequences of a replacement level population growth. We can probably imagine more positive consequences than negative ones. Our numbers and rate of growth are not our only problems but, as Senator Tydings put it, "A growing population makes the solution of nearly all of our problems more difficult and more expensive."[24]

A stationary population would strikingly affect our age composition. About 30 percent of our population today is under 15 years of age, while about 10 percent are 65 and older. With a stationary population, these age categories would be about even, with about 20 percent in each.[25] Some claim that an older age composition would harm us by slowing down the rate of new ideas and the pressures for social change. As a nation, we would, in short, become too conservative. Earlier, we discussed the political and economic consequences of a stable

[24]Westoff, pp. 352–353.

[25]Westoff, pp. 335–336.

population—as well as the consequences of overpopulation. Our economic system has for so long been based on the idea of economic growth that the decline in opportunities in a society no longer geared to expansion would require major social readjustments. We will need all the thought and imagination we can muster to minimize the negative consequences and take full advantage of the positive ones.

We have seen that social demographic studies can tell us much about the people of a society, how many there are, and what are their characteristics such as age, sex, and marital status. Such studies reveal how the numbers and characteristics of people are changing and how these changes affect and are affected by the society. Demographic studies show us where people live and how many move about within a geographic territory, and why they do so. But we need to know more about how people live, particularly how they organize themselves into groupings we call the city and the particular problems they face as they become urbanized. These topics are covered in the next chapter.

SUMMARY POINTS AND QUESTIONS

1. Demographers study the characteristics of a population and the possible effects of population change and growth.

> *What are some types of population characteristics?*

> *In what ways can demographic information be put to practical use?*

2. Demographic statistics are gathered in three ways: (1) by censuses; (2) by registration of certain events, such as birth and deaths; and (3) by surveys.

> *How does each of these methods actually work?*

> *What advantages and disadvantages are inherent in each method?*

3. Three basic demographic processes are *fertility, mortality,* and *migration.* Fertility is measured by the crude birth rate and by the fertility rate.

> *How are each of these rates calculated?*

4. A number of social factors affect fertility. These include socioeconomic status, rural-urban residence, religion, and race.

> *In what specific ways do each of these factors affect fertility?*

> *What explanations can you give as to why each of these factors affects fertility?*

5. The second demographic process, mortality, is measured by the crude death rate and the infant mortality rate; life expectancy also can shed light on a group's mortality pattern.

Why is the infant mortality rate considered an index of the health of a society?

What is the difference between life span and life expectancy?

A group has been found to have a 10–year increase in life expectancy at birth. Does this mean that if formerly males at age 60 lived five additional years they will now, on the average, live 15 years? Explain.

6. The third demographic process, migration, might be viewed in terms of immigration and internal migration.

What are some of the major migration trends taking place in the United States?

Discuss some demographic effects on communities resulting from the fact that 36 million Americans move each year.

7. World population growth is increasing at a fast rate. For example, the world had a population of 500 million in the year 1650, 1 billion in 1850, 2 billion in 1930, and 3.8 billion in 1974.

What factors account for the increasing rate of population growth?

What problems might occur if the world reaches a population of 7 billion, which is projected for the year 2000?

8. For the United States, it is projected that population size will be 320 million by the year 2000, 440 million by 2020, and 600 million for 2050.

How might this increase of population affect the quality of life in the United States?

What would be some effects if our population did not increase?

9. Two concepts that help us understand population size effects are the *maximum* population size, which refers to the total number of people that could survive at a subsistence level of living, and the *optimum* population size, which refers to the ideal size that would permit a society to provide a good life for its members.

What do you think is the maximum population size of the United States? The optimum population size?

What do you think might happen if the population went over the maximum population size?

10. One objective for controlling population size is to achieve replacement level fertility. Some ways suggested for accomplishing this control include education, more family planning centers, new roles for women, incentives and penalities, and some form of coercive controls.

How would you evaluate each of these means for meeting the objective of replacement level fertility?

Considering the staggering size of projected future populations, do you think that coercive controls such as sterilization or licensing might be necessary?

SUGGESTED READINGS

Adelstein, Michael E. and Jean G. Pival, eds. *Ecocide and Population.* New York: St. Martin's Press, 1971. Essays on population from an ecological perspective. Deals with the effect of our population on our natural environment.

Borrie, W. D. *The Growth and Control of World Population.* London: Weidenfield and Nicolson, 1970. Presents a world overview of the major demographic patterns, movements, and policies. Contains numerous migratory and population maps and statistics.

Brown, Harrison and Edward Hutchings, Jr., eds. *Are Our Descendants Doomed?* New York: Viking Press, 1972. A series of essays dealing with the problems that an over-populated world will face and some of the methods that might be used to alleviate the consequences of projected population growth.

Ford, Thomas R. and Gordon Dejong, eds. *Social Demography.* Englewood Cliffs, N.J.: Prentice-Hall, 1970. An excellent general treatment of the field of social demography.

Freedman, Ronald, ed. *Population: The Vital Revolution.* Garden City, N.Y.: Doubleday, 1964. Essays on population trends, migration, and fertility organized in terms of specific world regions.

Hardin, Garrett, ed. *Population, Evolution and Birth Control.* San Francisco: W. H. Freeman, 1969. A reader on population problems, the evolution of man, and the feasibility of birth control to prevent overpopulation.

Spiegelman, Mortimer. *Introduction to Demography.* Cambridge, Mass.: Harvard University Press, 1968. A basic text on demography. It deals with the processes of fertility, mortality and migration and the methodological procedures used to collect data on those processes.

Stockwell, Edward G. *Population and People.* Chicago: Quadrangle Books, 1970. Deals with migration, mortality, and fertility in relation to the composition and distribution of the population in today's world, and the resulting consequences.

If you're white, middle class, well educated, fairly affluent, have two or more children, and you live in the city, what are you? A statistical minority, for one thing. Most others like you are in the suburbs. Even many working class people have moved there. Large cities are now mostly the home of the poor—including many whites of various ethnic roots, but also almost all blacks and other nonwhites. Were suburbs produced by some panic flight of whites away from the racial minorities? Not really. Suburbs are not new; they've grown as the middle class grew, became wealthier and could afford to leave the increasingly crowded and polluted cities. Meanwhile the central cities, the source of income for most suburbanites, stagnate and decay. They have a poor residential population in need of public services and a commuting, well-off, working population that can't be taxed by the city on the money it makes there.

14

THE CITY

The inner city is dying. Gracious old mansions, lived in for generations by the city's leading citizens, are being abandoned rapidly. The middle-class families that leave them head for the newer areas outside the old city. . . . Behind them into the decaying city come the poor families of the rural areas of the south. As each middle-class family leaves, the vacated house is soon divided into tenements, and five to ten rural families jam into it. The process is accelerating, and the inner city is probably on its way to becoming an overcrowded slum where young, jobless men in increasing numbers, peddle pot.[1]

Richard Holbrooke

A multiple choice test: The city described above is: (a) New York, (b) Detroit, (C) Chicago, (d) all of the above, (e) none of the above. The correct answer is "none of the above." The city is Fes, Morocco, founded in A.D. 808, the exotic walled city described in the fourteenth century as one of the wonders of its time, and over 800 years old when the Pilgrims landed at Plymouth. Our description was written in 1972 by Richard Holbrooke, who spent two years in Morocco directing the Peace Corps there.

That the description of a deteriorating Moroccan city could be applied to many places in the United States may give us little consolation. Yet it is good to be reminded that cities have been around for a long time and that urban problems are not uniquely American. A brief overview of the origin of cities and worldwide trends in urbanization should give us insight into what created cities. It will also help us to understand their growth and, at times, their decline. Surely these remarkable changes in the settlement patterns of our species are not haphazard. Once we know something of the origin and growth of cities,

[1]Richard Holbrooke, "An Extraordinary City Fights for its Life," The Washington Post, 24 April 1972, p. A-20.

we can deal with urbanism in the United States. Although the origins of cities may seem only remotely relevant to the problems of pollution and congestion facing urban America in the 1970s, it is fascinating to explore why and where it all began.[2]

THE ORIGIN OF CITIES

For most of human history people have either settled in small groups on the land that gave them sustenance or wandered in nomad tribes in constant search of fruit and game. Only about 7000 years ago did the first cities arise. A city is a large gathering of people. Cities produce and distribute nonagricultural goods and services. Essentially three conditions are needed before cities can come into being: first, a regular and recurring agricultural surplus; second, sufficient technology; and third, social organization.

Not until families could consistently produce more food than they needed could some people do something other than produce food. Technology, in the form of rude farming implements and practices, not only helped to create the agricultural surplus, but, in the form of the wheel and domesticated draft animals, allowed the surplus to be transported from the producers to the consumers. Technology also enabled city workers to produce goods of value for those in the hinterland.

Farm surpluses and technology were not in themselves enough. We also had to develop a system of roles that would permit food and other goods to be traded for each other in an orderly manner. Division of labor was needed so desired goods could be manufactured and distributed. We needed social organization. Drawing upon the concentration of manpower, early cities frequently offered military protection. In exchange for food and fiber, therefore, city dwellers provided a variety of services for the rural people. Frequently, however, it was not an even exchange, for the city people could exert power over isolated families in the hinterland.

Because an agricultural surplus was so basic a need, the earliest cities arose in the fertile valleys of the Tigris and Euphrates rivers and in parts of India. Later, as commerce became more important, seaport cities grew up in many parts of the world. These early cities were quite small, and even later ones were small by contemporary standards. Ancient Babylon probably had no more than 25,000 people; whereas Athens, which reached its peak during the fifth century B.C., probably contained only 150,000 people. But thousands of years ago the die was cast. We, the nomads of the forest, the cave dwellers, the primitive farmers, had begun to live in cities.

[2]For an account of the origin and history of cities see Lewis Mumford, The City in History (New York: Harcourt, Brace, Jovanovich, 1961).

These freeway ramps and loops symbolize an ancient fact about cities: their roots are in trade, which requires a technology for transportation of goods.

WORLD URBANIZATION TRENDS

As we briefly scan the last 2000 years of human history, keep in mind that our species, *homo sapiens*, has been around for at least 100,000 years. Also keep in mind that there are two measures of world urbanization: first, the number of cities and their sizes; second, the proportion of the people, in the world or in a particular part of it, living in these cities.[3]

At the birth of Christ there were about 12 cities in the Mediterranean area, each with no more than 100,000 inhabitants. Probably in Asia a few cities approached this size. By the second century A.D., when Rome was at the peak of its power, its population was somewhere between 250,000 and 1 million people. At about this time there were other cities around the world with populations up to 20,000. Records are understandably imprecise, but the best estimate is that at the time of Christ there were 250 million people on earth, and a generous estimate would be that one–half of one percent of them were living in cities with populations of 20,000 or more.

---

[3]For the history of cities, see Mumford; Ralph Turner, *The Great Cultural Traditions* (New York: McGraw-Hill, 1941); and Henri Pirenne, *Medieval Cities* (Princeton: Princeton University Press, 1925).

The collapse of the Roman Empire in A.D. 476 dramatically affected civilization and cities. The decline of the mighty Roman political organization cast an eclipse on the cultural skies of Western Europe. Trade and commerce, no longer centrally controlled, came to a virtual standstill during the Dark Ages. Although historians no longer consider the Dark Ages to have been completely "dark," the distinction that the phrase suggests is still sound. Cities lost their importance as centers of art and intellectual life, and their populations gradually declined. The population of the once glorious city of Rome was reduced to about 20,000.

The eclipse of the cities lasted for about 800 years, until the beginning of the Renaissance in the thirteenth century. At about this time printing with movable type was invented, and interest in the fine arts and scholarships was rekindled. Trade within Europe was restored, and cities were once again centers of events.

The real growth of cities was not to come until the Industrial Revolution, in the later eighteenth century. Steam, the newfound source of power, proved to be efficient and relatively cheap, but it had to be used close to where it was produced. The workers were collected into an immense place, and their looms and other machines were fed the magic power of steam. The factory system was born and with it the factory town and the factory city. The numerous workers in the city were at the same time both producers of huge quantities of goods desired by the rural population, and a market for food and fiber. Meanwhile agricultural techniques were improving. Many farm laborers found themselves out of work and responded to the lure—however illusionary it may later have seemed—of better work and better living in the cities. Everything thus fitted together to produce one of the greatest migrations in human history, the trek of huge numbers of people from rural areas to the cities. We are now up to the relatively recent past, and as we treat this period we concentrate on urban growth in the United States.

URBANISM IN THE UNITED STATES

Statistical information on cities in our country is abundant, some of it going back to 1790. By consulting records of the census held every 10 years, you could find the land area of Albuquerque or the number of people per square mile in Youngstown. The population of specific cities is analyzed according to the median age of inhabitants, their race, sex, death rate, and so on. Much of this information is of use to urban specialists. The informed citizen should be acquainted with the *Statistical Abstract of the United States,* which contains condensed information from the censuses and special surveys.[4]

[4]U.S. Bureau of the Census, *Statistical Abstract of the United States* (Washington, D.C.: U.S. Government Printing Office, yearly).

Our general question in this section is, How urbanized is our society? To answer this question, we must phrase more specific ones: What proportion of the population lives in urban areas? How many cities are there in the United States and how has this picture changed? In what size cities do Americans live? How is the population currently distributed among farm, suburban, and central city residence? What proportion of the population lives in places that are socially and economically linked to a city?

THE RURAL-URBAN SHIFT

According to the census definition, any place that is incorporated as a city, village, borough, or town and that has at least 2500 inhabitants is considered to be urban. Recently, unincorporated places of this population size have also been designated urban. Some exceptions exist, but if you live in a place with at least 2499 other people, that place is urban. Smaller places and farms are classified as rural.

Within the perspective of human history, 170 years can be either a long or a short time. In Table 14-1, we can see the contrast between 1800, when a little over 300,000 people, or 6 percent of the population, were living in urban areas, and 1970, when almost 150 million people, or almost three-fourths of the population, were urbanites. It can be noted also that in 1920 a simple plurality of the population were living in urban areas. Fifty years later the urban population was almost 75 percent. And we can expect still more change in the same direction. By the year 2000, which is not all that far off, the best estimate is that 90 percent of us will be living in urban places.

TABLE 14-1. Growth of Urban Population, 1800–1970

Year	Number of People in Urban Areas	Proportion of Total Population[a]
1800	322,371	6%
1820	693,255	7
1840	1,845,055	11
1860	6,216,518	20
1880	14,129,735	28
1900	30,214,832	40
1910	42,064,001	46
1920	54,253,282	51
1930	69,160,599	56
1940	74,705,338	57
1950	96,846,817	64
1960	125,268,750	70
1970	149,324,930	74

[a]Rounded to nearest full percentage point.

Source: U.S. Bureau of the Census, *1970 Census of Population, U.S. Summary* (Washington, D.C.: U.S. Government Printing Office, 1970), p. 42.

Few places in the United States today are unaffected by the spread of urban technology; by the year 2000 less than 10 percent of us are expected to be living in rural areas.

Another way to see the rural-to-urban change in our society is to look at how both cities in general and large cities in particular have increased in number since the turn of the century. As is shown in Table 14-2, 70 years ago there were fewer than 2000 urban places; now there are a little over 7000. In 1900 there were only six cities in the United States with populations of a half million or more, now there are twenty-six. Only 15.6 percent of urban dwellers, as indicated in Table 14-3, live in cities with populations of 500,000 and more. And this proportion has not changed much since 1920; the big increase since the turn of the century is in the proportion of the population that lives in cities with under 100,000 inhabitants.

Americans are often said to be deserting their cities. True, the central cities have not grown as fast as their surrounding suburban areas, but these suburban

TABLE 14-2. Number and Size of Cities, 1900-1970

Size Classification	Number of Cities							
	1900	1910	1920	1930	1940	1950	1960	1970
1,000,000 or more	3	3	3	5	5	5	5	6
500,000–1,000,000	3	5	9	8	9	13	16	20
100,000–500,000	32	42	56	80	78	88	111	130
50,000–100,000	40	60	77	98	107	126	201	240
25,000–50,000	83	119	143	185	213	252	432	520
Under 25,000	1579	2037	2437	2802	3072	4278	5276	6146
All urban places	1740	2266	2725	3179	3485	4764	6041	7062

Source: U.S. Bureau of the Census, *1970 Census of the Population, U.S. Summary* (Washington, D.C.: U.S. Government Printing Office, 1970), p. 46.

areas are integrally related to the cities. Figure 14-1 shows clearly what has happened over the last 30 years; suburbanites, once the smallest category of the population, have become the largest. This is one reason why later in this chapter the suburbs receive considerable attention.

Another indicator of how highly urbanized our nation has become is the proportion of the population that lives in standard metropolitan statistical areas (SMSAs). A SMSA usually consists of a city of at least 50,000 inhabitants, the county in which the central city is located, and any adjacent counties that are found to be metropolitan in nature and are socially and economically tied to

TABLE 14-3. Urban Population of the United States, 1900-1970[a]

	1900	1910	1920	1930	1940	1950	1960	1970
Percent in cities of 1,000,000 or more	8	9	10	12	12	12	10	9
Percent in cities of 500,000 to 1,000,000	2	3	6	5	5	6	6	6
Percent in cities of 100,000 to 500,000	8	10	10	13	12	12	13	12
Percent in cities of under 100,000	21	24	25	27	28	35	41	46
Percent in cities, all sizes	40	46	51	56	57	64	70	74

[a]Percents rounded to nearest full point.

Source: U.S. Bureau of the Census, *1970 Census of Population, U.S. Summary* (Washington, D.C.: U.S. Government Printing Office, 1970), p. 46. Prior to 1950 some large and densely settled areas were not classified as urban because they were unincorporated. The data in this table use the current definition of urban for 1950 and beyond. The data prior to 1960 do not include the population of Alaska and Hawaii.

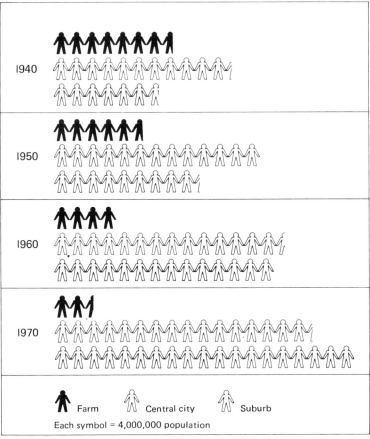

Figure 14-1. Farm, City, and Suburban Population, 1940–1970. Rural nonfarm dwellers, and urban residents outside of metropolitan areas, are not included in this chart. Some farm dwellers are also included in the suburban category. Definition of central city and suburb for the years 1940–1960 are according to the 1960 Census. The 1970 figures reflect some slight changes in the definitions that were used in the 1970 Census. Reproduced by permission. Carl Behrens, "Where Will the Next 50 Million Americans Live?" Population Bulletin, Vol. 27, No. 5 (Washington, D.C.: Population Reference Bureau, October 1971), p. 9.

the central city. In 1970 there were 263 SMSAs in the United States, 148 of them having populations of 200,000 or more. In the same year over 150 million Americans, or over 70 percent of the population, were living in SMSAs. Thus, the bulk of our population lives in places that are economically and socially integrated with a city.

URBAN ECOLOGY: THE CITY AS A SYSTEM

In the 1920s several sociologists at the University of Chicago, notably Robert E. Park, Ernest W. Burgess, and Roderick D. McKenzie, began studying the American city. They concentrated on the *spatial pattern* of cities, how their spatial arrangements got to be the way they are, and how they are likely to change. Through the efforts of these and other pioneers, the subfield of sociology, *human ecology*, came into existence.

Today *ecology* is an "in" term. To many it means little more than not throwing beer cans along the highways, not flushing soapsuds down the drain unless they are clearly biodegradable, or not cutting down too many trees for newsprint. Beyond these popular notions there is a broader concept that somehow deals with the interrelationship of all organisms. It was Charles Darwin, writing in 1859, who first described this interrelationship of living things as the "web of life," and it was Darwin who recognized the different forms this interrelationship could take—sometimes a struggle for existence among species, sometimes cooperation, and sometimes a process of help.[5] Darwin also dealt with how these processes affected the geographic distribution of species, that is, how the picture of an area could change through the interaction of species.

Possibly because plants do not run away when you try to study them, plant scientists were the first to recognize how important the interdependence of species was, and to develop a science of interdependence, plant ecology. Animal ecology followed, but not until 1921 was the concept of human ecology used in a sociology text.[6] The term *urban ecology* is now often used instead because so much of human ecology research deals with how humans in and around cities interact and are interdependent, and with how these processes affect the spatial patterning of activities in cities.

SEEING THE CITY AS A PIECE OF NATURE

It is not surprising that urban ecologists, as latecomers to the field of ecology, adapted to human populations many of the concepts of plant ecology. While plant ecologists dealt with the *invasion* by one species into an area previously dominated by another, urban ecologists use the concept *invasion* to designate the intrustion of new types of population units or kinds of activities into an area. Some examples include the establishment of a few stores or offices in

[5]Charles Darwin, *Origin of Species* (Cambridge, Mass.: Harvard University Press, 1964).

[6]Robert E. Park and Ernest W. Burgess, *An Introduction to the Science of Sociology* (Chicago: University of Chicago Press, 1921), pp. 161–216.

Invasion: Competition for building space in a residential neighborhood impinges on this homeowner. Eventual replacement of this home by apartments seems inevitable.

what was once an area of single-family homes, or the movement of a few black families into an all-white area. If the residential area becomes predominantly commercial, or the all-white suburb eventually becomes predominantly black, the process is completed, for the time being at least, and we refer to it as *succession.*

Just as an area in which a hardwood forest has succeeded a stand of softwood trees presents a *new configuration,* so does an area where businesses displace homes or one ethnic group displaces another. The competition for space within an urban area is presumably no less orderly than is the competition for space among plants and animals. Urban ecologists thus study the processes that occur among segments of the urban population, the processes that affect urban activities, and the ways in which these processes affect the spatial pattern of the city.

From his studies of Chicago, sociologist Ernest Burgess theorized that American cities could be depicted as a series of concentric zones, as presented in Figure 14-2. The central business district, called the Loop in Chicago, is at the center, and each of the other zones was hypothesized to have more or less distinct populations and land use. Other theories of the structure and growth of cities

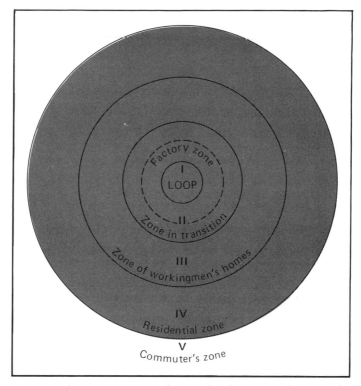

Figure 14-2. Burgess' Concentric Zone Theory of Urban Growth. Reproduced by permission, from Robert E. Park, Ernest W. Burgess and Robert D. McKenzie, The City (Chicago: University of Chicago Press, 1925), p. 51.

have been advanced, such as sociologist Homer Hoyt's sector theory, also shown in Figure 14-3.[7] Understandably, none of these theories adequately describes all American cities. Rivers or mountains may effectively prevent growth in certain directions. The spatial arrangement of a city also may be affected by the values or traditions of the inhabitants. In Boston, as sociologist Walter Firey has shown, the Common remains a large park in the center of the business district, even though economically the land could be put to better use.[8]

Sociologist Alvin Boskoff's diagram of an urban region, shown in Figure 14-4, takes us beyond the city and its immediate surrounding areas to show how even a smaller city, called a *satellite,* can be socially and economically linked with a large city. Within the scope of this chapter we cannot give more than an

[7]Homer Hoyt, "The Structure of American Cities in the Post-War Era," *American Journal of Sociology* 48 (January 1943), 475–492.

[8]Walter Firey, *Land Use in Central Boston* (Cambridge, Mass.: Harvard University Press, 1947), ch. 4.

Make a map of the various zones of your community. Which spatial theory best fits your community?

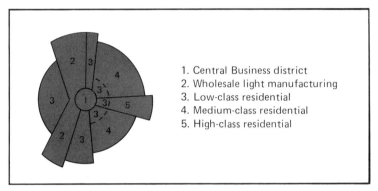

1. Central Business district
2. Wholesale light manufacturing
3. Low-class residential
4. Medium-class residential
5. High-class residential

Figure 14-3. Hoyt's Sector Theory of Urban Growth. By permission from the Annals of the American Academy of Political and Social Science, 242 (Nov., 1945), 13, in C. D. Harris and E. L. Ullman, "The Nature of Cities."

indication of how areas of a city are functionally interrelated, nor can we analyze the various segments of a city and show how they relate to one another. It should suffice for us to say here that cities are complex centers of socioeconomic interaction, and that every city in history has fitted into a larger network of such interaction, whether on a national or an international scale. Raising crops and animals are the work of the rural areas, while manufacturing, trade, commerce, and transportation, are the work of cities.

Before we study further the elements of urban areas, we should add that sociologists have studied other aspects of the city besides its ecology. A number of important studies have dealt with the power and class structures of cities and towns. Some of the most interesting include Robert and Helen Lynd's *Middletown* and *Middletown in Transition*, W. Lloyd Warner's *The Status System of a Modern Community*, John Dollard's *Caste and Class in a Southern Town*, and William Dobriner's *Class in Suburbia*. Jane Jacobs says that her book, *The Death and Life of Great American Cities*, is "an attack on current city planning and rebuilding." It is more than this, for it contains many insightful and fresh ideas on the use of sidewalks and parks, the advantages of mixing residential and commercial uses in the same section of the city, social life in the slum, and many other topics. Sociologists have given the city much study in the past and continue to do so.

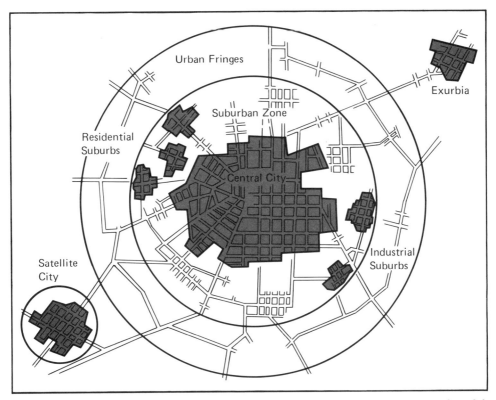

Figure 14-4. A Simplified Ecological Diagram of the Urban Region. Reproduced by permission from Alvin Boskoff, The Sociology of Urban Regions, *2nd Ed., © 1970, p. 107. By permission of Prentice-Hall, Inc., Englewood Cliffs, N.J.*

SLUMS AND GHETTOS: PURGATORIES VERSUS HELLS

Within the central city, just beyond the business district, is the area that Burgess called *Zone Two* or the *Zone in Transition.* Earlier in the history of the city this zone was usually a residential area, but it is now becoming a part of the business district with stores, shops, and office buildings. If the business district actually does expand to take over this area, the value of the land will increase. While waiting for the expansion, most landlords do not consider it good economics to keep up or improve residences that they believe will soon be torn down. So they rent out the houses or apartments for the best price they can get and hope that in time they can sell the property at an inflated price. Because the growth of central business districts has slowed, however, areas around them really may not be in transition. They could be destined to remain slums for a long time.

SLUMS: HELLS WITH AN ESCAPE HATCH

Even though the rats may be as large and the roaches as pesky in one as in the other, it is useful to distinguish between a slum and a ghetto. At its worst, a slum may consist of woefully deteriorated buildings with leaky roofs, sagging floors, and hazardous electrical wiring. To produce more rental income, the older homes or apartments may have been cut up into extremely small units producing severe overcrowding. People from several apartments may have to share toilets and sinks, and sometimes even these indoor facilities are lacking. Not all slums are this bad, but by definition none is a decent place to live in.

Socially, slums are no more desirable. Knifings, shootings, and crimes of other sorts are all more prevalent in the slums than in other sections of the city. So are divorce, desertion, prostitution, some forms of mental illness, suicide, and drug use. No wonder that some people consider the larger society criminal for allowing the slum dwellers to destroy themselves and one another, either physically or psychologically.

In the past, migrants from foreign countries or from rural areas settled in the slums of the city, usually because they could not afford to live anywhere else. As their economic lot improved they moved out. True, the Irish, Italians, and other ethnic groups at times had difficulty finding homes in better sections of the city, but the pressures to keep them out of such areas were not extreme. And herein lies a difference between a ghetto and a slum.

GHETTOS: HELLS WITH NO WAY OUT

Ghetto first described parts of European cities where Jews were required to live; they could not, by law, live elsewhere. Today *ghetto* is a tragic but apt description of some sections in American cities. Blacks, the poor, and particularly poor blacks live in these areas and almost no one else does. The laws on the books do not require them to do so, but social and economic factors that have had the force of law, have all but created a wall around our urban ghettos. Despite open-housing laws, blacks find it exceedingly difficult to find housing outside the ghetto. And many simply cannot afford to buy or rent in the suburbs. The term *ghetto* thus implies a forced segregation, and it often implies the slum conditions we described above. Even a suburb or good apartment complex with a virtually all-black population is technically a ghetto if forced segregation accounts for the lack of racial mixture.

Overcrowding in slums and ghettos creates competition not only for housing units but for all kinds of living space.

We have had no shortage of rhetoric on what to do about our urban ghettos; nor, to be fair, have we lacked noble plans and efforts. But we still have the ghettos. Attempts to improve the lot of ghetto dwellers fall into two categories: One, remove the ghetto by providing decent integrated housing elsewhere; or, two, rebuild the ghettos. There are problems with both approaches. And to make matters worse, both may be missing the crux of the problem.

INTEGRATED HOUSING OUTSIDE THE GHETTO

That all future housing for the poor should be located outside existing ghettos sounds like a reasonable and humane goal, and quite in keeping with our democratic ideals. The big trouble is that so far it has not worked, at least not very well. Black ghettos are growing larger; between 1960 and 1970 blacks in the

---

List the services provided by a municipality and show which areas of the city benefit from these services. Does high quality service correlate with high income level areas?

---

central cities increased by 3.2 million, mostly in the already black ghettos.[9] By contrast, the number of blacks who live in or have moved to integrated areas outside the central city is scarcely noticeable.

Few homes are built within the central city by the private sector at a price that the urban poor of any race can afford. Public housing is usually located near the central cities, partly because people in other sections refuse to allow the poor to live among them. In addition, much public housing is racially segregated; integrated housing outside the ghetto helps only a small number of the more affluent blacks. A good case can be made for not abandoning the struggle to create integrated housing outside the ghetto at prices people can afford to pay. In the immediate future, though, this approach seems unlikely to tear down the ghetto walls.

URBAN RENEWAL

Urban renewal may sound like a way to rebuild and renovate the ghettos and slums. Curiously, rebuilding projects under the Urban Renewal Act of 1954, which is still in effect, do not necessarily clear the slums. For one thing, the local urban renewal agency has the power to decide what is a slum. Once an area has been labeled a slum, the city can then buy the land, raze the property, and secure low–interest federal loans for rebuilding. Often, the areas being renewed are the best of the slums. Part of the city is beautified, but the worst of the slums remain. The criterion for renewal often seems to be not whether slum dwellers need better housing but whether the area in question has the potential for producing income for the city.

Urban renewal can ignore human needs in still other ways. The Act requires the local agency to demonstrate that "decent, safe, and sanitary" housing is available elsewhere in the city, and to help relocate the people who are being evicted by urban renewal. Nevertheless, the new locations may not be any better than the old ones, and the forced relocation can destroy a neighborhood and break up long–established interaction patterns. (The acute anguish of some people who were forced out of an inner–city Boston neighborhood is vividly described

[9]Sandor Halebsky, ed., *The Sociology of the City* (New York: Charles Scribner's Sons, 1973), p. 81.

Urban renewal planners are often unaware that stoops and streets are part of the social space of poor urban dwellers.

by Marc Fried in his article "Grieving for a Lost Home."[10]) Middle–class planners seem unaware of the attachment the poor have to their neighborhoods, and particularly how they define the streets and alleys as part of their social space. Edward Ryan describes this aspect of life in the slums:

> Social life has an almost uninterrupted flow between apartment and street: children are sent in the street to play, women lean out of windows to watch and take part in street activity, women go "out on the street" to talk with friends, men and boys meet on the corners at night and families sit on the steps and talk with their neighbors at night when the weather is warm.[11]

[10]Marc Fried, "Grieving for a Lost Home," in Leonard J. Duhl, M.D., ed., *The Urban Condition* (New York: Basic Books, 1963), ch. 12.

[11]Quoted in Marc Fried and Peggy Gleicher, "Some Sources of Residential Satisfaction in an Urban Slum," in Halebsky, p. 408.

The decaying portions of our cities must be saved and revived. But true renovation of the ghettos would require much more than rebuilding dilapidated housing. Parks, playgrounds, libraries, and schools would have to be added or improved to make the ghetto a decent place in which to live. Because ghetto rebuilding would continue racial segregation, some people are opposed to it. But urban renewal has so far failed in meeting human needs chiefly because slum and ghetto inhabitants have little power and can exert little influence over the decisions that affect their lives.

REDUCING POVERTY

The problem of ghettos and slums cannot be disentangled from the problem of poverty. A massive attack on poverty would make slums and ghettos less oppressive to their inhabitants, and it would give many people greater choice about where and how they are to live. The differences in family income between those inside and those outside the central city are a telling sign of the magnitude of effort needed. In 1971 blacks living in the central cities of large metropolitan areas had a median family income of $7247, while whites outside the cities of these same metropolitan areas had a median family income of $12,865.[12] In smaller metropolitan areas, white suburbanite families had a median income about $5000 higher than that of black central city dwellers. More than 3 million black families live in the central cities of metropolitan areas. Relieving this large group from poverty is an enormous task; among other things new jobs would have to be created, better job training programs would be needed, as would various welfare measures. Because inner-city black families have incomes $4000 below that of inner city whites and $5000 below that of white suburbanites, they cannot afford to move out of the ghettos, either to better sections of the city or to the suburbs.

SUBURBS

The next time you are at the beach make a pile of sand, then pour more sand on the center of the cone. Some will remain at the center, making the pile higher, but much will spread out in a ring around the base. In the same way, while skyscraper office buildings and high-rise apartments have created upward growth in our city centers, most city growth has been outward in an ever-expanding ring of suburbs around its edges.

Those who consider the growth of suburbs a recent plot against the central city seem to miss the basic fact that sizable growth of urban populations demands

[12]U.S. Bureau of the Census, *Current Population Reports*, Series P-60, no. 85 (December 1972), p. 1.

Find out what urban renewal projects are in your city. Assess their effects on the people who lived in the area and the city in general.

---

outward growth. There is no plot, and the outward movement has not exactly been recent. New York began to decentralize as early as 1850, and some 22 other cities did so around the turn of the century. As the urban historians Charles Glaab and Theodore Brown point out, the movement of population from the center of Philadelphia was proportionally greater in the years from 1860 to 1910 than it was between 1900 and 1950.[13] Following these early beginnings, the suburbs grew in great spurts in the 1920s, when the automobile allowed commuting to and from the central city. After World War II the unmet needs for housing that built up during the war, coupled with greater general affluence and with government supported home–loan plans, produced further growth of suburbs, this time of unprecedented proportions.

THE MYTH OF SUBURBIA

Both as part of the growth pattern of urban areas and as settlement groups we have invented to satisfy our needs, the suburbs are fascinating to the sociologist, as they are also to novelists and journalists.[14] It is amazing how many ways the popular view of the suburbs and suburbanites differs from the reality of the suburbs discovered by sociologists.

The suburb that intrigues novelists, and presumably their readers, is often a colony of mass–produced houses whose occupants are as indistinguishable from one another as are their homes. The typical suburbanite is described as a status seeker *par excellence,* moving to the suburbs to display and enjoy the material fruits of his past efforts. Once there, he works at an exhausting pace to keep up with his neighbors in gathering a bewildering display of appliances, gadgets, and furnishings. Meanwhile, the truly successful family moves to a better suburb where the race continues, but on the higher materialistic plane of backyard swimming pools, country club memberships, and expensive cars. Suburbanites are described either as lonely or as too much caught up in the affairs of their neighbors. If the stereotype is to be believed, suburbanites undergo

[13]Charles N. Glaab and Theodore A. Brown, "The Emergence of Metropolis," in Victor E. Ficker and Herbert S. Graves, eds., *Social Science and Urban Crisis* (New York: Macmillan, 1971), p. 24.

[14]See, for example, Richard E. Gordon et al., *The Split Level Trap* (New York: Bernard Geis Associates, 1961); John Keats, *The Crack in the Picture Window* (Boston: Houghton Mifflin, 1956); A. C. Spectorsky, *The Exurbanites* (Philadelphia: Lippincott, 1955); Peter Wyden, *Suburbia's Coddled Kids* (Garden City, N.Y.: Doubleday, 1960); and John McPartland, *No Down Payment* (New York: Simon and Schuster, 1957).

The myth of suburbia and the facts of suburbia collide. Do suburbanites differ much from their city cousins—other than by their chosen surroundings?

something approaching a religious conversion. That is, seemingly nice, ordinary people move to the suburbs and are mysteriously transformed into ultraconservative conformists, and racists to boot. They fled the city but now, although bored, alienated, and altogether disenchanted with suburban living, they have lost the will to flee, except perhaps to another suburb.

THE FACTS OF SUBURBIA

It is easy to debunk these extremely critical views of the suburbs. For the suburbs simply have not produced all the pathological people that could be predicted from the stereotype. Most sociologists have recognized the popular description of suburbia for what it is—a myth. But at least two sociologists have taken the myth seriously enough to conduct research on suburbia. Bennett Berger studied a suburb of San Jose, California.[15] He not only applied the general misconceptions about suburbs as hypotheses for proof or disproof, but he also conducted a detailed case study of the way of life of suburban blue collar families. The findings

[15]Bennett M. Berger, *Working Class Suburb* (Berkeley: University of California Press, 1960).

of his study were quite at odds with the conventional wisdom. The working class families who had moved to the suburb, Berger found, "had not been profoundly affected in any statistically identifiable or sociologically interesting way." Herbert Gans made a participant observation study of the Levittown near Philadelphia.[16] The suburbanites were happy, engaged in many family activities, and continued to visit relatives. They were neither in a status race with the neighbors nor unduly concerned about conformity. He, too, found the rule to be contentment without unwanted conformity.

An important reason why the sociological findings differ from the suburban myth is that sociological principles do not allow us to predict dramatic change in people, the so-called "conversion effect," as a result of a spatial move. You will recall that in our discussion of adult socialization we saw that people are required to take on new roles as they move into new and different social situations. But this process is not a "conversion." The adults who are being socialized—or, in suburbia, who are frequently socializing one another—bring with them their basic values and keep as much of their way of life as is considered appropriate.

Therefore, many sociological studies of the suburban movement have focused on the background of people who move to the suburbs and their motives for doing so. From such studies there emerges a sociological profile of suburban people, including their age, class, race, and so on. Compared and contrasted with profiles of populations from other parts of the urban area, these profiles show the suburb to be a functional part of the larger social system.

THE PUSH-PULL OF CITIES AND SUBURBS

Sociologists commonly categorize motives for moving to the suburbs into those that *push* people *away* from the central city and those that *pull* them *toward* the outskirts. When the combination of push and pull factors is sufficiently strong, people move. Of course, many people have never lived in a central city; having grown up in one or more suburbs, upon marriage they settle in another suburb. No push factors are involved for them unless they have mentally weighed living in an urban environment but have opted for the suburban style. In still other instances no pushes from the city are involved. A few years ago, for example, several hundred employees were transferred from an IBM plant in Lexington, Kentucky to one in Austin, Texas. Few, if any, of those families could have settled in the central city of Austin, for adequate middle-income family housing is not being built in our cities. And so these families moved from the suburbs of Lexington to the suburbs of Austin. They did not flee anything or anybody.

[16]Herbert J. Gans, *The Levittowners* (New York: Pantheon Books, 1967).

Suburbia—quiet streets with lawns, good schools, and convenient shopping centers are all part of the vision.

What, then, do people not like about the city, and what draws them to the suburbs? The factors that usually push people out of the cities are known to anyone who has lived or thought of living in a central city: old and rundown buildings and streets; air pollution, noise, and traffic congestion; high crime rates and the age and condition of the schools. And everywhere there are crowds. Central to our cultural heritage is the idea that the good life is to be found in rural areas and small towns. The closest most Americans come to this vision is suburbia. Various studies have found that those who move to the suburbs place a high value on family living and what they consider the good life for all family members.[17] They want roomier homes than the city provides, and they consider owning a home important. Quiet streets, yards with trees and grass, good schools, and convenient shopping centers with ample parking are all part of the vision. Suburbanites also expect that they and their children will find friends among neighboring families who share these values.

Millions of Americans invest a great deal of time and money in achieving the values of suburban living, and in general they are not disappointed. As we

[17]Wendell Bell, "Social Choice, Life Styles, and Suburban Residence," in William M. Dobriner, ed., *The Suburban Community* (New York: G. P. Putnam's Sons, 1958). See Berger. See also Gans.

Conduct an attitude survey among middle class, middle aged men in at least a moderate sized city to determine whether they would prefer to live in a city or in a rural area. For those that say they prefer a farm or small town, ask as many questions as neceesary to determine if they really prefer country living. Have they ever lived in the country? What would they do for a living? Have they talked over their plans with other family members? Have they investigated costs or time factors? Have they looked at rural property? All things considered, how much confidence would you place in the answer to the stated preference for rural living?

noted earlier, studies consistently find that people in the suburbs have a sense of well-being and are content with their lot. There are problems, to be sure, but much of their dream has come true.

LIVING PATTERNS: DAYDREAMS VERSUS FACTS

Do people live where they want to live? Gallup pollsters asked people, "If you could live anywhere in the United States that you wanted to, would you prefer a city, suburban area, small town, or farm?" Although the categories do not allow an exact comparison with census definitions of cities, SMSAs, or rural areas, we can still form some idea of the discrepancies between where people live and where they would like to live.

Rural living appeals to over *half* of all Americans, as shown in Table 14-4, but only about a *quarter* of Americans live in rural areas. Five times as many people say they would like to live on a farm as actually do. Conversely, only 13 percent say they prefer to live in a city, but 54 percent live in cities of over 100,000 population.

Some people could move if they wanted to, just as some people can, and do, move to Australia or New Zealand. Yet most people who would like to live in rural areas are prevented by the scarcity of rural jobs and the difficulties in commuting long distances to work in the city. Then, too, small towns no longer would be small if a third of our population, roughtly 70 million people, moved to them. The Gallup poll does show little enchantment with urban living. The proportion preferring the city has gone down considerably over the various years the public was polled on their preferences: 22 percent in 1966, 18 percent in 1970, 17 percent in 1971, and 13 percent in 1972 preferred city living.

The difference between where people live and where they say they would like to live points up a persistent problem in sociological research. We have data on what people *do*—they live in cities; and we have data on what they *say*—many

TABLE 14–4. Where Americans Live and Would Like to Live, in Percentages[a]

	Preferred Size of Place	Actual Size of Place	
City	13%	Central city	32%
		Urban fringe	27
Suburbs	31	Urban but out-side urbanized area	15
Small town	32	Rural nonfarm	22
Farm	23	Farm	5

[a]Rounded to nearest full point.

Source: *Gallup Index*, December, 1972, p. 22; and U.S. Bureau of the Census, *Statistical Abstract of the United States: 1972* (Washington, D.C.: U.S. Government Printing Office, 1972), pp. 16 and 584.

want to live on farms and in small towns. How do we interpret what they say? Do the statements reflect strong desires or nostalgic dreams? And how do we interpret the discrepancy between actual behavior and stated preferences? Are most Americans extremely unhappy about where they live? These would make interesting topics for further research, and we might be able to answer some of these questions. We could ask those people now living in cities but stating a preference for rural living how long they have felt this way, how strongly they feel about it, how frequently, if ever, they priced or inspected farms, whether or not they know the commuting time from the nearest small town to their place of work, and so forth.

SOCIAL CHARACTERISTICS OF THE SUBURBS

Not everyone in our cities has the values that send people to suburbia to seek the good life, nor can everyone who wishes to afford to. Thus, the suburbs gather certain kinds of people, mainly working, middle, and upper class, as opposed to lower class. Among the working class there is an overrepresentation of foreman, craftsmen, and other more highly skilled workers. In our society the upper class are few in number, so it stands to reason that the suburbs are chiefly middle class.

Suburbanites have a higher median family income and a higher level of educational attainment than people in the central city. Home ownership is high. A high proportion of suburban college–age children are enrolled in college because the family values education and can afford to pay for it. Divorce and separation rates are low. Less clearly related to social class in the suburbs is

Amidst the urban discord and ugliness many live who claim to dream of country living. Strong desires or nostalgic dreams?

the concentration of families with children and the rarity of single people and childless couples.

Racial segregation is quite apparent in the suburbs, but this is not due primarily to economic factors. In their book, *Negroes in Cities,* Karl and Alma Taeuber conclude that economic factors figure little in segregation.[18] In one way or another, blacks who could afford to live in white suburbs are kept out. Deep-rooted fears and prejudices keep most American suburbs all-white, or nearly so. People continue to fear that property values will tumble if a black family moves into an all-white neighborhood, despite studies that show that, if anything, prices go up.[19] Regardless of income increases among blacks, therefore, it is likely that many suburbs will continue to be all-white, at least for quite awhile.

[18]Karl Taeuber and Alma Taeuber, *Negroes in Cities* (Chicago: Aldine, 1965), p. 94.

[19]See Luigi M. Laurenti, *Property Values and Race* (Berkeley: University of California Press, 1960); and William F. Ladd, "Effect of Integration on Property Values," *American Economic Review* 52 (September 1962), 801–808.

THE DYSFUNCTIONS OF SUBURBAN SEGREGATION

The self-segregation of white, primarily middle class suburban families makes it difficult for the suburbs to be a truly functional part of the larger urban community. The suburbs are economically tied to the central cities, for most suburbanites commute there to earn a living. But social and sometimes political separation could, in time, lead to real polarization, as blacks and as urban poor on the one hand and the more affluent suburbanites on the other hand, view one another with suspicion and distrust. This is not the way to achieve the good life, let alone orderly growth and change.

The urban community might be functionally integrated by legally annexing the suburbs to the central city. This annexation is not always possible, though, because some suburbs have incorporated as separate entities, and others, such as the suburbs of St. Louis, Washington, New York, and Cincinnati, lie across the state line, thereby making annexation virtually impossible. One answer to functional segregation is some from of *metropolitan government* for the whole urban area, although suburbs and central cities separated by state lines are not open to this solution. Even without the problem of state lines, the polarization between the city and the suburbs can stand in the way of metropolitan government. Suburbanites fear the domination of minorities in the central city who, in turn, suspect that any changes will reflect the interests of the more powerful white suburbanites. The suburbs need the city, for no small suburban unit can possibly supply jobs for all its workers or organize such large-scale projects as flood control and public health services. The city needs the suburbs as a place to house many of its workers and as a source of financial support for urban services used by suburbanites.

PLANNING OUR URBAN FUTURE

The suburban movement is likely to continue. Middle class people are not returning to the city in any appreciable number; they like the suburbs too much. During the next 25 years we will add approximately 50 million people to our population. Most of them will live in urban areas, primarily in suburbs. We can hope that the 90 percent of our future population that will, for the most part, be living, working, buying, selling, worshiping, and playing in and around cities will suffer from fewer of the tensions and frustrations of urban living than is usual today.

Such a change will not happen by itself. We must seek to improve urban living, and we need sound planning to fulfill this commitment. In the physical work, the funds, and the new ideas needed, it is difficult to estimate the magnitude

In Reston, Virginia, many people feel that some dreams of urban planners
have been realized. By what criteria would you evaluate this planned
community?

of such a commitment because we have never made one. Its scope and effort
would probably have to equal our efforts so far devoted to exploring outer space.
Improving the urban condition would have to be a high–priority national goal.
We would need political leadership to guide and direct the commitment with
realism and enthusiasm. And we would need planning of the most imaginative
and comprehensive sort.

URBAN PLANNING: THE MAJOR CHALLENGE

In one sense urban planning is very old; in another sense it has scarcely been
tried. It all depends on what you mean by "planning." In the fifth century B.C.,
the Greek architect Hippodamus laid out the design for Piraeus, the port of Athens.
In the early nineteenth century the New York state legislature appointed a
commission to develop a plan for Manhattan Island. The commission recom-
mended a gridiron layout, and did not ignore human needs, acknowledging that
"a city is to be composed of the habitations of men, and that straight sided
and right angled houses are the most cheap to build and the most convenient
to live in."[20] Our nation's capital, with its gridiron arrangement of streets and

[20]Quoted in Christopher Tunnard and Henry Hope Reed, *American Skyline* (New York: New American Library,
1956), p. 57.

diagonal avenues radiating from the Capitol and the White House, was laid out by Pierre L'Enfant.

By "urban ·planning" sociologists mean something far more comprehensive than laying out streets or even locating parks and playgrounds, organizing welfare service, or establishing traffic flow patterns. Ideally, planning should begin with human values, with the question, "What do we want our urban areas to be like?" The sequence of steps needed to create the desired urban condition should be spelled out in enough detail to make their implications clear. Lawrence Haworth, for example, has defined a good city as one "whose institutions are flexible, voluntary, and controllable,"[21] and in which there is a sense of community. Haworth stresses individual freedom: People have a right to accept or reject the activities available in a city and a right to control the destiny of their settlements. It is hard to fault these ideas as abstract principles. But putting them into practice may be difficult and even divisive.

PLANNING VERSUS OTHER VALUES: THE INESCAPABLE COMPROMISES?

Should people be completely free to settle wherever they wish? Already some American cities are attempting to curb their growth, or at least to discourage further growth. There is doubt as to whether population limits can be set by law. Legal or not, the wishes of the people in a given city to halt growth could clearly conflict with the desires of others to move into the area. There is also doubt about whether restricting growth is practical. In Russia, for example, it was decided in 1931 that both Moscow and Leningrad had reached their ideal sizes and further growth would be actively discouraged.[22] In 1931 each city had a population of between 2 and 3 million inhabitants; by the 1960s each had over 6 million. Of course, deciding on the ideal size of a city or urban area is not the only problem in planning the desirable urban condition. Even so, contemplating the ideal can reveal the difficulty of trying to create an environment that contains all elements of the good life. It seems that when some elements are planned in, such as fixed size, other elements, such as freedom of movement and personal choice of location, sometimes have to be excluded.

The best contribution urban sociologists can make to urban planning is to stress that planning starts with the human values that individuals and groups want incorporated into their settlement patterns. The sociologist is also in a position to recognize two other points: One, to carry out plans requires that many different sorts of activities be carried on simultaneously; and two, planning

[21]Lawrence Haworth, *The Good City* (Bloomington, Ind.: Indiana University Press, 1963), p. 77.

[22]Quoted in Barbara Ward, "Cities for 3,000 Million People," *The Economist* 245 (July 8 1967), 116.

WILL THE FOLKS WHO BROUGHT YOU ACUPUNCTURE BRING YOU CRIME-FREE CITIES?

In the 23 years between 1949 and 1972, fear of crime in the streets of our central cities rose 550 percent. Four percent of respondents to a sample survey in 1949 named crime as the major problem in their cities (of 500,000 people or more in size). In 1974 crime was named as the major problem by 22 percent. In 1968 31 percent of city dwellers were fearful of walking in their own neighborhoods at night. In 1974 49 percent felt that fear. Seventeen percent of city dwellers are also fearful of being attacked in their own homes. And all of these fears are felt more by blacks than by whites.

Fully one-third of the people living in densely populated areas of the United States have been touched by urban crime in the last 12 months. They have been mugged, robbed, raped, or suffered property loss. Crime is a way of life in the central city, both for the criminals and for those who have been or fear to be victims.

For older people it's probably difficult to remember the good old days when the major urban problems were such nuisances as corrupt politicians, traffic congestion, high taxes, and poor housing. For younger people it's probably hard to believe that most urban crime was confined to smoke-filled rooms in City Hall. Oddly enough, at least one large city of the world has been transformed in the last 25 years from a worldwide symbol of crime to a virtually crime-free city of 10 million people.

Shanghai, China, had even lent its name to crime. To shanghai someone was to drug or intoxicate a man and kidnap him for involuntary service at sea. But when the communists came to power in 1949, Shanghai's days of crime were over. Or so it is claimed.

How was this transformation accomplished? By what sociologists call resocializing and communist spokesmen call ideological education. Sixty thousand criminals and prostitutes had been rounded up, reeducated, and resettled, with jobs, by 1953. In 1972 foreign visitors on their own unescorted journeys throughout the city could find no police other than those directing traffic. What could account for the success of such resocializing? Is there something about a classless society that drastically reduces the motivation for antisocial behavior? Or did the authorities use techniques in their resocializing that are contrary to our democratic values? What the secret is—if we could make use of it without radically altering our political values—would be well worth studying.

In the future all urban planning should start from the human values people want incorporated into their living patterns.

should be as broad and comprehensive as possible. Both of these points are illustrated by the creation of "new towns." (To a planner, *new town* does not mean simply a town that is new, but rather a community that is planned to be an integrated entity.) The new town of Columbia, Maryland, is an example of a city developed with human values and human needs in mind.[23] Located between Washington, D.C. and Baltimore, Columbia is designed for a population of 100,000. Eventually it will consist of ten villages, each with five neighborhoods. Elementary schools are located in each neighborhood so that each child can walk to school. Buses run on their own rights–of–way, forests and streams have been preserved, cultural activities are provided, and a unique system of comprehensive medical services is being developed. The careful, comprehensive plan for Columbia clearly gave full attention to the convenience and freedom of its residents and so far seems to be working well. Yet as a nation we cannot devote all of our efforts to the creation of new towns, neglecting the many problems in our existing urban areas.

In our discussion of slums and suburbs, we saw that the sections of an urban area are functionally interrelated and interdependent. The families in residential

[23]For a fuller description of Columbia, see James W. Rouse, "The City of Columbia," in Ficker and Graves, pp. 423–431.

areas need incomes from the business areas, and the commercial areas need customers from the residential areas. Not only are the problems of one section the problems of all, but the solutions for one area may create problems for another. Planning therefore must be as comprehensive as possible, based on the broadest socioeconomic unit possible. Thus, some political changes, such as the creation of a metropolitan government whose power goes beyond the legally defined city, have much to recommend them. But even a metropolitan government may not deal with a large enough socioeconomic unit. The creation of Columbia, Maryland, is a possible case in point. Surely when it reaches its population maximum of 100,000 it will have effects on Washington, D.C., Baltimore, and their many suburbs. Although sociologists do not have the final answer to our nation's urban problems, their perspectives should allow all of us to get a better grasp on the full dimensions of the problem.

When urban sociology got its start in the United States around 1920, scarcely more than half of our population lived in cities. Early research, as we have seen in this chapter, was devoted to the ecology of cities: that is, how their spatial arrangement arose and then changed. Today, about three–fourths of our population lives in urban areas. Since 1920 both the number of our cities and the number of our urban problems have increased significantly. Basic to our urban problems are the past discrimination and segregation that created slums and ghettos and our present treatment of racial and other minorities that perpetuate those blighted areas. Of course, minority group relations create problems other than urban ones, as we will see in the chapter that follows.

SUMMARY POINTS AND QUESTIONS

1. For the city to survive and flourish, three factors were necessary: a regular agricultural surplus, a production and transportation technology, and some form of a division of labor.

> *Why were these factors necessary?*
>
> *What additional factors are necessary for the survival of the modern metropolis?*

2. Urbanization has taken place in stages: (1) the growth of the ancient city until the collapse of Rome; (2) the dispersal of the population during the Dark Ages; (3) the restoration and growth of the city during the Renaissance; and (4) the emergence of the modern city as a response to the Industrial Revolution.

> *What direction is the city taking today?*
>
> *Considering the new technologies invented since the Industrial Revolution, what new stage might we be moving into today?*

3. Two indicators of urbanization in the United States are the proportion of the population living in urban areas (a political jurisdiction of 2500 or more), and the proportion of the population living in SMSA's (a city of 50,000 or more and its adjacent counties).

What other indicators might also provide a good picture of urbanization?

4. A growing field within sociology is urban ecology, which studies the spatial patterns in a city by using such concepts as invasion, competition, and succession.

How would you define each of these concepts?

Apply them to areas of a city with which you are acquainted.

5. Two theories by urban ecologists are Burgess's concentric zone theory and Hoyt's sector theory.

What usefulness do these theories have?

How might they be applied in order to understand the growth and development of a city?

6. Urban studies seem to center around the problems of the slum and the ghetto. While *slum* is used to describe a physically deteriorating part of the city, *ghetto* implies forced segregation.

What are the major problems that slum and ghetto dwellers face?

What factors operate to keep a ghetto intact?

7. Two ways of dealing with ghettos or slum areas have been to move the ghetto dweller into integrated housing outside the ghetto and to rebuild slums through urban renewal.

Why have these programs failed?

What alternative programs would you suggest?

8. Since the invention and widespread use of the automobile, suburbanization or dispersion of the population outward to the periphery of the city has been a major process in the United States.

What types of persons are moving to the suburbs? Why these types?

What attraction do the suburbs have compared with the city?

9. The suburbs have a middle class complexion in terms of the values held and in terms of the economic ability of the suburbanite to pursue those values.

What are the values that have been associated with the middle class?

10. Considering the urban problems the United States faces, urban planning now appears to be a necessity.

What factors must be taken into account by urban planners?

Can you give an example of how the values and ideas of urban planners have come into conflict with those of groups in a community?

SUGGESTED READINGS

Banfield, Edward. *The Unheavenly City.* Little, Brown, 1970. An unorthodox view of the city and the problems of urban poverty, crime, and riots.

Boskoff, Alvin. *The Sociology of Urban Regions.* New York: Appleton–Century–Crofts, 1970. A demographic approach to the city. It essentially deals with urban problems as a regional ecological problem.

Burgess, Ernest W. and Donald Bogue, eds. *Contributions to Urban Sociology.* Chicago: University of Chicago Press, 1964. A reader in urban sociology that includes 42 articles divided into four areas: urban ecology and demography, urban social organization and mass phenomena, ethnic and racial groups in urban society, and urban social problems.

Clark, Kenneth B. *Dark Ghetto.* New York: Harper & Row, 1965. Analyzes the problems of the ghetto dweller in relation to the educational, economic, political, and religious institutions of American society.

Glaab, Charles and Theodore Brown. *The History of Urban America.* New York: Macmillan, 1967. A survey of the development of the American city from the colonial period to the 1950s, dealing with such issues as the effects of immigration, bossism, and reformism on the structure of the city.

Haar, Charles M., ed. *The End of Innocence: A Suburban Reader.* Glenview, Ill.: Scott, Foresman, 1972. A collection of essays on living in suburbia, the relation of the suburbs to the city, and the future of the suburbs.

Jacobs, Jane. *The Death and Life of Great American Cities.* New York: Random House, 1961. An excellent, readable depiction of what cities are like and what they could be like.

Thomlinson, Ralph. *Urban Structure.* New York: Random House, 1969. A survey of the different approaches to the study of city life and how these approaches might be related to regional and urban planning.

The word **barbarian** comes to us from one that the ancient Greeks used to mean both **foreign and ignorant:** To be non-Greek was to be out of luck. Ethnocentrism is clearly an ancient human trait. In our own society in recent times we've been constantly aware of the social irritant of racism. Blacks and other nonwhites have been struggling, often with little success, for their rights and just rewards. Where does racism come from? Originally from ignorance and error. We notice differences between ourselves and others, and we treat the others as inferior. In a biological sense, though, there is one human species containing groups with only superficial differences. Race is therefore a social invention. There are no built-in social or intellectual differences among what are called races. Racism is a different story. Your life chances are closely related to your social race—in school, at work, as a parent, and on and on.

15

MINORITY GROUP RELATIONS

Little Indian, Sioux or Crow,
Little frosty Eskimo,
Little Turk or Japanee,
Oh! don't you wish that you were me? . . .

You have curious things to eat,
I am fed on proper meat;
You must dwell beyond the foam,
But I am safe and live at home.
Robert Louis Stevenson[1]

Most of human history is marked by ethnocentrism, and evidence from our dim prehistory suggests that this sense of the difference between "us" and "them" is as old as human groups. The childish rhyme above suggests that such differences in kind are also differences in quality: "We" are *better* than "they." It should be clear that ethnocentrism has played a large role in the history of our society and culture, and continues to play such a role. As a predominantly white society with a predominantly Christian culture, Americans are visible in the world picture as a minority of "haves" in a world of "have nots":[2]

> Only about one-third of the world population is white, but whites control about 70 percent of the total wealth.

> Only about one-third of the world's people are Christian; the other two-thirds is mostly Jewish, Moslem, Hindu, Buddhist, or professes no religious belief.

> Americans make up 6 percent of the world's population, but control nearly half of the world's wealth.

[1]Robert Louis Stevenson, "Foreign Children" in *Gaily We Parade,* John Edmund Brewton, ed. (New York: Macmillan, 1940), pp. 154–155.

[2] Adapted from Dr. Henry Leiper's "A Town Called World," *Read* XVI, No. 12 (February 15, 1967), pp. 10-13.

> Americans have a life expectancy of more than 70 years; the rest of the world less than 40 years.
>
> Americans (6 percent) produce about 16 percent of the world's food supply and eat all but 0.5 percent of it. (Americans have ten times more to eat than others in the world.)
>
> Americans use 10 times more electric power, 20 times more coal, 21 times more oil, 30 times more steel, and 30 times more general equipment than everyone else in the world.

Think for a moment about what might happen if we suddenly had to go without the oil, steel, and power on which our technology depends so heavily. How would this affect our current position of world leadership? How would the people of other nations think of us and feel about us? What if the nonwhites who are two-thirds of the world's population organized into an effective majority? How would whites feel then? Do you find such possibilities disturbing? If so, do you think it's because we're somehow *entitled* to our favored position—and one so immensely more favored than any other's? If you think so, why?

DOMINANT AND SUBORDINATE GROUPS

We are living in a world in which a minority racial group dominates. (Although it did not always; white peoples spent the first four-fifths of human history in comparatively primitive cultures while other ethnic groups flourished.) This domination by a minority is as characteristic of our society as it is of the rest of the world. White males are a numerical minority in our society, yet ours has always been a white, male-dominated society. Moreover, it has long been both racist and sexist, that is, discriminating against nonwhites and against women.

Racists and sexists are not merely aware of differences among races or between sexes; they also believe the differences are part of the basic inferiority of the other races or sex. In any society the dominant group regards itself as superior and frequently interacts with minority groups as inferiors.

Minority groups in such a dominant-subordinate relationship have cultural or physical traits that subject them to social, political, and economic discrimination by the dominant group. Members of minority groups are excluded from having full membership rights, privileges, and responsibilities in their society and so have poorer life chances (as we discussed in Chapter 7). In their book *Black Power,* Stokely Carmichael and Charles Hamilton defined racism as "the predication of decisions and policies on considerations of race for the purpose of subordinating a racial group."[3] Probably most members of the dominant group

[3]Stokely Carmichael and Charles Hamilton, *Black Power* (New York: Vintage Books, 1967), p. 3.

> **Select someone you know quite well (or yourself), and try to analyze this person's ethnocentric views. How prejudiced are they toward other races? Toward women? Toward men? Do they view others in stereotyped groups or as individuals judged by their own worth? Are their views similar to those of their own family members? How did these views evolve? How easy would they be to change? How would you suggest their trying to change them?**

would deny having anything to do with a *purposeful subordination* of a minority group, be it racial, sexual, or whatever. If pressed, they might admit to having inherited a system of policies based on the decisions of those before them or of those in power today.

RACISM: A SOCIAL CREATION

Because our socialization can prevent us from being fully aware of how we affect another person, we may put others down without even knowing it. As we found in Chapter 4 and elsewhere, socialization in childhood is a complex process, of which conscious teaching is only a part. So it is natural for members of a dominant group to pick up attitudes toward other groups without being aware of acquiring such attitudes.

To see whether you have attitudes about other groups that you're not aware of, we can look at a slice of majority–minority group relations from the viewpoints of numerous minority groups as mock-seriously compiled by the Foundation for Change, Inc.[4]

> Black is . . . going to court to be judged by a jury of your peers and finding that all your peers look bleached.
>
> Indian is . . . learning in school that your country was "discovered" by Christopher Columbus.
>
> Chicano is . . . learning in school that the pioneers "settled" the West 200 years after your ancestors were living there.
>
> Puerto Rican is . . . wondering why white tourists get brown on your island's beaches while you get pale in a mainland ghetto.
>
> A Racist, Southern Style is . . . someone who allows Blacks to live close as long as they don't get "uppity."
>
> A Racist, Northern Style is . . . someone who allows Blacks to get "uppity" as long as they don't live close.

[4]"Definitions of Racism," in *Viewpoint: Newsletter Series for Classroom Use* (New York: Foundation For Change, Inc., July 1972).

Our society is beginning to realize how deeply within it—its norms, values, and social institutions—the seeds of white racism are buried. Our thinking, our attitudes, our actions, and even our institutional structures force persons or groups to be systematically subordinated for physically insignificant but culturally quite significant characteristics such as skin color.

Even preschool children, whether black or white, learn to sort people by skin color and already begin to attach value judgments. Prejudiced racial attitudes are learned not only in the home or in small face-to-face groups, but also in the community and in broader experiences children have away from home. Once children have begun school they are exposed to numerous other influences on their behavior and thinking. Even if parents are unprejudiced, the school and the larger community can work against the parents' efforts.

Such a likelihood is compounded by the circumstances we saw in Chapter 10; there is little racial integration in our neighborhoods and schools. In segregated environments, children often learn attitudes toward minorities without any exposure to members of those minorities that could dispell those attitudes. In recent years legislation has been passed to revise the social structure of our institutions to provide equal opportunities for all groups and individuals. In practice, though, equal opportunity is frequently a myth. The white majority still dominates major social institutions and has the power to implement racially discriminating practices. When it uses this power, such a society is practicing white racism.

THE TWO FACES OF RACISM: INDIVIDUAL AND INSTITUTIONAL

Racism is either individual or institutional. Although we can describe the two forms separately, they go hand in glove. No society will be found with one form but not the other, although a society in the midst of reforming itself may manifest quicker success in reducing one than the other. *Individual racism* takes the form of acts by one or more individuals against individuals of another race; whereas *institutional racism* is built into our very institutions and therefore into the overall relations between the dominant race and the subordinate race or races. Acts of individual racism include such things as lynchings, bombings, and harassing minority group children newly integrated into a dominant-group school. Less violent but more frequent forms of behavior indicate how dominant-group members feel about minority group members—the names they are called by, the tone of voice in which they are spoken to, the reactions they often experience when they are in dominant group neighborhoods, and the like.

How do individual and institutional acts of racism differ? Which kind of racism is implicit in this photograph?

Institutional racism, on the other hand, is less open. No specific act can be singled out, for the entire circumstances of a minority group member's life may be the result of it. Evidence of such racism is revealed in segregated schools, churches, and housing; discriminatory practices in employment and promotion; and mass media and textbooks which, being controlled by whites, sometimes ignore or distort the role of minority group members.

Institutional racism usually operates through well-established and respected procedures. For this reason it is difficult to identify or even bring to public awareness, much less to change. Hence, as we found in Chapter 14, our large cities have ghettos where low-income minorities attempt to survive in spite of inadequate housing, food, clothing, income and other physical needs, not to mention unfulfilled social and psychological needs. Moreover, we saw in the chapter that these circumstances are both destructive to the ghettoized minorities

In a community with which you are familiar, select at least one type
of institutional racism—for example, housing. Determine whether or
not there is a law in this community that prohibits segregated
housing. Is there a state law that prohibits it? How well is this law
enforced? To what extent is institutional racism practiced in this
community with respect to housing? In other words, how common is
it for minority families to live in "white" suburbs and vice versa? Do
they feel welcome? In what ways?

and dangerous for the future of all society. The National Advisory Commission
on Civil Disorders, called to study the urban riots of 1967, reported in 1968 that:[5]

> Our nation is moving toward two societies, one black, one white—
> separate and unequal . . . but choice is still possible. . . . The alternative
> . . . is the realization of common opportunities for all within a single
> society. This alternative will require a commitment to national action.
> . . . From every American it will require new attitudes, new under-
> standings, and, above all, new will. . . .
>
> Segregation and poverty have created in the racial ghetto a destructive
> environment totally unknown to most white Americans. What white
> Americans have never fully understood—but what the Negro can never
> forget—is that white society is deeply implicated in the ghetto. White
> institutions created it, white institutions maintain it, and white society
> condones it.

White America did not agree. Only a few weeks after these findings were
made public, Gallup pollsters randomly asked 1500 white Americans, "Who do
you think is *more* to blame for the present conditions in which Negroes find
themselves—white people or Negroes themselves?"[6] As you may have surmised,
"Negroes themselves" were cited as the main cause (58 percent). Only 23 percent
blamed whites, and 19 percent had no opinion. Most whites denied any discrimination against blacks in their home communities. Most of those who blamed
whites for the present circumstances were college graduates, although only a
third of the college educated respondents blamed whites. We could conclude,
then, that[7]

---

[5]*Report of the National Advisory Commission on Civil Disorders* (Washington, D.C.: U.S. Government Printing
Office, 1968), pp. 1–2.

[6]The data reported here are from the *Gallup Opinion Index* (July 1968), pp. 17–22.

[7]Norval D. Glenn, "The Kerner Report, Social Scientists, and the American Public: Introduction to a Symposium,"
in Norval D. Glenn and Charles M. Bonjean, *Blacks in the United States* (San Francisco: Chandler Publishing
Co. 1969), p. 516.

In view of these data, it is not surprising that most whites expressed little sympathy for Negro participants in ghetto violence, and especially little sympathy for looters. Fifty–eight percent said police should shoot looters on sight—a position one is not likely to take if he feels that he, or a majority of whites, are to any great extent responsible for the behavior of the looters. . . . The feeling that whites owe Negroes a social debt for past wrongs appears to be very rare, even among the more liberal segments of the white lay public.

Even today this unsympathetic feeling prevails and is sometimes voiced in reaction to forced adoption of Affirmative Action plans (i.e., special efforts to hire blacks and other minorities to correct their absence from, or underrepresentation in, certain kinds of employment). Although social legislation is making some headway, minority groups still do not receive an equitable share of the social benefits of society. Such racism, both individual and institutional, severely restricts both the physical and psychological development of individuals.

THE LIFE CHANCES OF MINORITIES

Love of money may be the root of all evil, but having an adequate supply of it would help to remedy many problems of minorities; for being a member of a minority usually means being poor. In addition, as blacks and other minorities move into the inner cities, whites move out to the suburbs. The suburbs are as white as the ghettos are black: In 1960 three cities had more than a 50 percent black population, while in 1970, 16 did.[8]

Even with the same amount of education and training, black workers have always earned less than white workers. Table 15–1, presenting the median family income in 1970, indicates that this trend is still true. Despite legislation to the contrary, equal pay for equal work is not a reality in the United States for nonwhites.

TABLE 15–1. Median Family Income in 1970

Regions	Black	White	Black Income as % of White Income
United States	$6279	$10,236	61%
Northeast	7774	10,939	71
North Central	7718	10,508	73
South	5226	9240	57
West	8001	10,382	77

Source: U.S. Bureau of the Census, Report No. 2, *We the Black Americans* (Washington, D.C.: U.S. Government Printing Office, 1972).

[8]Bureau of the Census, Report No. 2, *We the Black Americans* (Washington, D.C.: U.S. Government Printing Office, July 1972), p. 4.

THE IMPACT OF POVERTY ON THE BLACK FAMILY

Black family incomes are less than those of whites because "black families are nearly three times as likely to be headed by a woman as white families. Husband-wife families, regardless of race, tend to have incomes double those of families headed by women."[9] Many low-income families are headed not just by the mother of the children, but by her mother and other female relatives who live together. Strong female family ties develop in many low-income families, often to the extent that even after a young woman marries she maintains stronger ties to her mother than to her husband. This is a form of "old age insurance" for the females of the family.

This family pattern is related chiefly to the economic status of minority members. When it comes to family situations the low-income male seems to have the greatest identity problem in our society—particularly if he is black. He sees himself at the bottom of the stratification scale with no hope of moving up. He earns too little to support a wife and children, yet he desires to marry and have children. His frequent failure in the husband-father role is further complicated when his children lose respect for his authority. Consequently, he often loses respect for himself and leaves the home or expresses his sexual prowess with other women. Many times the father may develop a more affectionate relationship with his children after he has left the family. But sometimes after his departure a series of other men may develop relationships with the mother and her family.

THE SCHOOLS: A PATH AND A BARRIER FOR NONWHITES

The socioeconomic sources of family disintegration among blacks are gradually becoming less severe. More blacks are finishing high school than in the past, and more of them are finding better-paying jobs. In 1960 only 36 percent of black males and 41 percent of black females finished high school, while in 1970 54 percent and 58 percent, respectively, did so.[10] Census data for 1970 show that the number of blacks in white-collar and skilled jobs was 72 percent higher than the 1960 figure.[11] Nevertheless, even though black men make up 10 percent of the total labor force, they are still a minor percentage of the professional labor force.

These improvements in black job status have come about partly through education and partly through the migration of many blacks from the low-wage areas of the South to the higher-wage areas of the North. Education is one of

[9]*We the Black Americans*, p. 7.
[10]*We the Black Americans*, p. 2.
[11]*We the Black Americans*, p. 8.

The low-income male seems to have the greatest identity problem in our society—particularly if he is black.

the institutions that incorporates racism into its policies and practices. For this reason, education is doing less than it can to improve black socioeconomic circumstances. Racial segregation of residential areas produces racially segregated schools, and little is being done to reduce either form of segregation today. The compromise solution of busing children across lines of residential segregation to produce integrated schools has been a source of extreme political controversy and some would like to see it abandoned.

In addition, even schools with an integrated student population can maintain a basic form of segregation (called *tracking*) that has significant consequences for the minority child's future. That is, students are assigned to their classes according to their tested abilities. But performance on tests cannot be separated from socialized attitudes toward education and toward oneself. Therefore, the practice of separating students on such grounds simply magnifies the problem; in effect students are told what the school thinks of them and what they should think of themselves. This segregation by testing ability—which usually produces segregation by socioeconomic class and by race—has the further devastating effect of depriving the slower students of the stimulation they can receive from the quicker ones. Research has proven that slower students generally benefit from

> **Select an organization with which you are familiar. What steps have they taken to reduce racism within their structure and policies? Do they provide equal opportunities for all persons (racial minorities, women, etc.) in their hiring, promotion and other personnel policies? Do they have an Affirmative Action plan, for instance, with goals to pursue hiring more minority group members?**

intermixture with more able students. In such situations slower students register measurably improved test scores and levels of motivation. Moreover, teachers who instruct classes of both capable and slower students tend to set higher expectations for all their students than if the class contained only slow learners.

This same benefit of "intellectual integration" is demonstrated by comparing segregated and desegregated schools, as Christopher Jencks did in one study:[12]

> Poor black sixth-graders in overwhelmingly middle-class schools were about 20 months ahead of poor black sixth-graders in overwhelmingly lower-class schools. Poor students in schools of intermediate socioeconomic composition fell neatly in between.

Yet even if schools and classrooms were both desegregated, equal educational opportunities for whites and nonwhites would not open up as easily as might be expected:[13]

> . . . white student achievement appears more closely to reflect parents' educational levels, whereas the scholastic performance of black students is more highly associated with parents' economic conditions. From this it is possible to infer that poverty factors, such as inadequate shelter, clothing, nutrition, and health care, may weigh so heavily upon a black child that there is only meager opportunity for parental educational factors to influence the child's school performance. . . . The policy implication of the above is that attempting to alleviate black students' poverty by means such as providing employment, health services, and other economically oriented programs to the family may be a necessary pre-condition for increasing school achievement.

Even though enforcement of social legislation in recent years has helped to raise the standards of nonwhite housing, wages, education, and the like, vast

[12]Frederick Mostellar and Daniel P. Moynihan, *On Equality of Educational Opportunity* (New York: Vintage Books, 1972), p. 87.

[13]James W. Guthrie and Thomas C. Thomas, "I. Policy Implications of the Coleman Report Reanalyses," *Phi Delta Kappan* (May 1973), p. 603.

inequalities still exist. Many whites feel that nonwhites should be pleased with the overall improvements. But nonwhites are not pleased because, compared with whites, they are still deprived. However far we have yet to go, the goal of equal opportunity no longer can be considered an impossibility; more progress will be made, for social legislation is changing our institutional structures.

THE SPECTRUM OF ETHNIC AND RACIAL RELATIONS

Relationships between dominant and minority social groups cover a broad range, from inhuman extermination of minorities to complete integration of groups as social equals. The dominant group may take from the subordinate group what they need or want: their farming skills, technology, or wealth. And then, regarding them as of no further use and possibly even a threat, the dominant group may gradually or swiftly annihilate them, as the American colonists and pioneers tried to do to the Indians, the Nazi Germans to the Jews, and the Nigerians to the Biafrans. Or instead of being put to death, minority groups may be put into slavery that deprives them of freedom but preserves their lives for their usefulness to the dominant group, as we find in our own history.

Closely related to subjugation are segregation and discrimination, which are not forms of slavery but of exploitation. Many of you are familiar with segregated schools, and your parents will remember segregated churches, restaurants, theaters, restrooms, drinking fountains, swimming pools, and parks. Accompanying such dominant–subordinate relations is a set of roles for each group to play in dealing with the other. The subordinate group can be expected to *act* subordinate, the dominant group to act dominant. Such role divisions were once much in evidence in our society. A Southern black man was not expected to feel insulted when called "boy" or, if he were elderly, "uncle." In the North such roles were far less obvious and less formalized, but a black knew better than to try to rent an apartment in a certain neighborhood, to apply for certain jobs, and the like.

Our own society, as we have seen, has reached a stage in which, however unevenly matched socioeconomically, the dominant and subordinate groups have entered into *competition* for the material and nonmaterial benefits of society. This stage will probably evolve into a *pluralist* stage, in which, after a period of unrest and change, groups may be distinguishable by ethnic cultural background but will be treated as equal to one another. Each group will at once maintain its own identity and fit into the larger society, as American Indians, chicanos, and blacks are now trying to do.

Protests and civil rights legislation of the 1960s began building into the social structure the right and opportunity for minority groups to be different yet equal.

Why does most of the domestic help in our society come from black and other minority groups? Does this photograph show dominant–subordinate relationships?

They are no longer segregated by law (although in many areas they still are by practice). Nonwhites can now legally attend the same schools, hold the same kinds of jobs, and earn the same amount of money as whites can. Whites still dominate American society, but if pluralism prevails they will become simply one of the many ethnic groups. Despite these changes, the culture of the larger society probably would continue to be dominated by white ethnic cultures, with other ethnic groups socializing their young into both their own subculture and that of the larger society.

Pluralism is one stage of *integration,* but in the recent past integration has come to mean *assimilation.* That is, two or more groups blend into one, which is what the early Northern European immigrants achieved gradually within our society. Hence, there can be confusion about what people mean when they advocate racial or ethnic integration. They can mean the right of equal opportunity for the same jobs, schools, and housing, or they can mean ever–increasing numbers of interracial marriages until two or more races have ceased to be distinguishable from one another.

Black Panthers demonstrating in New York City characterize the self-pride of minorities who feel that assimilation into the mainstream culture is not necessarily desirable.

There seems to be little support in our society for this last stage, racial assimilation, from either whites or nonwhites. As minority groups struggle to develop self-pride and their own identities, they show no interest in becoming culturally or racially different from what they are. The change they want is that society grant them their rights to equality. Yet integration even in this pluralist sense has come far more slowly and difficultly for racial minorities than for cultural minorities.

RACIAL CHARACTERISTICS: SKIN DEEP OR IN THE EYE OF THE BEHOLDER?

Perhaps the main reason that racial integration has been taking much longer than other forms—say, the integration of the Irish—is that black or brown or red or yellow skin sets a person noticeably apart from other members of society. The Irish Catholic looks much like the German Lutheran. Not so, however, with the black person, who also carries the stigma of the days of slavery and subjugation.

Usually we think of the primary races as three in number (Caucasoid, Mongoloid, and Negroid), with most people in the world being some combination of these. Despite such distinctions, enough intermarriage has taken place in the United States for many "blacks" to pass as "whites." In fact, the psychologist Earl Baughman holds that[14]

> . . . in biology, of course, cross–mating often produces a superior product, but racists refuse to consider such a possibility for "homo sapiens." White racists, for example, express the fear that interracial reproduction will lead to "mongrelization" of what they call the white race. In point of fact, however, geneticists have shown that completely random mating of American whites and blacks would result in the virtual elimination of the black American as we now know him. This is so, of course, because black Americans comprise only slightly more than 10% of the total population, and most blacks already have significant numbers of white genes. In the most basic sense, then, black racists have more to fear from a completely free mixing of the races than do white racists.

Perhaps it would be more accurate to use the term *social race* because society has developed the need to distinguish among races, has attached significance to differences such as in skin color, and has socialized its young to see these differences and attach meaning to them. There is one human species (and biologically one human race) as evidenced by the fact that no matter what our skin color and hair texture may be, our anatomies are identical. Furthermore, we can interbreed and produce offspring, while, say, a wolf and a fox cannot because they are not of the same species or genetic make–up.

Thus, all human beings are essentially the same, and the only racial differences pertain to inessentials like skin color, hair texture, and so forth. Moreover, even these superficial differences are only a matter of degree. For example, skin color is determined by two chemicals called carotene (yellow tinge) and melanin (brown tinge). Everyone except albinos has both of these chemicals in his or her skin, and the proportion of melanin and carotene determines color.

In a similar context, scientists have identified four main types of blood: A, O, B, and AB. These blood types do not determine race, nor does skin color determine blood type. All blood types are present in all racial groups in similar proportions, as are other physical factors such as height and shape of head. The shape of the head does not determine brain size, nor does brain size determine the degree of intelligence. (The world's largest brain belongs to an imbecile!)

[14]E. Earl Baughman, *Black Americans, A Psychological Analysis* (New York: Academic Press, 1971), p. 3.

Arthur R. Jensen, an educational psychologist from the University of California in Berkeley, presented evidence to support the thesis that a person's IQ is primarily determined by his genes. Many people proclaim him a racist, but because of his training in social science research, he cannot be completely ignored. Using Jensen's thesis (which you may want to research more completely), conduct a survey among students and faculty on campus to determine the number in each category that are for and against "Jensenism." You may want to conduct a similar survey off campus to determine any differences between academic and nonacademic persons.

THE MYTH OF RACIAL INTELLIGENCE

Some people, such as psychologist Arthur Jensen, believe that research findings show that whites and blacks have significantly different intellectual abilities which are genetically based.[15] The differences that do appear, however, have generally not been conclusively proven to have a genetic source. Most studies indicate that every racial group tends to fit the normal curve, having the bulk of its members within the "normal" range and smaller percentages at either extreme. These normal curves of the various racial groups overlap so much that no one group, white or other, can be proven innately more intelligent. Hence, there is no scientific justification, as some claim there is, for segregation in our schools because many nonwhite children are "smarter" than many white children, and vice versa. Although many nonwhites can score lower on IQ tests than whites, their unfamiliarity with the kinds of things being tested is the problem. It is reasonable to expect that an immigrant would have a lower IQ score when tested in America with American tests than when tested in his or her homeland.

If we could hold all other variables constant while we measure intelligence, there probably would be no significant differences between ethnic groups. The greatest differences would be among income groups. For this reason it is unfair to compare IQ scores of middle income and low income persons, especially because IQ tests relate mainly to middle class standards foreign to those in low income groups. What, in fact, we are measuring is innate intelligence plus what has happened to us since our birth. Since nonwhites in America have poorer life chances, might we not expect them to have poorer scores on IQ tests too?

[15]A. R. Jensen, "How Much Can We Boost IQ and Scholastic Achievement?", *Harvard Educational Review* 39 (1969) 1–123.

TRENDS AMONG U.S. MINORITY GROUPS

Nonwhites are not genetically inferior to whites. Even so, they have continued to lag behind whites year after year as a result of differences in income, education, housing, cultural advantages, and other such opportunities. Many people claim that nonwhites are solely responsible for their circumstances. After all, once this nation was established every immigrant group except the English was discriminated against and stereotyped as inferior when it first came to our shores. Yet they all proved themselves through their own efforts and came to be fully accepted. Why, for instance, didn't the blacks work hard to make a good life for themselves like our forefathers of only a few generations ago? The answer is that some doors were not open to them. Black people became a free people too late to reap the benefits of a good living, much to the relief of many immigrants and working class people who feared the end of slavery as the beginning of fierce competition for jobs. The big cities no longer had an abundance of jobs requiring little or no skills that were waiting for the early immigrants. And, of course, few blacks had the skills that many immigrants had brought with them from their native country. In addition, many blacks, skilled or not, were the unfortunate victims of racial discrimination. For slavery can be justified only by a belief that the slave is innately inferior, somehow not really human. Such a belief was not found only in the South, nor was it erased anywhere simply by freeing the slaves. Machines do many jobs today, so when the unskilled black, Puerto Rican, or Indian migrates to the city in search of a better life, he or she finds instead unemployment and poverty.

As a social force minorities were once all but invisible. When they were noticed it was only to persuade them to hurry their assimilation into the American culture—unless, of course, they were racially undesirable. Some groups tried without invitation and failed. Blacks, many Mexican Americans and Puerto Ricans are examples. Others, like the American Indian, refused to become assimilated. In recent years those who once tried but failed have worked energetically to revive their own identities and restore their consciousness of their roots. We can look briefly at how this process works for each minority group and how it affects the group's relation to the larger society.

INDIAN AMERICANS

Few people learn in school exactly how much the Europeans assimilated American Indian agriculture, both for survival here by the early colonists and for new ideas back in Europe. Some people jokingly allow that Squanto was the first County Agricultural Agent in the new world. (A county agent is a government

The automobile parked beside a teepee illustrates a dilemma of American Indians today—How much of the "white" culture do they really want?

worker whose job is to advise the farmers and other growers in a county about agriculture and to pass on new practical knowledge and ideas.)

Few Indian Americans voluntarily converted to Christianity. To make matters worse, they did not believe in ownership of land. For these two reasons, among others, the settlers and pioneers found it easy to justify pushing the Indians aside in pursuit of land. After all, they were savages who refused to see the good and the right even when it was presented to them by missionaries. We still send missionaries, teachers, government agents, and even soldiers to help "civilize" the Indians. Until recently we sent their children off to distant boarding schools for long periods of time, where they would forget their native language, customs, and ceremonies. Now we just bus them to white schools where they do not learn anything very positive about their own heritage.

As the American Indians say, the government is spending millions of dollars to *change* them, not to *help* them. They remain the poorest of all minority groups. Some Indians have tried to become assimilated into the larger culture, and a few have succeeded. Others have not been completely accepted and live on the fringes of both groups. Some quietly survive, practicing their traditional ways, while others protest loudly, and even violently, for the right to be both Indian and American.

People of Mexican extraction, both legal residents and illegal aliens, still make up the bulk of farm laborers in Southwestern states.

As a group, the American Indians have assimilated the material culture of our society, but still cling to their own nonmaterial culture, their own philosophy of life. They have some special rights that other American citizens do not have because our government has always treated Indian reservations as parts of an autonomous nation. Many Indians still live in tribal communities and are fighting to maintain them. After all, such communities represent their tradition, their identity, and for good reason. If they were to be assimilated, their tribal communities would disappear into history. They would lose their own identity.

MEXICAN AMERICANS

The 1970 Census counted five million Mexican Americans, but members of this minority group believe that twice this number are living primarily in the Southwest. After the Mexican War, about 70,000 people who were a mixture of Indian and Spanish automatically became part of the United States territory. Traditionally they were farmers or ranchers, having been well–established in these vocations more than 200 years before the European settlers arrived in the West. Again we borrowed from their culture, learning much about ranching and farming, and adopting their words into our language, words like *rodeo, corral, bronco,* and many others. Over the years Mexican Americans have farmed and followed the harvests as migrant farm laborers. Those who dropped out of the migrant agricultural labor force sought employment in large cities like Chicago, or settled in Wisconsin, Michigan, Washington, Oregon, and Florida in addition to the major concentration in the Southwest. These Mexican Americans exchanged their problems as rural migrant laborers for those of an underprivileged urban minority group. Overall, Americans of Mexican descent have become so fragmented that it is difficult to generalize about them.

Much like the rest of society, the Mexican American minority in Southern California, for instance, has changed with the times from the traditional folk culture to a more urbanized one that is moving toward middle class status.[16] In the process the traditional family structure has been weakened and juvenile delinquency has become a problem. Mexican Americans lagged behind in education because many clung to Spanish as the first language, in conflict with the old, uniform educational policy in our society that English is the primary language. (This policy is losing favor in many culturally mixed parts of the country, and many court decisions are helping it on its way to extinction.)

Today many Mexican immigrants come from the middle class of the more industrialized sections of Mexico. Most of these immigrants who settle in the urban neighborhoods of Southern California fit into blue collar and white collar jobs. Along with veterans of World War II and later wars who attended college on the GI Bill and went on to professional jobs, these new, middle class immigrants are breaking down social barriers. In recent years more and more well-trained Mexican American professionals have been returning to positions of leadership in the old Mexican American neighborhoods, or *barrios*, where they help to solve the long-standing problems of their people. The picture for this minority group is beginning to brighten somewhat—in Southern California, at least. Only time will tell whether they will become accepted and fully assimilated like other nationality groups, or, since their motherland is so close by, whether they will retain their own heritage and remain a minority group in a pluralistic America.

PUERTO RICANS

Puerto Ricans have many of the same hardships of other minorities. Most live in the ghetto areas of New York City, to which they have been migrating for over half a century to escape the hardships of their homeland, a Caribbean island under partial U.S. control. Their heritage is a mixture of Taino Indian, Spanish, and Black African; some have French, Italian, and Irish ancestry from later settlements on the island. Much like Mexican Americans, the Puerto Ricans

[16]Fernando Penalosa, "The Changing Mexican-American in Southern California," in *Majority and Minority*, ed. Norman R. Yetman and C. Hoy Steele (Boston: Allyn & Bacon, 1971), pp. 321-333.

have tried to better themselves through education, hoping to enter medical and other professions so they can help their own people better themselves both in Puerto Rico and on the mainland. But often poverty is too great an obstacle and they, too, suffer from poor education, high unemployment rates, and racial prejudice.

JAPANESE AMERICANS

This national and racial group suffered much discrimination during World War II when they were bodily evacuated from the Pacific Coast and placed in relocation camps. It was claimed that because so many of them lived on the coast they were potential collaborators with the Japanese military, yet no grounds for such expectations were ever established. Furthermore, many Japanese Americans had been born in this country, and—perhaps bitterest of all ironies—many of the families in the camps had sons who were fighting and dying in the American armed forces. Because no German American or Italian American was ever placed in such a camp, or even forced to move away from either coast, the conclusion is inescapable that this was an episode of racist hysteria, pure and simple. Consequently, Japanese Americans were expected to have a difficult adjustment period after their release as a result of strong anti–Oriental prejudices and discrimination on the West Coast. To avoid this difficulty many Japanese Americans migrated eastward to large metropolitan areas. Yet they were traditionally small farmers, and their culture was considered to be alien to the majority; so again problems were anticipated.

Fortunately, the expected problems were rare, partly because the Eastern communities did not have a built-in rejection of the Orientals. In fact, research on Japanese Americans in the Chicago area indicated they were well accepted by their neighbors, employers, landlords, and most other middle class Americans with whom they interacted. Most Japanese Americans completed high school, went on to college or vocational training, and held professional or skilled jobs that were respected in the community.

Research shows that while there are marked differences in the American middle class and the Japanese cultures, both share many basic values and norms: "politeness, respect for authority and parental wishes, duty to community, diligence, cleanliness and neatness, emphasis on personal achievement of long–range goals, importance of keeping up appearances and others."[17] Not only are Japanese and middle class American values and goals similar, so are their personality developments. Both are highly sensitive to cues from others and adapt their behavior accordingly by suppressing their real emotions. Thus, even though some factors were working against the Japanese Americans (racial visibility, alien

---

[17]William Caudill and George DeVos, "Achievement, Culture and Personality: The Case of the Japanese Americans" in *Majority and Minority*, ed. Norman R. Yetman and C. Hoy Steele (Boston: Allyn & Bacon, 1971), pp. 302–303.

A family of Japanese Americans stoically waits to be relocated to a detention camp in California during World War II.

culture, and a general American prejudice against foreigners), the compatibility of the Japanese and the American middle class value systems allowed them to find their niche, just as such similarities have helped Chinese, Filipino, and other Orientals living in America.

AMERICAN JEWS

In an ethnological sense the Jews have held a confused position in the world. They were once considered by many to be a race, then later to be a dispersed nation (which is historically correct). They are, in fact, many nationalities, and people of every social race include Jews among them. Jews are simply people who adhere to the Jewish religion or to its concomitant cultural traditions. They combine ancient values and norms with the folkways and mores of their countries of birth or adoption.

Discrimination against Jews extends far back into history. For centuries European Christians maintained a vicious stereotype of them. They were rigidly controlled as to where they could live, how they could earn a living, and with whom they could mingle. Although they settled all over Europe, for centuries they were so carefully isolated that little intermingling took place with the dominant group until the preceding century or so. For these and other reasons the Jews developed a separatist urban history and became proficient in managing their own small businesses. They arrived in the United States in large numbers at just the right time to benefit from their specialized background. Many quickly moved into middle and upper middle class positions, despite prejudice and discrimination.

In recent decades Jews have experienced less discrimination in our society, although prejudice and stereotyping have been resistant to extinction. The probable cause for their improved status is the greater feeling of ecumenism among religious believers, and the overall decline in the importance of religion in our society. For the prejudice against the Jews seems to have been based chiefly on religious grounds. The Jews had rejected the divinity of Jesus Christ, and, so it was vulgarized, had betrayed him by calling for his execution by the Romans. Other elements of the Jewish stereotype were likewise the creation of the dominant group, the Christians. Jews were considered "unclean" (spiritually) for the reasons just given, so Jews were restricted to occupations that were apparently necessary to the economy but perilous to the Christian soul. Thus, from being forced into these trades and occupations, the Jews later acquired the stereotype of greed and obsession with money.

BLACKS

Blacks comprise the largest minority group in America. When race, discrimination, prejudice, or minority group are mentioned, blacks usually come to mind because "you name it, they've had it." Judith Kramer summarizes the plight of the American black community in one sentence: "Without a communal ideology to define an independent identity there can only be socialization into the nonidentity of personal invisibility and racial visibility."[18] That is, the black minority group has no identifiable culture or heritage of their own that is acceptable to them. Before their ancestry of slavery they had a "pagan," primitive tribal culture that most American blacks cannot identify with. Besides, this culture can't be transported from the past and from the African continent to our society, rural or urban, any more than a German American could transport the culture of the nomadic hordes that wandered pre–Christian Europe. Thus, parents have no cultural heritage to hold up for their young.

Ironically, before a minority group can become acculturated into the larger society it must first have a culture of its own. The culture that blacks once had was traumatically torn from them and systematically broken down during their many generations of slavery. But when they tried to take on the culture of the larger society they began to see themselves as inferior beings—for why else were they slaves? The recent emergence of free African nations, coupled

[18]Judith R. Kramer, *The American Minority Community* (New York: Thomas Y. Crowell, 1970), pp. 214–215.

"Soul" expresses the achievements of the lower class way of life:
the dignity, strength, courage, and shrewdness to survive.

with Black Nationalism, Black Power, and other such movements has helped
many blacks to begin to identify with a living, usable tradition. As Kramer says,
this "communal ideology" would lend support and meaning to a person's life
so he or she might better "define an independent identity."

Until such a "communal ideology" is established, as Kramer says, black people
are not seen as individuals. They are given a categorical status, based upon
their skin color (their "racial visibility"), and are judged by this minority group
status and stereotype rather than by their own merits. Before long, even people
with untapped resources and abilities may begin to hold themselves in the low
esteem of their racial stereotypes.

One sign that a positive self–identity is developing among blacks was the
popular emergence, beginning a few years ago, of the notion of "soul." "Soul"

idealizes the achievements and superiority of the lower class way of life: the dignity, strength, courage, and shrewdness required to survive in a ghetto of a racist society, combined with compassion and loyalty for one's "brothers and sisters." Notions like "soul" and "black pride," and slogans like "black is beautiful" can be the prelude to forming a personal identity. Whatever their limitations as guides for action, they acknowledge the black person's wounds and the strength that has enabled black people to have survived for so long. They help to undo some of the injuries to self-identity that come from being treated as a "personal invisibility."

We have found that one detail in the pattern of human interaction encompassed by a society can be the failure or the refusal to interact, as happens when a dominant racial or ethnic group treats members of a subordinate group according to stereotypes. If we treat a person as a stereotype of his or her race, religion, nationality, or sex, we are denying that person's individual identity. And if members of a dominant group treat every member of another subordinate group by the stereotype they were socialized to hold, the individual reality of every one of those people has been denied. Until a few decades ago, and then changing only slowly, such was the history of racial and ethnic relations in our society. Although not every society has at all times had subordinate minority groups—primitive tribal societies, for example, have usually been quite homogeneous—every known society has had to deal with some form of *deviancy*, behavior that strays too far from the culture's norms to be tolerated. What constitutes deviant behavior differs from society to society, as does how it is handled, but the occurrence of deviancy itself seems universal. The next chapter examines this social phenomenon at length.

SUMMARY POINTS AND QUESTIONS

1. Minority groups are defined as social aggregates with distinctive cultural or physical traits. These traits serve as a basis for discrimination.

> *Who defines these distinctive traits?*
>
> *How important are these traits? How do you define important in this context?*

2. Racial attitudes are often deeply embedded in the norms, literature, laws, and institutions of a society. They are passed from generation to generation through the process of socialization.

> *How is it possible to change the content of socialization so that negative racial attitudes are eliminated?*

CULTURE-FREE SOCIAL RESEARCH:
THE IMPOSSIBLE DREAM?

"All men are created equal" has been the source of abiding confusion and controversy. What does the statement mean? With equal rights before the law? With equal talents, abilities, and intelligence? The writers of the Declaration of Independence had the first meaning in mind. The second meaning seems to be unconsciously held by many Western intellectuals. In this view our intelligence is determined by our upbringing, not by our genes.

Few people completely dismiss heredity as a factor in intelligence, but most people give it far less importance than much evidence seems to warrant. As only one example, identical twins who are raised separately show IQs much closer to their parents' than to their foster parents', and much closer to their twin's than to their foster brothers' and sisters'.

The question of the components of intelligence is surrounded by controversy. This controversy was fanned to fury in 1969 when Arthur Jensen published an article in which he claimed that blacks' intelligence was, on the average, somewhat lower than whites' intelligence. The reason, Jensen maintained, is more hereditary than environmental. It has long been known that IQ tests are culturally biased—that they favor members of certain social classes over others. So differences between blacks and whites in tested intelligence have been attributed to cultural bias.

Jensen tried to correct for such bias in several ways. He compared blacks and whites of the same income, occupational, or educational level. The difference was narrower than the overall average difference, but it was there. He tried constructing "culture-free" (as opposed to culturally biased) tests. The tested differences between black and white children increased as the tests became more abstract. Some of Jensen's critics view culture-free tests as an impossibility: Removing obviously cultural questions like "Who wrote Faust?" only appears to remove culture. These critics claim that certain abilities, such as using abstractions, are themselves culturally based.

Jensen did not publish his report to make trouble. He was suggesting certain reforms in education to improve the learning of blacks and other culturally disadvantaged students. The controversy that he unwittingly began is extremely complex and has not yet been brought to any conclusion, so certainly no judgments can be made here. But one question for further study that has been raised by the controversy is whether social scientists themselves can ever escape their cultural bias.

3. Two types of racism are *individual* racism, which involves an overt act by one or more individuals against some other individuals of another racial group, and *institutionalized* racism, which is covert and found within institutionalized practices, norms, and laws.

> *What are some historical examples of individual racism?*
>
> *Of institutionalized racism?*
>
> *Why is institutionalized racism covert?*

4. The life chances of minority groups are impaired by such factors as economic discrimination, the failure of educational institutions to provide equality of opportunity, and the ghetto conditions in which minority groups often live.

> *How does each of these factors operate to reduce life chances of minority group numbers?*
>
> *How are the factors interrelated?*

5. The relationship between dominant and subordinate groups may take several forms. These include annihilation, subjugation, segregation and discrimination, competition, pluralism, and integration.

> *How would you define each of these forms?*
>
> *How do they work?*

6. Although race is defined in terms of physical traits, the traits which are selected as distinctive differ from society to society and over historical time.

> *Why did race ever become a factor affecting relationships between persons?*
>
> *Who benefits from a situation in which one group is defined as racially different?*

7. Three distinct minority groups that have not been assimilated into American society are the American Indians, the Mexican Americans and the Puerto Ricans.

> *What specific reasons can you give for the failure of each of these groups to be assimilated in American society?*
>
> *What particular problems does each of the groups face?*

8. On the other hand, Japanese Americans and American Jews have become assimilated more rapidly than other minority groups.

> *What distinctive cultural traits have aided these groups in becoming part of the mainstream of American society?*
>
> *What problems do they still face?*

9. Blacks make up the largest minority group in the United States. Usually when we think of racism, we think in terms of black–white relationships.

> *What directions has black culture been taking?*

10. In the past decade, Americans have been becoming more aware of racial discrimination resulting in certain changes in American institutions.

> *What major changes are taking place?*
>
> *In what areas has there been little change?*

SUGGESTED READINGS

Brown, Claude. *Manchild in the Promised Land.* New York: Macmillan, 1966. An autobiography about the author's experience in growing up in Harlem.

Burma, John. *Mexican–Americans in the United States.* Cambridge, Mass.: Schenkman, 1970. A collection of essays on the relationship of Mexican–Americans to American social, political, economic, and cultural institutions.

Fanon, Frantz. *Black Skins, White Masks.* New York: Grove Press, 1967. A study of the psychological problems that the black man experiences living in a white world. This study is accomplished by dealing with literature, dreams and case histories.

Fitzpatrick, Joseph. *Puerto Rican Americans.* New York: Random House, 1971. A book about Puerto Ricans in New York City. It specifically centers on the events and the meaning of migration both to the migrants and the neighborhoods they enter.

Himes, Joseph. *Racial and Ethnic Relations.* Dubuque, Iowa: William C. Brown, 1974. A general work on minorities. It covers minority and dominant group relationships, minority subcultures, and political policy aimed at intergroup relations.

Levine, Stuart and Nancy Lurie, eds. *The American Indian Today.* Deland, Fla.: Everett Edwards, 1968. Essays on the culture and the values of American Indians, the conflict between these values and those of the dominant culture, and the Indians' attempt to preserve their heritage.

Lewis, Oscar. *La Vida.* New York: Random House, 1965. An intensive study of one Puerto Rican family. Uses this as a vehicle for understanding the conditions of poverty both in San Juan and New York City, and the specific problems that the Puerto Rican faces.

Lincoln, C. Eric. *The Black Muslims in America.* Boston: Beacon Press, 1961. Discusses the rise of Black nationalism and the relationship of the Black Muslims to the black community.

Myrdal, Gunnar. *An American Dilemma, Vols. I and II.* New York: Harper & Row, 1944. An analysis of the American social structure and normative structure, and the role in which it places the black. It points out the contradiction of the ideal of equality and the status of the black.

Petersen, William. *Japanese–Americans.* New York: Random House, 1971. Discusses the migration of Japanese to the United States, the problems they faced such as dual nationality and incarceration during WW II, and their attempt to become an integrated part of American Society.

Yaffe, James. *The American Jews.* New York: Random House, 1968. Presents an interesting discussion on Jewish culture and values and their operation within American society. Deals with various myths about Jews, the merchant image, and the problems of survival faced by Judaism.

What do a longhair member of a rural Oregon commune, a catatonic schizophrenic, a bank robber, a heroin addict, and a homosexual have in common in our society? They're all deviants. What creates a deviant? Society does, by deciding what behavior is tolerable and what is not. What makes some people behave in such ways? Sociologists lack any single theory that answers for all forms of deviance. And no theory explains why some people become deviants and others don't. But three theories answer some questions about deviancy: The anomic theory traces it to a misfit between cultural ends and institutional means; the deviant subculture theory supposes that alternative values and norms sway some people; and labeling theory suggests that people who think themselves normal but are caught in so-called deviant acts are labeled deviant and then assume the deviant role.

16

DEVIANCY: GOING BEYOND
THE NORM

". . . And how do you know that you're mad?"

"To begin with," said the Cat, "a dog's not mad. You grant that?"

"I suppose so," said Alice.

"Well, then," the Cat went on, "you see a dog growls when it's angry and wags its tail when it's pleased. Now *I* growl when I'm pleased, and wag my tail when I'm angry. Therefore I'm mad."

Lewis Carroll

Lewis Carroll was not a psychologist nor a sociologist, so we'll never know why the Cheshire Cat began his reasoning from the premise that "a dog's not mad." Was the Cat simply being good-natured and giving his long-time natural foe the benefit of the doubt? Or was everyone in Wonderland socialized to believe that a wagging tail expresses pleasure and a growl means anger? Or were such norms, like everything else in Wonderland, established arbitrarily? Probably this last likelihood is the case. In fact, Wonderland is such a hectic, arbitrary place, populated by lunatic, unpredictable people, that the only true deviant there was Alice herself.

She was not deviant in her own society, though, and a second look at the Cat's reasoning will show us why. Deviancy is a social creation: What is deviant in a society is simply whatever behavior or characteristics depart sufficiently from norms to exceed the tolerance of that society. (Here the comparison with Wonderland breaks down: The reasons for punishing people in that society are as arbitrary and unpredictable as everything else there.) Alice is deviant in Wonderland because she is sane, because she assumes that people have reasons for their behavior and she persists in trying to find them. In our society such an assumption and such efforts at understanding are not deviant. (If they were deviant, sociologists would be found in asylums instead of on college campuses.)

DEVIANCY A UNIVERSAL SOCIAL TRAIT

No human society escapes deviancy; within each society some individuals cannot or will not conform to its behavioral expectations. As Simon Dinitz puts it:

> For whatever reasons, some persons act, at times at least, in so bizarre, eccentric, outlandish, abhorrent, dangerous, or merely unique and annoying a manner that they cannot readily be tolerated. Thus, every society must somehow deal with its saints and sinners, its kooks and clowns, and its dependent, disruptive, inadequate, and aberrant members.[1]

You can see that all the adjectives Dinitz uses to describe intolerable behavior express a value judgment or social definition: They are not simply descriptive terms; rather they describe a *judgment* of some behavior rather than the behavior itself.

Not all forms of behavior that stray from the norms of society are necessarily considered deviant by that society. Different societies tolerate different aberrations, and the same society may tolerate an act at one time but not at another. Killing and plundering are deviant sometimes but not at other times. Behavior that expresses what we call "mental illness" may be thought of by other societies as rare but acceptable supernatural abilities.

THE SOCIAL CATEGORIES OF DEVIANCY

Society, then, defines as deviant any forms of unusual behavior that are undesirable. Having defined some behavior as deviant, societies attempt to prevent such behavior by socialization. If deviancy occurs, societies try to prevent its recurrence by punishing the deviant individual.

Because deviancy is as much a form of social behavior as conforming to norms is, it has been much studied by sociologists. They have sought to understand how it comes about, what its social or group bases are, and how the frequency of certain types of deviant behavior is related to conditions within a society. In all these efforts sociologists have experienced somewhat less success than in their studies of other areas of social interaction. Perhaps part of the problem is the method of categorizing deviancy that sociologists have inherited from presociological efforts to explain such behavior. The two major categories are the deviant as criminal and as sick. A third category, the deviant as dropout, has also become pertinent to our times.

[1] Simon Dinitz et al., eds., *Deviance: Studies in the Process of Stigmatization and Societal Reaction* (New York: Oxford University Press, 1969), p. 3.

Police still spend many man hours arresting those who commit victimless crimes. Do you think prostitution should be decriminalized?

THE DEVIANT AS A CRIMINAL

Some behavior is deviant because it violates criminal law—whether an offense against a person such as murder, rape, or assault, or an offense against property such as theft or destruction through vandalism or neglect.[2] Because by this standard a deviant is anyone who commits a crime the frequency of that criminal act does not affect the definition. Even if many people cheat on their income taxes or smoke marijuana, these acts are still crimes and therefore are deviant. Thus, by this definition, even if a given act were statistically "normal" (that is, committed by an overwhelming majority of those in a society) it is still deviant.

Some crimes have victims; other crimes do not.[3] Crimes against persons or property, or in which someone has been hurt or wronged, have victims. Homosexual acts, or heterosexual prostitution, between consenting adults, use or abuse

[2]For an elaboration of this point see Mark Lefton et al., eds., *Approaches to Deviancy* (New York: Appleton-Century-Crofts, 1968), pp. 46–48.

[3]Edwin M. Schur, *Crimes Without Victims* (Englewood Cliffs, N.J.: Prentice-Hall, 1965).

of drugs, and gambling do not properly have victims. Nonetheless, they are crimes. Thus, our society treats some forms of behavior as intolerable whether someone else has suffered involuntarily from that behavior. In effect, then, criminal behavior is deviant simply because it is defined as such on the statute books. Other forms of behavior are deviant for a different reason: because they presumably express, or symptomize, something deviant within the person.

THE DEVIANT AS SICK

There is nothing illegal about going into a catatonic trance, or believing yourself to be a famous historical person and acting accordingly, or changing your mood from great excitement to severe depression. These forms of behavior are considered to be symptoms of mental illness and are judged to be socially disruptive or possibly dangerous and thus deviant.[4]

Unlike criminal deviants, the mentally ill are not held responsible for their actions; they are considered "sick." Some forms of behavior have remained deviant but have changed their categories of deviancy. Alcoholism is generally considered a sickness rather than a crime,[5] as is homosexuality, although state legislatures allow it to remain a crime. The dual social status of homosexuality as both a crime and a sickness is further complicated because gay people in general do not consider themselves sick and in need of treatment. Although some physicians and lay people continue to define homosexuality as pathological, many are changing their views. In 1974 a body of psychiatrists decided by vote that homosexuality was no longer to be considered a sickness.

The deviant–as–sick model assumes that we can distinguish the mentally sick from the well, but there is some doubt that we always can.[6] Psychiatrists often differ on diagnoses. To cite a bizarre example, psychiatrist D. L. Rosenhan conducted a participant observation experiment in which eight sane persons had themselves admitted to different mental hospitals by falsely complaining that they had been hearing voices.[7] Seven were diagnosed as schizophrenic, one as manic depressive. Once admitted, these persons acted their normal selves while in the wards; their only deception had been their initial false claims. They spent their time in the wards observing and taking notes. Yet in no case was their deception detected by doctors, nurses, or ward attendants, although 35 of the 118 "real" patients on the ward of one hospital suspected that the pseudo-

---

[4]Dinitz, pp. 16–18.

[5]Elwin M. Jellinek, *The Disease Concept of Alcoholism* (New Haven: Hill House Press, 1960).

[6]Szasz makes the point that some of those labeled mentally ill are simply troublesome persons who lack the power to stay out of mental hospitals. See Thomas Szasz, *The Myth of Mental Illness* (New York: Harper & Row, 1961); and also his *The Manufacture of Madness* (New York: Dell, 1970).

[7]D. L. Rosenhan, "On Being Sane in Insane Places," *Science* 179 (January 19, 1973), 250–258.

Deviant behavior is often the major subject in novels and movies. Using a novel or a movie in which a deviant is the hero or antihero, describe how deviancy is portrayed, show how the central character comes into conflict with society, and show how this conflict is resolved.

---

patient was not sick. In fact, one patient came close to the truth by asserting that the pseudopatient was not crazy but was a professor checking up on hospitals. The hospital staff observing the same behavior recorded it as "persistent obsessive note-taking behavior." What the patients considered sane behavior the staff considered mentally deranged. The so-called sick were pretty good diagnosticians. The discharge records of the incorrectly diagnosed schizophrenics bore the notation "schizophrenia in remission." In other words, these normal people were still considered mentally ill when they left the hospitals.

Are such behaviors as hallucination, anxiety, depression, and mental anguish sufficiently different from normal behavior to make the diagnosis "mental illness" meaningful? Extreme cases such as the catatonic who remains in a trancelike condition for months are clearly distinguishable from normal kinds of behavior, but others are not so clear. Yet less extreme cases that are labeled mental illness do not guarantee that the person is much different from other people. The sick may not *really* be deviant; that is, such individuals may not exhibit behavior that is very different from behavior of the average person.

SOCIAL DROPOUTS AS DEVIANTS

Not all types of deviancy in the United States are considered neatly either criminal or sick. Some are considered both, such as the "criminally insane." Homosexuality is by some or possibly many viewed as a sickness, while in most states homosexual behavior is still against the law and thus criminal. Compulsive gambling can be considered both a sickness and a crime.

Still other types of behavior are defined as socially undesirable but are neither crimes nor sicknesses. Alienated people, mostly young, who reject the "straight" life and seek escape in a rural commune are considered by many to be deviants (as were hobos years ago when they were numerous). Their deviancy lies in their basic values and life style, which are at odds with the dominant culture. These differences produce feelings of distrust, suspicion, and sometimes fear in members of the larger society. The behavior of such alienated individuals is considered odd, strange, or wrong, and therefore deviant.

Nothing deviant about living in the country. But the life style and values of some who do are thought deviant by others.

Many people hold that those who choose alternate life styles and values are responsible for their behavior. They feel that the values of the dominant culture were rejected voluntarily by those who could have chosen to accept them. Others sense that such rejections may have roots in some profound difficulties in the larger society. There is no agreement among sociologists on what theory explains why deviancy in its various forms occurs.

SOCIAL THEORIES OF DEVIANCY

Sociologists rely most heavily on three theories to explain deviancy: the anomic theory, the deviant subculture theory, and the labeling theory. As we shall discover, no one of the theories fully explains deviancy, and each provides some element of explanation that the others lack.

THE THEORY OF ANOMIE

In his study of different rates of suicide in the late 1890s the French sociologist Emile Durkheim used the concept *anomie*—literally translated, "normlessness," the condition of being without norms.[8] Durkheim discovered that *rates* of suicide could be linked to social conditions, to confusion and contradiction in norms and roles, such as during wars or otherwise politically or economically unsettled times. Such suicides he named *anomic* suicides, for they were related to anomie.

Another sociologist, Robert K. Merton, later adapted the concept of anomie to describe a condition in a society or a social system in which the culturally shared goals do not fit together with the institutionalized means for achieving the goals.[9] The disharmony between cultural goals and institutional means has two chief sources: The institutional means for achieving the cultural goals either are confused and ambiguous or are inaccessible.

In the first case, the goal becomes so important that the accepted institutional means are abandoned. Recent American history has shown many instances of this form of anomie, from the Watergate scandals in which electoral victory was sought at the price of democratic norms that elected officials are sworn to uphold, to cases of gigantic stock and insurance frauds on the scale of many millions of dollars.

In the second case, when means to achieving goals are inaccessible to some groups, the lower classes in our society may accept the goal of economic success but find themselves unable to get or keep jobs that will allow them to reach the goal. Early in their working lives many people learn that they will never be able to consume goods and services at anything close to rates of other, successful people.

Thus, the condition of anomie is a confusion about norms. The anomie theory holds that the greater the degree of anomie within a society, the more individuals will turn to deviant behavior as a way out of the difficult situation. The deviant behavior could take different, broad forms, depending on the kind of disharmony between means and ends, and social reactions to it.[10] Merton has described four strategies for meeting anomic conditions. The first strategy he calls *innovation*.

Part of the American dream is economic success. Society holds out this goal to all but withholds the means for achieving the goal from many. Some people who accept the goal but find the means to achieve it blocked adopt new and culturally disapproved means of achieving the goal. Merton calls this activity

[8]Emile Durkheim, *Suicide: A Study in Sociology* ed., George Simpson (New York: Free Press, 1951).

[9]For a discussion of anomie and the various reactions to it see Robert K. Merton, *Social Theory and Social Structure* (New York: Free Press, 1968), Chs. 6 and 7.

[10]See studies in Marshall B. Clinard, ed., *Anomie and Deviant Behavior* (New York: Free Press, 1964); and Richard A. Cloward, "Illegitimate Means, Anomie and Deviant Behavior," *American Sociological Review* 24 (April 1959), 164–176.

In Merton's concept of anomie, the wino and hobo are retreatists—they are unwilling or unable to live by the rules of the majority society.

innovation. Some crime and juvenile delinquency can best be understood as a subgroup's reaction to frustration, for the young or the poor want the same things that middle and upper class people want, money and what it can buy.

Cheating in college is no doubt motivated by an acceptance of the goal but not the means. The ultimate goal of a college degree and intermediate ones of receiving passing grades are accepted, but anything goes to reach these goals. Perhaps the course is defined as irrelevant or a "mere requirement." Or the instructor may unwittingly encourage cynicism about approved means by stressing the value of independent thinking or the mastery of general principles while suggesting the opposite by the trivia on his tests. Although the approved means to achieve the approved goal have not been blocked, a certain ambivalence has been created about them.

If both the goals and the means are rejected, the deviant behavior can take the form of *retreatism,* Merton's second strategy for anomie. People say in effect that they do not want the prize and are not going to run the race. In one way or another they drop out. The wino on Skid Row and the hobo are retreatists. Some forms of mental illness represent retreatism. A more recent form of retreatism is the rural communes set up to allow their members to function usefully outside the materialistic, individualistic values of modern American society and to seek a better way of life.

The third strategy is *rebellion*—active attempt to change society's goals. In pursuing rebellion some may get into trouble with the law. Even if peaceful demonstrators and other rebels avoid legal trouble, they are often distrusted as deviants by the larger society. But if they were to succeed in changing society, there would be new norms and the old rebels would no longer be deviant.

The fourth strategy for anomie is *ritualism:* The individual rejects the culturally approved goals but conforms to the means. Such conformity is ritualistic because it involves going through the motions rather than commitment to goals, like the behavior of people who attend church services out of habit or respect of social pressure but have no commitment to the goals or basic values of the religion. Ritualists in society can be considered prone to deviant behavior because they lack commitment to the goals their behavior serves and are thus susceptible to other goals and norms. Their conformity is only an appearance. They are unstable types, needing only a triggering event or idea to reveal themselves as in fact anomic.

Innovation, retreatism, rebellion, and ritualism thus are different forms of reaction to anomic conditions of society.[11] The behavior accompanying these reactions either is deviant or could easily become so. According to the anomie theory, if confusion or contradictions surround society's means for achieving its basic goals, high rates of deviant behavior will result. Nevertheless, the theory does not explain why some individuals in a society adopt deviant behavior while most others do not.

DEVIANT SUBCULTURE THEORY

Within a society subgroups with their own distinct cultures can sometimes be found.[12] They are called *subcultures* because they have the elements of a culture but exist within the larger society and its dominant culture. Subcultures range from, say, Ukrainian Americans living in a large city to motorcycle gangs, jazz musicians, and rock groups. If its values and norms contradict or conflict with those of the dominant culture, the subculture is a *contraculture*. The deviant subculture theory holds that deviant subcultures are what transmit and perpetuate deviancy within a society. According to this theory people who are members of certain subcultures or have sufficient contact with members will come to learn their values and norms much as any values and norms are learned. Edwin H. Sutherland, a criminologist, developed the concept of *differential association* to explain how criminal behavior is learned.[13] By his theory, within a society

---

[11]Our discussion of these reactions has followed Merton's *Social Theory and Social Structure*.

[12]Albert K. Cohen, *Deviance and Control* (Englewood Cliffs, N.J.: Prentice-Hall, 1966).

[13]Edwin H. Sutherland and Donald R. Cressey, *Principles of Criminology* (New York: J. B. Lippincott, 1966).

Would you categorize these people as members of a subculture or contraculture? Why or why not?

some people have greater opportunity than others to associate with criminals and delinquents and thus learn not only criminal values but even criminal skills and techniques. According to the deviant subculture theory, the very behavior that is condemned by the larger society is supported and rewarded within the subgroup.

The deviant subculture theory is mainly concerned with how deviancy is transmitted. Once a recognizable subgroup and its subculture is at odds with the dominant culture, the deviant behavior of members can find approval and be reinforced. In addition, through differential association some are attracted to the subgroup and adopt its behavior patterns. But the theory does not explain

---

Visit police or criminal court. Report on the proceedings. What crimes are tried? What types of sentences are handed down by the judge? What types of interaction take place among those involved in the proceedings?

---

how deviant behavior or deviant subcultures arose in the first place. Subcultures seem to arise frequently because deviants or potential deviants keep each other's company. Around college campuses, for example, we find subgroups whose culture includes the use of marijuana and other drugs. About a decade ago such groups began to emerge as people with common attitudes and a common stance toward the "straight" society banded together. Once formed, the groups reinforce, support, and reward the behavior that brought them together in the first place.

LABELING THEORY

One of the most recent attempts to understand deviancy is by theorizing about how people in the larger society react to norm-violating behavior, what they do about it, and what effects their actions and reactions have on those who performed the behavior.[14] The act itself is played down, and emphasis is placed on the label—delinquent, psychopath, criminal, homosexual—that society gives to a person known to have committed the act. Labeling theorists make a fundamental distinction between what they call *primary* deviancy and *secondary* deviancy. Primary deviancy is simply rule-breaking or norm violation. At this stage offenders do not think of themselves as deviants but somehow rationalize their behavior to fit into a socially acceptable role.

But if this behavior becomes known to others who label it deviant, the self-concepts of offenders are likely to change. As we have seen, our selves are social creations and our sense of self is always more or less susceptible to the influence of others. No longer will the offenders think of themselves as normal persons who occasionally break rules, just as "everybody else" does. They are now deviants. For example, the young man who feels somewhat attracted to other men and has had a few homosexual experiences may have worried about his sexual identity but perhaps still thought of himself as basically heterosexual. What happens if he is caught in a homosexual act and is arrested

[14]For examples of the works of labeling theorists see Howard S. Becker, *Outsiders: Studies in the Sociology of Deviance* (New York: Free Press, 1963); Erving Goffman, *Stigma* (Englewood Cliffs, N.J.: Prentice-Hall, 1963); and Edwin M. Schur, *Labeling Deviant Behavior* (New York: Harper & Row, 1972).

and charged with homosexuality? He has been officially labeled a homosexual, and his employer, friends of both sexes, parents, and others are likely to think of him as a homosexual and react to him as one. Perhaps he will now find acceptance only among homosexuals. Thus, a self–fulfilling prophecy may be at work; for having been given the label homosexual he is more likely to adopt homosexual behavior than if he had not been so labeled.

The behavior he adopted as the result of labeling is his *secondary* deviancy. This is how society creates deviants, by labeling people on the basis of single, discovered acts of primary deviancy. Howard S. Becker, a labeling theorist, contends that:

> Social groups create deviance by making rules whose infractions constitute deviance, and by applying those rules to particular people and labeling them as outsiders. . . . The deviant is one to whom the label has successfully been applied.[15]

Again this theory also does not explain how some people are moved to the acts of primary deviancy and others are not.

NEEDED: INTEGRATION OF THE THREE THEORIES

We have seen that while each of the theories purporting to explain deviant behavior has merit, none alone can explain all deviancy. Perhaps further research will link the theories together.[16] For instance, there could be a chain reaction from anomie to labeling to subcultural influences. In a society suffering from considerable anomie, strain on individuals will produce norm–breaking behavior. If this behavior comes to the attention of conformists within the society, the norm–breaking individuals are likely to be labeled deviant. The pool of labeled deviants, in turn, is a potential subgroup of deviants who could support and reward one another's behavior and serve as a recruiting force for more deviants.

Even linking the three dominant theories of deviance cannot completely explain the phenomenon; many fundamental variables remain unexplained. Why do some people respond to anomie or deviant subcultures, or practice primary deviancy, and others do not? Why do many persons whose behavior should be explained by these theories violate their predictions, like individuals who do not respond to labeling by acts of secondary deviancy?

[15]Becker, p. 9.

[16]For an attempt to link anomie, subcultural, and labeling theories see Ira L. Reiss, "Premarital Sex as Deviant Behavior: An Application of Current Approaches to Deviance," *American Sociological Review* 35 (February 1970), 78–87.

MAJOR FORMS OF DEVIANCY IN THE UNITED STATES

As we have seen throughout this book and as newspapers, television, and perhaps your own direct experiences have demonstrated, our society is in the midst of change, uncertainty, and great unrest. We have not only major social problems, such as energy crises, urban deterioration, and racial discrimination, we also face major problems of deviancy. We now look at three major areas of deviancy in our society and at how well the theories we just examined can explain them.

DRUG ABUSE

The deviant use of drugs in our society has become well known in recent years—not only in the broadening popularity of marijuana but also in heroin addiction and in the growing use of many drugs by high school students. Various forms of drug abuse simply do not fit within one neat definition; for some nonaddicting, otherwise illegal drugs can be used by prescription and under a doctor's guidance. Many people are addicted to drugs, but the drugs themselves, such as barbiturates to induce sleep or amphetamines to help dieters, are legal when prescribed. Marijuana is illegal but is neither physiologically nor psychologically addicting. And alcohol, which is respectable in most circles as a social lubricant and is legal almost everywhere, is our most abused drug.

Although an estimated nine million people are addicted to alcohol—that is, are alcoholics—alcohol receives almost none of the attention directed to drug abuse. This lack of attention is probably because it has been so long among us as a respectable form of emotional and social release of tensions, whereas even the nonaddicting drugs are novel and exotic, something to be shied away from and kept illegal to discourage their use. For these reasons we concentrate here on the drugs that many people in our society consider the objects of deviant use—heroin, hallucinogens such as LSD (lysergic acid diethylamide), hashish, cocaine, and marijuana. These are the commonest drugs, and they are all illegal to possess or use.

Prevalence of Drug Abuse No one knows how many drug abusers or even drug addicts there are in the United States. A fairly recent study conducted by the National Institutes of Mental Health found 18,080 users of addictive drugs (chiefly heroin) in a 40-block area of Harlem. Most users in this country are between the ages of 20 and 35, but in Harlem researchers discovered 2000 users aged

7 through 15.[17] Despite the reputation of heroin as a dangerous, addicting drug, and despite efforts to dry up its supply, heroin addicts in the United States number at least 300,000.

LSD has been called a "mind-expanding" drug because the user frequently sees strange sights and beautiful colors and experiences various unusual, intense, sensations. The incidence of severe mental disorders and suicide and the frequent need for extended hospital care following the use of LSD are well documented. Flashbacks, or the return to the LSD state without taking the drug, also have been verified. Nevertheless, its use continued among young people, even high school students. A survey in 1970 found that 14 percent of college students had tried LSD at least once, although more recently the drug has become less popular.[18]

The most widely used illegal, mind-altering drug is marijuana. One study found that 40 percent of college students had smoked pot but higher percentages have been reported for specific colleges.[19] The number of people who have tried marijuana and the number who smoke it regularly is staggering, but its use, as we have noted, is nonaddictive and does not by itself lead to the use of harder drugs.

Anomie Theory and Drug Abuse Two reactions to an anomic social condition, retreatism and rebellion, seem to explain drug abuse. Many heroin addicts exhibit a retreatist reaction when the means of achieving goals are blocked. Frustrated and disappointed in life, they seek personal escape in drugs and find life intolerable without them. Some LSD users are also retreatists, while others and many marijuana users react rebelliously to the anomie they perceive. Some of them reject the individualistic, materialistic goals of society and feel that freedom of expression and openness in human relations are higher values.

Deviant Subculture Theory There is clear evidence of a drug subculture in the United States. Of course, a sophisticated social organization is needed to produce and distribute the illegal drugs. For many drug users there is also a common culture of shared values, dress styles, music, and jargon. Although some of these features do not belong exclusively to the drug culture, studies such as Isidor Chein's *The Road to H* have shown that people are introduced to drug use not by a pusher but through contact with unconventional groups.[20] Bingham Dai's study of drug users in Chicago revealed that over half of them had personal

[17]*Associated Press,* June 12, 1970.

[18]*Gallup Opinion Index: 1971* (Princeton, N.J.: Gallup International).

[19]*Gallup Opinion Index: 1971.*

[20]Isidor Chein, *The Road to H: Narcotics, Delinquency and Public Policy* (New York: Basic Books, 1964).

acquaintances with other users and could identify many more.[21] Thus, once there is a subgroup of drug users their way of life can be transmitted to others who themselves fail to find a place in the conventional world. Despite the need to keep their drug use secret, the drug culture is sufficiently visible to attract new members. Even so, the deviant subculture theory does not fully explain why people ever start to use drugs; for not all those who are aware of the subculture seek to attach themselves to it. One researcher, Harold Firestone, has suggested that those young people whose careers are blocked by dropping out of school or by juvenile delinquency are particularly susceptible to the lures of the drug culture.[22]

Labeling Theory Labeling theory has almost nothing to contribute to an understaning of drug abuse. Like the other two theories it fails to explain why people start using drugs. In addition, it fails to explain why people become long-term regular users. Only a tiny fraction of marijuana users, for example, are ever apprehended. For this reason their prolonged primary deviancy never becomes secondary deviancy. The same is true for most acid users, many amphetamine users, and quite a few heroin addicts. Marijuana and LSD users consider the laws to be wrong, so their persistent use of their chosen drug or drugs cannot be considered secondary deviancy. And since heroin is physically addicting, it is useless to speculate whether the addict is engaged in primary or secondary deviancy. He or she is simply "hooked."

HOMOSEXUALITY

In 49 of our 50 states a homosexual act is a criminal act. Many people think such behavior is deviant not because it violates criminal statutes but because they feel it is immoral, sinful, or against nature. In one study, for example, 180 people of different ages, sexes, occupations, religions, and races were given the following instructions on a questionnaire: "In the following spaces please list those things or types of persons whom you regard as deviant."[23] They were not furnished with a list of types of deviancy. The most frequent response, given by almost half of the people, was "homosexual"; 12 percent listed "lesbian" and 11 percent wrote "pervert." These are the things that came to their minds when they saw the word "deviant."

Why do so many people in our society think first of homosexuality or lesbianism when they hear the word deviant? In some societies, such as ancient

---

[21]Bingham Dai, *Opium Addiction in Chicago* (Montclair, N.J.: Patterson Smith, 1970).

[22]Harold Firestone, "Cats, Kicks, and Colors," *Social Problems* 15 (July 1957), 3–13.

[23]J. L. Simmons, "Public Stereotypes of Deviants," *Social Problems* 13 (Fall 1965), 224.

As the Gay Liberation Movement gains momentum, can we expect people to change their attitudes about what constitutes deviancy?

Greece and Rome, homosexuality was freely practiced and not considered wrong. Some American Indian tribes created a special role for the homosexual male, sometimes referred to as "squaw man." He was considered different from other men and from women, but he was not looked upon with horror or disgust. In 1967, the British Parliament repealed its laws that made homosexuality a criminal offense. Prior to the decision the appointed Wolfenden Commission had made a careful study of homosexuality, took expert testimony on its nature, prevalency, and causes, and heard arguments on homosexuality as a disease and on its effects on the family. The commission concluded that homosexual behavior between consenting adults in private should not be considered a criminal offense.[24]

[24]Report of the Committee on Homosexual Offenses and Prostitution, *Wolfenden Report* (New York: Lancer Books, 1964), p. 48.

Perhaps some day far fewer Americans will consider homosexuality deviant than do today. Already, as we mentioned, the American Psychiatric Association has moved that homosexuality no longer is classified by its members as a form of mental illness. We might have misgivings about deciding matters of health (mental or physical) by votes at a convention. Nevertheless, that vote indicates at least two things. First, attitudes'toward homosexuality are changing among those closest to the study and attempted treatment of it. Second, the evidence is still ambiguous enough, and controversial enough, that such a matter had to be decided by vote rather than by the traditional presentation of over-whelmingly convincing research reports.

This odd occurrence—bestowing mental health by vote—perhaps can give us some insight into the social origins of deviancy. Clearly, murder, rape, and theft are deviant because they assault at least two, if not all three, of the basic social functions societies seek to fulfill. Murder ends the victim's physical life and injures social order within and among groups. Rape is a violent assault on the victim's psychological condition and often upon her physical survival. And theft, depending upon its seriousness, can have harmful consequences for all three functions.

Perhaps such a deviancy as homosexuality has never had such firm grounds for social intolerance. The Bible is interpreted as condemning homosexuality, and interpretation of the Bible was for many centuries a source of many mores and folkways. But we have seen such practices as divorce, abortion, and ex-tramarital sexual relations become increasingly acceptable in our society. Is it possible that now, when sex is not considered only justifiable as a means of producing offspring—and when the Bible no longer is the source of our secular laws—we lack any reasons to consider homosexuality deviant?

To answer this question sociologists will have to do some historical delving into the past of our culture and society. Meanwhile, sickness or not, homosex-uality is still a crime almost everywhere in our society. And, interestingly enough, there seems to be more reaction to male homosexuality than to female homosex-uality. Perhaps this is because our society, and the social sciences as well, have been male–dominated, and because male sexuality, or masculinity, is much more rigidly defined as exclusively heterosexual in our society than is female sexuality. Women can show each other much more affection through many more intimate physical gestures (hugging, kissing, etc.) than men can.

Prevalence of Male Homosexuality Because homosexual experience is essen-tially a private matter, it is almost impossible to estimate the extent of this type of deviancy. In addition, the definition of what is a homosexual greatly affects conclusions regarding the incidence and prevalence of it. Kinsey found, for example, that about 4 percent of the adult, white males were exclusively homosexual throughout their lives.[25] He found also that about 37 percent of the males had some homosexual experience, to the point of orgasm, between adolescence and age 45. Then there are those who can be called latent homosexuals in that they are aroused by homosexual stimuli, or recognize that they have a strong sexual preference for other males but never give active sexual expression to the preference. How can we develop theories to account for homosexuality unless we are clear about what behavior—sporadic or life long—we are trying to explain? Are we seeking to explain why 4 percent of American males are exclusively homosexual or why over a third have had at least one homosexual experience? To date, sociological theories of deviance seem unable to explain the original cause of a person's homosexual behavior. The deviant subculture theory allows us to understand better the life cycle and life style of some homosexuals. The labeling theory is useful for understanding how social influences move individuals from the commission of a few deviant acts to accepting the role of deviant.

Labeling Theory According to the labeling theory the fairly large minority of males who have had only a few homosexual experiences would be described as primary deviants. Despite such encounters most could continue to think of themselves as basically heterosexual. The entrance into secondary deviancy can take different forms. It is not always caused by public discovery of their primary deviancy by police, family, or friends. Some sociologists believe that, just as we develop a self through socialization, we can take the role of the generalized other in respect to our primary deviant acts and decide for ourselves that we are deviant. From then on our acts can be considered secondary deviant acts.

There are some weaknesses in the variant on labeling theory that holds that a person can progress from primary to secondary deviancy by his concept of himself as a homosexual rather than by society's labeling him as such. This variant assumes that inside every homosexual there is a heterosexual male begging to be let out. That is, if only this person who was practicing primary homosexual acts hadn't come to *think* of himself as a homosexual he would eventually have become heterosexual. There is no evidence that this assumption is correct. So this "internal labeling theory" has to be treated for now with skepticism. Whatever the source of homosexual behavior is, Kinsey found that of the 550 practicing, exclusive homosexuals three-fourths were not known by society to be homosexuals. The labeling theory, then, could not apply to them.

In some instances labeling theory can explain how people become secondary homosexual deviants. A young man may be experimenting with homosexual

---

[25]Alfred C. Kinsey et al., *Sexual Behavior in the Human Male* (Philadelphia: W. B. Saunders, 1948), pp. 650–651.

behavior and may be concerned with his sexual identity. If he is apprehended and charged with homosexuality or receives a dishonorable discharge from the armed forces because of his homosexual behavior, he might accept the label. Had he not been labeled publicly he might have given up his homosexual practices, as do most of the young men who experiment with it.

The label of homosexual, when applied to a person by society, frequently can be a terrible cross to bear, despite current efforts to deal with the situation openly and honestly. A person who candidly admits that he is a homosexual may find himself shunned by his friends and almost disowned by his parents. Occupationally he may be hurt, for many employers do not want "that kind" of person around. If his homosexuality is known, it is unlikely that he could obtain a government position involving the handling of confidential or sensitive materials, for there is the fear, justified or not, that he would be subject to blackmail.

Deviant Subculture Theory The homosexual subculture is surprisingly visible for one based on a deviant activity. The banding together of those who share a common value has positive effects for the individual homosexual. In the homosexual group the behavior that society considers wrong meets with approval; homosexuality is normal. In homosexual groups there is typically much gossip about sex and bragging about sexual encounters. This serves to reaffirm for participants the subcultural value that homosexuality is acceptable, even good. The emotional support gained from belonging to such a group has a strong psychological value. The individual finds that not only does the group reward his homosexuality but that it will help him to find means of expressing it. He learns how to solicit, how to give recognition cues to others, and which are the bars, parks, street corners, or public toilets where sexual contacts can be made.[26] The homosexual subgroup thus performs a socialization function.

Visible signs of the homosexual subculture include the gay bars, restaurants, and in some cities entire neighborhoods; the many magazines published for homosexuals; their formal organizations; and, of course, the Gay Liberation Front which fights for the rights of homosexuals as persons. The network of homosexual groups across the nation is less visible but exists nonetheless. Although a study of homosexual subcultures reveals how homosexuals live, what values they hold, and the norms and folkways they have developed to assure adherence to their central values, the deviant subculture theory does not explain why people choose the homosexual way of life in the first place.

[26]For studies bearing on the subculture of homosexuality see Laud Humphreys, *Tearoom Trade: Impersonal Sex in Public Places* (Chicago: Aldine, 1970); Maurice Leznoff and William Westley, "The Homosexual Community," *Social Problems* 3 (April 1956), 257–63; and Albert J. Reiss, Jr., "The Social Integration of Queers and Peers," *Social Problems* 9 (Fall 1961), 102–120.

CRIME AND JUVENILE DELINQUENCY

In a technical sense no one is a criminal until he or she has been found guilty of breaking a criminal law. In a sociological sense, though, anyone who has committed an act defined as a crime has engaged in deviant behavior, whether or not the act is discovered or the person is apprehended, arrested, or convicted. Legally, juvenile delinquency includes all deviant acts that, if committed by adults, would be criminal, and also includes some acts by minors that would not be crimes if committed by adults. Such acts include staying out all night, even with no evidence of specific wrongdoing; truancy from school; curfew violation; and refusal to obey parents. Most Americans are well aware that there is considerable adult crime and juvenile delinquency in our society. Unfortunately the true extent of either is virtually impossible to assess.

The Extent of Criminal Deviancy In the United States, on a typical day in 1972 there were 51 homicides, 127 forcible rapes, 1065 aggravated assaults, 1026 robberies, 6425 burglaries, 5035 larcenies, and 2414 auto thefts. These are only the crimes reported to the police. Many crimes, particularly rapes but also other, less serious ones, are simply never reported. Another sign of the extent of criminal deviancy is the annual number of arrests. As indicated by the figures for 1972, in Table 16–1, the number of arrests is staggering.

Note that a high percentage of those arrested for a number of the crimes are under 18 years of age and are male. As a matter of fact, the largest number of those arrested for all crimes were 16 years of age. Seventeen–year–old youths comprised the second largest group, followed by those 15 and 18 years of age. For juvenile delinquency the ratio of boys to girls has been dropping and is now about 4 to 1. Adult arrests are holding at about 10 men to 1 woman.

Official records of arrests and convictions reveal that lower class individuals have a far greater chance of being labeled a criminal or delinquent than those of other classes. But some studies, in which young people report on their own behavior, show that the social class differences are not as great as the official records would indicate.[27] Crime and delinquency rates for blacks have been estimated to be two to five times higher than the rates for whites. Theories attempting to explain criminal deviancy must take into account what is statistically known about such deviants. That is, they are far more likely to be male than female, are more likely to be young than old, and are more likely to be black than white.

[27]See, for example, F. Ivan Nye et al., "Socio-Economic Status and Delinquent Behavior," *American Journal of Sociology* 63 (January 1958), 381–389; and Lamar T. Empey and Maynard L. Erickson, "Hidden Delinquency and Social Status," *Social Forces* 44 (June 1966), 546–554.

TABLE 16–1. Persons Arrested by Major Crimes in the United States, 1972, by Age and Sex[a]

Offense	Number of Persons Arrested	Male	Female	Under 18	Over 18
Criminal Homicide					
(a) Murder and nonnegligent manslaughter	15,049			11	88
(b) Manslaughter by negligence	2986			9	91
Forcible Rape	19,374	100		20	80
Robbery	109,217	94	7	32	68
Aggravated Assault	155,581	87	13	18	83
Burglary	314,393	95	5	51	49
Larceny	678,673	70	30	50	50
Auto Theft	121,842	94	6	54	46
Other Assaults	307,638	86	14	20	80
Arson	10,645	91	10	58	42
Forgery and counterfeiting	44,313	75	25	10	90
Fraud	96,713	70	30	4	96
Embezzlement	6744	74	26	6	94
Stolen property; buying, receiving, possessing	71,754	90	10	31	69
Vandalism	129,724	92	8	71	29
Weapons; carrying, possessing, etc.	119,671	93	7	16	84
Prostitution and commercialized vice	44,744	26	74	3	97
Sex offenses (except forcible rape and prostitution)	51,124	91	9	22	79
Narcotic drug law violations	431,608	85	15	23	77
Gambling	70,064	91	9	3	98
Offenses against family and children	52,935	91	9	2	98
Driving while intoxicated	604,291	93	7	1	99
Liquor laws	207,675	86	14	37	63
Drunkenness	1,384,734	93	7	3	97
Disorderly conduct	582,513	86	15	22	78
Vagrancy	55,680	65	35	10	90
All other offenses (except traffic)	966,722	84	16	27	73
Suspicion	41,475	76	24	30	70
Curfew and loitering law violations	116,126	80	20	100	
Runaways	199,185	44	56	100	

[a]Percentages have been rounded off and may not add to 100.

Source: Federal Bureau of Investigation, *Crime in the United States, Uniform Crime Reports, 1972* (Washington, D.C.: U.S. Government Printing Office, 1973), adapted from pages 128, 129.

What is considered delinquent behavior for juveniles in our society? Why is there a distinction between deviant acts as committed by juveniles and adults?

Anomie Theory and Criminal Deviancy If it is assumed that the success goals of American society are shared by all or most people, regardless of class background, then anomie theory could explain much of criminal deviancy. As we noted in Chapter 7, lower class youth, for example, often find little real acceptance in the schools, which usually reflect middle class values and norms. Teachers are likely to expect "trouble" from lower class students, and frequently get it. The curriculum and extracurricular activities are geared to the presumed needs of the middle class. The educational route to success is not exactly blocked to lower class youth, but it is certainly strewn with obstacles. Those who drop out of school either cannot find decent jobs or work in low–paying, menial positions. Illegal activities, then, are one means of achieving material success.

As a general explanation of criminal deviancy anomie theory presents several difficulties. First, sociologists are in disagreement as to the extent to which lower class people accept the success goals of American society. If they do not accept the goals, then it can hardly be said that lower class deviants are choosing illegal means to reach prescribed goals. The higher rate of criminal activity among blacks would fit the anomie theory, since by any reasonable perspective the opportunities for success are fewer for blacks than whites. This explanation

---

Divide your community into police precincts and make a map showing how the number and types of crime differ by precinct. What demographic factors correlate with crime?

---

rests on the assumption that the criminally delinquent blacks accept the cultural success goals, which may or may not be true.

In addition, why should males be so much more likely than females to perceive society as anomic? Traditionally, of course, many women did not aspire to an occupational role. Their economic success was tied to the activities of their husbands. Should not lower class women be extremely frustrated, then, to know that they could never have the good things of life because legitimate means of achieving them are unavailable to their husbands? If they experience such frustrations, why is there so much less criminal deviancy among women?

Finally, some types of crimes do not fit in well with the anomie theory of deviancy. Vandalism, malicious destruction of public property, sex crimes, or gang violence, for example, bring no financial reward to the perpetrators. All of these crimes may be related to frustrations inherent in society, but they do not fit the scheme of reaction to unattainable material success goals.

Subculture Theory and Criminal Deviancy In some ways the deviant subculture theory is in contradiction to anomie theory. That is, some authorities believe that a fairly well-developed criminal subculture perpetuates the criminal way of life. Furthermore, some feel that there is a close connection between lower class culture and crime. Such authorities do not subscribe to the notion that the success goal cuts across all classes and groups. Walter Miller, for example, believes that the culture of the lower class is relatively distinct from that of the middle class.[28] Lower class culture is said to contain such primary concerns as toughness, trouble, excitement, and "fate." These concerns can be easily translated into delinquent or criminal behavior. The deviant subculture is seen almost as an offshoot of the lower class culture. The toughness and courage required for delinquency or crime is also necessary for some lower class jobs.

Whether or not one ties criminal deviancy to the lower class culture, it is apparent that in practically all communities groups of delinquents and criminals have developed something akin to a distinct way of life. As with other deviants, the criminal subculture consists of a set of values, attitudes, and beliefs that guide the behavior of participants. The culture defines appropriate role models,

[28]Walter B. Miller, "Lower-Class Culture as a Generating Milieu of Gang Delinquency," *Journal of Social Issues* 14, No. 3 (1958), 5–19.

Visit a prison or mental hospital. Report on the programs and treatments that are used to rehabilitate and reorient inmates back into the community. How would you evaluate the success of these programs?

---

that is, successful criminals and delinquents. An individual who wants to be accepted into the criminal subculture can imitate the role models' behavior, and through association with others can learn the values and behavior rewarded by the subgroup. The more involved he becomes with the subculture, the more he rejects and is rejected by the noncriminal world. It is difficult to tell how much recruitment to the ranks of criminals and delinquents is done by the criminal subculture.

Labeling Theory and Criminal Deviancy As with other types of deviancy, labeling theory works better for explaining criminal and delinquent careers than it does for isolating the original causes of deviancy. It is well known that many young males break criminal laws and thus are primary deviants. Many are never caught, however, and of those who are caught many never receive formal punishment for their behavior. The majority give up their sporadic acts of delinquency and go on to live law-abiding lives. But if society officially labels the person a delinquent, the result is likely to be quite different. Thrown in with delinquents in a detention facility, he is likely to begin to think of himself as one of them. He makes new friends who praise and reward his behavior and more than likely can teach him to be a better delinquent. As his delinquency continues, the social stamp becomes firmer in the sense of sterner punishments, more rejection by nondelinquents, and greater stigmatization. The label "delinquent" was first earned by the person's behavior, but once the process was started the label itself pushed him more and more in the deviant direction.

WHITE COLLAR CRIME: CRIME BY "NONCRIMINALS"

Labeling theory is particularly useful for showing how those who commit what are called white collar crimes are not usually labeled "criminal." Edwin H. Sutherland defined white collar crime as "crime committed by a person of respectability and high social status in the course of his occupation."[29] The concept now includes various nonviolent crimes committed usually by middle

[29]Quoted in Dinitz, p. 100.

THE AMERICAN WAY—FAIR PLAY
VERSUS ANOMIC INNOVATION?

Once the most important element of "the American Way" was the value of fair play: "It doesn't matter if you win or lose. It's how you play the game." But much of American society now seems to operate by a different value, expressed by a professional football coach: "Winning isn't the most important thing. It's the only thing."

This is a blunt statement of Robert K. Merton's anomic theory of social deviancy. The cultural goal becomes so important that the means resorted to become unimportant. This principle was expressed time and again during the investigations into President Nixon's 1972 campaign practices. The need was to get President Nixon reelected at all costs.

Speculations about "why Watergate happened" have gone far and wide—the Cold War mentality; alienation of one group from another and the growth of fear and mistrust among them; and so on. And granted the stakes are often high—whether immense political power or "the good of the country." But what about when the stakes are infinitely smaller?

In 1972 the annual Soap Box Derby—of all the unlikely things—erupted in scandal. The Derby is a downhill race among unpowered cars piloted by youngsters. The contest rules require that the cars be designed and built by their young pilots. The winner of the 1972 Derby was disqualified when it was discovered that his car had a concealed electromagnet to give it superior initial acceleration. Not only that, it was later discovered the car had been designed and built by the boy's uncle, who also had installed the magnet.

Cheating and thieving have always been with us. And competitiveness has always been an important value in our society. But today it seems that the obsession with winning at all costs has extended into more and more areas of group interaction. Even in areas where the victory is only symbolic, where the financial or other rewards are insignificant, winning has often become "the only thing." How has our society or our socializing changed to produce this anomic pattern (as Merton would call it) in our behavior? Have we become alienated to the point that "playing the game" with each other—whether in sports, politics, or business—is often worthless without the sure promise of victory? Have secondary relations come to so dominate our social interaction that we feel closer to the goals than to each other?

What effect do you think President Ford's pardon of Nixon has had on the American people's view of white-collar crime?

and upper class people, often but not always in connection with their occupation. False advertising, antitrust violations, price–fixing, income tax evasion, embezzlement, bribery, and other crimes. (Street crimes such as muggings, robbery, and rape are not considered white collar crimes regardless of the social class of the offender.)

The person who commits a white collar crime usually does not think of himself as a criminal and is not so stigmatized by society. Many Americans probably thought of Billy Sol Estes, who was convicted of a $30 million fertilizer swindle, as a "wheeler-dealer" who happened to get caught. Price–fixing is often rationalized as being part of the business game. Even those who go to prison for income tax evasion manage to escape the label "criminal." Several of those sentenced to brief prison terms for their roles in Watergate complained that in prison they were "treated like common criminals." Nevertheless, in spite of having committed crimes, they generally can resume their respectable lives after release from prison. It is unlikely that conviction for a white collar cime results in a life of crime. The white collar criminal, in other words, rarely becomes a secondary deviant. Is this perhaps because the middle class does not consider such crimes as deviant?

If many middle class people indeed do not consider white collar crime deviant, can we expect the same social trend that widening marijuana use generated? Will there be pressure to "decriminalize" white collar crime? Probably there won't be because these are not victimless crimes, as marijuana use is. Yet the leniency that many people feel toward crimes that middle and upper class people commit might give us some insight into deviancy. We are socialized to consider certain behavior deviant, but we feel more sternly about some forms of deviancy than about others. A comparison of our society at two different periods would reveal not only different frequencies of certain kinds of deviant behavior but also different attitudes toward them. Although deviancy will probably always be with us in some form or another, it, too, like everything else in our society, has undergone change.

The study of deviancy is a fitting way to conclude this text. It illustrates the sociological approach to the study of human interaction. The anomic, the deviant subculture, and the labeling theory represent efforts to seek explanations for deviant behavior not in the individual but in human groups. Indeed, the very definition of deviancy—forms of unusual behavior considered undesirable by society—is social. The study of deviant behavior also illustrates how sociologists work to further their understanding of human interaction. Theories, even though logical, are not merely accepted but are tested with the hard facts of observed behavior. If white collar crime, for example, cannot be adequately explained by the labeling theory of deviancy, the theory needs to be modified or reformulated. The study of deviancy shows, too, the necessity for understanding basic sociological concepts before working in applied areas. An understanding of how, through socialization, the culture of a society enters the individual and shapes his or her personality is at the root of the deviant subculture theory. Finally, the study of deviant behavior illustrates the excitement of sociology. Working in an area of clear benefit to society, we can recognize the validity of the sociological approach, even if we must admit that final answers are not possible and that there is much work yet to be done.

SUMMARY POINTS AND QUESTIONS

1. Deviant behavior or characteristics refer to that which departs from the average or normative. More conventionally it refers to behavior that is disapproved by a society as being beyond certain limits, and so it is sanctioned negatively.

> *Because deviancy is relative to a society, can you give an example of behavior that is considered deviant in our society but not in another society?*
>
> *Why do you think it is deviant in our society?*

2. Even if there is no victim, one criterion for deviancy is that a law has been broken.

> *What are some examples of victimless crime?*
>
> *Why are such actions made illegal by a society?*

3. If behavior is irrational or bizarre, and beyond certain normative limits set by a society, it is defined as sick deviant behavior. This is exemplified by mental illness.

> *How does a society deal with persons labeled as sick deviants?*

4. Behavior that is at odds with the values or norms of a dominant culture might also be labeled deviant. The rejection of the value of materialism by those involved in the hippie movement is an example of this type of deviancy.

> *What other groups or movements might be considered forms of deviancy?*
>
> *To what extent are deviant social movements agents of social change?*

5. There are three major theories used by sociologists to explain deviancy. These are *anomie theory*, *deviant subculture theory*, and *labeling theory*. Anomie is defined by Robert Merton as a condition in a society in which there is a disharmony between culturally shared goals and the institutionalized means for achieving them.

> *What are the major cultural defined goals in American culture?*
>
> *What are some ways that the prescribed means do not function as ways to achieve these goals?*
>
> *According to Merton, what are four types of reaction that might occur in an anomic situation?*

6. One proponent of deviant subculture theory is Edwin Sutherland. He posited the theory of *differential association*, which states that deviance is learned in association with a deviant subculture.

> *What are the limitations of this theory?*
>
> *What types of deviancy does it fail to offer adequate explanations?*

7. Labeling theory, on the other hand, focuses on what happens to a person when he is labeled as a deviant. It views deviancy in stages. *Primary deviancy* is the rule-breaking or norm violation, and *secondary deviance* is the stage at which the individual is defined as deviant and begins to view himself as deviant.

> *How can the concepts of self-fulfilling prophecy and looking-glass self be related to labeling theory?*
>
> *What are the limitations of this theory?*

522

8. In the United States, one prevalent form of deviancy is the use of illegal drugs. Drug use is considered deviant when it is a violation of law.

> *How prevalent is drug use in the United States?*
>
> *How could anomie theory, deviant subculture theory, and labeling theory be applied to explain this phenomenon?*

9. Although in some societies homosexuality is not viewed as deviant behavior, it is in the United States.

> *Why is there such an aversion to homosexuality in the United States?*
>
> *How might labeling theory and deviant subculture theory be used to reach a better understanding of homosexuality?*

10. Crime and juvenile delinquency are considered to be major social problems in the United States.

> *How would anomie theory explain the prevalence of crime and delinquency in the United States?*
>
> *How would labeling theory and deviant subculture theory explain the continuing increase in crime rates?*
>
> *With these theories, what programs might be devised that would reduce crime and delinquency rates?*

SUGGESTED READINGS

Buckner, H. Taylor, ed. *Deviance, Reality, and Change.* New York: Random House, 1971. Readings on a variety of deviant forms of behavior and the social control of such behavior.

Cloward, Richard and Lloyd E. Ohlin. *Delinquency and Opportunity.* New York: Free Press, 1960. Deals with delinquency subcultures, particularly the gang.

Cressey, Donald R. and David A. Ward, eds. *Delinquency, Crime, and Social Processes.* New York, Harper & Row, 1969. A book of readings centered on the criminal from a subcultural perspective.

Dinitz, Simon, Russell R. Dynes, and Alfred C. Clark, eds. *Deviance.* New York: Oxford University Press, 1969. A reader covering a wide variety of topics in the area of deviancy, including crime, riots, alcoholism, drug addiction, homosexuality, and victimless forms of deviation.

Lofland, John. *Deviance and Identity.* Englewood Cliffs, N.J.: Prentice-Hall, 1969. Deals with effects of being labeled a deviant on the individual's identity, his self-conception, and his relationships.

Merton, Robert K. *Social Theory and Social Structure.* Chs. 6 and 7, New York: Free Press, 1968. These two chapters present the development of anomie theory and deal with types of reaction to anomie.

Schofield, Michael. *Sociological Aspects of Homosexuality*. Boston: Little, Brown, 1965. A thorough research study on homosexuality. It views factors associated with homosexuality and how society deals with homosexuality.

Sutherland, Edwin H. *White Collar Crime*. New York: Holt, Rinehart, and Winston, 1961. A study of corporate and other forms of white collar crime and the presentation of the theory of differential association as an explanation of some types of crime.

NAME INDEX

SUBJECT INDEX